FOR THE HEATHEN ARE WRONG

By EUGENE BAGGER

This is a kind of autobiography. It is the story of the growth of a mind— the personal adventure of a man who took time out to think.

Some years ago Eugene Bagger, roving American newspaper writer, went on a six weeks' vacation in a tiny Provençal village along the Mediterranean coast. He stayed six years. He gave up being in a hurry. He threw away a journalistic career that bored him. This delightful and disturbing book is the distillation of those six thoughtful years. The more he thought about sick Europe, the surer he felt that *civilizations die when religions die.*

But first of all Mr. Bagger had to reconvert himself. A realist "without a drop of mysticism in his makeup", he found his way to the eternal truths of Christianity by a strictly intellectual, rationalistic process. He turned back in his reading—to

...ant, Descartes, Bacon. The ...his reconversion to Roman ...m is exciting personal ...narrative of ideas.

...re many delights wrapped ...he solid core of serious ...Mr. Bagger is cosmopolite ...convert, epicure as well as ...er. The account of his six- ...own is but part of a life ...made him intimate with ...he world's most charming ...writes, provocatively, of ...Adler, Stendhal and detec- ...s, landscapes and food and ...account of the fall of ...hich he saw, perfectly ...bewilderment of the *petit* ...nose world came tumbling.

But what makes "For the Heathen Are Wrong" truly important is that it deals with world ideas. To all of us who are wondering "what comes after?" while the guns are still blazing, it is a vital experience.

FOR THE HEATHEN ARE WRONG

FOR THE HEATHEN
ARE WRONG

An Impersonal Autobiography by

EUGENE BAGGER

For if any man think himself to be
something, whereas he is nothing, he
deceiveth himself. But let every one
prove his own work. . . .

— GALATIANS vi. 3–4

LITTLE, BROWN AND COMPANY · *BOSTON*

1941

To the Beloved Memory
of
G. K. C.

Paien unt tort e chrestiens unt dreit.

                         LA CHANSON DE ROLAND, LXXIX

The author is grateful to the editors of *Harper's Magazine* and the *Atlantic Monthly* for permission to reprint here material which has appeared in their pages.

CONTENTS

FOR THE HEATHEN ARE WRONG

I. New Lives for Old

On the eighteenth day of July of the year 1940, at six o'clock in the afternoon, I stepped off the gangplank of the *S.S. Manhattan* and entered the United States via the West 19th Street Docks, New York. I was, as I did so, an anomaly, and a symptom of the prevailing anomalous state of the world. For I was a citizen of the United States; New York had been my home for many years; and yet here I came as an immigrant, facing the unknown, with no particular place to go to, with my way to make in a new world, as so many young men must — only I was not young, but well advanced into middle age, and I was coming back to a world which seemed all the newer and more frightening because I had been familiar with it when it looked very, very different. I was, in other words, a repatriated expatriate, and, as such, one of the motley company that had filled, more or less, the ship that, sent by the United States Government to save the lives and portable possessions of Americans from the collapse of the Old World, incidentally severed, by her departure from the Tagus, the last physical bond that had linked American civilization with that of the mother continent. For whether we expatriates had been misfits in our own country, or its emissaries and cultural ambassadors abroad, — either case could be argued; I myself have often argued both, — the one stark fact was that we were expatriates no more. Our exile, or our mission, was over. The explosion that had rent Europe to pieces had sent us flying, and deposited us, dazzled and dazed, on the West 19th Street Docks, New York, to start our lives over again, at our time of life, if we knew how.

My particular attempt to build myself a new existence out of the wreckage of what has gone forever takes the form of writing this book. On the title page I call it an autobiography, because everybody knows what an autobiography is; but it would be more to the point to call it an account of the End of Our Time in terms of one man's life.

2

Cnossus, as everybody knows, or ought to know, was the capital of the Minoan Empire in Crete, or rather of the three Minoan Empires which succeeded one another, all before the end of the second millennium B.C.; but of the three I am only concerned with the third. Now the most curious thing about Cnossus was that it was, in almost every respect except size, more like New York than any other capital of the past, whether distant or all but recent. It was more like the New York of today than had been Athens, or the Rome of the Emperors, or medieval Florence, or even the Córdoba and Kairouan of the Caliphs, though the last-named was built on an enormous scale and laid out in the checkerboard fashion; and it was certainly more like New York than was the London or Paris of the eighteenth century. For though Cnossus had no rapid transit, needing none because of her smaller area, nor any sky-scrapers, because land was not dear and the population not over-centralized as in our days, nor yet electricity, nor any other kind of power-generating system worked by the solar heat stored in oil or coal, it had most of the other things that make life effortless and pleasant in the twentieth-century metropolis of America. It had great palaces, cunningly planned and commodious, containing luxurious offices, apartments, assembly halls, and so on. These palaces were centrally heated in winter, by a circulation of hot air, and had resplendent bathrooms, showers, and swimming pools, with supplies of water both hot and cold; and they even had some sort of ventilating system in addition to windows and doors — conduits of fresh air which must be regarded as the precursors of air conditioning some 3500 years before the thing was reinvented in a more perfect form in our own United States.

The drainage and sanitary arrangements of those old Minoan palaces were admirable, and it has been stated by good authority that in respect of general comfort, cleanliness, and hygiene, both public and private, the city of Cnossus, which I repeat flourished no less than thirty-five centuries ago, possessed standards which mankind was not to attain again anywhere and at any time until the end of the nineteenth century. Nor were beauty and art sacrificed to utility and plumbing; for the walls of those palaces were adorned by magnificent paintings, and the halls and courts and public squares and gardens sported beautiful statues galore, both sacred and profane. We also know, precisely by the report of those frescoes, that social life in Cnossus was as brilliant and entertaining as (though we may hope less expensive than) in the Manhattan of our day. For we see representations both of functions of State and of private foregatherings of high society, and — this is perhaps the most striking and astonishing feature of all — these affairs were attended by ladies as well as by men, although in later ages, in Greece and elsewhere, women were usually kept in segregation, as in the Orient. What is more, the ladies who paraded their beauty at those Minoan parties wore, not the severe draperies of white linen or woolen cloth that we associate with the later classical times, but tight-fitting bodices and very full skirts which accentuated height and the smallness of the waist, made of very rich materials of bright coloring, arranged harmoniously or else to contrast, like those worn at the Ritz-Carlton or the Waldorf-Astoria. And, while we have no evidence that cocktails were served at those 2000 B.C. affairs, we have no evidence to the contrary either, and we know that they enjoyed wine with their sophisticated meals, and they probably had ices and sherbets. Further, we know that the Cnossians were regular all-round sport fans. They had a kind of bull-fight which was more like our Western rodeo than the deadly Spanish variety, and they loved wrestling matches and boxing, and other contests, and attended them in vast crowds.

Finally we know that their supplies of food and other necessities were elaborately organized on a large scale, though the business was not, as in our day, in the hands of a few very rich men known familiarly and more or less affectionately as wheat kings, beer kings, pork kings, beef kings, soap kings, baking-powder kings, oil kings, and so forth, but in the hands of one man, the King. So if we disregard this one commercial detail, and also the absence of ear-splitting noises and asphyxiating smells, it is perhaps not too farfetched to say that the life of the Minoan metropolis of thirty-five centuries ago, and the life of the American metropolis of today, resemble one another more than either resembles the life of the cramped, crowded, uncomfortable, unhygienic, and generally dismal European towns of say the seventeenth century of our era; which is a pretty astounding thing if one comes to ponder it.

And all that splendor, all that beauty, all that ingenious planning and managing of common human happiness, came to an end overnight. Cnossus, and all it stood for, was destroyed as a mighty tree is destroyed by a stroke of lightning.

"The last age of Minoan culture ended suddenly and disastrously. A little before the close of the fifteenth century B.C. (1420?) complete destruction fell upon the great people of Cnossus, and all the old centres of Cretan civilization were plundered and burnt. The Minoan culture still lingered on in an impoverished and weakened form, but had lost its imperial power. Crete had sunk into a dependency of mainland Greece, and the last period of the Aegean culture was not Minoan but Mycenean."

Thus Mr. Christopher Dawson, the great English historian and philosopher of culture, on pages 181–182 of his *The Age of the Gods,* a most learned and fascinating treatise, in general terms, of the rise and fall of the archaic civilizations (of which the Minoan only formed a smaller variant) that lighted up the stage of history when there were as yet no Greeks in Greece; and when the site on which Rome was to be built was marked by nothing but possibly a ford across a muddy river, used by buffalo and boar, and perhaps some lonely and disease-ridden savage in skins pursuing an uncertain and dangerous meal; and when the ancestors of the Germans ate roots and acorns, and the ancestors of other Germans.

And we know what we know of the splendors of Cnossus, not from old books, for the Minoan civilization had been wiped out so completely that its only record preserved by the old writers was the legend of the Minotaur, but from excavations which only the other day cleared away all the earth and rock debris that finished off the job begun by the Nordic Achaeans.

All of which, the reader might say, is very interesting, and it may even be true; but what on earth has it got to do with this impersonal autobiography which was foisted on me as such, at so many dollars and cents?

Just this.

On a certain afternoon of August, in this year of grace 1940, I was standing, with my wife, at the window of the thirty-eighth story of a great apartment building in Manhattan, and we were looking out on and admiring what is the proudest, and one of the most beautiful, of all the monuments erected by the human genius to its own greater glory, namely, this great city of ours, New York. There were all those stupendous towers glistening in the sun, the Waldorf-Astoria and Empire State and the Chrysler Building and General Electric and Rockefeller Center and all the rest; and there was the mighty sweep of Fifth Avenue, and the green expanse of Central Park with its great trees and its lakes, and in the distance the heights of Westchester and the fantastic Triborough Bridge, and a glimpse of the Sound, with Long Island beyond. Now we had both of us seen a great many of the most admirable sites and sights of the Old World, but we agreed that the one that spread before our eyes was as good as any of those others, at least insofar as they were made by the hand of man. And yet, far from being cheered and uplifted by all this beauty and magnificence, we both felt depressed and unhappy. For we had but recently arrived from Europe as refugees on board the *Manhattan*; and we had left a good many of our most cherished belongings in our home at Arcachon in Southwestern France, and lost part of such money as we possessed in the collapse of France, and had the rest tied up by the wartime regulations in England; there were also other reasons of a personal nature into which I need not go. But what made us feel far more wretched and hopeless than our own personal losses was something that did not concern us alone.

For we knew, and did not even have to say it to each other, having said it many times before, that if there ever had been such a thing as an object lesson in history, we were It. For we had lived in France for the past three years, more or less, and had friends and our closest relations in England; and we had lost our pleasant and comfortable home, and were now here, strangers, with little more than our bare lives. *And we knew how and why it all happened,* for we had been on the spot, and had kept our eyes open, and had seen Armageddon looming below the horizon, though we had never expected such a catastrophe as was eventually to overtake the whole of Europe. And if there was one thing we knew with as much certitude as it is possible for the finite human mind to attain, it was this: What had happened in France happened because everybody in that country, ourselves included, thought and said that it could not happen in France.

And here we were in America, offering ourselves as a horrible example, and trying to tell our story to people; and some listened with interest, while others were frankly bored by what we had to say; but their comment was invariably the same single sentence: —

"It cannot happen here."

This was the main reason, this general incredulity which we knew only too well was but the worst form of credulity, and at its best an irrational faith in a lucky star, that made us feel so miserable. Now I had spent the last ten or twelve years doing not much but smoking my pipe and reading books, mostly about things that had happened long ago, and thoughts that other men had thought; and as I stood there, at that high window, and looked out on New York, things that I had read came back to my mind. And I said to my wife, who I knew would understand exactly what I meant without my having to explain: —

"*This is Cnossus.*"

I know very well that when I said that I exaggerated a good deal, and things are not nearly as bad as that. I know that the historic parallel or analogy which my remark implied is anything but accurate, not only because it exaggerates the actual danger that hangs over the heads of Americans, but also because it leaves all sorts of circumstances and factors out of account that it ought to take in, and smuggles in other circumstances and factors that have no legitimate business in this business. And I could easily find half a dozen flaws in my own analogy in as many minutes and show that New York is not Cnossus, and the Germans are not the Dorians, and the Atlantic is not the Aegean, and so forth; so no learned critic need tower over me and accuse me of trying to sell the great American public a historico-philosophical pup of the kind sold by that great breeder and merchant of pups of this particular class, the late Dr. Oswald Spengler.

But once we have discounted all that must be discounted, there remains from my analogy this: —

New York, insofar as it is the modern Cnossus, is not the only one. Paris was another. France was part of that great twentieth-century Western civilization which is our own equivalent of the Minoan culture and that of its greater hinterland in Egypt and Asia.

And Paris, and France, are no more. They have been destroyed overnight, like that old Cnossus, and by an enemy far more implacable and far more thorough than were those Achaeans and Dorians. And we, my wife and I, and many friends of ours who have come over with us in the same boat, were there when the Dorians arrived and Cnossus fell, and the great sack of a splendid old civilization by the marauders began.

Our existence, and our presence in America, are a warning to Americans to look to their fences and defenses, not to allow themselves to be taken by surprise, and above all to discount and to *distrust* those in their midst who shout, till their lungs burst, that America is already safe and need do nothing. To this extent a book written by me cannot escape having a political ax to grind; not by what it says, but by what it is. But once I have acknowledged this much, I will emphatically repudiate any imputation that this book was written as a piece of political propaganda. Not that I think there is anything wrong with propagandizing the right cause.

I expect to do a good deal of propaganda once I have got this book off my chest; nor will I leave the reader in any doubt as to the side on which I stand. But in this particular book I advocate nothing. I do not tell Americans what they must do and what they must not, nor for whom to vote, nor what letters to write to their Congressmen, nor anything else of a practical nature and application; though there is nothing to stop them from drawing such conclusions as appear to them reasonable. And the reader will see that I live up consistently to this pledge of abstention.

What I, on the other hand, do intend to tell in this book is how France fell and why; and generally how and why we have come to be where we are. I know that many books are being written at this moment, and some have already been published, that seek to answer these very questions. But I will say with a clear conscience, and without fear of bragging or extolling myself in any way, that the method by which I have arrived at my conclusions is different from the method employed by most of my brethren and competitors. For they claim authenticity for their answers on the ground of their knowledge of inside facts, and their accurate and unprejudiced reporting of such facts; and this approach to the subject seems to me wholly legitimate and necessary. But I, for my part, expressly disclaim any knowledge of inside facts. I have nothing to reveal, in the respectable journalistic or historical sense of the word, for I know nothing of the facts that others don't know, and what I know I know by reading the newspapers, and from what my friends who write those newspapers have told me.

On the other hand, what I have to relate about the events that happened in France, and the causes and trends that had led up to them, is not what was new and distinctive in them, but what was very old, and the repetition or echo of what had already happened before, and more than once, in the course of history. I have nothing to say about what Daladier said, or Gamelin did not do; for this has already been related by those who know far more about these things than I do. But I shall have something to say of what the rulers of Cnossus, and of the Old Kingdom of Egypt, and the

Middle Kingdom for that matter, and the rulers of Rome in the third, fourth, and fifth centuries of our era, said and did; for their thoughts and deeds have occupied my horizon for many years, and have to my mind confirmed the saying of the great Rabbi ben Akiba that there is nothing new under the sun; though others also have made the same point, not infrequently. The question that I am interested in, above all, is this: What is it that makes things such as happened in France within the last ten months happen all over again in the course of centuries? What is it that causes the race of men to commit the same mistakes, makes them put their trust in the same false gods in certain recurrent historic constellations, ever so many times between the beginning and the end of Time? Is it some blind fatality, some cycle of the unknowing and unfeeling forces in our blood, as Spengler asserts? It is questions such as these that I have sought to answer, to the best of my ability; and though it would be ridiculous for me to try to squeeze my conclusions, that is to say the gist of this book, into a sentence or two of the first chapter, I want to state here and now that I consider the answers proffered by Spengler, and by all other fatalists, naturalists, and materialists, wholly false. The view that I shall suggest in these pages is that history is made and unmade by the free mind of man, who passes in this manner through the ordeal imposed on him by an omnipotent, omniscient, and all-good transcendent God. Some day I intend to write another book to demonstrate this view, but in these pages I merely propose to throw it at the reader; he may take it or leave it.

And I can imagine some clerk, by which I mean a cleric and scribe, and not a young man who mixes ice-cream sodas in a drugstore, who, having somehow escaped from the destruction of Cnossus, made his way across the sea to the delta of the Nile, or a city of the Hittite Empire, and told the men who gave him refuge that he saw it all happen, and that the Ahhiyava, that is to say the Nordic Achaeans, were on their way, let all good men beware. I can also imagine the Egyptian high priests, or the Hittite politicians, saying to him, Thank you very much for the intelligence, but it can't happen here.

Well, perhaps it can't. But anyway I shall try to relate how it happened, and why; and to do this in my own way, which is the only way I can do it.

3

Our home at Pyla-sur-Mer, forty miles southwest of Bordeaux, one hundred and fifty miles north of the Spanish frontier, had five rooms, a bathroom, and the usual offices, as the English "To Let" advertisements have it. A commonplace enough home, like that of any moderately well-off retired American surburban couple living by themselves and devoid of social ambitions. The one feature that distinguished the house from dozens of its neighbors was that it was furnished in the English taste, which means rather more simply and much more comfortably than the average French villa; and that the walls of the rooms were restfully distempered in white or creamy yellow, in place of the gay multi-colored papering that the middle-class French seem to love. There was a garden, consisting of some roses, camellias, and arbutus, one lovely cedar, and, for the rest, of the tall pines that had been there for a hundred and fifty years before a local promoter with vision *à l'américaine* invented Pyla-sur-Mer, fashionable offshoot of the almost-fashionable yet pleasant enough resort into which the old fishing and oyster-breeding port of Arcachon had blossomed toward the end of the last century. All the neighboring gardens were fenced-off fragments of the magnificent pinewoods into which some crabbed long-misunderstood genius of the early nineteenth century had transformed the endless sandy waste of the Landes, thus bringing high prosperity, in the form of pit props and resin, to what had been one of the poorest regions of France. Two minutes from our front door the civilizing efforts of the visionary in the American style came to an abrupt end; for the next hundred square miles or so the forest had remained delightfully unpromoted.

There was my workroom — six or seven hours a day of it, behind my Corona; there were my books. My wife took the dog for a walk along the sandy beach that stretched for unbroken miles along the vast lagoon called Bassin d'Arcachon, home of fishing smacks and oyster beds, bounded on the far side by the narrow tongue of pine-crested Cap Ferret; beyond boomed the Atlantic. Sometimes my wife took the dog into the woods, for a change. Madeleine cooked lunch, in the commendable manner of her native Bigorre, the country of Lourdes. In the afternoon, authentic Southerners, we had a siesta. After that, a walk in the forest. Then another two hours' communion with the Corona. After dinner, the wireless; the crossword puzzle of the London *Times*. (We were awful snobs about this, refusing to touch any other kind with a fifty-foot pencil.) At eleven o'clock I took the dog into the garden. On the lead. For Tosca was sixteen years old now, though lifelong strict dieting and plenty of exercise had preserved her girlish figure; most people put her age at six. She was the most ladylike of wire-haired fox-terrier bitches: she never barked; she never performed parlor tricks; she was small, graceful, and dignified, like an eighteenth-century French marquise with powdered hair. Despite her age she was still a tireless hiker; but she did not know that she could not fight cats any more, and chased them on sight; hence the lead. After our outing, an hour or so with detective stories, selected by my wife with scrupulous care from the *Times* library in London.

Such was our routine. It did not hurt anybody, least of all the great German people. On June 16, 1940, we went to bed, as usual. There were, as usual, drinks in the refrigerator, and fruit salad. Orange juice for breakfast, and sliced bacon. What could be more peaceful, more suburban, more American? We might have been three miles from Cleveland, Ohio, somewhere on Lake Erie.

The next night, that of June 17, we spent in a trench reinforced by sandbags, my wife sitting on a suitcase, Tosca on her lap; we counted the bombs as they fell, and wondered how near they were falling; we listened to the D.C.A., which is French for antiaircraft gunnery. Not all night, only the first half; during the second half we sat in the front seat of the Ford; the back was loaded with suit-cases up to the roof. My wife dozed; I made an effort not to, in case the raiders returned. For the next three weeks that Ford was our home. Then Lisbon, *S.S. Manhattan*, New York.

The change had been abrupt. Up to a fortnight before our flight, Pyla, like Arcachon, had no blackout to speak of. We had plenty of everything, though once or twice we had to wait a day or two for our half-pound of coffee. Sugar cards had just been issued; we were destined never to use them. Prices had been going up, though not spectacularly; but then prices had been going up as far back as we could remember, war or no war. At Arcachon there were some convalescent officers and soldiers, but not wounded, just sick. Gasoline was rationed, but we had no time for joy rides anyway. As far as the external aspect of things went, up to the middle of May at any rate, it was difficult to realize that there was a war on.

And yet our very presence at Pyla-sur-Mer was itself an effect of the invisible war. We had not chosen Pyla-sur-Mer. It had been chosen for us, in a manner of speaking, by no less a person than Mussolini, nine months before.

For the home we had to leave on the morning of June 17, be-cause the Germans wanted *Lebensraum*, was not the first home we had lost, but the second, within ten months. We had had an-other, and we had been driven from it, by that Italian nonbellig-erency which meant sitting on the fence while the Germans did the work. This other home had been at Mougins, just behind Cannes, where the road, lined by olive groves and vineyards and acres planted with orange blossom and jasmine, begins to rise and braces itself for its terrific upward sweep behind Grasse, and the crossing of the Alpine passes into Dauphiny, Savoy, and Switzer-land.

Our Mougins home had been even more peaceful than the Pyla one; it had certainly been more spacious and more comfortable, for it had to contain accommodation for the boys' holidays; when we were at Pyla, Hitler had canceled all holidays abroad for Eng-lish undergraduates and schoolboys. We followed, at Mougins, much the same routine that I have already described at Pyla. It was a blessed place for work. The distempered walls of my workroom toned down the white blaze of the sun, as it filtered through the dark brown lattice, to a deep orange. The window was high above my desk; I had to stand up if I wanted to look out on the olive groves and the classic line of the Esterel faintly trembling in the heat of the horizon; but it was good to know that those olive groves were just outside, that the Esterel was out there. A perfect workroom. It had only one fault. It was fifty miles from the frontier of a country which had once battered and subjugated the Teutons and had now become their abject slave and accomplice; a country which was to invent the term "nonbelligerency," and was thereby to infuse new meaning into the till then stupid and detestable word, Dago.

4

I said that our *bastide* was a peaceful place. Yet since September 1938 we, like the rest of Europe, had been living under the shadow of war. My wife and seventeen-year-old stepson were then doing a cure at Châtel-Guyon, in Auvergne, about thirty miles south of Vichy, of which the place was an up-coming young rival. It offered the best treatment in all Europe, so the doctors said, for liver and intestinal troubles. Joe had just had a very serious operation. The treatment was supposed to take twenty-five days. The two of them had had fifteen when the Sudetenland sore, long festering, broke wide open. Chamberlain had flown to Godesberg and back. On Saturday, September 24, France mobilized. Our doctor, saying good-by in a lieutenant colonel's uniform, advised us to leave at once. Next day we drove across the Swiss frontier, a matter of 450 miles between breakfast and dinner, crossing the mountains of the Forez and the Jura into the bargain.

Appeasement ended the Sudetenland rumpus. We spent the next three months at Geneva, at that hotel behind the huge tragic white house of cards which occupies what is probably the grandest hotel site in the world; for its horizon has Mont Blanc, and the other white giants of the Savoy Alps, for a backdrop rising in breath-tightening majesty behind the green domes of the Chablais foothills. I had been to Geneva before, on three or four short visits; this was the first time that I stayed, and I came to love its rarefied, too translucent, too spiritual, precisian air, where the two native trades that thrive most are a careful and elegant literary exegesis, and watchmaking; and I see now that I had to go to Geneva to understand, for the first time, New England and its tradition. I walked those three miles into town, and back, every day along the lake; to my mind it is the most glorious town walk in the world, though sad, for its beauty seems to be cut off by the moment, to lack future, like lovely things in a museum. I turned one of the rooms which during the League session had been used as an office by the British delegation into a small library, and worked away. On Sunday afternoons we took walks in the foothills of the Jura, which began at the back door of the hotel grounds. Several times we walked into France, only three miles distant; there were no formalities; sometimes they asked to see our passports, at other times they didn't. Once or twice we walked to Ferney, the village which had joined the name of Voltaire to its own, because he had lived there. In my opinion he did a good deal of harm in and to this world, though he meant well; to his own parish he was a Maecenas and a benefactor, financing the whole show and building libraries and hospitals like an American oil millionaire. He was very rich, for like George Bernard Shaw in our own day he knew how to dress up a cherished commonplace as a startling paradox, and combined the reformer's high-burning flame with an infallible knack for producing best sellers. Of all his works the one I admire most is his house at Ferney-Voltaire, in its garden at the foot of the Jura. When I saw it I wished it were mine; now I am glad that it isn't.

Toward the end of December, month of black fogs and glacial winds in Geneva, my wife and I migrated, with her two boys down from Harrow for the Christmas "vac," to Aix-en-Provence. It is, as de Brosses, writing in the middle of the eighteenth century, had already perceived, one of the most beautiful towns in France, with its seventeenth-century palaces and fountains and gemlike, perfectly proportioned little squares. The palaces are still there, and the squares, and so are the surrounding hills with their cypresses and dry rubble walls and parasol pines, and the brave promontory of the Mont-Sainte-Victoire towering abruptly above the Provençal plain; the mountain at the foot of which the legions of Marius, two thousand years ago, slaughtered one hundred thousand Germans — not nearly enough, as we have learned since; the mountain beloved, and painted many a time, by Cézanne, citizen of Aix. But when I first knew the place, some twelve years earlier, it was an adorable sleepy little retreat. Arriving from the north, one sat on the terrace of the café of the Cours Mirabeau, a short thoroughfare but one of the most beautiful in the world, with its immemorial clipped plane trees, its moss-grown fountains spouting medicinal warm water, and its lovely baroque mansions with their delicate ironwork; it was like sitting in the antechamber of the southern paradise which is the Department of the Var with its wine-red earth, its hills covered with pine and ilex and chestnut, its terraced olive groves, its cherry and peach orchards, its vineyards, heaths, and sea. . . . That café is still there; but twelve years of the skyrocketing development of road transports had turned the little university town, *Ateno dóu Miéjour*, the Athens of the Provençal South, into a prosperous center of the trucking industry and the motor-coach network, or, in nonbusiness English, into a howling hell of klaxons, loud-speakers, and black clouds of Diesel fumes. A Communist municipal council grown fat on the proceeds of tourist taxation has seen fit to erect a garbage-disposal plant less than a mile from the best hotel. . . .

In the first days of March we were installed in that lovely little *bastide*, four miles north of Cannes at the foot of the hill upon which stands the pleasant little town of Mougins. The house had belonged to Picabia, the fashionable Franco-Spanish painter; a dozen of his drawings still adorned the walls, but I preferred the cartoons and fashion plates from the days of Louis-Philippe, and the two sepias by Hubert-Robert, one of the fall of Sodom, the

other a classical landscape, unnamed. What we liked best were
the almond trees and the *Pyrus japonica*, now in full bloom, outside our porch; and the olive trees in the field beyond, and the smell
of wood smoke in the evening, and the terraced heights and the
clock tower on top of that Mons Aegitna of the Romans which an
age with a slurring tongue calls Mougins. In the corner of the hills
up northwest we could see the terrifying gap of Gourdon, with its
perpendicular cliff dropping three thousand feet on the ice-green
waters of the Loup rushing forth from the high mountains. . . .
All my life I had been dreaming of just such a place to work in;
now I had found it, and I worked away.

Then Hitler discovered that in spite of appeasement he was still
unappeased, and marched into Prague. For some days — or was
it weeks? — we lived glued to the wireless. In the little road that
wound past our front gate battalions of French infantry were
marching to their swift, gay, insolent clarion tunes, the brightest
military music in the world. How we loved that music — and
how we believed in it! As long as those clarions could be heard the
world was safe. Tall Senegalese were building log barriers that
could be swung into place at a moment's notice. I suppose they
were meant to stop tanks; I suppose they supposed in those days
that one could stop tanks with log barricades. They were merry
friendly fellows, those helmeted coal-black legionaries, flashing
ivory smiles on us and patting our dog as we walked by; we loved
them, and were praying for them; for weren't they living proof of
how France was loved, and that she could do what Rome once had
done, could civilize far-flung tribes to protect our common civilization?

The boys had come down from England for the Easter holiday.
One morning, a long-promised treat, we took the motor coach to
Le Trayas and then went for a hike in the Esterel, the mountains
that all the socialites and all the tourists who sit in cafés on the
Cannes sea front know as the most spectacular backdrop in the
world. Years ago I had lived at Le Trayas; for six years, uninter-
rupted save for an occasional motor trip or a month in Paris. I
thought, and think to this day, that the Esterel, especially inland,

is the most beautiful region in the world; not objectively speaking — such superlatives must be a matter of taste — but to *me*. On the steep slopes the air trembles with the heat among the pines, and the world is one vast fragrance blended of resin and wild thyme and rosemary. There is the coolness and unbelievable tranquillity of the gorges, with their dark-red porphyry crags rising like sculpted towers of a primeval Gothic, each with a solitary pine for a flagstaff; three or four ice-cold springs and a torrent in the bottom of the Mal Infernet — all the water there is within forty square miles; a thick carpet of pine needles to walk on, and from the summits and *cols* blue horizons inland, ridge behind ridge, and to the east and south the dark imperial purple of the Mediterranean. I had always been skeptical about Homer's wine-colored sea until I saw it from between half-closed eyelids as I lay prostrate on a flat stone under the Pic d'Aurèle. The Roman road, Via Aurelia, connecting Italy with the Gauls and Spain, is still winding around the flanks of the mountain, parts of it converted into a narrow, ill-kept, and dangerous macadam motor road, but parts with the old gray Roman bricks still intact underneath the herbage. . . . The Sainte-Baume, the little cave where Saint Honorat, apostle of the coast, once lived, is still there; so are the trees that nurtured him, fig trees and wild cherry, and his fountain, behind the neck of the gigantic red iguana which is Cap Roux. . . . Many people find the Esterel barren and sad; I may be prejudiced, seeing that rocky jungle of maritime pine and ilex and cork oak, of ling and broom and brier and lentisk, through the spectacles of memories that are more than half dream. . . . With all its wild solitude the Esterel landscape is not romantic but classical; its small-scaled moderation and the severely composed rhythm of its contours make it the quintessence of the Hellenic and Latin South. Some say it is just like Corsica, only less grand; others are reminded of the Apennines, and still others of Greece. I imagine that my friend Ludwig Lewisohn was right, too, when he likened its vistas to those of the Holy Land.

We had a great day, Martin and Joe and I, carrying our sandwiches in rucksacks, supplementing our bottles of red Corsican wine with water from two of those very rare springs without knowledge of which a day's outing in the Esterel may become very unpleasant indeed. . . . My wife hadn't felt up to climbing, and stayed at home with Tosca — Tosca who had spent six years of her youth chasing the cats of Le Trayas, and the rare squirrels of the Mont de l'Ours and the Hubac de l'Escale, and had known the paths of the Esterel as a town dog knows his back alley; but she was fifteen now, and though she still would enjoy a ten-mile hike in flat country, the stiff gradients of the Esterel with their crumbling rocky soil were no more for her. We picnicked on the flat rocks, in the shadow of the tall red porphyry "needles" of the Mal Infernet gorge, so called because, according to tradition, in the Middle Ages they had a leper colony there. . . . A lovely meadow where two streams meet, a lusher green than the rest of the region because there is always some water, is to this day called Aire des Morts, the Area of the Dead. . . .

We slept in the shade, and climbed up to the ridge, and clambered down to Le Trayas, and at six o'clock we were seated in the homeward bus. We changed at Cannes for the Mougins coach. Alighting near the *bastide*, we found the Grasse road blocked by troops; a regiment of mountain artillery, with light cannon strapped onto the backs of mules, on its way to guard the frontier of the Alps. . . . A steel-helmeted officer on horseback, reining in his mount, stood out, brave silhouette of the power of France, against the sunset sky.

We heard next day that they were fixing machine-gun nests in the *calanques*, the little deep green fiords of the Esterel with their gravel beaches where I used to swim my two miles a day in the old times. We also heard that there were now heavy guns on the summits, trained seaward to protect the Gulf of Cannes; God knows how they had got them up there. The crisis of the conquest of Czechoslovakia blew over, much to the regret of Arno Dosch-Fleurot, who in his Cannes flat yearned to exchange his blue flannel blazer for the khaki of the war correspondent, and who was outlining, over a demitasse, magnificent plans for a campaign in Africa, "if I were the German General Staff." But old Colonel

Clifford Harmon, founder of the International League of Aviators, and of Harmon, New York, was pleased; he did not want to move again, as he had had to do last September; he was now comfortably re-enthroned in his penthouse flat on top of the Martinez, busily corresponding with New York about the publication of his memoirs. I liked the first chapter best, the one narrating how, at the age of ten, he had run away from his father's fort in the old Indian Territory, and lived on horseback with the Comanches until the U. S. Cavalry found him a fortnight later. He now had his fleet of shining Cadillacs in the garage downstairs, as the children and grandchildren of his old Comanche friends, now millionaire oil-well owners back in Oklahoma, had theirs.

5

I went on working. Those were the happiest months of my life, and oddly enough I knew it at the time; I was telling my wife that it was too good to be true. In August my wife went to Châtel-Guyon, the spa in Auvergne; Joe, from England, joined her there; they were to resume the cure which Hitler had interrupted the year before. Probably it was a mistake — I mean their going to Châtel-Guyon; for it is quite plain now that Hitler was determined that Esther and Joe should never complete that cure of theirs. . . . Martin and I were making gorgeous plans for a motor trip to join them on September 2; we were to drive up the Alps to Die, another lovely terraced town that I had been longing to see, and to descend from there the valley of the Drôme; cross the Rhône at Valence, rush the high road up the Cévennes plateau; lunch at the little restaurant at Lamastre, three thousand feet up; deploy into Auvergne by the superb valley of the upper Dore. Then Riom, Châtel-Guyon, and all the delights of the landscape and architecture of Auvergne, most primeval and most mysterious of French provinces, with its extinct volcanoes, its tarns, and its many noble Romanesque churches. . . . The high point of the itinerary was the lunch at Lamastre; for that little restaurant was kept by the nephew of Escoffier, king of French chefs, and was reputed to be the best in France.

On August 22 I opened the morning paper, and knew that all was over. Hitler had concluded the pact with Russia. Within the next ten minutes I telegraphed to my wife: "Return immediately wire arrival." I had no reply. Next day I tried to telephone; the operator said it would take twenty-four hours to get the connection; all over France everybody was trying to telephone to somebody. In the evening the phone rang; it was my wife, who, by an incredible fluke, found the line open and only had to wait a few minutes for the call. She was coming back on Saturday. At 7 A.M. on Saturday I was at Cannes station. Thousands of people thronged the platforms. The last summer holiday of European civilization had come to an end. Esther and Joe arrived at eleven, after an uneventful and even cosy trip; the rush had been northward, Parisward.

Sunday morning. At eleven I was sitting at my desk, making my last stab, for months to come, at work. Joe came into the study. "Two ladies from the Consulate at Nice." The two ladies wore the Riviera summer uniform — open-necked sports shirts, shorts, and sandals; I noted that even judged by the high standards of the United States Foreign Service they had remarkably pretty legs. They were not, as I had thought, consular employees, but volunteers; whenever anything happens in the world, there are always American ladies who will volunteer to do something about it. They wanted to know, in behalf of the Consul, what we expected to do in case of evacuation. When I said that we had a car they suddenly lost all interest in us, and departed.

At 7 P.M. on Tuesday, August 29, after thirty-six hours of suspense, I drove to Nice to seek consular advice. The twenty miles from Cannes to Nice used to be the busiest bit of country road on the Continent; its emptiness, even at that early hour, was ominous. Just before Antibes a soldier, standing in the middle of the road, stopped me. "There are mules ahead." "Well, what of it?" "Yes, but these are mules who have never seen a car; they have just come down from the Alps, to be requisitioned. You must drive very slowly and carefully." Sure enough, for a couple of hundred yards the road was lined with mules; some stood up on their hind legs, the others stood on their heads, two peasants or soldiers struggling to keep down each mule. I drove through at four miles an hour, trying to look like a pedestrian.

At 8 A.M. the consular lobby in the Boulevard Victor-Hugo was black with people — German Jews, Austrian Jews, Czechoslovaks both Aryan and non-Aryan. They were all waiting for U. S. visas. At 9:10 A.M. an official shouted in French, "No visas today, please go, everybody." He had to shout it three times before the lobby emptied. I was left in possession with a great big heavy Chicago Czech. I had arrived first, and he knew it, but he cut in ahead. "I have my first papers. I want reservation on United States Government battleship to evacuate me." It took the tall patient American girl ten minutes to make him understand that (*a*) the U. S. Government was not sending any warships to evacuate anybody, and (*b*) even if the U. S. Government were sending warships they would not evacuate *him*, seeing that he was not an American citizen. "But I have my first papers, I come to Europe with State Department permission on business. I make much money. I want reservation on battleship. Battleships is much safer." At last he was evacuated, from the Consulate if not from Europe. Then the consular young lady stated her case. "For the time being there is no indication that Cannes will be evacuated. But the situation may change at any moment. In any case they will probably requisition all cars. Suppose they take your car away, and a week later Italy comes in and you are ordered to leave your house. You will be allowed fifteen pounds of baggage per person. You will lose all your possessions. This Consulate advises all Americans to leave at once in the direction of Bordeaux."

The argument seemed unanswerable. In an hour's time I was at home. In the afternoon we put Martin and Joe on the Paris train. This was imperative, for, with mobilization imminent, passenger traffic might be stopped at any moment. Throngs at the station. I found a smartly dressed young man arguing, in English, with

Martin. "I am South American. I lose all money at casino. But I have big Auburn car, very fine car, very fast car. You and your brother pay me first-class rail fare. I drive you to Paris." Martin, shyest and sweetest-tempered of Oxford undergraduates, was up against it until I stepped in with an emphatic No, thank you. The boys left. They arrived at Dover in pretty nearly the normal train time; but we were to learn this only some three weeks later.

We spent the next day packing our suitcases. Emily the cook, who had been born at Genoa but who had lived most of her life at Cannes, was to remain in charge; for we hoped, indeed expected, to return in a few days' time. Just the same I had the American Express call for my library, to be kept in storage until further instructions. The books had been packed into two large, specially made wooden cases on the Sunday. Martin and Joe had done an excellent job of it, but this again I was only to find out two months later, when I next saw those cases. Joseph, the Italian gardener, and I loaded up the car in the evening. We found we had to take out the back seat, to make room for the luggage. We went to bed late, for the last time in that Provençal home of ours.

II. The Bridge of St. Gilles

IN the year 1919 two ignorant and conceited old men, the one a self-worshiping visionary American professor, the other a stubborn and wily Welsh lawyer, closed their ears to the pleading of a great soldier and threw away the fruits of Allied victory by contriving, between them, the worst peace treaty in history. A treaty that did all it could to perpetuate German hostility and German unity (which means German striking power) at the same time; a treaty that tried to wrest from the German people its means of livelihood, but did not destroy its capacity for restoring and perfecting its military organization. It was because Wilson and Lloyd George had known nothing about European history, and overruled Marshal Foch, who knew a good deal, that my wife and I found ourselves, at ten o'clock in the morning of August 31, 1939, on the road to Grasse in a car heavily loaded with suitcases and boxes and bags. A good part of our portable belongings, but not all; for we expected — well, we did not really know what we expected; only we could not believe that our peaceful and harmless existence had really come to an end, and hoped for a miracle to save it and to enable us to return to our home.

Our immediate goal was Marseille, there to call on my old friend, Consul General John P. Hurley, and to base our further plans on what he had to say. Now the road to Marseille from our *bastide* at the foot of the hill of Mougins lay by way of Cannes, and thence either by the seashore Corniche which skirted, or else by the great inland highway which traversed, the Esterel, to Fréjus, Brignoles, and Trets. But we figured that both the Corniche route and that of the Col des Adrets might be encumbered by army columns on their way to Menton and the Italian frontier, and decided that we should do better if we went farther inland, by way of Grasse and

Draguignan, along a road a little longer and even more tortuous than the other two, but very lovely and probably deserted. We found both the loveliness and the solitude. The region between Grasse and Les Arcs, where we were to rejoin the main highway, is among the sweetest in Provence, and among the most Provençal, though few foreigners ever trouble to seek it out, since it boasts no stereotyped "attractions." There are landscapes that look their best under a gray sky and even in the rain; we had found the upper end of the Lake of Geneva to be an instance of such, for in sunshine the great 8000-foot rock of Grammont, with the blue expanse of water lapping at its bottom, looks rather like a picture postcard, whereas just before a thunderstorm it has a terrifying grandeur not popular with either the makers or the purchasers of picture post-cards. But then the Grammont, and the Rochers de Naye, and that stupendous gap through which the young Rhône rushes out of the Valais like a mad stallion, to go to sleep, as it were, floating down Lake Leman to the locks and weirs of Geneva, all this is quintes-sentially romantic country, which is probably why Ruskin thought it the most beautiful corner of Europe. Whereas Provence is classi-cal, and at its best in the full blaze of that sun which God had used in making it what it is — a country not of wild thrills and nameless dis-contents and dreams of things that never were on land or sea, but of that contentment which comes to man from recognizing his limitations, from seeing the world in clear contours, from loving and enjoying the small and near-by things for what they are; a country whose very forests are like artfully planned gardens of God. And should the reader object to my use of the labels "roman-tic" and "classical," and say that these are mere names, and what do they mean anyway, I would remind him that I have just explained what they mean; and should he further object to my dragging in these meditations when he was led to expect an account of our wartime flight across Provence, I would say that we were ponder-ing just these things during the first hour or two of that flight, and I am being conscientiously historical. For one cannot drive through Provençal country for hours on end and go on fretting about the next piece of practical business on hand.

What I had wanted to say before I wandered off into recollections of Lake Leman and the difference between classical and romantic was merely that it was a gray day, and the Draguignan country did not look its most characteristic self, as it would have done in the golden light of the last day of August had the sun been out. Nor is the epithet "golden" an idle one in this context, for everybody who knows the Provençal coast knows that at the height of summer the sunlight there is not golden but a blinding white, like the glare of molten metal; but it turns into a mellow gold as the days grow shorter with the approach of the autumn equinox. Anyway, it was a gray day, and I shall remember the road from Grasse to Les Arcs as long as I live, as I last saw it under a gray sky, with the little villages perched on their hilltops to the north — Callas and Fayence, and the rest: Callas, where that rich red wine came from, and Fayence, where my friend Dr. Compain, he who had once saved the life of Tosca when she was very ill, had his property. And there were the cypresses of the churchyard of Draguignan behind its white wall, and the little *bistro* of M. and Mme. Blacas, in the main street; the gentle, thrifty old couple with whom I used to discuss the crops in the old days, and from whom I once bought those great eighteenth-century oil jars for the garden, Hellenic in their perfection of form and finish, and used to buy that nice dry white wine which came from Sète, at about ten cents a quart. They were dead now, and there was a world war about to begin, so we went on to Les Arcs, and past the little café opposite the station where many years ago I had been handed my French driving license, and past the ditch into which I had swerved my little Citroën on the way to the driving test. That corner of the maritime Provence, the triangle formed by Draguignan, Fréjus, and Grasse, the country enclosed by the rivers Argens and Siagne, the chain of Tanneron, and the sea, had been home to me for six years, and then again for nearly three; and I knew every bit of it, its people and its villages, its vineyards and its heaths, its rocks and trees and streams, as I know no other part of the world. All that was behind me now, in space as well as in time; and I had good reasons to think that I should never see any of it again.

It was only after we had struck the main road, beyond Les Arcs, that signs of anything unusual afoot began to appear. In each of the little towns we knew so well — Vidauban, Le Luc, Brignoles, and the rest — the main square was transformed into a military car park; middle-aged reservists, in the old horizon blue of the last war, were sorting and renumbering an amazing variety of lorries and vans and busses and small touring cars, all just requisitioned. The traffic was not, on the whole, abnormal, but twice we narrowly avoided getting entangled in army transport columns, which seemed to make a point of swooping down on us in crooked village main streets. Just beyond Pourcieux we turned off the broad national highway and took to the narrow road which approaches Marseille from the northeast, by way of Trets and Plan-de-Cuques. The hill country we were now traversing is, like all the Marseille region, very different from the rest of maritime Provence; the warm red tints of the sandy soil of the Var yield to gray clay, the friendly wine-colored porphyry to the white desolation of limestone and granite; in the gorges the poplar and willow, rare elsewhere in the deep South, introduce an incongruous Northern note. But this day I had not much thought for the landscape, for I was anxious to reach Marseille before the Consulate closed. As we went on I became aware of a vague feeling that something was wrong; but it was not until we were within ten miles of the city, that is to say already within its suburban fringe, when the malaise had intensified into something like real terror, that I realized what was wrong. For the last twenty or twenty-five miles we had not met, or passed, a single car.

Now I should explain here that Marseille is the second largest city of France, and the greatest seaport not only of France but of the whole Mediterranean, and one of the most important in the world; its population, with the wide belt of suburbs, is well over the million; and this huge agglomeration, through which used to pass most of the trade of continental Western Europe with the Near and Middle East, as did also much of the oil coming from overseas, is shut off from the land by a ring of mountains, so that the enormous traffic was forced to flow by one or other of six narrow roads, each of which formed a regular bottleneck for the first fifteen or twenty miles. For this reason Marseille was, of all the great cities of Europe, the most unpleasant to approach by car. It so happens, moreover, that while on the whole the French are among the best drivers in the world, the Marseillais are undoubtedly among the worst; we used to joke in the old days, when we had not much else to worry about, that in some of the Marseille streets the traffic moves on two levels, as at Grand Central in New York, only there is no elevated roadway — they simply drive on top of one another, and some of them scramble out alive.

So we realized, all of a sudden, that what had at first bothered and then terrified us was that we had the whole road to ourselves, literally to ourselves, for there were no pedestrians either, not so much as a dog or cat for miles on end; the empty shining streetcar tracks added to the sense of desolation; the windows of the two rows of houses were blank cavities under a leaden sky, and the only sounds to be heard were the humming of our engine and the swishing of our tires. It was as if all life but our own had departed from the whole planet, and as if we were headed for one of the craters of the moon; and we positively sighed with relief when at the top of the Canebière a taxi, dashing out of a side street, shot across our path at fifty miles an hour and cleared our bumpers by an inch amidst the screeching of our brakes; for then we knew that this was, after all, Marseille. As I look back now, that drive of ten miles along the dead boulevards of what I remembered as the busiest town in Europe stands out both as a portent, which I felt it to be then and there, and also as the weirdest of all my memories of the war, more disturbing than the burst of the bombs above the suburbs of Bordeaux.

2

We reached the Consulate at a quarter to five. There was Mr. Hurley, calm, kindly, and to the point, as I had always known him, looking cool in his fresh silk suit in the midst of a wilted and harassed world. We had not met for thirteen years; for when we stayed at Aix, only twenty-five miles distant, in the first months of the year, and I discovered that he was now Consul General at Marseille, he happened to be off to the United States on leave, and he had only just returned. We spoke of the old Vienna days, when the world seemed young and was flushed with the hopes of the recent Allied victory, and with the easy money of the inflation; it was he who reminded me that for about a year we used to meet practically daily, after lunch, in that cosy little café in the Spiegel-gasse, behind the tall spire of St. Stephen's, to discuss, over a demitasse and a cigar, the way the world was going; and little did we dream in those days of the abyss toward which that pleasant old world was even then headed, though raw-faced young men in brown shirts and with hooked crosses on their armlets were already marching and brawling in the working-class suburbs of Vienna.

But now we had little time for reminiscences. He was horrified when I told him that my wife had no American visa; my excuse was that I had meant to finish my book, that eternally just-about-to-be-finished old book, by the end of the year, and to return to the United States then, and my wife was to follow me after a visit to her people in England; and we both had thought that there was plenty of time. So did, for that matter, the British and the French Government, and so do still on the very day when I write this the people of the United States; but this point was not raised. He advised me to apply for the visa at once, and to drift, in easy stages, toward Bordeaux, whence we might be evacuated in U. S. ships in an emergency. I spoke about our pleasant home at Mougins, and the possessions we had left behind, and of our lease that was still running until November, and of our hope that Mussolini would not turn traitor to the Western World of which Italy formed a part. Mr. Hurley stuck to his advice, "Go west"; but he said we might await developments at Nimes, which was only about 120 miles from Marseille and a very pleasant town with comfortable hotels. And I said that we did not like towns, but that we might go another hundred miles further west to Lamalou-les-Bains in the foothills of the Cévennes, a quiet little resort which we had visited before, and loved. So Mr. Hurley gave us his blessing, and we were to return next morning to arrange for the visa, and then to start on our westward trek. We slept in a crude little hotel that night, for the one we tried to book rooms at was full of returning colonials; and we had our first experience of a great city in a blackout, or what in those untutored days passed for a blackout; and we wondered, for the first but not the last time, whether we should be awakened by dropping bombs.

So next morning we returned to the Consulate, and learned what an easy job a camel had if he wanted to pass through the eye of a needle; for in doing so he was not required to produce his birth certificate, in two copies, a certificate of marriage, a judicial record, a certificate of morals, a certificate of health, a letter from his bank manager attesting that he could support himself on the far side of the needle; and on top of all this, two witnesses to prove that he was the camel he claimed to be, and not a quite different camel. Of all the papers demanded, the medical certificate was the only one that we could acquire on the spot; all the others had to be collected from London, Paris, and Geneva, and there was a jolly little world war waiting to break out just around the corner; so the prospects were not so good. The best thing we could do, in the circumstances, was to have some lunch, and, leaving our car in front of the Consulate because I hated to drive in a town where other cars were apt to climb on the roof of my own, we took a taxi to Basso's, fervently hoping that the driver would stick to the ground level.

Now Basso's was not the best restaurant in Marseille; I knew at least four that I preferred; but it was very Marseille-ish, with its glass verandah facing the bustle of the Old Port and the ugly old Sardine, as the enormous thin ironwork footbridge spanning its entrance well above masthead height was called. We went to Basso's because I thought that this might well be the last time we ever had a meal at Marseille; for the sight, rather than the flavor. It was Friday, and, like good Provençals, we ordered bouillabaisse.

We were in the midst of it when the gray-haired headwaiter, whom I had known for many years, stepped up and said that the radio had just announced that early that morning the Germans had invaded Poland, and that general mobilization had just been ordered in France. He added that he had fought in the last war, hoping that it was to be the last. "Now I am fifty-two; and I have to go back tonight, to fight 'em again. My two sons are going too. Is the bouillabaisse all right, sir?"

I finished that bouillabaisse; not because I craved it, far from it, but somehow I felt that I owed finishing it to that gray-haired headwaiter who had inquired whether I liked it, although at the age of fifty-two he was being uprooted from his comfortable prosperous existence, and was going back that evening "to fight 'em again." My wife saw the point, but she did not finish her lunch; she was thinking of her sons back in England.

We had to see the doctor recommended by the Consulate, about my wife's certificate. He lived a mile and a half from the Old Port. It was very hot and close. We hailed a passing taxi. It did not stop. We hailed another. Same result. Three or four whizzed by, full of people with suitcases; then a column of empty ones. I spoke to a policeman. "Don't you know? The empty ones are on their way to the requisitioning centers. The full ones are on their way to the station, *avec des mobilisés*. This is war." We had an appointment with that doctor; we had to run that mile and a half across town in the stuffy heat, carrying Tosca. When I thought that we were near our goal I spoke to a passer-by, to make sure. He was a little round man, blue-eyed, about forty, decently dressed in the black beloved by the Marseillais; he looked like a comfortable neighborhood grocer. He answered my query, and then asked, "You English?" "American." "Bravo," was the unexpected comment. "I have just heard on the radio that your President Roosevelt has called a council of war and has ordered general mobilization. We are allies again! We shall show those dirty Boches! *Vive Pershing! Lafayette, nous voilà!* Tonight I join my regiment. You come and fight too. *Vive l'Amérique!*" He embraced me; we parted with mutual felicitations and benedictions. I had not the heart to disillusion him; I wondered what he might have heard on the wireless that he could so flagrantly misconstrue. I had no idea what President Roosevelt was going to do, but I was pretty sure that he was not going to order general mobilization.

We saw the doctor; he testified that my wife was not a congenital half-wit, nor a paralytic; we returned to the Consulate. Mr. Hurley was out; there was not much we could do but write for my wife's papers to London. At half past three we left Marseille by the Salon road. This is the first lap of the main oil route of France. Normally, the huge tank lorries, each with a trailer even larger than itself, used to leave Marseille every day about midday. They struck the main Paris road at Sénas, south of Avignon, about 3 P.M., and traveled all night. I never found out just how they worked the thing, but I figured that the crews slept during the day, for I never met these enormous oil convoys on the roads of the Center or the North before 4 or 5 P.M. Now this road, past Sénas, was the main route from Paris to the Riviera, following the Rhône from Lyon down; a first-class, beautifully planned and kept road, four-track along most of its length, traversing picturesque and varied country. I used to know it in the old pre-road-transport days, when, apart from tourist traffic, it was practically empty along its whole six hundred miles. Once you had cleared Fontainebleau, and outside the not too numerous towns and villages, your speed was limited solely by what your engine could do. When I, after an absence of four years, returned to France in 1937 I drove down this road to the coast. It was February, and dark from Montélimar onward. It was also unmitigated hell, with an unending, unbroken column of oil trucks, each a good twelve tons with its trailer, bearing down on you at forty miles an hour, blinding you with their headlights, choking you with their black Diesel fumes. Subsequently I made it a rule never to be caught on that road north of Sénas after noon; any sort and length of detour was preferable. Well, here we were on this dreaded road, where it was the narrowest, at 4 P.M.; but there was not a single oil truck to be seen. There were plenty of private cars, all northbound, and some military cars full of officers in khaki darting at full speed in and out of the traffic. But we had not the impression of a flight; had there been a bullfight scheduled at Arles next day, the road would have looked much the same.

3

As a matter of fact, looking back on that 1200-mile trek of ours across France, from the extreme southeast to the extreme southwest, a trek of which what I have described so far was barely the first lap, I realize that we considered it, at the time, a lark rather than a tragic exodus. True, there was uncertainty ahead, and our pleasant home, full of cherished little things, behind us; and the car was stuffed full of luggage, to remind us that this was no ordinary joy ride. I remember that we regarded, and referred to, ourselves as refugees. But it was refugeedom de luxe, and we never for a moment thought that it might have any but a happy ending. During the first week at any rate we fully expected to return to Mougins. In the months that followed, when we had decided not to, we often cursed ourselves for mugs, and our decision for silly panicking, and thought, and expressed, unkind thoughts about the U. S. Consular Service for having been so emphatic against our going back. On the other hand we were absolutely certain that Britain and France were going to settle Hitler's hash, sooner or later, and the whole thing was hardly more than a temporary inconvenience, and the outcome well worth a little discomfort; we were also, in a sense, relieved that the inevitable had happened at last, that the blow which we had been predicting for years had now fallen, and that we were still alive and things around us were pretty much what they had always been. In a word, we had altogether lost contact with reality, and lived in a curiously elated and yet passive mental state blended of thrill, apprehension, and the sense of our own impotence. On the one hand, the fact that this trip was not our own choice but had been forced upon us constituted a real grievance. On the other hand, there was that

exhilaration which always accompanies one's being relieved of responsibility and the obligation of taking the initiative. We lived
from day to day, comfortably enough; we had money in our
pockets to last us six or even eight weeks; and we could do nothing
about anything. I should not analyze our state of mind at such length
had it been ours alone. But I am sure it was typical, the state of mind
of thousands, if not millions, sharing our predicament: we were
trapped by a danger that we had foreseen for years but had done
nothing to avert; it involved immediate disturbance but no unbearable hardship, and this produced the illusion, almost, of a change
for the better. All this has historical importance. It was, as we
know now, on the one hand the euphoria of the old European
civilization, the exalted lightheaded feeling which some say heralds
the approach of death; but on the other hand it was merely part of
the war of nerves, the mock sense of security into which Hitler
had lulled us all before he was ready to strike.

We slept that night at Arles, in our pleasant old haunt the Hôtel
Jules-César. At ten in the morning we were on our way, crossing
the bridge of the Grand-Rhône into the great island of the
Camargue. How I longed to go out of our way and run down
southeast to Les Saintes-Maries, and to see the little that was left
of the fine Abbey of Psalmodi, and to explore, before it was too
late, the vast lagoon of Vacarés, scene of that moving masterpiece
of the great Provençal poet, Joseph d'Arbaud, *La Bèstio dóu
Vacarés*, fifteenth-century account of the lonely half-clerk (cleric,
not shop assistant), half-cowboy, of how he met, in the fens, the
Beast: the last of the demigods, an authentic Satyr and disciple of
Pan; he was old and tired now, and begged for food, and felt that
the end was near; but all his power had not left him, and one day,
before the end came, he played on his flute, and all the million
beasts of the great Delta, the savage bulls and cows, the wild-
running white ponies, the otters and beavers and foxes and wild
boars, and all the birds, the flamingoes and herons and bustards,
the cranes and mallards and shrikes and magpies and kestrels and
the rest of them, rose and gathered in great converging columns,
and followed him in a thunderous pagan cavalcade. . . . For this

was Provence, westernmost outpost of the Hellenic soul; it was only fit that the last survivor of the semi-divine race of the children of Pan that had once peopled the wooded slopes and valleys of Hellas should come here to die, near the spot where the "holy Marys," Mary the Magdalen, and Mary the mother of James, and the Mary whose real name was Salome, and Sarah their Egyptian maidservant, had landed from their little boat on the coast of Gaul.

For twelve years I had meant to explore the Camargue; I had crossed it more times than I could remember, and knew Aigues-Mortes and Le Grau-du-Roi, in its western corner; but somehow I never managed to turn south after crossing the bridge which the officials and the tourists call that of Trinquetaille, but the people call Trenco-Taio, and so I never saw the fortress-church on the shore where the gypsies foregather in May, to honor their patron, Sarah the Egyptian maidservant, nor the country of the thousand lagoons where the *gardians* on their white ponies, quaint survivors of a prehistoric equine race extinct elsewhere, herd their savage cattle, and clouds of flamingoes darken the setting sun. I had always said to myself, there was plenty of time . . . But I had deceived myself. It was too late now; once more, as so often before, I passed the turning to Les Saintes-Maries on the left, and we crossed the Little Rhône at St. Gilles, and were in Languedoc. Then Lunel, and Montpellier, where the empty silence of the great square facing the Théatre, in ordinary times one of the noisiest spots in the world, with its idle chatting crowds and clanging trams and cars klaxoning away for the fun of it, was rather unnerving. . . .

After Montpellier the road forks. On the left it follows the great lagoon of Thau, with the houses of Sète glistening on the heights of the far shore, and forks again at Narbonne toward Spain on one hand, and Toulouse and the North on the other. On the right it rises slowly until you find yourself in the midst of the mountains that the traveler across the plain glimpses on the horizon on his right without quite believing in their existence: isolated peaks, some shaped like cones pointed or truncated, and others like vaulted domes and colossal eggs, and still others like staggered pyramids and swaying towers and gigantic mushrooms; a whole forest of such

fantastic indigo cloud-shapes — in short, the Cévennes. We took the
fork on our right, and at one o'clock we reached the mountain
village of Gignac. In the plane-shaded square about thirty cars,
and half a dozen coaches, were parked in front of the little inn;
in ordinary times this would have meant merely that it was a very
good little inn. We entered the usual low-ceilinged dining room
with its tile floor and paper-clothed tables, and the welcoming
and welcome sizzle from the kitchen in the rear. It was full of
people, commercial travelers (why are commercial travelers the
most unmistakable profession all over the world?), glum heavy
unshaven farmers, four or five coach drivers and conductors, in
shirt sleeves, with their leather satchels and ticket punchers slung
over the backs of their chairs, and three colonels, one with his
lady.

It was a memorable meal, and now that the age of such meals, in
little French village inns, has passed, perhaps forever, to allot to it
a word or two in the general record has become part of the historian's official duty. . . . Trout that tasted as if it had been
flung straight from its mountain stream into the blistering panful
of butter — as it probably had been; two kinds of sausage, a long
thin one of chestnut-fed pork, rather like the best American farm
sausage but smoked, and small fat ones, contrived of chicken's
breast and truffles. There were other good things too, but these
stand out, and it all cost, for two people, with a bottle of iced
and most commendable *vin rosé* of the region, one dollar and forty
cents. . . . I asked to see the *patron*, which is French not for the
guest but for the boss; for I knew that French innkeepers love
nothing more than a word of expert appreciation. He came, a tall
man in the customary white smock and linen cap which mark,
but do not make, the *chef*; I made my cheering speech; but he was
not cheered. "Look at all this," he said bitterly. "*I* made this.
It took me thirty years to build *this* up. Yes, I know that my sausage
and my *quenelles* are unique, and my trout the tastiest in Hérault.
Hundreds of people know it too. They come here in their cars not
only from Montpellier and Béziers, but from Nîmes and Carcassonne and even Toulouse. A hundred miles, to eat my *quenelles*.

And now I must leave it all. Tomorrow I go to Toulon. I am in the navy." I tried to comfort him by saying that lucky was the warship over whose galley he was to preside. "That's what *you* think!" he snorted. "In the navy, they make me an engineer."

4

At four o'clock we arrived at Lamalou. As I have already said, it is a little spa in the foothills of the Cévennes; it is situated just off the main road that leads from Montpellier to Toulouse by way of Clermont, Bédarieux, and Mazamet. Just past Bédarieux you turn north, if you don't miss the turning, and drive about three quarters of a mile in an avenue of Lombardy poplars; and then you are in Lamalou.

Your first impression of Lamalou-les-Bains is that it is not much of a place, and your first impression, for once, penetrates to the soul of the matter; for it is part of the soul of Lamalou that it understates itself. It is, in the shade of its magnificent centenarian planes and chestnuts, architecturally so nondescript as to be almost unnoticeable. Just some gray-shuttered old houses, most of them hotels, left over from the last third of the last century, a period not marked by either its taste or its daring in building; a few modest cafés, with iron tables and chairs, painted blue or red, on the sidewalk; a few little shops; a bandstand in front of a one-storied assembly hall, with large plate windows, called the casino; an "*établissement thermal*," where the guests take the treatment, identified by a tall chimney behind and a damp smell, like that of a steam-filled bathroom, in front; a whitewashed little church — that is all. Not a building in the whole place that you would accord a second glance; not one that you could recall if you turned away your head. I knew four or five such little towns in the France that was before the war, or in the France that was, for short; I loved them all, and love them still. For these places existed outside time. They resisted change because they did not notice it. In such places nothing ever happened; they were pure space — that is to say, pure contemplation, the projection, onto this tormented earth of ours, of that angelic essence which is understanding unmoved by the will and the passions. But that is, perhaps, the voice of nostalgic regret for what has gone forever, overstating its case. Anyway, when I first knew Lamalou-les-Bains, which was three or four months before the time of our arrival just mentioned, I added it to the list of the three or four places in one of which I hoped to spend my old age. Most people would translate this panegyric into plain American by saying that Lamalou is one of those Godforsaken, one-horse, two-by-four, backwoods towns a thousand miles from anywhere; which of course covers with fair accuracy part of what I mean, though not all. It leaves out, among other things, the oft-noted fact that there is no accounting for tastes. It also leaves out the chestnut forests that clothe the surrounding slopes, and the heather-covered plateau, broken only by the low rubble walls marking the fields, which guides the eye, once you have climbed those slopes, toward a far horizon of serrated peaks. It also leaves out the sunlight, which in the Cévennes has a tinge of aquamarine green, very different from the rosy opalescence of Provençal skies.

I have often thought that if I were allowed to live my life over again, I should want to spend my youth in New York (which is just what I have done). For a town-born, town-bred young man with imagination New York is a good place, for it is a frontier town: it is situated on the frontier of the unexpected; there is, in a very real sense, more high adventure in New York than in the jungle of the Amazon, where adventure merely means keeping alive against odds. I used to think, in the places of which I have just spoken, such as Lamalou, or Uzès, which also possesses the inestimable quality of timelessness, though it differs from the former by its man-made proud beauty — I used to think in those places, how pleasant it would be to retire there, at the age of seventy, and to look back on and write about life in New York. Little did I suspect in those days that I was destined to look back on and write about life in Lamalou, and Uzès, on the thirty-eighth floor of a Manhattan apartment hotel.

I also said, a little while ago, that nothing ever happened at Lamalou. Well, one thing did happen at Lamalou. On Sunday, the third of September, A.D. 1939, just about lunch time, Auguste, the hotel valet, came to us as we were sitting in the hotel garden over a peaceful *apéritif*, and announced that Great Britain had just declared war on Germany.

5

As I look back on that first week of the last European war, I see the great plane trees of Lamalou, and the green sunlight seeping into my room through the foliage of the age-old chestnut trees behind the hotel, in the little park where children played and an old priest or two read his breviary, a park that had no fence or boundary toward the north but merged imperceptibly into ten thousand square miles of mountain and primeval forest. I see the little hotel garden with its faded crimson and yellow sunshades and little tables and chairs on the grass-tufted crazy pavement, where we sat and drank vermouth before luncheon and dinner. The rest is a blank. For we were marooned, as effectually as, if less irrevocably than, if Lamalou had been on Pitcairn Island or Tristan da Cunha. But this isolation, the most complete and most poignant of which I have recollection in all my life, did not spring from that timeless quality of the little town of which I have spoken. Those places outside time which I loved were, among other things, lookout towers; it was perhaps their greatest charm that one could watch from them the antics of men who lived and scrambled and wearied themselves to death for nothing, or very little, within time; the follies and futilities of the human race, so called. Now we looked out on nothing. Our island was surrounded by a blank wall, of which we did not know, at the time, the name, though we have had ample opportunity, and reason, to learn it since. It was the frustration and even paralysis of the complex organism which provides the news without which, unfortunately but most certainly, modern society cannot live. It began on the first day of the war, and endured till that last day of which it had hastened the advent.

There is such a thing as too much information, and a very dangerous thing it is. The mass of Americans know nothing of what is going on around them in the world, because their brains are soddened by spates of newsprint, loosened on them four or five or six times a day, and by the ceaseless droning flood of the radio. The people of wartime France knew nothing of what was going on around them in the world, because their governors told them nothing; by and by they came to take no news to be an attempt to conceal bad news, and this sapped their confidence, which had not been much of a muchness anyway, for reasons of which I expect to treat further on. Uncertainty is the mother of panic; its fathers were, among others, in the France of 1939–1940 (for its begetting was a co-operative enterprise), the gentlemen who were paid, by the masses of French taxpayers, to provide certitude through the various information centers monopolized by the French State. During those first weeks of the war the mails were disorganized, for the post-office staffs had been depleted by the mobilization, and the trains were needed for the troops and their supplies. This was both inevitable and excusable; and there was an excellent case for reducing the size of newspapers. But the really essential information can be easily conveyed on a single daily sheet; it need not be a large sheet. The Paris newspapers, let alone the London ones, did not arrive at all. All we received was that single sheet, sometimes from Montpellier, sometimes from Toulouse; and it contained no essential information, but only an official bulletin or two, and other rubbish of that sort. I realize now that they could not have told us much in those early days, even if they had wanted to. But they told us nothing, and it was very disturbing. At 7 P.M. we could listen, for the price of an *apéritif*, to the radio in one of the cafés; though those who grudged the price could hear it too, standing outside. It told us nothing at all. Gentlemen employed, or sponsored, by the Third Republic made polished speeches about the necessity, and inevitability, of victory.

On the second day of the war, or maybe the third, I wrote to

Ambassador Bullitt in Paris. He and I had been friends in those old Vienna days, when both of us, and the world around us, were young, and later when he had that charming little house of his off the Avenue Victor-Hugo. Then we drifted apart, and the next I heard of him he was Ambassador at Moscow. I now asked him to give me something to do — any sort of work, paid or unpaid, for the Government. I found my enforced idleness the hardest part of the immediate situation to bear; I felt that in times like those we were living in, everybody ought to do something directly and practically useful. In making this offer I made the very mistake, though with far less fateful results, that was to characterize the whole conduct of the war on the Allied side, and to cost France her freedom. I was thinking of the current war in terms of the last. I felt from the outset, in fact I had felt it for five or six years before the war began, that this was to be the last stand of white civilization against the new machine-strengthened barbarism represented by Germany and Russia; that the stakes were the lives of us all, and everything that made those lives worth living. And, feeling this, I could not imagine for a moment that the United States could keep out of it for long. Oh yes, I remembered the *Lusitania;* and I knew that the *Lusitania* was nothing compared with the issues of *this* war. I also remembered that in that last war the Government of the United States had offered ample scope to men with special knowledge who were prepared to serve the nation for little pay or none. So I wrote to William Bullitt. He replied at once, very kindly; I need not say to what effect. But it was only a month later that I received his letter; it took the P. O. all that time to catch up with our wanderings.

One afternoon I was having a talk with Auguste, the hotel valet, in the garden. He had fought in the last war, but in this he had not, so far, been called to the colors. He was a man about forty-five, of some sound schooling, sober and hard-thinking and surprisingly knowledgeable, a type that in his walk of life could only be met with in France. He knew more history than ninety per cent of our legislators. We discussed the current happenings that we knew nothing about, when we were joined by one of the few remaining guests, a small, dark-haired, swarthy-complexioned lady of about sixty. She had a limp, was dressed in black, and had a face and general presence rather like a frail and unsuccessful bird of prey. She was, she had told us, the widow of a general who had fought in the last war. One of us happened to mention the thousands of Spanish Communist and anarchist militiamen who were interned in concentration camps in Southwest France, and deplored the expense and danger that their presence constituted for the country. This gave the little old lady her cue. She said that the only thing to do with these prisoners was to let the Senegalese troops loose on them, with their long sharp knives. Now I had no love for these prisoners; in my opinion it was the urgent duty of the French authorities to get rid of them as quickly as possible. What I disliked was the pop-eyed relish with which the old lady imitated the swish of the long Senegalese knives across human jugular veins. To change the subject, I said how difficult was the position, in wartime, of a foreigner like myself, past useful military age and without the least experience of soldiering, who wanted to serve France; driving an ambulance was about the only job open to the likes of us. The old lady interrupted me. "Speaking of cutting throats, the Spanish Communist prisoners are not the only ones . . . It is delightful to meet a foreigner like you, Monsieur, one who loves France and wants to serve her. Unfortunately there are the others. Ah! I knew them, in the last war. One in particular I remember, in that little fishing village on the Mediterranean coast — I am not at liberty to name it. He was a writer, too." (A meaningful glance at Auguste.) "He too spoke our language almost without an accent. He too had a good deal to say about his love for France. He was, in a word, of just the most dangerous sort. You might think that they could not do much harm in one of these little seaside villages, or in a place like Lamalou" (another glance at Auguste) *"but it's just there that you would be wrong.* Well, I shan't bore you with details. *I watched him* . . . There were mysterious flashes, at night, on that deserted little beach . . . I saw it all. The gendarmes nabbed him in time. Ah, Monsieur, this is what you can do for France: watch out for soft-spoken foreigners who say they love France." She gave

Auguste another long look, and tap-tapped away with her stick. When she was out of earshot, Auguste the valet slapped me on the back, three times, good and hard, and burst into Homeric laughter.

6

Six days passed. We received no mail. We cabled to London, to our people. There was no answer. We heard, on the wireless, about the *Athenia*, and saw in the Montpellier news sheet that French troops were fighting in the Saar. One morning there was a rumor that German aeroplanes had flown in the night over Nimes. They did not drop bombs, a thing we could not understand; for we had been led to expect that this war was to be one long unceasing aerial bombardment. We took walks on the heights, and loved them, though we were in a sort of daze. We did not know that those were to be our last mountain walks in France; what we did know was that we had come to the end of something, and that at our feet gaped the Unknown.

When we had arrived, there were still four or five guests at the hotel; the rest had scattered at the news of mobilization. Now they were all gone; on Thursday evening the *patron* (he was an Alsatian, and had heard from his wife, who managed their hotel in a little town near the German frontier, that she had stayed put and was now a Red Cross nurse) told us that all the hotels at Lamalou had been requisitioned by the army, and were to be turned into hospitals; but we could stay until Sunday if we wanted to. We did not want to; we could not stand inaction any longer. There had been no news about Italy. This we took to be good news. Italy was not going to fight; something that many people in France, especially those who like ourselves belonged politically to the Right, had confidently foretold. Why shouldn't we return to our home at Mougins? We decided that we would.

In the morning I went to the *mairie*, to have our identity cards visaed. This was something new, the first war measure to affect us. For in times of peace foreigners had to have their identity cards stamped only when they changed their residence or left France. We had not changed our residence, but were returning to it. I told the two officials how we loved their region, and that we were sure to return next summer, with the boys, for a long holiday. After Hitler had been properly licked. One of them stamped our papers, "leaving for Marseille." For we meant to stop at Marseille, to see Mr. Hurley once more.

We left after lunch, not across the mountains, via Clermont-l'Hérault, as we had come, but by the lower road that rejoined the Béziers–Montpellier highway. We had been over it before, and it was a very beautiful road. We saw no sign of the war until we reached Lunel; there we ran into great activity — hundreds of horses and mules were being requisitioned. We recrossed the two Rhônes, and reached Arles about seven. The manager and head porter of the Jules-César greeted us as old friends; we seemed to make a habit of it.

My wife lay down to rest a little before dinner. I crossed the boulevard, and sat down in the café opposite the hotel, for an *apéritif*. There is no dusk in Provence; once the sun has set, darkness descends in a few moments. It had descended now, and it was very dark indeed; for Arles was a great garrison town, and they were strict about the blackout. The arc lights of the boulevard had been replaced by tiny dark blue bulbs; the cars which drove past had only their side lamps lit, and these too were varnished dark blue. But the people of Arles crowded the sidewalks, walking up and down, chatting; as they had done in the Latin towns of the South for the past two thousand years. The terrace of the café was crowded with officers, discussing the war. Now I am not a visionary nor a mystic, but a hard-boiled realist, yet for once, sitting there in the dark, I had a vision.

Years ago, when I had first explored Provence, I thought that I had discovered the meaning of Provence, and with it the meaning of European history; and it was this: There were two races in Europe, two great group allegiances determined not, as the pseudo-scientists of Hitlerism said, by blood, but by historic and intellectual heritage. There were the Builders: hard-working, sober-minded people, small of stature and dark of coloring, who saw the things of this world in great clear-cut precise patterns, despised strong drink but loved wine, and lived by agriculture and commerce in their great cities that studded the coasts of the inland sea. They had a gracious dry climate which enabled them to work out of doors, and to travel, all the year around, and encouraged clear vision in the things of the mind; and they had discovered, twenty-five or thirty centuries ago, that there was a context in this universe that man had found ready-made, the way things were and ought to be, and this unalterable context was the Law whereby men must live. These men hated fighting, but had found that the only way to avoid having to fight was to fight better than the enemy; and they constructed a great Empire surrounded by an iron wall, a wall composed of small dark soldiers who had steel breast-plates and muscles of steel, and fought extremely well in closed ranks according to scientific rules. As long as this wall held, the Empire was safe, and the small dark sober-living men could go about their occupations and administer the Law, which was the same for all, and worship God who was their Father.

But outside that wall there lived another race, and this I called the race of Raiders. Great heavy men with straw-colored hair and bodies of a faded yet shiny pink, fundamentally stupid yet also extremely cunning when hunger or fear whipped them out of their habitual stupor; but their dominant quality was laziness. Their climate was harsh and wet and their earth covered by thousands and thousands of square miles of primeval forest, where it was not marshland; and they did nothing to improve their earth, or their general condition, for they needed a prod from the outside to make a start, and for many centuries this prod was not forthcoming. They hated work, for the rewards of work among them were scanty, and left it to their women; they fuddled their brains with strong fermented drink, for they could not bear to look their inclement world in the face, and not having discovered the art of thinking, they were extremely bored with each other and with themselves. When they were hungry they went forth to slay the wild beasts around them, aurochs and stag and boar, and gorged themselves on bloody meat until they could not move; then they lay down in their smelly dens, and slept it off. They were extremely brave, for they had not discovered that life was something to prize and to guard; life or death, it was all the same to them, but they loved a fight, and loved loot; so they spent most of their time, when they did not sleep or gorge, quarreling among themselves, and beating out one another's brains. But the time came when they received news about that other race that lived in resplendent cities beyond the two great rivers and the high mountains, and wallowed in wealth. So they organized raiding parties, and slipped across the frontier where they could, and collected some booty; but they found to their great surprise that though any one of their own numbers was a match, in hand-to-hand fighting, for two of the small dark helmeted men, five hundred of these latter could make mincemeat of a thousand giant raiders. But the rewards of the forays were enormous, and the numbers of the raiders were ever on the increase, while after a time the number of the defenders, and also their spirits, seemed to shrink. And this went on for centuries.

The moment came when the Raiders had settled down, and shed the worst of their bestial ways, and began to learn from the older race the ways both of peace and of war; and after a few centuries more they had become outwardly quite civilized and in some fields of prowess even surpassed their masters. But underneath the crust of civilization one thing did not change, and this was their spirit. They had acquired all the old arts, and invented some new ones, but one thing they could never learn, and never understand: the Law, and why it should be obeyed not only by the weak, who could be made to obey, but also by the strong. To them the idea that man could not make his own law, but had to discover a Law that pre-existed him and was independent of his wishes and interests, remained forever unfathomable, and not understanding it, they despised it. They used the word Law, but in their own sense, and this was their own Will. Men were allowed to do what they were able to do; for if they were stronger than the rest, who could stop them? This was the most natural rule in the world, the only natural rule. In times of peace they wrote long and learned books to prove this; and this was when they were too weak to do anything else. Whenever they felt strong, they returned to their old ways, and raided the Others. And this was the history of Europe for the last two thousand years.

Now it had taken me years to figure all this out, partly by reading books and partly by just sitting and smoking my pipe in a garden that was hidden on the hillside among the pinewoods and overlooked the Provençal sea, but I *saw* the whole thing in a flash, as one sees a painting, one day as I was gazing at the Pont du Gard, that triple sequence of orange-tinted arches that spans the emerald river and the gray-green heath somewhere between the towns of Uzès and Remoulins, and is the simplest, and in its astounding simplicity the most beautiful, of all the monuments left to posterity by what I called the Race of Builders. And oddly enough I had thus seen the thing before I properly understood it. That is to say, as I was gazing at that old aqueduct which does not carry water any more to Nîmes, but merely a trickle of tourist cars and a few farmers' trucks along its lowest span, I suddenly *knew* what it meant, in the same way in which I know "This is I," for instance, the way that learned men call intuition. I did all the figuring and piecing together afterwards. And many a time since, as also repeatedly in this book, I have asserted that I discovered the meaning of Europe by discovering the meaning of Provence, and this in a sense is true, for Provence was the first *provincia* of the race of Builders; they had begun to construct European civilization, as an extension of their old home town, right there, and Provence still looks it, or looked it when I saw it last. But in another sense it is not true that I discovered all this in Provence, for the Pont du Gard is in Languedoc; but most people don't know where Languedoc is, though they may have heard of Provence; so I call it Provence, as many better men than I have done before me, including Henry James and other shining lights of English and American letters who did not realize that there is no Provence on the right bank of the Rhône.

Now the vision which I saw at or about a quarter to eight on the evening of Friday, September 8, 1939, as I was sitting on the terrace of the café in the Boulevard des Lices, opposite the Hôtel Jules-César at Arles, had all this behind it, but was not nearly as long and as complicated as all this. It was in fact very simple and short, and was not a vision at all in the occultistic sense of the word, but merely a keener perception, aided by the darkness, of what was around me, a poignant sensing of the moment in terms of twenty centuries. There were all those officers sitting, and talking a Latin tongue, around me, and there was Arles, with its Cathedral and its cloisters, its Roman arena and statues, and its Greek theater and statues, and its ruin of the palace of Constantine, and its Gallo-Roman cemetery, and all the rest. And there was a war on. There surged, in the Northeast, the menacing masses of the Raiders. And I knew that it was the same war, the war of two thousand years ago that has never ceased since, except for brief intervals while the Raiders, once more beaten back, gathered strength for the new attack. It was the same Germany, and the same Rome. That was all, and I finished my drink and went across the road and sat down to dinner with my wife.

7

At noon, next day, we saw Mr. Hurley at the Consulate at Marseille. He advised us very firmly indeed against returning to Mougins. We must be prepared for all eventualities, including a hurried evacuation; and Bordeaux was the place for this. He warned us that Bordeaux was crowded with Americans; but we might find rooms in a near-by town or village. He took me to a large map on the wall of one of the offices and sketched out an itinerary. I caught the name of Arcachon. I asked: "Why shouldn't we go to Arcachon?" And Mr. Hurley said, "I don't see any reason why you shouldn't." Now I knew nothing about Arcachon, except that some celebrated small oysters came from there; but the oysters had nothing to do with it. Some time ago I had seen an article, in *L'Illustration*, I believe, about Arcachon and its *mondain* pleasures. We disliked intensely the *mondain* pleasures of French seaside resorts; but I figured that the summer season was over and also that there was a war on, so we should be safe from that point of view. What had caught my fancy was a half-page reproduction of a photograph on which the sand dunes showed up very silvery and the lighthouse very white and the pines and the sea very dark. And Arcachon was only forty miles from Bordeaux, and had many hotels. I said good-by to Mr. Hurley.

After lunch we went to the police, to have our identity cards stamped. About six hundred people were lined up at the entrance, most of them Italian workmen and their women. I spoke to a sergeant. "You want to stay in Marseille?" "No, we have just arrived and we want to leave at once." "Well, why don't you? You don't want to stand here in line until tomorrow noon? Scram!" We thanked the sergeant, and scrammed.

It was well past three o'clock by then, and we wanted to sleep at Carcassonne. Two hundred miles. We drove along the Salon road, for the fourth time within a week. It was crowded with cars, and this time it did not look like an excursion to the bullfight at Arles. It looked like flight. For the first time we saw cars stuffed with bedding and kitchen utensils, with perambulators and bicycles strapped to the baggage grid and mattresses on the roof. It was the mild prelude to that mad scramble of millions toward a non-existent safety which nine months later was to prove one of the main causes of the French *débâcle*. It was on the evening of June 18, in the midst of the Bordeaux nightmare, that I listened to the broadcast of some French cabinet minister or other (what matter whether his name was Nebuchadnezzar or Pomaret?) ordering people, under severe penalties, to stay put. Nobody paid any attention to him, and it was too late anyway, too late by nine months; the mass migration which clogged the roads of France had by then done the work of Hitler. In the afternoon of September 9, of which I write, the early exodus of the more nervous inhabitants of Marseille meant to me little beyond the comparatively simple task of leaving behind a long file of low-powered French touring cars in a Ford V8. God forgive me, but I enjoyed it.

We stopped for a drink at the Jules-César at Arles. The people of the hotel had come to regard us as a cross between star boarders and a great joke. The manager offered us special rates for a long stay. We had to go on. It was a little past six o'clock when we crossed the Little Rhône, for the fourth time in a week, and possibly for the last time in this life. But I hope not. The Rhône, to me, is a symbol. For ten years, and more, it had flowed in and out of my life. I know it better than any other river in the world. It is the river of the Roman Valais; of the Romanesque Kingdom of Burgundy; of Gallo-Roman Lyon, Vienne, Valence; of the Avignon of the Popes; of *Provincia Romana;* of that "humble disciple of the great Homer," *umble escoulan dóu grand Oumèro,* the most Hellenic, and also most Latin, of modern poets, Mistral. I have followed the Rhône along its course as he had followed the path of the peasant girl Mirèio. The Roman river. More Roman, in our day, than the Tiber, on the banks of which a stocky mongrel with a negroid skull prattles of pure race and lords it, as the lieutenant of the successor of Odoacer, over a people of blustering degenerate auxiliaries of the progeny of Odoacer's hordes. I hope to see the Rhône again, from that bridge of St. Gilles, and from that high terrace behind the palace of the Popes at Avignon whence the eye sweeps all that Roman country which stretches from the Alps to the Cévennes; and when I next see it, all will be well, for our civilization will have been saved by that last outpost of Rome which is England.

8

That evening we dined at Pézenas, that sprawling village beyond the lagoon of Thau which in the seventeenth century had been the elegant summer residence of the Montpellier nobility, and had seen the first nights of some of Molière's plays. The old palaces are still there, inhabited by vintners and artisans. We left at nine o'clock in the dark, and I had my first taste of driving with headlights covered by a thick blue varnish. This was part of the universal blackout, to prevent hostile aircraft from spotting the cities by the headlights on converging roads; and it was extremely unpleasant. On the outskirts of Béziers a policeman's whistle stopped us. "Your headlights!" "What the hell, I have no headlights! They are blue, and dipped at that!" "You cannot use them at all. You must drive with your side lamps." My side lamps were varnished blue, too. And all street lights were out. And Béziers is a large and populous town, flanking a tall hill, and even in daytime it is pretty difficult to pick your way through it, unless you know the place. Well, I knew the place, but not in a blackout. I managed to reach the main square, at the pace of a paralytic snail. I knew, fortunately, that the center of the main square is occupied by some sort of monument surrounded by some sort of garden, and that I had to drive around it. What I had forgotten were the tables. Three or four cafés, flanking the square in a row, had their tables pushed out into the middle of the *route nationale*. All the tables were occupied. Waiters were dashing to and fro in the dark, bumping with their trays into one another. I had to navigate between mugs of beer and glasses of Pernod and shoals of demitasse. All I had to guide me in the pitch-dark was the glowing cigarette tips of the guests. I am happy to say that I did not touch a thing, or a body; but when I had got through and was coasting down the hill I blew hard, and several times. At the foot of the hill I stopped and scraped the varnish off my side lamps. A policeman came up. "What are you doing?" "Well, I reckon I shall need these lamps when I have to drive through the restaurants at Narbonne." He laughed, and wished me good luck. As a matter of fact at Narbonne the national highway skirts the town, and there were no Pernods to miss.

We reached Carcassonne at midnight, after an uneventful last lap whose fifty miles seemed like the endless passages of a bad dream in the spectral glimmer of our blue headlamps. To our surprise the Hôtel de la Cité, one of our best-beloved stopping places of happier days, was all but empty; it was to close down in a day or two.

The road from Carcassonne to Bordeaux runs by way of Toulouse and Agen, due northwest; but I thought next morning that a little detour would not do any harm; I suspected that this was to be the end of my fifteen years' touring career in France, and I felt it might as well wind up with a flourish. Today I am only sorry that I did not make the flourish a little longer, and more elaborate; so we decided to go to Bordeaux by way of Toulouse, St. Gaudens, and Pau, which was rather as if one went from New York to Cleveland by way of Buffalo, Harrisburg, and Louisville, though of course the French distances are on a smaller scale.

We left a little before noon, which gave us an easy run before lunch to Castelnaudary, twenty-five miles along a wide and almost straight road. Five miles this side of Castelnaudary we found our way blocked by two large military lorries which had run into, and upset, one another. So we followed a car full of local people which made a complicated detour by lanes and cart tracks across the fields and piloted us into the town. Now Castelnaudary was a place which I had been wanting to visit for many years. It boasted a castle which had belonged to Henry IV, who some say was the greatest of French kings, in the seventeenth century. I was not, however, interested in visiting this castle; I had found out long ago that very few old castles in the world are worth the time travelers spend in them, unless they contain paintings or tapestries, for one hall or dungeon is pretty much like another, and a sample will last me a very long time. The particular attraction, for me, of Castelnaudary was a quite different aspect of the private life of this Henry. Every French schoolboy knows that he was a great social reformer, much concerned with the welfare of the common people, and the most famous plank of his platform stipulated a boiled chicken dinner for every peasant in the realm at least on Sundays. This is why boiled chicken is always called, on the bills of fare of French eating places, *poule au pot Henri-Quatre*, and a very tasty dish it can be, though very often it is not.

Now, while boiled chicken was thus being used by King Henry for political purposes, rather like the full dinner pail of other politicians nearer home, his own tastes lay in a different direction, and he used to come to Castelnaudary for prolonged week ends to indulge them. For Castelnaudary is the center of a district where they breed geese of exceptional merit; and the good King's favorite dish was the *cassoulet*, which stands or falls, as it were, with the geese that enter into its composition. I know exactly how *cassoulet* is made, and am prepared to prepare it any time I have the ingredients at my disposal; nor is this a rash vow, for the gooseflesh required must be treated in advance in a very special way, and I am not likely to find chunks of it in my fan mail, sent by a reader who wants to hold me to my promise. So, since this is not a cookery book, I shall merely say here that *cassoulet* is neither more nor less than the French edition of Boston baked beans, left in the oven overnight, but with a layer of alternating pieces of breast of goose and of a certain rich pork sausage taking the place of the plain salt pork. There are people, even French people, who find this delicacy rather overpowering, and it is certainly not a course that one wants to see on one's table three times a week, but to my own taste it is much the finest dish invented by the culinary genius of the French South, which to me means the finest dish to be found in France; for in matters of cooking, as in most others, I am a case-hardened *méridional*, or Southerner, and though I feel pretty much at home anywhere in France, except in French Flanders and Brittany which I don't know at all, I feel that I have arrived where I really belong when I cross the imaginary line that runs from Bordeaux, by way of Périgueux, Aurillac, Le Puy, and Valence, to Gap and the Italian frontier. (I am now speaking of the French frontier as it was before the war, and as it shall be again when Hitler and Mussolini are but an accursed memory, unless our civilization perishes altogether. But enough said of what I feel and what I hope.)

Well, for diverse reasons it took me many years to arrive at lunch time in front of the little hotel at Castelnaudary kept by a benefactor of the human race called M. Fourcade; but here we were, and we were by no means alone on our pilgrimage. For the little dining room was filled to capacity by about a hundred people, all of whom seemed to share my own opinion about *cassoulet*; but the handsome dark proprietress found a table for us presently, and we sat down to the serious business on hand. There were many local people in the room, that is to say people of the Toulouse country, who look and talk like Spaniards, rolling their *r*'s very hard and keeping their speech on a level, instead of rushing up and down the scale as if they were trying to catch their own thoughts, like Northerners. But there were a good many Parisians too, very smartly dressed women with Pekingese dogs on their laps, and these — the women, I mean — were a sign of the war; so were the many young soldiers in uniform who were evidently celebrating their joining the colors. There were also several officers, majors and colonels and a general or two, rubbing shoulders, quite literally in the packed room, with the conscripts; for we were in France, a country where equality existed in small hotel dining rooms too, and not only on the platforms of electioneering assemblages. We were served our *cassoulet*, and in the midst of it we were addressed by two young soldiers who sat at the next table with their fathers and mothers and sisters, very obviously prosperous peasants, but not of the region, as we soon verified. For the soldiers told us that they had come in their cars from Villefranche in Rouergue, a distance of about a hundred miles, to join their unit; and they were greatly pleased when they heard that we knew their town and countryside. They all said that *cassoulet* was an excellent dish in its way, but not to be compared with their own *confit de canard*, which is duckling potted in its own fat, and is usually served with green peas. We discussed this, and when I ventured to say that on the whole I preferred goose, they shook their heads solemnly, and one of the young girls remarked sagely that there is no accounting for tastes.

9

Way back in '25 or '26 I once saw, in the grounds of an Austrian castle, — it may have been the old Emperor's at Ischl, but I cannot guarantee it, — a large sundial laid out on a lawn, bearing the inscription, in bold lettering, ULTIMA FORSAN. "The last, maybe": meaning that it was time for you to pull yourself together and to bring order into your accounts, for the hour that you beheld on that dial might well be your last. I was a flippant person then, mistakenly believing that flippancy was the best way to enjoy life, and almost entirely uninstructed in the things that matter; but that medieval device on that comparatively modern dial gave me a shock. For I realized then that my whole life was organized, insofar as it was organized at all, on the basis of the certainty that I should live forever; and a fine sort of a certainty it was, if one came to look at it. Well, as at 4 P.M. on Sunday, September 10, 1939, my wife and I were crossing the Garonne bridge at Toulouse in our car, I thought of that device, and thought that although I had learnt a great many things since I saw it somewhere in Austria, I was in many ways still the same old procrastinator I had been, always preferring inaction to action with the excuse that there was, after all, plenty of time. For here we were, driving through Toulouse without stopping, and with the odds being in favor of our never seeing Toulouse again.

Now at the risk of irritating the reader, who by now might well exclaim, "What is this, a book about the collapse of European civilization, or a lament for the places where this fellow did not stop because he was in a hurry?" I will say a word or two about Toulouse. I have heard many people say that it is a distinctly disagreeable town, crude and violent in its ways; and this judgment would seem to be borne out by its history, which contains quite an unusual amount of rioting and massacre and cold-blooded assassination, rather like that of Edinburgh. It is also true that Toulouse is a large city, and was, before the deluge, a prosperous one, making much money out of commerce and industry and all that; and much business prosperity tends to make a city ugly and vulgar in an old country like France, where it means the tearing down of beautiful old buildings and the remodeling of the whole place in the deplorable taste of backgroundless money-grabbers and their politician allies; though in a new country like the United States municipal affluence tends to work the opposite way, as witness the great cities of the Middle West, which are certainly better to look at today than they were fifty years ago; though in the old states of the Atlantic seaboard the position is much the same as it was in France.

Yet, when I had reviewed the whole case against Toulouse, I still wanted to see it, and even to explore it, very much, for it contains one of the finest Romanesque churches in France, and some other churches that are quite good if not of the front rank, but above all it contains some of the best Renaissance architecture in France, both municipal and private, and some very rich museums. Also, it is the capital of what is, unofficially, called the Red Languedoc, an expression with two meanings, one of which, the political, did not interest me in this context, but the other, the architectural, did. For the western and northern regions of the great province of Languedoc, the country of Toulouse and the Albigeois, are characterized by practically all of their grand old churches and palaces and so forth being built of red brick, a material not much favored elsewhere in France, but certainly suited, in its fiery emphasis and in its ineptitude for and indifference to all finely shaded chiaroscuro, to the passionate character of the Languedoc people and the tragic abandon, so different from the measured tranquillity of Provence, of the Languedoc landscape. You cannot know what red brick can be and do until you have seen the Cathedral of Albi. Yet another reason for my wanting to explore Toulouse was that Henry James has much to say about it in his *A Little Tour in France*, which to my mind is one of the most interesting, perhaps *the* most interesting, of his books, because it allows you a good look at Henry James off his guard, and confirms some of your suspicions about the quality of his mind, and his character, that curious blend of gentleness and fatuous, old-maidish ruthlessness. It is, in other words, not a very reliable guide to France, but a most revealing guide to Henry James, and I used to think what great fun it would be to follow in his footsteps from the châteaux of the Loire down south to Narbonne and then up north again by the Rhône Valley and to check him up, and to base an analysis of his novels on what he missed, and what he saw, in

France. Now the things that struck me when I read *A Little Tour in France* were, first, that Henry James was essentially and fundamentally a late Victorian English governess, who saw the world from the point of view of the vicar's garden party, but a governess with quite unaccountable, frequent and beautiful, flashes of genius; and second, that he combined such a governess's fanatical love of neatness in small unimportant things, such as the correct alignment of doilies on a luncheon table, with a fundamental dislike and incomprehension of essential order and of transcendent values which, however paradoxical the word may sound when applied to such a mild and genteel creature, are almost diabolical.

Well, the point that I have been trying to make for the last two pages or so is that we did not stop at Toulouse, but drove through, because I felt that it was too late and we could not afford to stay; but I realize now that this feeling was merely a sort of mental nervous indigestion brought about by the shock of the war, and that it would have made no difference whatsoever if we had stopped for a couple of days, then and there. So all I remember of Toulouse is a very wide boulevard with white globe-shaped lights rather like those of the lake shore at Geneva, the bridge of the Garonne from which we saw some unexpected meadows right in the middle of the town, and the winding river spanned by many bridges, and in the distance the tower of St. Sernin with its curious outside spiral galleries. Then we drove along one of the straightest roads that I have ever seen, due southwest and following the Garonne, but upstream, and at a respectful distance. At St. Martory this road turned almost due west, and ran parallel with the great chain of the Pyrenees which shut off the horizon just a few miles away on the left; and I shall not try to tell you what the Pyrenees looked like, for several reasons, one of them being that I should not know how, for it was my first glimpse of these western ranges, though many years before I had traveled among them further east, on the French Catalan side, in Roussillon and Vallespir and Cerdagne; and I was very tired now, and I do not remember that afternoon's drive with the clarity of detail with which I remember most things, thus crowding my brain with items that more practical people keep in reference books and card indexes. What I do remember, though, is that I thought at the time that this road from St. Martory to Tarbes, which follows the wall of the Pyrenees as a town street follows a row of houses, was the most beautiful road that I had seen in France, with the exception of the one that drops down the great canyon of the Ardèche from beyond Le Puy to Aubenas, and that other road from Thonon, on Lake Leman, that first follows the valley of the Drance and then passes along a crest under Mont Blanc apparently so close that you think you can reach out and touch it, although there is a valley thirty miles wide in between.

But as I said I don't remember details; and I see that afternoon as a sort of emerald haze shot with gold, which was the slanting sheaves of sunlight, and powdered with silver, the snow on distant peaks and ridges. We stopped at Tarbes for a drink, and to listen to the municipal radio in the main square which was blaring out news so loud that we could not understand a word of it; and I thought it a good omen that we passed through the native town of the great Maréchal Foch. Then we left Bigorre, which is the country of Lourdes, and were in Béarn, which had been the original kingdom of the good King Henry IV when he was a beginner, and gives its name to a very agreeable sauce flavored with tarragon, which for aught I know may have been invented by the aforesaid King, a great lover of the pleasures of the table, as already indicated.

At seven we arrived at Pau, and were amazed, though we had heard about it before, by its spacious beauty and the magnificence of its site on a ridge which is separated by a narrow valley from the chain of the Pyrenees. In fact we liked the place so much that we said to each other, was there any reason why we should not stay on, instead of proceeding to Arcachon, and await developments for a while? Bordeaux, we reasoned, was only five hours' drive, and we could make it in a hurry if necessary.

In the morning we went to the police, to have our identity papers stamped. An official with a high stiff collar and a Charlie

Chaplin mustache examined the cards carefully through his pince-nez, and then said in tones as close-clipped as the mustache: "According to your last visa you were going to Marseille. I do not see any Marseille stamp. This is serious. Where have you been?" I explained, patiently, that we *had* passed through Marseille, but that the police there had said it would be sheer waste of time to have the cards visaed, and had told us to run along. The official's face remained wholly expressionless, and when I had finished he said, "This is serious. You will have to come back on Wednesday." Now he did not say this menacingly, but rather gloomily and even sadly, as who should say, "You see, it is not my fault, you ought to have known better, now your head will have to be cut off, and then where will you be?" I tried to argue with him, but he merely repeated, "*C'est bien grave, il faut repasser mercredi.*"

When we were outside I told my wife that I would not repass on Wednesday. The trouble with the official was evidently that he was a fundamentally stupid man, and scared out of such wits as he possessed by the responsibility of an unprecedented situation. We had better go on to Arcachon after all. We discussed the matter with the hotel manager, a very friendly man who confirmed my diagnosis that the police official had felt out of his depth, and had not really meant any harm. The manager advised us to stay, which of course was what a hotel manager would do; but I had a pretty comprehensive notion of what a police official, French or other, might do in wartime if he felt out of his depth, so we left Pau about four that afternoon, though we should have loved to stay. We drove across the hills of western Béarn and down into the Landes, which are reclaimed sandy wastes all planted with pines for many hundreds of square miles. We called this the pit-prop country, after an excellent detective story by Freeman Wills Crofts, the scene of which was laid in the region; and about eight that evening we arrived at Arcachon, the place which, though we had no idea of this at the time, was to be our home for the next nine months, but probably would not have been anything of the sort if the police official at Pau had not been a stupid man.

III. Prelude to Disaster

DURING the first six weeks of our life at Arcachon the fact of the war was brought home to us mainly by the discomforts involved in having our identity cards revalidated and in obtaining safe-conducts and road permits; by the lateness and general undependability of the mails from England; and by a rather languidly observed blackout. Afterwards we had our road permits in our pockets, the postal service had improved, and the blackout regulations came to be completely ignored. By December, as far as external indications and the daily routine of our life went, it had become quite easy to forget that there was a war on; and we know today that this general easing of the earlier tension was not something that just happened that way, but was part of the superb stage management of Hitler.

To the aggregate life of the town of Arcachon the war had made little enough difference. Two or three of the best hotels had been requisitioned immediately, for military hospitals; but until the end of April they remained empty except for their skeleton staffs, and were practically negligible as visible symptoms of the war. The hotels that stayed open were abnormally crowded. A large proportion of the hotel visitors, as well as of the villa dwellers, were Slavs: some well-to-do Czechs who had left their country after the German occupation, a few not so well-to-do White Russians, and a conspicuous number of Poles. The presence of most of these latter had nothing to do with the war. For many years Arcachon, a double-purpose resort with its "winter town" on top of the hill and encroaching upon the forest, and its "summer town" grown up along the sandy shore, had boasted a considerable colony of wealthy Poles, partly retired merchants and the like, partly people engaged in business at Paris or near-by Bor-

deaux who spent their winter and summer holidays here. I meant
to find out what had originally attracted these Poles, but somehow
I never got down to it; the parish church of Notre-Dame des
Passes had, in one of its chapels, a beautiful copy of the famous
Black Virgin of Czestochowa, a late medieval painting on a wood
panel which we were told the Germans had destroyed. This original Polish colony formed the nucleus of a constantly increasing
one of war refugees; in the more fashionable cafés of Arcachon
one could hear almost as much Polish spoken as French. There was
also a Polish Consul; I never met him in the course of our nine
months' stay, but he was to play an important part in my life just
the same, as will be seen.

Years ago there had been an English colony, as attested by the
little ivy-grown Anglican church and some street names like
Avenue des Anglais; for some reason or other this colony had all
but completely vanished. According to one theory they had been
lured away, since the last war, by the newfangled custom of
wintering where the snow is thickest; but by and by we guessed
that the peculiar ways of some of the local property owners and
tradespeople must have been at least partly responsible for the
exodus. Soon after our arrival we had some first-hand experience of
those ways; and later we were told, by French friends, that the
Arcachonnais have a reputation for that special gloomy rapacity
which Anglo-Saxon tourist mythology used to attribute to the
French at large. As the months passed we found that the people
of Arcachon were not very different from people anywhere else;
that is to say, some were nice and others were not. There were
those whom we detested; there were a few others whom we came
to like and to respect, and from whom, when all was over, we
parted with a heavy heart.

We had fallen in love on sight with the Arcachon landscape, so
reminiscent of Cape Cod with its dunes and sand cliffs and pines
and lighthouses; but our decision to stay for the winter was taken
on grounds of a different order. My last talk with one of the Vice-
consuls at Marseille had made it clear that it would take at least
two months to obtain a visa for my wife. On the other hand, soon

after our arrival at Arcachon I was informed at the United States Lines office in Bordeaux that in two months' time there would probably be no more sailings; this, indeed, proved to be the case. Now on this matter of taking ship our family counsels had been divided anyway. I was anxious to return to New York at the earliest possible moment because I felt that resuming the work that had gone so well at Mougins was impossible under wartime conditions. Since 1933 I had been working on a new philosophy of history, based on a synthesis of the Catholic Realism of Saint Thomas Aquinas and of modern Pragmatism. For the first time in six years I had felt, in the precarious peace of our Bastide de Mai six months earlier, that I had mastered the task begun in 1933 with a few bright ideas in my head but without the requisite fund of solid knowledge. All that remained was the actual writing of the book, and at the rate at which I was working during the spring and early summer I expected to finish the job by Christmas, and to sail for the United States with the manuscript to show for my seventeen years' absence and apparent unproductiveness. During the last days of August, when the signing of the Russo-German pact had made war inevitable, I realized that the only thing for me to do was to take the first boat and to finish my book in some university town of New England or the Middle West. But there were those two boys, aged nineteen and eighteen, back in England, liable to be called up for service in the army; and my wife was naturally reluctant to put the Atlantic between them and herself. She would have best liked to return to England, but this solution was impracticable for several reasons, one of which, the ban put by the U. S. Government on the travel of American citizens from one belligerent country to another, was decisive. Thus our staying at Arcachon for the next few months was conceived as a compromise between my wife's pull to England and my own pull to the United States, a compromise to which we reconciled ourselves all the more readily as we had no doubt that the Allies would win the war within a year. I remember saying, jokingly, — because in those days we could still joke about the war, — to one of the American Vice-consuls at Bordeaux that I was, apart from the newspaper correspondents, probably the only American citizen to remain in Europe not in spite but because of the war.

The hotel where we had stopped on our arrival was crowded, uncomfortable, indifferently kept, and, considering its disadvantages, ridiculously expensive. We were so anxious to leave it that we took literally the first house that we could find. It stood on the beach of Pyla, five miles from Arcachon proper, and had a view of dazzling loveliness over the lagoon, the great sand cliff known as the Grande Dune at the far end, and the tremendous white-capped rollers of the Atlantic thundering against the sandbanks which defended the entrance of our small inland sea. All this, and the fact that the house was brand-new and furnished scantily but in good taste, instead of being filled up with Louis-Quinze chairs, plush horses, and herds of china elephants in the way of most French *villas meublées*, bribed us into forgetting to ascertain whether there were any blankets on the beds, and to inquire into some other equally essential but prosaic details, until it was too late. We were made to pay through the nose for our trustfulness. After this rather nerve-racking experiment we rented the charming, comfortable, and elaborately equipped little Basque house, on the edge of the great forest, which I have described in the first chapter. It belonged to the Bordeaux-born widow of a Polish nobleman, recently defunct; we leased it for three months, with option of renewal; it would have been much cheaper to sign a long lease, but the war made long-range plans impossible.

Our cook Emily was now in our midst once more. She brought with her, from Cannes, the possessions which we had left behind, including my six hundred books and the back seat of our car. Emily was not only a first-class artist in her own line, but also a most capable organizer and manager, and an all-around worker of amazing capacity. To join us she had traveled from Cannes during two nights and a day, changing those slow and crowded wartime trains three times; once they had to stop on the open line for three hours, with German planes circling overhead; but the raiders, in those days, merely took photographs. After this harrying journey of thirty-six hours, which would have reduced me to jelly, if it had not given me apoplexy at an early stage, she arrived smiling, rosy, and unruffled, like a fat little queen after her morning bath, and proceeded to cook dinner without as much as sitting down for ten minutes' rest. Born of peasant stock in a village near Genoa, she had spent most of her forty-seven years at Nice and Cannes; her husband, also Italian, had served in the French army during the last war, and had fallen in battle. Her only son, Dante, a handsome, gentle youth with charming manners, a first-rate driver and good mechanic, had been our valet during our first month at Mougins; but the mobilization of the Czechoslovak crisis snapped him up, and he was never released; we missed him, and he came to spend his three leaves with us.

Some years ago an English family whom she had served at Cannes took Emily back to Somerset, but she did not stay long; she disliked both the climate and her fellow servants, whom she considered lazy and incompetent. She returned to France with her repertoire enlarged by oxtail stew, baked jam roll, and two or three other English delicacies. Her bête noire in that household near Yeovil had been the gardener. He held with growing green peas as big as possible, whereas Emily believed in cooking them young; this clash of views resulted in Emily's stealing the key to the kitchen garden at night, and sneaking out to plunder vegetables for next day's luncheon. We suspected that another thing she had brought back with her from England was a thorough understanding of English speech, but this the sly and malicious peasant in her would never admit. She could do, and do to perfection, some American dishes such as Southern fried chicken and oven-baked ham; she told us that she had been taught these by another former employer, Mr. Dudley Field Malone, of New York. Nevertheless we discovered, after a while, that her range was circumscribed by certain rather astonishing idiosyncrasies: her scrambled eggs were never what scrambled eggs should be, and whatever way she might set out to cook tomatoes, somehow they always appeared on the table fried in oil. Where she could not be surpassed was in the Piedmontese and Provençal cooking of her own Mediterranean coast, dishes like the *soupe aux poissons* of the fishermen, a chowder made of all sorts of small fish cooked and passed through a sieve, and *potage au pistou*, a thick, dark green vegetable soup flavored with that pungent Southern herb, basil. Her greatest masterpiece, however, was just plain roast leg of mutton — at least it looked plain, but it tasted like a *pouèmo en lengo d'O*, a Provençal poem made flesh, or a quintessence of the gray-green Southern heath; it had strands of rosemary pulled through it with a long needle, and sprigs of thyme and specks of marjoram, and a bashful clove or two of garlic. Her characteristic Latin, and peasant, virtue as a cook was her knowledge and cunning employment of herbs; she used to run out into the woods to collect them; only, like all virtuosi, she tended to excess in her art, and it was difficult to persuade her to let a plain roast of pork speak for itself.

We were delighted to have her with us again, but after a while we noticed a subtle change. For two or three days she would serve indifferently cooked meals, then excel herself with some chef-d'oeuvre, and then relapse into mediocrity; she had spells of grumbling; we caught her in petty and wholly unnecessary lies. It did not take us long to figure out what was the matter. She hated Arcachon; she was out of her element; she was homesick as hell. At Cannes she was known to, and admired by, everybody in her own world; she was a personage — more, she was the queen of the Marché Forville, that choicest and most delightful, also the most expensive, of food markets in all France. When I drove her in, twice a week, at eight in the morning, she did her shopping as if she were holding a levee, surrounded by kowtowing stall keepers — Madame Émilie this, Madame Émilie that; she did not gossip — she received homage, and sat in judgment. Here, at Arcachon, she was a mere foreigner and stranger, twice over — Italian by birth, Provençal by allegiance; she used to complain to me that the natives spoke French as if it were Spanish, forgetting that she herself spoke a kind of coastwise Italian as if it had been French. Toward the end of April she returned to Cannes, for an amply earned fortnight's holiday at her own flat; a few days later we had a letter from her, saying that she would not come back;

we had expected it, and felt relieved. She had one vice, an unexpected one in an Italian peasant: she was fantastically extravagant, having been spoiled by the large careless ways of her former
employers, all wealthy English or American Riviera-dwellers. To
her credit be it said, she never made us feel that she regarded us,
as she doubtless did, as mere pikers, and her service with us as a
comedown in the world. I hope her son Dante weathered the war
and is now safe.

2

The holdup staged by the villainous landlady was a piece of bad
luck suffered in wartime, but not strictly speaking a wartime hardship. It was through the business of the road permits that the war
messed up our lives during those first weeks at Pyla-sur-Mer.

Now we had realized from the outset that living in a country
at war would involve us in all sorts of inconvenience. We were
prepared, we were even eager, to prove our love for France by
making sacrifices for her. But one's eagerness to make sacrifices is
apt to wear thin if the particular form of sacrifice one is called upon
to make consists in standing about in a street queue, or in a dingy,
crowded, and unventilated little lobby, three or four hours a day,
for no other purpose than to have a small and not even particularly
painful flea bite administered to one at the end of the waiting; and
if one has to go through this procedure seventeen times in nineteen days, on the ground that the fleas have not been sufficiently
trained to the business of biting in the proper place in the required
manner, and must get into their stride. And this was exactly what
was going on in those first weeks of the war, except that the
official posters and newspaper announcements referred not to fleas
and flea bites, but to the revalidation of identity cards and the
issuance of safe-conducts and travel permits.

In those first few weeks we thought of these matters mainly in
terms of what they meant to us personally: fretting, fatigue, and

waste of time. Yet I saw only too clearly even then that the all-pervading muddle and the squandering of everybody's time and nervous energy were merely the wartime extension, multiplication, and exacerbation of those normal practices of French official-dom for which the French themselves had long ago coined the expressive and contemptuous terms *paperasserie* and *chinoiserie*, and which had made France notoriously the worst-governed country in Western Europe. I knew, moreover, that these methods, so clearly at variance with the neatness and the beautifully organized economy of the French mind, had resulted from, and their suppression or amelioration was prevented by, the permanent necessity, under the Third Republic, of providing soft if poorly paid jobs for two or three million voters of the Radical, Socialist, and Communist tickets. Things had been, and were, done badly in official France because they were being done by far too many unskilled people who got into one another's way, and sought to maintain the appearance of being desperately busy and majestically idle at the same time. And I recall that the war was not yet three weeks old when we began to wonder whether all that terrific expenditure of bureaucratic time and vitality on unimportant and often ludicrous results did not constitute a fatal drain on the national resources, every ounce of which ought to have been invested in the major instruments of winning the war; and whether this tragic extravagance of misapplied effort was not a symptom and a symbol of something radically wrong and dangerous not only in the physical organization but in the very psychological make-up of France.

My misgivings in this respect antedated the war. For years I had seen and judged French politics in the light of the writings of Charles Maurras, the philosopher of Royalism and leader of the Nationalist Right. I rejected some extremist clauses of his doctrine, and had my mental reservations as to others. I was repelled by the foul tactics zestfully employed by some of his followers. But there was no doubt in my mind that his judgment as to the fundamental rottenness of the Third Republic was correct; and his condemnation of the philosophy of liberalism as a distortion of reality by wishful thinking coincided with conclusions which I had worked out from premises vastly different from, and implacably hostile to, his own Comtist foundations. I had also accepted his distinction between the "legal country," which was that of the machine run by the republican politicians, bureaucrats, professors, and their backers in high finance and industry, and the "real country," which was that of the sound, sober, realistic, hard-working, hard-thinking core of the French nation — peasantry, artisans, small bourgeoisie, professional people, and what had remained of the landed gentry and nobility, these seemingly divergent elements being held together by a Catholic tradition and outlook, even in the instances of those who were not actual practising Catholics, and by an intransigent conservative nationalism. And I had no doubt in those days as to the fundamental rightness of this essential France, a France which possessed real existence by dint of culture, mind, thought, religion, tradition, history, and not by dint of the Barbarian simulacrum of Race or the materialistic fiction of Blood. Nor have I any such doubt today, though the real France be eclipsed, and trodden under by the Barbarian invader and his native accomplices.

But enough of this diversion. Whatever misgivings I may have had concerning the evil heritage of the Front Populaire, the ravages of the Red Tapeworm, the slowness, wastefulness, inefficacy of the bureaucratic machine, there was always one thought to vouchsafe a brighter future. There was the French army. The best army in the world. It would have been better if the bureaucrats and politicians had not bungled things. But, thank God, there was one organization, one institution, one body of men in France that did not bungle things. The army. We could depend on the generals; we could depend on Gamelin. . . .

In strict fairness to French officialdom, it should be stated that the presence in France, at the outbreak of the war, of three to four million foreigners (the estimates used to vary and I have no means now of verifying my figures) constituted a problem which was at the time thought to present extraordinary difficulties, and which today we know to have been outright insoluble. The great majority of these foreigners had entered France within the last decade, and were Reds of diverse origin and shade: Italian anti-Fascists, German Socialists and Communists and parlor pinks, Russian Trotskyites, Spanish Communists, syndicalists, anarchists, and P.O.U.M. adherents. Always hospitable to the victims of political or religious persecution, France had, since the last war, replaced, as a receptacle for refugees, a Switzerland that had learned the lesson of some unpleasant experiences and had begun to insist on sifting those whom she let pass through her gates. That a large proportion of the German fugitives from Nazi terror were in reality Nazi agents in disguise had been evident long before the war to those who had eyes to see and ears to hear and brains unfuddled by populitarian catchwords. Up to August 22, 1939, the Communists, French and foreign alike, acting under orders from Moscow, had been the loudest advocates of a war against Hitler at any price and to a finish. Once the Russo-German treaty had been signed Moscow changed her orders, and thenceforth the Communists were much the most dangerous among Hitler's auxiliaries in France, conducting espionage, military, industrial, and political, organizing sabotage, and spreading defeatism in all its conceivable forms. There, too, lies a lesson for these United States.

On the outbreak of the war a meticulous checking-up on and sifting of these foreign masses, and a thoroughgoing control of their occupations and movements, became self-evidently a matter of life or death for the French state. The check-up took the form, in the first place, of revising the identity cards that all foreign residents of France were required to possess. Foreigners were ordered to call at the nearest police station, to have their cards stamped, or to apply for them if they had neglected to do so before, and to have their fingerprints taken. The control of movements was based on dividing France into military and nonmilitary zones. In the latter, people of French nationality could move about unrestricted, while foreigners had to apply either for safe-conducts, valid for a single motivated journey between two specified points, or for what were called *permis de circulation*, granted for a period of three months and a limited area to foreigners in good standing who gave acceptable reasons for wanting them. Foreigners who wanted to drive their cars had to have authorization. In the military zones special permits were exacted from all, Frenchmen and foreigners alike.

With the principle of these measures no bona fide foreign resident could quarrel. As to the scope of the restrictions, the only criticism that foreigners like myself, who had the interest of France at heart, could make was that they were not nearly far-reaching enough. We should have been prepared to accept, without a murmur, rules much more stringent for the sake of the safety of France. What disgusted us and made us feel rebellious was the manner in which these comparatively mild regulations were administered in practice.

The restrictions were to come into effect on Thursday, September 21. It happened to be the day on which we were to move into our ill-starred apartment on the beach of Pyla. On Wednesday I went to the police at Arcachon, to report our change of address; this we were supposed to do in France even in time of peace. The official, on hearing that we were moving to Pyla, told me that in that case I had to report, also, at the police of La Teste, the township of which Pyla formed part.

Here I must explain the geography of the region. Arcachon is situated in the broad northern tip of a small peninsula. The neck of the peninsula is comprised in the township of La Teste-de-Buech. La Teste itself is an insignificant village, without shopping facilities; it lies in the eastern end of the neck, while Pyla occupies its western edge, alongside the lagoon. Pyla residents must do their buying in Arcachon, which is a town of some importance and also a spa, with a good market and passable shops. The distance from the center of Arcachon to Pyla is about five miles, but the road connecting the two is just a suburban boulevard, comprised within the city limits. Arcachon merges into Pyla without any visible boundary.

I drove out to the police station at La Teste, registered our new address, had our identity cards stamped, and said that I might as well apply for our road permits, since I should be required to do so on the morrow. We needed these permits for occasional trips to Bordeaux, forty miles away, to keep in touch with the American and British Consulates. The policeman said that I could file my application upstairs, at the *mairie*.

Upstairs I was directed to a *guichet*, behind which officiated a heavy-featured, bespectacled lady who looked like, and probably was, an ex-schoolteacher and Communist intellectual. I shall call her Mme. Dessus, because that was not her name.

I stated my errand. The lady said, "You must come back tomorrow and bring four photographs of yourself and two of your wife. Your own *permis* must be made out for a driver; that of your lady, for a passenger." I said, "That will be all right; I'll come back tomorrow." She said, "You realize, of course, that you will have to come on foot, for foreigners are not allowed to drive their cars even within their own township without authorization. Your permits will be good for Arcachon and Bordeaux. You will have them in a week's time."

I could not believe my ears. "Do you mean to say, in the first place, that I shall have to walk here from Pyla three miles, and back; and in the second place, that during the next week we shall not be allowed to go to Arcachon? You realize that we cannot do our marketing at Pyla."

Mme. Dessus said, "Exactly. As to coming here, you *might* catch a bus; they don't run regularly just now. But you certainly cannot go to Arcachon until you receive your permit."

I tried to argue; she was politely adamant. After half an hour's bickering I got angry, and said, "I am now going over to the *gendarmerie*. I trust they will show some sense." At the headquarters of the local *brigade* a fat and smiling sergeant assured me that the lady at the *mairie* had exaggerated; those, to be sure, were the rules, but "we are reasonable people, we French. You can drive here and to Arcachon as often as you like, pending the arrival of your permits. If a gendarme stops you, refer him to me."

I went back to Mme. Dessus and reported what the sergeant had said. She looked sour. Next day I returned to the *mairie*, with my wife; we signed our applications, and handed over four photographs of myself, and two of hers. Within the next four days I was summoned four times: to sign my application in duplicate, to hand over some more photographs, and so forth. A week passed. Our applications had gone to Bordeaux; for the *mairie* was merely an intermediary, the permits were granted by the *commandant* of the *gendarmerie* division, and signed by the general in command of the Bordeaux district. The *facteur* came with the message that our permits were ready; would I call for them? I called with my wife; we signed receipts, were handed our permits, thanked the lady with the spectacles, and departed. Two days later the village policeman called once more. He was a very decent fellow; he had been a first lieutenant of infantry in the last war; he had taken his present job because he was obliged to live in the South on account of his health, and was not fit for service at the front. We got acquainted over the road permits; I offered him a drink occasionally; by the time we left Pyla he was my best friend in the place.

I said, "Any message from the lady?" He said, "She wants to see you." I went. The lady said, "Sorry to trouble you again, but it appears that you cannot use your car. You only have a driver's permit; you also need one as a passenger."

I felt slightly giddy. "Do you *really* mean to convey the idea that the paper I hold authorizes me to drive my car, but does not authorize me to ride in it while I drive?"

She said, "I admit that it sounds odd, but it is a fact. Kindly read our instructions."

I read her instructions; she had construed them correctly. In addition to my own motorist's permit I was required to possess one similar to that of my wife. I signed the application, in duplicate; Mme. Dessus asked for three photographs; I insisted on giving her six. My passenger's permit arrived a few days later; needless to say, I did not stop driving my car in the meantime, and had no trouble.

Our permits were valid for three months. A week before they expired I called at the *mairie* to renew them. I signed my application; my wife signed hers; we turned around to leave, when Mme. Dessus stopped us. "One minute. The regulations state that when you file an application for renewal you have to hand in your old permit."

I said, "But our permits are good for another week. We came here today precisely so as not to be without them while the new ones are being made out."

Mme. Dessus said, "I am sorry, but the regulations say that you cannot keep your old permit once you have applied for a new one."

I said, "Piffle. I am going to keep my permit until I get the new one, and I am going to Bordeaux straight away and shall see the *commandant* about it." Which I did, on the spot. The officer I saw said that Mme. Dessus was technically right, but that reason was on my side; he scribbled something across our permits and said we were welcome to keep them until the renewals arrived.

By this time I was working on a little book which proposed to put the French case for a Rhine frontier before the American public. That little discrepancy between Mme. Dessus's instructions and common sense cost me an afternoon's work, which I had planned to donate to the cause of France. It also cost me two dollars, for the price of rationed gasoline was now very high, more than double the prewar rate.

At this point the impatient, and incredulous, reader may well exclaim, "That will do, I've had enough of this permit business," and add that my experiences were of trifling importance even at the time, and are of no importance whatsoever from the historical standpoint; and why does this fellow anyway pad his book with anecdotal stuff like that, instead of telling us about the collapse of France?

The answer is that I am telling you about the collapse of France, and nothing else. For my tribulations over the road permits form an infinitesimally tiny episode in my own life, and did not make any difference to me in the long run; but they did make a difference to France. For consider. I was one of a well-defined category of foreign residents in that country, people who lived in France for lawful reasons which they could prove, on incomes from easily verifiable sources. Most of us were well known in one or several localities, to many French people and also to officials; and our dossiers, or files recording our means of subsistence, occupations, movements, pastimes, avocations, vices, friends, acquaintances, and habitual correspondents, had been in the possession of the French police for many years (mine, for instance, for at least twelve); for the French police used to be interested in all these things, and had an excellent indexing system. There were (I am guessing now, but conservatively) about one hundred thousand of us, with our families, in this particular category; and much the greatest number of us consisted of Britishers, that is to say nationals of France's ally, and of Americans. There were also, in those first months of the war, at least ten thousand Mmes. Dessus, male and female, working away at the *mairies* and police headquarters of diverse French cities, towns, and townships on the road permits of this particular category of well-established, well-known, and easily investigated foreigners. (There were probably far more than ten thousand; but I shall let it go at that.) There were also, in the little police station on the ground floor of the *mairie* of that quite insignificant village of the department of Gironde, La Teste-de-Buech, two policemen, one very old and nice, the other very young and rather stupid, dealing with nothing but identity cards and such; they had been kept very busy in September, but not afterwards; I had often occasion to look in on them, and every time I did so they sat there twiddling their thumbs.

Next, I would ask the reader to figure out and add up the working hours that Mme. Dessus spent on the matter of my road permits. When the reader has this total, I suggest that he divide it by two; for I may have been out of luck, and perhaps others had less trouble. Then let him multiply it by ten thousand, the very lowest putative number of the Mmes. Dessus in France. Then let him multiply the product of this last operation by forty thousand; for I shall assume, for the purpose of this argument, that the hundred thousand foreigners I am theorizing about contained a certain number of wives, children, sisters-in-law, aunts, half-wits, and so on, who had no direct dealings with the police.

The reader will now have a figure denoting working hours; and I am sure that this figure runs into millions, though I have no mind to check it. Of course, this figure was arrived at by a very rough-and-ready method of reckoning, and I should indeed hesitate to take my oath on it; but it is good enough to suggest what I am driving at.

I shall then beg the reader to remember that one of the reasons why the Germans had such a comparatively easy job in conquering the 1500-year-old realm of France was that the French fighting forces had nothing like the requisite number of aeroplanes and tanks, and that the moment came when the French artillery had no shells and the French infantry no cartridges left.

I would also recall that the efforts of my Mme. Dessus, and of the 9999 additional Mmes. Dessus whose existence I postulated, represented only a fraction of the energy spent on tasks, and in ways, not much more profitable, in a very large number of French administrative offices, state, departmental, and municipal. I would further recall that not only time and brawn, but also hard cash, were being thus frittered away, and squandered. Not long before the war I discussed French bureaucracy with a brilliant and extremely well-informed Frenchman who told me that if the French Republic reduced the number of officials employed in all those offices by seventy per cent (not, mind you, *to* seventy per cent, but *by:* that is to say, sacking seven officials out of every ten) there would be still far too many left; but there would be, also, a revolution. Well, probably that revolution would have been better for France than what happened in the end.

And if the reader still thinks that my tribulations over the road permits had nothing to do with the collapse of France, I shall ask my publisher to refund him the money he has paid for this book; though the chances are that he merely borrowed it.

I have only two more things to say, before I have finished, I trust forever, with this subject of the French road permits. One is that I do not, as I hope the reader has gathered, blame Mme. Dessus for anything, at least for anything that occurred in the course of our dealings; I have already said that she looked like a Communist intellectual, but that is another matter. I do not even blame the man who drew up her idiotic, wasteful, and quite impracticable instructions; I have a notion that he meant well. Nor do I blame the man who employed the man who drew up those instructions. What I do blame is the system of administration that prevailed under the Third Republic; only I do not want to go into this matter, but will refer the reader to a most instructive book by an ex-Premier of France, M. André Tardieu, published three or four years ago and entitled *La profession parlementaire*. I firmly believe that the Third Republic was not destroyed by Hitler, but by the Third Republic. Hitler only lent a hand.

The other thing is that we know now that all this business of checking and controlling the three million foreigners in France was a tragic farce, and that the French authorities might have saved themselves a good deal of trouble if they had known what we know today.

The men who sold out France to Hitler were not foreigners. They were all born in France, of good old French stock.

3

December had come; the war was three months old; and we, and with us another 150,000,000 people, were still wondering when it would begin. We could not understand why things were not happening, and were reduced to the wildest guesswork. Nobody knew what Hitler was up to, except, of course, Mme. Geneviève Tabouis, who had her own sources of information. In the happier times that were gone I used to get much fun out of collecting Mme. Tabouis's famous forecasts, and when I had about three months' crop I checked them in the light of what really did happen. Also, I once compiled a list of the people that she *must* have had on her payroll in order to know all the intimate details accompanying momentous deliberations and decisions that she used to describe with so much zest. Hitler's pet palmist, King George's golf professional, Stalin's manicurist, the Papal Secretary of State, the man who had the goods on Mussolini . . . I quote from memory; I left this list behind with other papers at Arcachon; I hope the Gestapo man into whose hands it eventually found its way enjoyed it too.

Our daily routine, which I described in Chapter I, had by now formed itself, more or less, and we dropped into it with much enjoyment of such little things, which four months earlier we should not even have noticed, as being able to keep our linen in chests of drawers instead of suitcases, and having good rich vegetable soup and fruit for dinner, instead of elaborate course meals at a hotel. I had begun to spend once more, as I said in the course of that description, my mornings, and a couple of hours after tea, in front of (or is it behind?) my trusty Corona. The phrase is literally accurate; for I was not using that Corona: I was just sitting, and brooding, and blaming myself, for sins both of commission and of omission. I had a plentiful stock of both kinds to draw upon.

For I could say to myself, with an absolute and tormenting truthfulness, that I was among the few people who had for years foreseen the inevitable fatality of this war. The number of those who imagined, and publicly protested, that they had foreseen it was of course, in that fourth month, pretty considerable. There are always plenty of people who are wise after the event, and are at the same time slightly hazy about their chronology; but the difference between them and me was just this: that I had tangible, recorded proof of my foresight; and it was a source of bitter self-reproach, not of pride. For it was in December 1934 — exactly five years prior to the time I am writing about — that I drew up a sixty-page outline of my "Philosophy of Freedom"; and in the last chapter of that outline I laid down my conviction, and my reasons for it, that we were on the eve of a gigantic struggle in which the stake was the survival of white civilization, and that in this struggle France and England, as the heirs of Rome, had to face Hitlerite Germany, as the complete practical realization of all the turbulent envy, greed, ambition, and immeasurable, truly blasphemous self-conceit which for two thousand years had made Teutondom the enemy of the rest of the human kind. And I had sent this outline, at Christmastide in the year 1934, to my old friend, Professor Oscar Jászi, of Oberlin College, Oberlin, Ohio, who read, analyzed, and commented upon it; and who was now an unimpeachable witness of both my clairvoyance and my damnable dereliction of duty.

This is not the place, or the time, to give a detailed summary of that book which, after the lapse of six years, still awaits completion; but for the sake of clarifying what is to follow I must briefly suggest some of the ideas that went into its making. My initial thesis was that the only true approach to the understanding of human history is the theological; by this I mean that each of the succeeding civilizations, that is to say, as far as Europe is concerned, the pre-antique, antique, medieval, and modern, is determined by a particular distinctive conception of man's relation to God and of the problem of Original Sin; one particular conception of this relation is expressed by the formula that there is no God, and that hence Original Sin does not exist; which is precisely the particular theological conception determining the civilization of Western Modernity. Now, by Original Sin I mean this: man's refusal to recognize that he is a being with limitations; his hankering after omnipotence; his willful transgression of a "Thus far, and no farther!" The story of the Fall in Genesis is but an allegorical representation of this trespass. Man cannot live without Power; but he is capable, by dint of his Mind, of attaining far more Power than is good for him. He may obey God's "Thus far!" or he may imagine that he can posit a valid "Thus far!" under his own sanction; but if he ignores this limit altogether, his Power will destroy him as surely as night follows day. Now man *knows*, because he has learned it in the course of thirty or forty or fifty thousand years of psychological development, that Power in itself is harmful (or sinful, as Christians put it); he feels, and he has always felt, that he must *justify* such power as he possesses by directing it toward salutary ends; the pragmatist Modern would say life-promoting ends where the Christian would say God-pleasing or divinely authorized ends. Justification of his own power is man's supreme psychological need, and justification of power is the same as solving the problem of Original Sin; if you say that Original Sin is a myth, you have solved, for yourself, the problem, in your own way.

Yet another way of solving the problem of Sin — that is, the problem of the existence and potency of evil, or the misuse of excess Power — is to say: "I am good; if I had my own way everything would be lovely; but *you* are evil, and whatever is wrong in the world is your fault. There are two Principles, the Good, or Myself; and the Evil, the not-Myself." I am not expecting the reader to believe all this, on the strength of my saying so; I have not attempted here to prove my ideas, but have merely thrown them about; it will take a book of about 500 pages to attempt to prove them, and I intend to write this book as soon as I have finished the one the reader is just on the point of hurling at the cat, on account of too much miaowing on the one hand and too much theology on the other. But now I can go on to quote the culminating passage of that outline which I sent to my friend Professor Jászi, of Oberlin, Ohio, sometime around Christmas in the year 1934: —

. . . For the true meaning of Hitlerism is this: it is the world-view of Power achieving its last corollary in and by a universal Destruction. By Hitlerism the German people has broken that deadlock in which European man landed himself by his equation of Power with Freedom, and which still enmeshes the "free" peoples of the West. The German people has saved itself from this breakdown by finding at last that solution of the problem of Freedom which had been inherent in all German history from the days of Arminius, which was first stated by Luther and finally formulated by Hitler: by destroying the last remnants of restraining Reason, and surrendering itself to the dominance of its Will at last completely free to create its own reality. The German people, in other words, have saved themselves, from the neurosis which paralyzes the West, into a releasing Madness. At last they can *act* because they are free, free as the paranoiac is free: they have unloaded all the guilt which inhibits freedom upon the Others, the not-I; but where Luther threw off his sins onto the shoulders of Christ, Hitler's Germany throws off *her* sins upon the shoulders of the Other-Race, of Jews and Latins and Anglo-Saxons. The Teuton is guiltless, because all the guilt belongs to that Mediterranean world which preempted all the best sites and drew up all the rules while the Teutons slept. Thus the meaning of Hitlerism, its fundamental, theological meaning, is this: "WE ARE GOOD, because we know that we are, and YOU ARE EVIL, because we know that you are; and it is the duty of Good to fight and to destroy Evil." Hitlerism is pure Manichaeism equipped with machine guns, aeroplanes, and poison gas; it is the final self-unfolding of a Faith which justifies itself and its power, and sets out to conquer and to crush whatever stands in its way. . . .

Thus the outstanding practical conclusion of my "Philosophy of Freedom" is this: *Delenda est Germania.* The notion that it is possible to come to terms with Nazi Germany by giving her what she wants — equality, armaments, Rhineland, colonies — is a fatal "protective fiction" which may yet cost Western civilization its very life. Seven years ago Léon Daudet wrote: "The moment will come when civilization will have to choose between the death of Germany and her own." *This moment has come.* The battle is on. If the peoples of the West wake up and stand firmly together they may yet crush Nazi Germany without resorting to the ordeal of arms; but that ordeal of arms must be reckoned with as a possibility, and faced when it comes.

Seeing that this was written in the winter of 1934, I ought to make it clear that Léon Daudet had written that prophetic line of his in 1927, in a brilliant little essay on his friend Charles Maurras; and also that when I said, "The battle is on," I meant the kind of battle which four years later was to be known as the war of nerves — that is, one fought by threats, mystification, bluff, surprise, broken pledges, lies, and an underhand, relentless, all-foreseeing seizure of all the strategic points of attack; a war of nerves of which I, indeed, did not know the name then, but which I privately reckoned, under the name "the Last Battle," from February 28, 1933, the day when the Reichstag was set on fire by Goering's men.

Now the trouble that in the month of December 1939 was gnawing at my mind was that while I had put on paper all those ideas, and a few more, five years earlier, in 1934, and made out as good a case for them as I could contrive in sixty typewritten pages, the book which was to bring them, in an organized and documented form that I hoped would carry conviction, before the world at large was still unwritten, and what was worse, though hardly surprising in the circumstances, unpublished. I shall not pretend that I am a better man than I am, and shall freely confess to a liberal allowance of vanity in my make-up; so, if I felt so wretched about that book's being unwritten and unpublished at a time when its predictions had proved themselves up to the hilt, it was partly because of the personal loss that my delinquency entailed. It would, for instance, have been nice to sit down to lunch with, say, Mr. Hilaire Belloc at the Reform Club, or the Athenaeum, and to know that there were two or three men in that dining room whispering to their table mates, "See those two chaps there? They knew all about it six years ago." But having admitted this, as it would, indeed, be most foolish not to, I shall say that my misery was not wholly at par with that of the fellow who had dreamed the name of the seventy-to-one Derby winner, but was too lazy to wire a bet to his bookmaker. I had no illusions about the effects of books such as mine would have been on public opinion at large. I knew well enough that the operative books are the books that sell, and that the selling books are the books that tell the public what it already knows and what it wants to hear expressed in a language a little more elaborate, and thereby impressive, than that of its own everyday colloquy — books like Mr. Wells's *Outline of History* or Mr. John Gunther's *Inside Europe*. I knew, in other words, that books, insofar as they were operative at all, were operative in the sense of articulating, and thereby strengthening, existing prejudices, not in the sense of changing the minds and hearts of men. I held this to be true even of those very rare books that seemingly changed the face of the world, whereas in reality they merely reflected an already changed face; nor was the epoch-making quality of such books either the function of literary merit or the proof of the lack of it; for some of them, like Bacon's *Novum Organum* and Luther's *The Liberty of the Christian Man*, were great masterpieces, while others, like Rousseau's *Contrat Social*, were dull twaddle, and still others, like Hitler's *Mein Kampf*, illiterate psychopathological screeching.

Now my "Philosophy of Freedom," the book that I did not publish six years ago, differed, as I had conceived it, from the general run of books on current politics in two ways: first, by its approach, which was by way of theology, a rather unfashionable form of mental exercise; second, unlike such books as that of Mr. John Gunther, and some others, it did not tell the reader, "You are right, you already know a good deal about it, only I know a little more; here is that little more, and now you know all," but it was to say, "You are entirely wrong about everything, your knowledge is out-of-date nineteenth-century superstition and wishful thinking, and unless you listen to what I have to say *you will probably die of it.*" I admit that this sort of stuff, and such a tone and trend, will not, as a rule, ingratiate a book with the large mass of book buyers; though I am aware that this admission may yet be used in evidence against me by the publishers to whom I shall submit it when it is finished. Yet I thought that my book might have had, with luck, say four thousand readers in England and in the United States; worse books than it, I mean better ones, had run as high. Out of these four thousand, say four hundred might have been scared into thinking seriously about ideas such as that you could not compromise with Nazi Germany, or that Hitler would attack us as soon as he considered himself strong enough; and among these four hundred there might have been three or four Members of Parliament, and even a United States Senator or two, who wanted to do something about it. From these calculations it was a mere step to kicking myself mentally, good and hard, on the somewhat megalomaniac ground that if I had done my duty Britain would today have three or four thousand aeroplanes more than she actually possessed, and the United States might have a trouser leg for each leg — I mean a navy sufficient to protect both the Atlantic and the Pacific approaches at the same time — instead of having two legs and only half a pair of trousers.

Moreover, the one thing that I was anxious to do at this time was to help France, the France that had been my home for many years and that I loved as if I had been her native-born son, and knew better than did many such sons. But there was only one way in which a man like myself could help France, and that was by writing books and articles about France in the United States. And this was yet another reason for cursing myself because I had not finished and published that book years ago; for it was evident that I could do far more for France if I had been known to the publishers, editors, and book reviewers of New York as the celebrated author of "The Philosophy of Freedom," instead of being known, as I was, to the suburban villa dwellers of Pyla-sur-Mer as the fat foreigner with the pipe and the little dog.

It was this bitter and ever-nagging sense of guilt, rather than the actual initial shock of the war, now worn rather thin, and its practical impact on this or that department of our everyday life, that hindered me in resuming my work where I had left it off at Mougins, three months before. Yet I realized that resuming work was the only thing that could save me, in every sense that I could think of; and by and by I reached a sort of *modus vivendi* with myself, a compromise between what I had been doing and wanted to do on the one hand, and what could be done in the given circumstances on the other. The moment was to come when I would pound away on my Corona once more, for hours on end and seven days a week, instead of using the poor thing merely as part of the *décor* of a rather bare room. But before I deal with that second phase of our existence at Pyla, insofar as it was intertwined with those larger events which were even then, unbeknownst to us, rolling on toward the final catastrophe, I wish to explain, as briefly as I can, my failure to finish that book in six years in a world where most of the writers that I knew, or knew of, finished one every six months. For this is, after all, an accounting for myself, or ἀπολογία, as the Greeks would say, and I want the record to be complete for its own sake, and know that I shall feel better myself once I have got certain things off my mind and out of my system.

There was, as I have already indicated, the beginning of all my trouble, which was simply that I had bitten off a bigger chunk than I could chew, let alone digest. A book on the philosophy of history must deal simply with everything that man has ever done, thought, and dreamed; a judicious selection is imperative, but possible only if one already has a fairly comprehensive view of all the fields from which to select, and also of what to select from each field. When I started out to write that book, I thought that I knew all about it. Later on I felt that the more I learned the less I knew; which sounds like a paradox but is a truism. Sir Isaac Newton somewhere expressed the same idea much better, but then he was Sir Isaac Newton; I haven't got the quotation handy.

But lack of knowledge was not my only difficulty. I have already let the cat out of the bag and said that the philosophy which I had constructed for myself, and which I now tried to apply to the task of making human history intelligible, was a kind of revised version of Thomism — of the official philosophy of the Roman Catholic Church: revised, that is to say, not in any of its fundamental, essential doctrines, for in that case it would, as every Catholic knows, have ceased to be a Catholic philosophy at all; but merely in the sense that I tried to get new use out of some of the discoveries and methods of modern scientific psychology by translating them into the language of those fundamental, unalterable, and eternal doctrines. Now one of the difficulties of writing philosophy that aspires to be Catholic is that one must weigh every word much more carefully than if one were to write anything else in the world, without exception. For according to Catholic philosophy Truth is One; it may be expressed in many ways, but your own chosen way either expresses it, or it does not; if your shot does not hit the mark, it misses it, which seems logical enough. Whereas according to the diverse other philosophic theories which have currency in the modern world, truth is many, and there is no way of settling whether one truth is *really* truer than another.

I am not trying to argue, here and now, that the Catholic standpoint is right, and that all the other standpoints are wrong. I merely try to point out that it is much easier to write if you believe that all you have to do is to say what you think, than if you believe that you are under the obligation to describe that which IS, is so, and cannot be otherwise. If you write philosophy in the non-Catholic way, you may miss the mark that you have set yourself, just by a little; but who is there to say that you have missed it at all? There is nothing to stop you from saying that your mark was precisely where you hit your target, and you may even be praised for your originality in diverging from the hackneyed practice of trying to hit the target in the very center. On the other hand, if you try to write in the Roman Catholic way, your Catholic critics will see at a glance whether you have scored a bull's-eye or not; and if you miss it too often and your average remains too low, they will politely suggest that perhaps marksmanship is not the best field for your talents, and will drop hints about the advantages of taking up golf. This may be an old-fashioned and narrow way of looking at things, or it may be simply common sense; but whichever it is, it does not encourage hurry in literary production.

Another way of putting what I was up against is to say that I was a lazy hound. As a matter of fact, I *was* lazy, and liked it. There were few things I enjoyed more than thinking about the great book of philosophy which I was going to write. I certainly preferred thinking about writing it to writing it. Very unoriginal of me. What I liked best of all, however, was just to sit and smoke a pipe, in some comfortable and quiet corner with a view of mountains or the sea. I used to call this philosophic contemplation. It may have been very wrong; my only defense is that it *was* philosophic contemplation.

But the reason which I like to think was the true reason for my not doing what I ought to have done, for not finishing that book before the outbreak of the war which it predicted, was this. I believe that it was written somewhere that I should not write that book before certain things happened to me, and to the world around me. I had, for instance, to lose my home, and many other things, first; and I had to lose the world that I loved, that mellow old world of my French hills and vales and gardens. It was written somewhere, and I could not change it but had to bide my time. And if the reader comments on this by saying that I am a fatalist and a believer in predestination, I will say that he is welcome to his mistake, but that I am nothing of the sort. I believe in free will, in the sense in which free will is expounded by the school of the Dominican Father Bañez rather than in the sense in which it is presented by the school of the Jesuit Father Molina; and my belief that some things stand written somewhere does not conflict with that Dominican version of free will known as the Thomist interpretation.

And should the reader, now thoroughly annoyed, exclaim, "To the devil with this tiresome Papist, first he fills three pages with ravings about a fat cook, and now he prates about free will and Dominicans and Jesuits, why doesn't he stick to his experiences in the war?" I would say merely that I am sorry, I thought this was my autobiography, not that of the reader, and that anyway he may go and look up what I tried to express in the above paragraph in an authority called the Book of Job; which is an authority usually quite acceptable to Protestants, and even to the milder brand of agnostic nurtured in the Protestant atmosphere of America.

IV. The Marseillaise of Ghosts

THIS is not a book of "revelations." I have no sort of inside story to tell. I never had, in the course of my nine months of this war in France, a peep "behind the scenes." I was not in touch with any important personage. I never interviewed a soul. I may have seen half a dozen generals, but I never spoke to one; I have held no converse with any officer above the rank of major, and nearer than seven hundred miles to the front. I am certainly not in the class of an Eternal Insider and owner of a dirigible second sight like Mme. Tabouis. Nor in the class of a serious special investigator like Miss Dorothy Thompson. Nor yet in the class of the permanent newspaper correspondents, always on the spot and up to the minute, like my good friends Mr. William Bird and Mr. William Henry Chamberlin, and some others.

What is more, I was not even an observer of the war in France, in the strict sense of the word. For an observer is a person who is looking for certain particular things, in a more or less methodical way. He knows what he is looking for, and does it according to a plan. He usually finds what he is looking for, since this world of ours contains a bit of everything. Hence the need for discounting certain aspects of science, which is based on purposeful observation; a need admitted and even emphasized by some of the best scientists. And I do not think that I should have made a particularly good observer had I tried to be one; for I am a person with a definite bias toward abstraction, interested more in the relations and likenesses and differences of things than in the things as such, in the hidden patterns which may be discovered behind the phenomena rather than in the ever-changing spectacle; which is the reason why, having tried my hand successively at philology, art theory, psychology, political and literary journalism, and history, I have eventually landed in philosophy, and feel now quite at home and have no intention of changing my residence.

Nor had I any idea, during those nine months in wartime France, that I should ever feel the urge to record and to report them. I have not kept a diary or made any occasional notes about anything that I saw or heard, though I am very sorry now that I did not. But I kept my eyes open; I was in constant touch, not only with people but with what might be called *the* people of an important and representative region; because I liked them and flattered myself by imagining that they liked me; because they were French, and I loved and understood France and identified myself with her destinies. I took things in, very often without being aware that I did. For, as I have already boasted more than once, I have an exceptional memory, photographic and retentive. I realize now that my mind registered pictures and sequences of pictures while I personally was doing nothing in particular beyond smoking my pipe, sitting in a café, or walking along the main street of Arcachon. And Arcachon was, in a very real sense, France.

I know now that insofar as I was an observer of wartime France (and I could not help being one to a certain extent, for I had once been a newspaperman, even though a dissatisfied and an unsatisfactory one) I was altogether wrong, and the victim of that universally practised self-deception which made up three fourths of the wartime psychology of France. In my capacity of observer I looked for certain particular things, and I found them. Grim determination to fight to a finish, at once heroic and businesslike. General eagerness to make no matter what sacrifices for the sake of eventual victory. Silent, tight-lipped, unquestioning, unswerving discipline. Universal understanding of the deepest spiritual issues about which the war was being fought. I saw all these things all around me all the time. Like better men than I; like Mr. Somerset Maugham, for instance, who wrote an excellent pamphlet about what he saw. The only trouble, as we know today, was that the things we saw were not there. They existed, in individuals; even in many thousands of individuals. They did not exist in the aggregate nation. What we did not know was the one important fact, and this was that the soul of France was sick; sickened by a century of that spiritual decay which underlay the material progress of the nineteenth century. The French are, beyond compare, the most intelligent, the most rational, the hardest-thinking people in the world. And they had been thinking hard in the wrong way for a very long time. They had been asking themselves, far too long, the one question that is fatal to both thought and action: "What is the use?" The question that will arise inevitably in a civilization built up on, and around, the idea that everything in this world is for man, the individual, the Self. The Self conceiving itself as its own ultimate purpose discovers, in time, that the Self as such is wholly purposeless.

The Germans had gone through all this, too. They had even had a much worse spell of it than any other people of the West. Until Hitler came, and told them what the use of it all was, and persuaded them. Hitler gave them an ideal, and a faith in that ideal. It was the wickedest ideal and the insanest faith that the world has ever seen. It was Evil. It was, in a literal sense that I am afraid few of my readers will be prepared to credit, of the Devil. But it *was* a faith. A people can fight, and conquer, only if it has faith, even faith in the Devil masquerading as God; for that faith will make all the works of the Devil appear grand, and worth living and dying for, in its eyes. A people cannot fight, it certainly cannot conquer, if it believes that maybe there is a God, maybe not, and asks what would be the use of Him even if He existed; for such a people, having devalued or "debunked" God, who is the supreme source of all value, will see enduring worth in nothing, and will live for the next meal, the next drink, and the next movie show; and such a people will be proud of being broad-minded enough to see that there is something to be said for the other fellow's point of view. Now if such a people, that lives only for the moment, is attacked by another people that has a firm faith in the Devil and all his works, and is prepared to die for its faith, the first people is bound to go under. War is not altogether a question of tanks and aeroplanes; though my argument covers even tanks and aeroplanes, for a people that has firm faith in the Devil and in its own vocation to do the Devil's work will provide itself with tanks and aeroplanes in good time, while a people that is asking itself what is the use will not. Nor is this a question of that famous "insidious propaganda" that we hear so much about. The French tried to propagandize the Germans; we know with what results. The German propaganda in France "went home" because, as the saying goes, there was nobody home. It filled the void that it found. Dr. Goebbels is, beyond question, one of the cleverest men that ever lived. Yet even a thousand Dr. Goebbelses (or Drs. Goebbels, if you prefer it that way; it is a revolting thought, whichever it is) would have been wholly wasted on the French of the time of Saint Louis.

2

But I have lapsed once more into theology. I must snap out of it, and give the reader Facts. For the reader, I know, likes facts and lives on them; so do we all, for that matter. But if by facts he means statistics of, say, aeroplane and tank production, or the ins and outs of the financial management of the successive French cabinets, or anything of that sort, I am afraid he is knocking on the wrong door when he reads this book. Those things are very important, but I know practically nothing about them. I am sure the breakdown of France could be written up, and accounted for, in terms of industrial statistics and financial policies; but not by me.

The facts which I propose to submit herewith are of another order than the material. They are, mostly, psychological facts, a brand with which I have played about in my time. And the outstanding psychological fact of France at war, and even before the war, was that some very important facts of the material order were not recognized by Frenchmen as facts at all, while a good many non-facts were regarded as facts.

There was, for instance, the ideology of Social Progress as fatally advocated by the Front Populaire and its Government under the eminent literary critic and collector of old silver who missed his vocation, M. Léon Blum. The idea that social progress is expected to translate into practical tangible reality is, very briefly, as follows: The advance of science in the last four hundred years has enabled men to turn the resources of nature into a vast reservoir of their own satisfactions, to be tapped at will. The fruits of this tremendous increase of human power must be distributed equitably to all men who contribute their share to the common effort.

There you have the whole idea in a nutshell; and it is a self-evidently just idea. It is also a wholly feasible, practicable, realizable idea. (Its justice may be argued in terms of the writings of Saint Thomas Aquinas, and has so been argued by three recent Popes; but that, for the moment, is irrelevant.)

But the idea of social progress, a just and practicable idea, is not the same as the ideology of social progress. The difference between an idea and an ideology is this: an idea is true if, insofar, and as long as, it sticks to the thing or fact which it seeks to describe. Whereas an ideology is nothing but a batch of ideas turned sour — that is, ideas from which the facts and things they seek to encase have run away; false ideas, though it would be very nice, for the people who accept them as true, if they were true. Or, in plain terse American, an ideology is a lot of empty wishful talk; though very often such talk is very potent in inducing people to do all the wrong things.

Now the Government of the French Popular Front did not try to realize the true and just and practicable idea of social progress. I doubt whether it knew what that idea was. The Popular Front Government did not say, "Let us organize production in a truly scientific way, so as to produce what we really need, and as much of it as we need; and then let us organize the distribution of what we have produced, in a scientific and just way, so that everybody shall obtain what he needs."

Instead of saying this, the Government of the Popular Front said to the people of France, "Vote for us, and you will get Something for Nothing; indeed, you will get Everything for Nothing."

Needless to say, the Government of the Popular Front did not put this idea in those words. But it did put that very idea in words that the people could understand and liked to hear. And if we look closely at what the spokesmen of the Popular Front did say, we shall find that it amounted to two main propositions, to wit: —

1. The only thing that matters to the people of France is social progress, and social progress means the increase, at once and *ad lib.*, of the material comforts and enjoyments of the workers.

2. The workers can obtain such an increase of their material comforts and enjoyments by reducing their output. The less you work, the less you produce. The less you produce, the more there will be to go round, and the greater will be your own share. To enjoy life you want higher wages, and more leisure. We shall give you higher wages, and more leisure, and you will enjoy life. It is very simple.

And the working people of France saw that it was very simple indeed, and voted for the Popular Front.

Now I shall not waste time by pointing out the folly of the notion that the workers can get more by producing less. A child can see that, provided it is not being educated by teachers appointed by the Popular Front; and it has already been pointed out by other thinkers, *ad nauseam*. But the proposition put forward by the Popular Front which I called No. 1 hides a much more subtle and much more dangerous fallacy, and many people in the United States accept it as gospel truth; so I feel it ought to be shown up as a fallacy.

The notion that social progress, conceived as the increase of the material comforts and enjoyments of everybody, is the only thing that matters is wholly false. I shall not, here and now, argue that it is false because there are other comforts and enjoyments than the material, and that the nonmaterial ones are also the more important ones. Let us, for the sake of this argument, ignore that aspect altogether. I shall accept, for the sake of this argument, the thesis that social progress consists in the increase of the material comforts of the masses.

What I deny is that such progress is the only thing that progressives need bother about.

It might be the only thing that they needed to bother about, in a world full of nice, reasonable, peaceable, well-meaning, well-behaved, intelligent, kindhearted, and altogether perfect progressives, such as M. Léon Blum himself. However, if the world were inhabited exclusively by such blatantly wise and righteous beings there would be no need for social progress, for in such a world the fruits of human power would be distributed equitably as a matter of course; everything would be perfect in such a world, and what is perfect cannot and need not progress.

But the France governed by M. Léon Blum and his friends was not placed in such a perfect world. France happened to exist in Europe where there were far more bad Nazis and Fascists than good progressives. France was part of a Europe in which her next-door neighbor was the Germany of Adolf Hitler. A Germany that, even before Adolf Hitler had become its God-appointed leader, had invaded France twice within the memory of men still alive; some ten times within the last hundred and fifty years; about a hundred times in twenty centuries. A Germany whose Government did not conceal, but widely advertised, an official philosophy according to which the Germans were superior to all the rest of mankind, entitled to all the good things of this earth, and determined to take those good things; a philosophy according to which it was the sacred duty of the German Government to give a solemn pledge if the interest of the German people demanded it, and to break the same solemn pledge if the interest of the German people demanded *that*. A Germany whose Government assured loudly France, and a dozen other countries, that it meant no harm whatsoever, and then assured, even more loudly, its own people that those assurances to France and the rest were but a sop to fools.

It should now be clear why I called the program advocated by the Popular Front an ideology, and not an idea. The program of the Popular Front, insofar as it asserted that the most important thing for the workers of France was higher wages and more leisure, left half the facts of the situation out of account, and that by far the most important half. And it is the lesson of I do not know how many times ten thousand years of the human past, and of six thousand years of recorded human history, from the Old Kingdom of

Egypt onward, that if men leave important facts of their situation out of account for too long, they end by destroying themselves. For the facts that we willfully ignore have a way of knocking us over the head when we least expect the blow.

Now let us suppose, for the sake of argument, that the Government of France, in the years 1936–1939, had adopted as its program not the ideology, but the idea of social progress. Then it would have begun by saying, "Let us ascertain first of all what France needs, then let us produce it in sufficient quantities, and then let us see that every Frenchman gets his proper share." The first thing that such a government would discover would have been the pretty obvious fact of the existence, nature, and avowed intentions of Nazi Germany next door. For it was this fact that dictated to France her greatest and most obvious need: the need for tanks, aeroplanes, cannon, ammunition, and all the other materials of war. Such a government (and it is not one the notion of which I, bloated with wisdom after the event, happened to concoct in an apartment facing Central Park, New York, on the sixth of September, 1940, in the course of writing this pseudo-autobiography; Charles Maurras had advocated just such a government for many years before the war, while the liberal press of France, England, and the United States was singing the praise of M. Léon Blum), such a government, I say, would, or might, have drawn up a short platform somewhat along these lines: —

1. Nothing matters until France has enough aeroplanes, tanks, cannon, ammunition, and so forth, for that settling of accounts with Germany which is merely a question of a very short time.

2. While these aeroplanes, tanks, and so on, are being manufactured at double-quick time, the Government shall see to it that every Frenchman who works for the security of the nation has a decent living, and that no Frenchman has a superfluity of the things that other Frenchmen need and lack.

3. Any Frenchman, whether capitalist, manufacturer, trade-union leader, film star, factory worker, lawyer, peasant, general, cabinet minister, or taxi driver, who is found guilty of interfering with the national effort, will be shot.

4. A reorganization of the whole national economy in the sense of an all-pervading social justice will take place as soon as the German danger is eliminated.

And should it occur to any reader to protest that those four planks of the imaginary platform of an imaginary government embody a well-known, hoary-with-age, and contemptible capitalist-Fascist dodge, that of making the workers work for the Fatherland, a small wage, and the hope of a better future, I would merely point out that millions of French workers who would not work for France under M. Blum are this very day working for Germany under Herr Hitler, and will have to go on thus working, or else die of starvation or under the fire of German machine guns, until Hitler has been destroyed by English power.

Now I have not been saying all this with the intention of disclosing the sensational secret that the mismanagement of the Front Populaire was largely responsible for the fatal shortage of war material at the outbreak of the war. I seem to have heard and read that disclosure before. What I believe has not been made quite so clear is this. The worst heritage of the Front Populaire was not the lack of war material, but a mental attitude in the working people of France which consisted in refusing to recognize disagreeable facts as facts, in regarding agreeable fancies as facts, and generally in thinking that one could think just as one pleased, without having regard to facts, and to the laws of thought. From the coming into power of the Front Populaire onward, the working people of France, and a good many other Frenchmen not strictly members of the working class, so called, lived in the conviction that anything was possible if you only wished it to exist, and if you voted right, that is to say, Left; that it was in the best interest of the workers to produce less, because it enabled them to have more; that the external menace did not exist, or at any rate did not concern the workers, who had a collective entity different from and independent of France; that it was necessary to fight Hitler to a finish because he oppressed the German workers, but that it was quite unnecessary to possess an army and armaments for the purpose of that fight; that it was, in other words, possible to will the end without willing the means, possible to have it both ways, possible to eat your cake and have it too. Such was the ideology of the Front Populaire, and it was greatly admired by many English and American intellectuals.

In justice to the Front Populaire, however, I shall add to this indictment that the Front Populaire did not invent this mental attitude, but merely profited by its existence, and went on encouraging it. Nor was this attitude the exclusive property of the working class, or of the Left Wing at large; on the contrary, its substance was shared pretty fully by the bourgeois Center, and by all but a small fraction of the Right. I will presently come to that; but I will say first that this mental attitude, which I call the divorce of the mind from Reality, and which Karl Marx called "false consciousness" in those who did not agree with him, was the goal toward which European thought had been drifting throughout the last century. For the notion of human omnipotence, which had taken hold of European mankind and had called itself faith in scientific progress, ended necessarily by persuading people that mere facts, and logical laws, constitute no valid barrier to their wishes. It was because the mass of the French people had got used to such undisciplined confusion of the real, the possible, and the desirable, to not distinguishing between what would be nice, if true, and what actually IS, that they raised the dreamers and hot-air merchants and self-seeking demagogues of the Popular Front to supreme power in the State. But I am aware that if it had not been M. Blum it would have been somebody else, by another name; though this does not absolve M. Blum of his share of responsibility for many things, done or left undone; and it is my conviction that it would have been better for France if M. Léon Blum had never been born, though he once wrote an essay on Stendhal which I enjoyed very much when I read it, and still think a fine book, though perhaps not quite as profound as I thought it then.

3

And now I shall say what I have to say about those aspects of the universal self-deception which were not peculiar to the Left Wing, but affected most Frenchmen, and also foreigners living in their midst like myself, regardless of their political sympathies and affiliations; and also a word or two about the partly tragic, partly vicious and contemptible folly which was to distinguish a certain section of the French Right and enlisted its adherents among the engineers of France's disaster, and turned them into the despicable and despised henchmen of France's oppressors. I can make this passage quite short, for this part of the story has already been told by others, and I include it in my record partly for the sake of rounding it out, and partly by way of anticipating the charge of partisanship, which I know will be hurled at me anyway, and which does not worry me overmuch.

I have already stated my conviction that a misjudgment of the realities, or what I called the divorce from Reality, was not the monopoly or distinguishing vice of this party or "wing" or that, but part of that general intellectual and moral nightmare which had descended on the whole of Western civilization, and was the consequence and penalty of four hundred years of hard thinking in the wrong way and from ill-conceived premises. Within this nightmare each party was clinging to the particular chimera or gargoyle which suited its fancy, and was begetting out of it its own specific litter of errors and distortions. But I would emphasize, at the same time, that in entering upon the record the fateful blindness that had struck that side of French political life which had my own sympathy, I am not actuated by any particular desire to see things from the other fellow's point of view. Ever since I began to think seriously about things in general, and to examine the processes of my thought as well as of the thought of others, I have believed that that excessive insistence on impartiality which one finds in most contemporary thinkers and near-thinkers, and which their public expects from them, is rather ridiculous, and is three fourths self-deception and one fourth hypocrisy. Any writer on any of the subjects usually called serious who claims to be taken seriously assumes the obligation, which is indeed imposed upon him by nothing less than the nature of the universe and the peculiar constitution of the human mind, to examine carefully, and to present scrupulously, the arguments that may be marshaled against his own case. But to weigh and to state objections is one thing, and to identify oneself with them quite another; and it is one of my firmest convictions, arrived at by years of worrying this particular problem of impartiality in judgment, that if you hold a conscientiously reasoned conviction on a subject that you regard as truly important, you are automatically barred from viewing that subject impartially, or indeed in any light but that of your own chosen standpoint; and that conversely, if you are really capable of "seeing both sides" of a question, you don't, in your heart, give a damn about that question, one way or the other. Recognizing and announcing his own bias is as close an approach to rectifying or getting rid of it as any man can hope to make, since the human mind is so constructed that it cannot grasp the multiplicity of being, or the infinitely numerous aspects of any single thing, all at once, but is obliged to select for its inspection a small area, or a few features, that are important or "interesting" at the moment, and to let the rest go; but selecting according to an interest is the same as having a bias.

This incapacity for a complete purging of thought from prejudice is to me so self-evident a note of the human estate as to be hardly worth making a fuss about. Yet I have found that my habit of stating my premises at the outset of a discourse or controversy, which to my mind gives my opponent an advantage by saving him the trouble of ferreting them out and by enabling him to come to grips without maneuvering for position, has earned me, among certain of my acquaintances, a reputation not only for bigotry, which I could understand, but also for a special intellectual dishonesty or trickiness, which is indeed beyond me, both in the colloquial and, I hope, in the literal sense.

The long and short of it is that I hold too much straining after, and protestation of, an unbiased judgment to be, most often, nothing but a sign of intellectual namby-pambiness, as well as a proof of ignorance as to the ways and limitations of the human mind; and as such it appears in many contemporary English novelists and essayists of the liberal persuasion, for the thing is eminently a liberal vice or superstition, and also very English. But in its most virulent instances the pose of referee in the mental prize fight of more or less evenly matched causes or ideas becomes a form of presumption; for what happens in such cases is that a little shrimp of an intellectual, encouraged by the praise (on the basis of reciprocity) of his fellows to mistake his own lack of mental guts for a mark of divine aloofness, plumps himself down in the seat of Judgment, and blows himself up until he thinks that he fills it. These excesses of the *furor judiciosus* are provoked, at times, by some exceptionally honest and clear-sighted writer's avowal that he is human enough to love some things and ideas and to hate others, and intelligent enough to perceive that if you love a certain idea because it is the truth, you are bound to hate its denial, because it is a lie. I am thinking particularly of certain gentlemen inhabiting the more literary precincts of the British press, who used to put G. K. Chesterton in his place every time they should have thanked him for the good deed of publishing yet another book.

However, let us return to the business on hand, from our excursion into an extraneous subject related to it only tangentially, but one that had the unexpected merit of taking us to the grave of Chesterton. And I trust the day will come when once more the mansions of the spirit will be regarded as at least as important as hospitals, laboratories, public washrooms, movie palaces, and railroad terminals, and when among the architects of those mansions Chesterton will occupy the place in English history which is his by right, and which today is accorded to him only by a few thousand eccentrics like myself; by people who are adjudged full of prejudice by our fellows, because after a careful study of the news in the best newspapers we have concluded that men have made a beastly mess of playing at God, and advocate that the cockeyed notions that led them to playing that stupid and lethal game, and that they never as much as glance at, not once in a lifetime, but swallow raw and wholesale, should be re-examined.

The great symbol whereby posterity, if any, will remember the tragic folly of the men who were responsible for the security of France and thus of Europe, and the tragic deception of those millions who put their trust in them, is of course the Maginot Line. I need not retell the wretched story, for it has been told many times; what I want to do is merely to fit the symbol into the picture I have been drawing. The men who governed France, and the men who commanded France's armies, had no knowledge of the world in which they, and we, were living: a world in which the Germans were building their seventy-ton tanks, and also the smaller ones, and organizing, equipping, and training their armored divisions, day and night, day and night, day and night, during the years that had preceded the war, and during the months that followed it. The ministers and generals of France were living in a world in which the Germans sat down and shook their fists at the Maginot Line, or else dashed their brains out against its steel and concrete wall. They had no inkling of a world in which the Germans would do nothing as lunatic as that, but would, as inevitably as water flows downhill and not up, seek to deliver a mortal blow beyond the point where that Line ended: northwest of Montmédy. Now it was five parts out of ten of the business of those men to know that world accurately, for you cannot expect to survive in an environment of which you are unable to calculate the behavior in advance. That, too, is the lesson of fifty thousand years of the human past, and of six thousand of human history. The environment of France was Germany. The governors of France were incapable of calculating in advance the behavior of Germany, even as the governors of Egypt, several millennia ago, had been unable to calculate the behavior of the Sea Peoples, and later that of the Hyksos hordes.

For man, knowledge is life, and the Unknown Factor the greatest enemy, and the purveyor of death. At the dawn of history the mind of man conceived the joss, the fetish, the Great Medicine, to

checkmate the Unknown Factor. Later on the mind of man discovered or invented religion, philosophy, science, and technology
to combat and to defeat the Unknown Factor. But in the periods
when the minds of a certain section of mankind had grown weary
and hopeless, they always reverted to the original medicine, which
was the Great Medicine. The Maginot Line was France's Great
Medicine, before the end came. And, in all justice, not only that of
France. Czechoslovakia, too, had had her Maginot Line, on a
smaller scale just as grand and just as perfect as that of her greater
ally. It fell without a shot to the Unknown Factor — the new evil
faith, the new strategy, the new tactics, of the old enemy Germany.
The Great Medicine of Denmark and Norway and Holland and
Belgium had been Social Progress, which we have already examined as such, and Neutrality. Nor has the tale of the Great
Medicine been fully told, to date; for the Great Medicine of our
own United States is the Atlantic Ocean, and a Neutrality which is
not even genuine, as was that of the fine, cultured, progressive
Ostrich Herd of Northwestern Europe, but a sham; for a country
that renders one of the belligerents "all aid short of war" is fighting
in that war and kids itself by believing that it isn't. That, however,
is not part of my story.

A Maginot Line that extended from the Fort l'Écluse, the
narrows of the Rhône breaking through the Jura into the wooded
gorges of Valromey and the valley of Bugey, to the North Sea
would have been a mere retarding factor in any case; thousands of
heavy tanks, working with minute accuracy in conjunction with
aeroplanes, which was the way of the German advance, would in
time have found its weak spots and smashed through. But the
Maginot Line, as it existed, did not extend from the narrows of the
Rhône to the North Sea. It began at Basle, and stopped at Montmédy. It entrusted the line of the Jura to the benevolence of God,
who, as we all know, helps only those who help themselves, and
to the small Swiss army, that of a country that was not an ally
of France, but yet another fanatic of the Great Medicine, Neutrality. The Maginot Line further entrusted I do not know how
many hundred miles of the northern frontier of France to the

benevolence of God, and to the neutrality of Belgium. The same northern frontier which was not even a steep and difficult system of mountains like the Jura, but flat country, for much the greatest part, and had as its only natural barrier worth the name the river Meuse, across which somebody was to forget to blow up the bridges when the moment came. That northern frontier through which the German armies had poured in 1914, only twenty-five years earlier, and more times before that than I can remember, but no more times than it was the business of the French Government and General Staff to recall.

Future ages, if any, will find much in the collapse of France to wonder about. But two things they will find incredible; though, since they will have been established beyond the shadow of doubt, they will have to be credited. One of these things is that the Maginot Line ended at Montmédy. The other is that the French statesmen and generals, and the French people, thought that this Maginot Line, which ended at Montmédy, formed an impregnable defense, and lived for nine months after the outbreak of the war as if the armored divisions of Hitler had been transferred to Saturn as soon as they had finished their job in Poland.

For it is not even as if the Germans had not given clear warning of what they were going to do if and when they tackled their job in France. The tank-*cum*-aeroplane business, the whole strategy and tactics of the armored divisions, had been given away in Poland. One might almost say that the Germans had been generous to the point of recklessness, the way they notified their enemies nine months ahead as to what they had in mind. They acted like the magician who warns the gentleman in the sixth seat, fourth row left, that in three minutes he will find an onion in his pocket. The Polish campaign had been just that sort of notice to France. And the generals, statesmen, and people of France said, "Bah! There is the Maginot Line." A Maginot Line that ended at Montmédy. Twenty-seven and a half miles southeast of Sedan, a place remembered by all Frenchmen in connection with another case of overconfidence. The great break-through on May 16, 1940, that settled the fate of France, was at Sedan.

And yet there was one soldier in France who, from the military point of view at least, had foreseen all. In 1934 a certain Colonel de Gaulle published a little book entitled *Vers l'armée de métier* (Toward a Professional Army). He demanded mechanization and the extension of the Maginot Line to the sea. He predicted the armored-unit-*cum*-aeroplane tactics, and he wrote that the best defense against massed tank attack was to attack first with massed tanks. In 1934 there was still time. As far as I know the only front-rank parliamentarian with influence on the ruling Left who took this little book seriously was M. Paul Reynaud. But the professional politicians feared that the extension of the power of professional soldiers, which the new ideas involved, might interfere with their fat little jobs. *Their* slogan was, "Safety first, for deputies." So the bill providing for the formation of motorized divisions was voted down in 1935, and that was that. But the German General Staff thought very highly of Colonel de Gaulle's book. He is now General de Gaulle, leader of all free Frenchmen, with an address in London.

I have seen no proof that any act of deliberate treachery had been committed by anybody in France up to June 17, 1940, the day when I lost such touch with events as I had had, and had to begin to do something to save the life of my wife and my little sixteen-year-old dog, and my own. Nor have I heard to date, which is the eighth of September, that anyone has seen such proof; and I have some friends who would know about these things.

But some man, or some men, must have been responsible for the altogether unbelievable fact that the Maginot Line ended at Montmédy. That there was no time and no money to continue it to the sea? Rot. It was the will that had been lacking. The men who for the last ten years — I say ten years, but I might as well say twenty — governed France were tired. Tired as the men who had governed Egypt in the years before the Sea Peoples landed, and of whom anybody may read just how tired they were, and how despairing, in several books that reprint the original record, now many thousand years old; one of these books being Mr. Christopher Dawson's *The Age of the Gods*, where I read that record — but the

Germans have the book at Arcachon. Tired as the governors of Rome had become by the year 400 of our era. They had asked themselves, those Egyptians, and those Romans (not to mention the rulers of Cnossus in Crete, to whom all that I have just said also applies; you could see the ruins of Cnossus if you had the fare, before the war, but now you can only read about them), they asked themselves, "What is the use of it all? We can do nothing but wait. The blow will come. We have probably deserved it."

I have no idea what the governors of France talked about when they were among themselves, between the years 1933, when Hitler came into power in Germany, and 1940, when he came into power in France. But I will say this — here was I, an outsider, a dilettante, a newspaperman who had given up being one because he ceased to believe that newspapers mattered, a writer whose books did not sell, for the excellent reason that he did not write them. And what I, sitting in my little flat in the Abbey Road, St. John's Wood, London, England, could figure out, in the month of December 1934, and put on paper: that Hitler was a Factor, a Danger, *the* Danger; that Hitler was the new Attila, but one who had come to stay; that Hitler would fight, and fight to a finish — is anybody going to tell me that there was not a man among the French cabinet ministers and ambassadors who, with the sources of information at his disposal, could figure out the same thing for himself, at the same time as I? I cannot believe it. At least a few of them must have known all about it, all along. Besides, there were the writings of Jacques Bainville and Charles Maurras, who had been drawing the same conclusions as I, though from rather different premises and by an entirely different method, for the past quarter century, and who, unlike myself, published their conclusions, instead of merely sending them in a letter to a friend in Ohio. I only discovered the writings of Bainville and Maurras in 1937, when, after four years' absence, I returned to France once more. Whereas the Frenchmen I speak of had those writings before them all the time.

But those Frenchmen must have been tired; for the faith had gone out of them. And the French people as a whole were tired too, and for the same reason, and ceased to look the facts in the face, but sought refuge in ideologies: that of M. Léon Blum, which I, on my part, rejected; and also that of M. André Maginot, which I, on my part, accepted as gospel truth, along with the rest. Though I, having those Egyptians and those Cnossians and Mycenaeans and Etruscans and Sumerians and Romans and all the rest of them before my mind all that time, and spending most of my days gnawing at the historical and psychological problems of the Unknown Factor and the Divorce from Reality, feel now that I ought to have known better; yet it would not have made any difference whatsoever if I had.

But the ideology of the Maginot Line did not exhaust the list of nonpartisan follies visited by the gods on those whom they were preparing to destroy. There was also the combined lunacy of the British blockade and of the inexhaustible and barely tapped resources of the British and French Empires. I call the faith in these two factors a lunacy, because though both were very important factors in winning the war eventually, to think that they were decisive factors was the same as to expect that after a while Hitler would, like a good fellow, lie down and die, and let Mr. Chamberlain and M. Daladier make obituary speeches from the platform of the Kroll Opera House in Berlin. Now to expect Hitler to do nothing while the blockade and the accelerated war supplies of the two great empires were strangling him was a folly even worse than the folly of the Maginot Line; for Hitler's whole past consisted in the repetition, half a dozen times between the Munich *Putsch* in the early twenties and the invasion of Poland in September 1939, of a single pattern: first to bluster; then to lie doggo; then to crouch; then to leap, strike, and kill. This was not the history of the Old Kingdom of Egypt, or of Cnossus, but of the last twenty years, not to say the last twenty minutes; yet everybody seemed to have forgotten all about it. But here I must give myself a pat on the back; for this was a lunacy to which I did not personally succumb, though my having steered clear of it did neither me nor anybody else the slightest good whatsoever. I never for a moment believed that the blockade and the superior potential in supplies and men of the Allies would win this war. I was firmly convinced that the war, at least the war on the Continent, could only be won by the superior army striking like lightning, and pulverizing the enemy's resistance in a few weeks. In this I was to be proved entirely right by the event. My only mistake was that I thought that the superior army was the French army, with its British ally. On the whole I find now that quite a few of the ideas I had concerning the French army were true, but unfortunately of the German army.

I have already hinted once or twice that my wife and I believed that the war would end by a stunning military victory of the Allies within a year. In retrospect it seems both tragic and incredible that we should have duped ourselves to this extent, but it is of some interest to record the mental process that resulted at the same time in what I might call our personally conducted tour in self-fooling and in our eschewing the prevailing false optimism about the blockade and the imperial war potential. I am telling this story, which has no bearing either on the larger events or on our personal fortunes, merely as a curiosity, partly because it throws light on the unexpected possibilities inherent in philosophical reasoning, and partly because it shows how easy it is for a man, the human mind being what it is, to be remarkably right and remarkably wrong in the same breath and in an oddly complex, wheels-within-wheels fashion.

It all began by my telling myself that the self-evident lesson of the Polish campaign was that the terrific striking power of modern armaments does not give the defense a dog's chance. I pondered this not as a military expert, for I knew absolutely nothing about army matters, but in my homely capacity as a student of philosophy, and it struck me that what had happened in Poland fell rather thrillingly in line with certain ideas that I had been trying to work out in my "Philosophy of Freedom": ideas such as that scientific progress, being essentially a grandiose imperialistic campaign waged by the Self against the universe, aims at the complete elimination of both space and time as obstacles to human wish-fulfillment, and that in the sphere of war elimination of time means that the aggressor has all the advantage, since such elimination takes the form of striking the enemy dead literally before he knows what has hit him. Now I reasoned that if I, a bookish person who had never fired a rifle in my life, could work this out, by a purely abstract philosophic argument, in a suburban villa seven hundred miles from the front, the Allied Commander-in-Chief and his general staff must know all about it as a matter of professional routine, and would never give Hitler a chance to do the thing a second time. I concluded that Gamelin was getting ready to act on this knowledge, that is to say, to deliver a smashing blow by tanks against the western frontier of Germany where it was the weakest; and that he was letting the editorial writers and newspaper experts put up a kind of smoke screen by all the talk about a five-year war, waged by means of the blockade and war manufactures in Canada, Australia, and Timbuctoo. It even flashed through my mind that the Maginot Line was being used by a brilliantly imaginative Allied Command as a gigantic red herring. I was wondering when Gamelin would begin; but I told myself that he knew what he was doing.

At the same time I went on believing that the Maginot Line was impregnable, and that no matter what happened France could not be invaded, let alone lose the war. And I wallowed in, and swallowed, like my neighbors, like millions of people from Lille and Rheims to San Francisco, all the official and semiofficial newspaper and radio hokum à la Tabouis about Hitler having lost his nerve and trying to save his face, or his bitter quarrels with his own generals as to what to do next; though I must add that I never for a moment was taken in by stupid wishful talk about driving a wedge between Hitler and the German people, the favorite early wartime drug of British Liberals and Labour, and even of some incorrigible self-befuddlers of the French Left. And I recall wondering at the time whether the *Altmark* incident was not the prelude to things beginning to happen. As a matter of fact it was just that; only the things that happened were not the things that I had expected to happen.

I am wondering now, as I put all this on record, what would have happened to me if I, in January or February, 1940, had written a letter to General Gamelin, explaining my ideas about the elimination of time as an aim common to modern science, voluntaristic logic, and the mechanism of dreams, as I had explained them back in 1934 to my friend Professor Jászi; and if I had suggested the application of these ideas to the conduct of the war by a massed attack of French tanks on Aix-la-Chapelle. I suppose that they would have put me into an asylum, in a segregated padded cell marked "Dangerous"; though it is possible that I should have been brought before a court-martial as an *agent provocateur* of the Fifth Column masquerading as a loony professor of philosophy. I am no great hand at the conduct of practical affairs, even where they concern me most vitally and intimately; but I am glad to say that it never occurred to me to write such a letter to General Gamelin. I had been cured of the habit of writing letters of this kind by an experience early in 1937, when I wrote one to somebody high in the favor of the United States Government, suggesting that the Department of State should organize within itself a small bureau of international psychology. I was thanked most politely for the suggestion, by return mail. Just recently I was greatly interested in a passage of an article by Colonel Donovan, published in a number of American newspapers under the auspices of the U. S. Navy Department on August 22, 1940, describing the psychological laboratories attached to the Nazi embassies all over Europe. Well, Fulton had suggested warships propelled by steam to Napoleon; and where are Fulton and Napoleon now? I shudder to think, especially as far as the latter is concerned; but that is neither here nor there.

And so I come to that chapter of the universal self-deception which to me is even more painful than the others already discussed; for it proves me to have been particularly foolish in a respect in which I prided myself on being particularly wise. I refer to that treachery on the Right which I now believe did France fully as much harm as the treachery on the Left, and which since the armistice has had the field of harming France entirely to itself. Now I list this treachery under the universal self-deception, but this does not mean that I seek in any way to excuse it; for I believe that while there was in it, as in the other manifestations of the same fundamental folly, a certain element of spontaneous and uncontrollable fatuity which hardly anyone living in a given atmosphere can escape, since it is precisely like a contagion in the air, it was, for the most part, an error induced by self-interest, or rather by supposed self-interest, the latter sort being fully as contemptible as the former, and also ridiculous. Just what the share of the men of the Right had been in bringing about the collapse of French resistance I do not pretend to know, and I doubt if anybody knows it as yet, though the matter is bound to be cleared up later on. The case against them is not nearly as crystal-clear as it is against the Communists, who conducted their campaign of sabotage and of spying, of undermining discipline in the army, of sowing distrust of the British ally, and despair as to the ultimate outcome, in the masses of the people, as the avowed emissaries and henchmen of a foreign power and ally of their country's enemy.

I believe that there were, among those who preached defeatism and coming to terms with Hitler from the Right, quite a number of honest but misguided people who thought that theirs was the best way to serve the ultimate interest of France; though I hasten to add that my belief in their good intentions would not induce me to put in a word for any of them, should they fall into the hands of General de Gaulle. I am the last person in the world to maintain that good intentions excuse the act and its results, and I do hope that when France is once more a free nation the men that I am speaking of will be dealt with according to their deserts, that is to say, lined up against a wall and shot, though I should not object to hanging them either, if that were thought more suitable. Nor can I believe that a man like the old Marshal Pétain, for instance, is to-day serving Hitler for what he gets out of it; nor do I suppose for a moment that Marshal Pétain *means* to serve Hitler; I am sure he thinks he is serving the best interests of France, though in fact he may be betraying them. It is also clear that some of the officials who remained at their posts after the collapse, and are now in charge of indispensable public services, did the right and patriotic thing from right and patriotic motives. But this applies mainly to the municipal officials and technicians and so forth, not to the men at the top of the ladder. I also believe that nothing can be said against good Frenchmen who, having found escape impossible, are now carrying on their occupations, whatever these may be, under the invader or under his native lieutenants; for such men are saving their lives so that they may later serve France.

But once all these allowances and exceptions have been listed, the fact remains that most of the men who today serve under Pétain in capacities of importance, or who actively support the Vichy regime, are men who believe, either that the Nazi dispensation, in an adapted form, is a good thing for France, or else that it is a good thing for their own pockets. Both kinds are traitors to France, to Europe, and to Christian civilization. They are to my mind no better than the Roman who went over to the Cherusci or Marcomanni or Goths, or the American who sided with the Sioux in their wars against the white men; I don't know if there ever were any such Americans, but I know that the Sioux had a far better case against the white man than the Nazis have against France, and yet I feel that the American who would desert to them was a renegade in a class infinitely worse than Benedict Arnold himself, for the English were white men and Christians. As to the Christian auxiliaries of the Arabs in Spain, they were renegades and traitors to their proper cause, but much less despicable than the native French *Gauleiters* of the Nazi usurper; for the Arabs were decent civilized people, if rather overrated by anti-Catholic historians, and certainly incomparably gentler and more humane than the new savages from beyond the Rhine.

But the worst that a person of my convictions may say of the men of Vichy, and above all of the multi-millionaire ex-Socialist from Châteldon, M. Pierre Laval, is that their existence and acts justify, in retrospect, the existence and some acts of the men of the Front Populaire, at least of those who were not Communists; for the Communists of France have for the last twenty years been doing the very work now carried on by M. Pierre Laval, that is to

say the work of Hitler. One might express the same notion by saying that the goings-on of the men of the French Right have turned
the world upside down; for they make the Left seem right.

4

By mid-December I had broken my little personal deadlock, and
made up my mind to write a short book, frankly propaganda, to
aid the French cause in the United States; and not only in the
United States. My initial thesis was to be that this war was, unlike
the war of 1914–1918, not one between two camps within the same
civilization, nor yet a war between civilization and savagery, for
that was a mere manner of speaking, a form of invective; but between two levels of civilization, the old European civilization and
something new which was also something very old, that grim and
bestial Teutonic pre-civilization which, turned by technology into
the greatest military power the world had ever seen, sought to
wipe off the face of the earth everything that opposed it and that
it could not gobble up. From this I would go on to show, by historical example and philosophical argument, that a war of this
kind could only end in the complete extermination of one or the
other side, something that the Germans had realized from the outset and were now shouting from the housetops, but that the Allies
had only just begun to grasp. Also, in such a war, I went on, neutrality was both meaningless in theory and impossible in practice,
for it was something that Nazi totalitarianism would not and *could
not* tolerate; and I supported this by an elaborate line of reasoning,
most of which has since been learned by heart, though not from
my book, by the peoples of Norway, Denmark, Belgium, and
Holland. All this was to be addressed, implicitly, to American
public opinion; for by this time I had come to accept as part of a
reality gone mad a fact which at first seemed to me so fantastic
as to be wholly incredible, the fact that the overwhelming majority
of the American people did not regard this war as a concern of its

own. And this, I reflected, was the same American people which on the one hand believed itself to be the foremost depositary and champion of human liberty and decency, and which on the other hand made paeans about the abolition of distance by the aeroplane part of its daily liturgy. It seemed to me that the foremost duty of any intelligent and patriotic American who knew the facts of the European situation was to contribute what he could to the effort to wake up America, for I realized that the greatest danger for the United States lay not in the armed power of Hitlerism, which we could double if we wanted to and tried, but in a mental paralysis that delayed action until it was too late.

The second half of my little book was to be aimed at English opinion as much as at American. For in the fourth month of the war I saw with incredulous consternation that an important section of British Liberals and Labour still believed that it was possible to win this war by driving a wedge between Hitler and the German people, or, as Lord Haw-Haw very reasonably put it, by persuading the German people to win it for England; and the same Liberals and Labourites also believed that once the war was over and Hitler had gone off to saw wood at some other Doorn, the Germans would suddenly turn democratic and elect Thomas Mann President of the German Republic and throw their arms into the Baltic and spend the rest of their lives talking about the Egyptian drug traffic in the big white international café at Geneva. We heard those charming sentiments expressed night after night in the broadcasts of the B.B.C. and met with them also in letters published in the London *Times*.

Now it was clear that English people who believed in those fairy stories could not be told too often the two most important truths about the political aspect of the war. The first was that Hitler cannot be separated from the German people, for Hitler *is* the German people. The second was the lesson brought home by all history and above all by the peace of Versailles: that Europe could not hope to keep a united Germany down, for a united Germany, however weakened, would arm herself in defiance of any difficulties and restrictions, and would in a short time become once more formidable; and that therefore the choice before Europe was between submitting to German domination and smashing German unity for good. Nor was a dismemberment of Germany the violent unnatural thing that the word betokened, for it meant merely the restoration of the old historic German federalism, under which the Germans were poor and powerless, but also happy, and their country was that of great philosophers, poets, and musicians. To cut up England or France into small autonomous districts would be to kill English or French nationality and culture. But to perform the same operation on Germany would be to restore to the various old regional and tribal units, Bavarian, Frankish, Saxon, Swabian, Thuringian, Austrian, and Rhenish, and also to a number of small but sturdy cultural centers rooted in dynastic history, their old life which had been trodden into the totalitarian dust by Hohenzollern Prussia long before the word "totalitarian" was invented; and this policy of the historic Germanies, as opposed to that of the unhistoric Reich, was one from which many pure-blooded Germans of old stock expected the salvation of their people.

For a quarter of a century some of the finest political brains of France, above all the historian Jacques Bainville and the royalist leader and publicist Charles Maurras, had advocated the program of this refederalization of a disarmed Germany, with a Rhine frontier for France guarded by an overwhelmingly strong French army, as the only guaranty of the security of France and of the survival of European civilization. It had been in the mind of the great Maréchal Foch when he demanded the march on Berlin and permanent annexation of the left bank of the Rhine, in which he had the support of General Pershing; but the English politicians were afraid of a French preponderance, and the framers of the worst peace treaty in history had different ideas — they left German unity intact, but inflicted excessive economic penalties, such as the Germans would not and could not pay, and the Allies could not and would not collect by forcible execution. And so Adolf Hitler came and made the most of both fateful mistakes of Versailles, the political leniency and the economic pound of flesh; and so we had the war of 1939, and all that was to follow, not because Versailles had been too hard on the Germans, but because it had been both mean and not hard enough. But neither the British nor the American public was ever made familiar with the full case for what came to be called the Bainville peace, a just designation but an unfortunate one from the point of view of publicity in the English-speaking lands. For the great historian Bainville was a man of the Action Française, that is to say the extreme Right, and all the men who reported French politics in the American newspapers, and most of those who performed the same function for England, had Leftist or at least Liberal sympathies; and to these men, who were nevertheless and without exception sincere friends of France, the intransigent anti-Germanism advocated by Bainville and Maurras was abhorrent partly because it was frankly militaristic, and chiefly because it was put forward by a group associated with Royalism, anti-democracy, anti-parliamentarism, and Jew-baiting.

I had realized as far back as 1934 that, the Germans being what they are, and Hitlerism being not a passing aberration but the natural climax of German evolution, the only security for European civilization lay in a strongly fortified Rhine frontier guarded by a France whose military supremacy was permanently established over a Germany restored to her immemorial pattern of loose federalism. But it was only in 1937 that I learned that these ideas had been formulated by Jacques Bainville before the last war was over; till then, living in my modest imitation ivory tower, I thought that I had invented them myself. And in the fourth month of the war I decided, though with many qualms and misgivings, that I would constitute myself the spokesman of these ideas in the United States, not because I thought that I was the right person, but because I knew that I was the only person, to tackle this particular job, no other writer having come forward to do it better than I could hope to. At the same time I felt that I was in a way not wholly unsuited to the task, for after all the expedients and demands of political strategy which I proposed to advocate were nothing but the practical corollaries of my own "Philosophy of Freedom," while the theoretical first part of the little book which I now proposed to write, that is to say the philosophical and psychological analysis of Hitlerism as the latest and most complete incarnation of the Teutonic spirit, was something that I could lift bodily out of the already typed-out section of that incomplete *magnum opus*. All I had to do was to loosen up a little the too closely knit philosophical argument and to translate it into words of two syllables from words of three or four. I did not realize then that it would have been much easier and quicker to disregard altogether what I had written and to write the whole thing anew according to my newly conceived purpose, and this aside has no importance for the general reader, but those who live by writing will know what I mean and will appreciate my quandary.

Before, however, I could settle down to do the job properly I had to solve an imminent practical problem, and this consisted in deciding where to do it. And since the reader might well ask what concern that intimate detail is of his, or of the history of the French collapse, I will remind him that I do not include intimate details in this narrative unless they are relevant to my larger subject; and it will be seen that my worries over such a purely personal matter as that of choosing a place to live in during the first half of 1940 (for that was the issue confronting us) were to produce the same sort of symbolic crop as my earlier troubles anent the road permits.

I have already said that the pressure of the war on our everyday life at Pyla had, by December, sunk to practically zero. We felt, however, that our tranquillity was too good to be true, and we realized that whether the Allies were to win by a long war of attrition or by a short one of smash and bang, a few months or even a few weeks might bring restrictions on civilian existence such as had been imposed in the war of 1914–1918. What weighed on our minds was not the possibility of having to miss this comfort or to waive that small luxury, but the inevitability of increasing contact with French officialdom over census matters, ration cards, road regulations, and so forth. At this time we dreaded such contacts far more than we dreaded German bombs.

Here was a good reason to consider leaving France, but not a decisive one. There were two others, more urgent. I had by then formed some notion of the beauties of the French war censorship, and while I had not the slightest doubt about being able to get the typescript of my book, when it was finished, through to the United States and to England, there was a substantial risk of getting it through with a delay of weeks, and such a delay might easily kill a topical book. I wished, not unnaturally, to find out in advance the proper time-saving procedure, and had we been living in Paris this would have been a matter of a telephone conversation or two with one of my American correspondent friends. But we were living four hundred miles from Paris, and my friends were very busy men, and to raise the point by correspondence seemed generally unsatisfactory. I addressed myself to some higher local officials, such as the chief of the city police at Arcachon and the commissioner of the port, and they were very charming and spent hours telephoning to the military authorities in Bordeaux, and then reported that nobody there knew anything about such matters. I began to think that if I wanted to do propaganda for France without wasting too much time on conferring with French officials, much the best thing I could do was to go to some place abroad.

Now we had been wanting, for purely personal reasons, to go to Portugal for some time; and my third practical difficulty seemed to make the long-planned trip inevitable. It concerned the period of immunity of my car from French customs duties, which was to expire about February 15 and could not be extended in the routine way. In December it would still have been comparatively easy to return the car by rail to England, but it would also have been very expensive, and at this time, which now seems to lie about a century back, life without an automobile seemed to us unthinkable. So it looked like Portugal or nothing, and I secured from London the documents required for driving the car across Spain and into Portugal, and called with my wife at the Portuguese Consulate in Bordeaux, for the first but not the last time in my life, to obtain visas; and it was then that I made the acquaintance of Senhor Mendes, the Consul, a man of charming manners destined to loom large in this narrative. We had to fill out forms and were told that we could return in a week's time and have the visas entered in our passports, and that Portugal would be enchanted to receive our visit.

Christmas, however, was approaching, and my wife flew to England, to spend three weeks with the boys and her parents near Guildford. Her departure involved us in a repetition, more or less, of the road-permit business, and in three expensive trips to Bordeaux; but we will let that pass. By the time she returned to Pyla, mid-January, I had changed my mind about Portugal. I wanted to see Portugal sometime, but I wanted much more to stay in France for the present if I could. For I loved France and it did not seem altogether decent to run away from a France at war just because life there was getting slightly less comfortable than it had been before. Also, the removal or rather migration would have meant the loss of about a month's working time, something I could not afford.

So one day I had an inspiration. I would go to Paris and put my case up to somebody in authority at the Ministry of Information. I would explain what I wanted to do to serve France, and that I would not accept any pay (not that there was much danger of my being offered any); and I would ask the Ministry to secure an extension of our customs immunity, and also to give me a road permit valid for the whole of the nonmilitary zone of France, so that I should be able to move about like a French civilian and need not spend days on end fighting petty officials for safe-conducts. In return for this latter favor I would propose to do a quick survey of the home front and to write an article or two about it for American magazines, or eventually a short book, that might help the French cause. And I would add that if for any reason these two requests, or either, could not be granted I was ready to remove myself to Portugal and to work for France with Lisbon as my headquarters.

This seemed to me an eminently fair offer, but my various friends, American, French, and of other nationality, were unanimous in calling me a fool for making it, when I discussed it with them after my arrival in Paris toward the end of January. To get there was not particularly easy, for I had to make four trips to the *mairie* of La

Teste and spend a whole day in Bordeaux to secure a safe-conduct, and I secured it in the end by threatening the bespectacled lady at the *mairie* with dire things if she further obstructed me in putting my services at the disposal of the French Republic.

On my arrival in Paris I did not call a conference of my friends to put my scheme to a vote, but I consulted them separately over a meal or a drink, and yet they all said exactly the same thing. This was that if I wanted to work for France by writing the sort of book I had in mind, it was a fine thing to do and they wished me luck, but that if I expected co-operation in the matter from the French Ministry of Information it merely showed that I was the combination of a hick, a newborn babe, a congenital half-wit, a purchaser of gold bricks, and a few other things all meaning ignoramus and dupe. For, they said, and they were in the position to know, the officials of the French Ministry of Information were not there to inform, nor yet to be informed, but principally to stop such information as might help France from getting about too fast, and apart from that, to draw salaries which, in all fairness be it said, were far from munificent.

My friends did not say these things in these same words, but the gist of what they said was the same, and some used expressions far stronger than I would care to put on paper. For most of these friends were American newspapermen who had spent the last five months of their lives in fighting a pitched battle and also a war of attrition against the official gentlemen of the censorship and the propaganda and the information center and God knows what those offices were all called; gentlemen who all seemed exceeding anxious to hinder the Germans in learning that the capital of France was Paris, a considerable city situated on the river Seine and containing several government offices; and whose whole philosophy of life seemed to be contained in the maxims "Any news is bad news" and "The public be damned." And yet, my friends added, these officials were, in private life, charming men, most intelligent and well-instructed; but once they stepped inside the Hôtel Continental they turned into French officials, and that meant people who . . . well, the reader ought to know by now what that meant. Most contemptuous of all was a friend who was not a newspaperman, nor an American, nor yet French, but one who had lived most of his life in France and loved France as one loves one's own country, and knew and was known to everybody and was generally a man of great culture, wide knowledge, and some influence. And this man said that if I really wanted to co-operate with the French Ministry of Information he would give me an introduction to the Boss, but I declined this, not judging it necessary for the support of my modest and crystal-clear proposal; and he also said that if I persisted in my purpose I would soon come to wish that I had never been born; and he wound up by muttering something about *fromage*, which is only French for cheese but suggests, in this context, fleshpots, slices of melon, lame ducks, and deserving Democrats.

Well, I thought of my bespectacled lady friend at the *mairie* of La Teste and said to myself, there must be something in what all these knowledgeable people say, but they probably lay it on thick because of constant irritation that has grown upon them. However, my contact will be short and I shan't have time to get my nerves frayed. So I called on a gentleman high up in the hierarchy of the Hôtel Continental, and explained my errand and showed him a ten-page outline of the book I proposed to write. The gentleman seemed genuinely interested, and was most understanding and scholarly, and I told myself that I was in luck, for he seemed to be definitely in sympathy with my Nationalist and Rightist ideas, and after all I might have run into some parlor-pink intellectual who had served his apprenticeship at the big white café in Geneva, and who would not have liked me at all. The gentleman did not even let me finish my little set piece but grasped it all when I was halfway through, and he said what I asked for was easy to grant and promised to see personally that I got all I wanted, and when my manuscript was finished I was only to post it to him and he would see it through the censorship in a day or two. One thing I emphasized was this: that if the Ministry of Information did not want, or had not the competence, to grant my requests or to arrange for their being granted, I would go to Portugal at once and do the work for France I proposed to do, anyway. But the gentleman said, not at all, not at all, it was preferable that I should stay in France.

So I went away very pleased with myself and said to all my friends, You were wrong, but they all said the same two words, namely, You wait. I took the train home to Arcachon and on the way I said to myself it was grand to be allowed to work for France, like a Frenchman born, and I already saw myself being kissed on both cheeks by M. Lebrun, the President of the French Republic, for what I had done for France; French Presidents sometimes do that in the more serious cases. When I got home to Pyla I wrote to the understanding gentleman to thank him for his kindness, and he wrote and confirmed his promises. So I spent most of my days hammering away at my Corona for France, and also watching for the *facteur* who would bring news from the Ministry of Information that the matter of my car was arranged and I did not have to pay five hundred dollars duty on an old Ford; and also that I had been granted the special road permit and could say good-by for evermore to the lady with the spectacles at La Teste.

Then one of my American correspondent friends came down from Paris and the idea was that he and I would travel together in my car and do a survey of the home front, and he would write it up for his big newspaper back home and I would write a pamphlet just as if I were Mr. Somerset Maugham. But my road permit had not arrived and my friend had to take uncomfortable and slow trains, and I asked myself in what way this delay was to help France to win the war. So I waited a little longer and then wrote a letter to inquire what had happened to my car extension and to my road permit, and received no reply. Then on March 31, which was eight weeks after my personal call at the Ministry, I had a letter from them, but signed by another gentleman, who wrote that my car extension had been granted; would I call at the office of the Director-General of Customs in Paris and attend to the matter? I wrote to the Paris agent of the Automobile Association of London, and asked him to call in my behalf as directed, and he called, and the Director-General of Customs said he had never heard of me. I wrote to the gentleman at the Ministry of Information and said there must have been a mistake, and anyway what had happened to my road permit? The gentleman wrote back and apologized for the mistake, and the agent of the A.A. went back to the Director of Customs and got me a nice new document for my car. I thanked the gentleman at the Ministry of Information and suggested very politely that theirs was a strange way of treating an American writer who had offered to work for the cause of France without pay; for I had written about my road permit three times and never received a word in reply. Nor did I receive one to this last letter, and I let the matter drop.

Of course all this caused me much annoyance and even anguish, for I was not used to being insulted by people to whom I proposed to do a good turn. But I went on writing my book to show America how right France was and what France needed to be secure; for I knew only too well that France was France, and the gentlemen who were nibbling at the cheese of the Hôtel Continental were quite a different matter. I also wrote a letter to one of my most knowing friends in Paris and said some personal enemy must have libeled me to the Ministry of Information. But my friend wrote back, Don't be a fool, it was just the Hôtel Continental way of doing business.

I did not believe my friend then, but I believe him now, and the other day when he came to see me in New York I told him so. He had lost all his furniture and books in Paris, and I had lost all my books and my wife's only fur coat and many clothes and other effects at Arcachon. In a delicate way the French Ministry of Information owes me compensation for what I lost, for I had proposed to them on February 5 that I would go to Portugal and work for France at Lisbon, but they advised me to stay in France; and afterwards I worked ten hours a day to fulfill my part of the bargain, but they only fulfilled one half of theirs, and for the rest neglected to answer my letters. But my friend and I spent a cosy half-hour talking, over a glass of grapejuice, which he prefers to beer, about the happy days when we both were trying to persuade the French Ministry of Information to let us tell the American people that France was right.

I trust the reader understands that I did not tell this story by way of airing a personal grievance, for it would be ridiculous to make a fuss about such trifling matters in the midst of the disaster that has overtaken the whole world. It is perfectly clear that France would not have won the war even if I had been allowed to write the little pamphlet about the home front, and encouraged to publish the short book about the Rhine frontier, by the mandarins of the Rue Rouget-de-Lisle. But it is my honest belief that France would have stood a better chance of winning the war if the Hôtel Continental front had been held not by those mandarins but by an altogether different type of man. So the story I have just told should be regarded as a kind of allegory, like my wholly truthful fairy tale about the bespectacled lady who sat in a cage in a little village of the province of Guyenne, which is now called the Department of Gironde.

Yet another consequence of my gratuitous and ill-starred assumption that maybe the propaganda center of the French Government was interested in doing French propaganda abroad was that I did not apply for our Portuguese and Spanish visas in January or February of this year, when I might have obtained them in five minutes by paying down a few dollars. What this, in itself not very spectacular, negligence was to mean to us later on will be related in the next chapter. But I would say here that when on the morning of June 17, 1940, I drove with my wife and little dog to Bordeaux, to secure those visas at long last, I had 60,000 words of my book neatly typed, out of a proposed 90,000, in a wooden box at Pyla. Three days later, when we returned to our house for twenty minutes, I ordered Madeleine the cook to burn that manuscript at once, and to burn it thoroughly; for the Germans had crossed the Loire at La Charité and other places, and their motorcycles were faster than our old Ford, and if they had overtaken us with that manuscript in the car it would have been just too bad. Madeleine burned it, and I had only worked on it four or five months; but I had packed the thought of ten years into it, and I was sorry to know that it was burning as I drove out of our garden for the last time. But I hoped then and I hope still that that was not the end of my work for France.

5

The Allied adventure in Norway, clotheshorse of so many hopes, collapsed on May 5. Our days at Pyla, and the days of the civilization of free men on the continent of Europe, were numbered, and were rushing toward their fullness. The ineptitude of Franco-British leadership hung over our heads like a thick black cloud. The lightning invasion of Scandinavia, and even more its brilliant follow-through, had by this time convinced all but the most addle-brained addicts to the conjectural dope dealt out by semi-official spokesmen in Paris and London that whatever may have been the cause of the seven months' all-quiet on the Western Front, it was not lack of imagination, fear of initiative, or the progressive paralysis of senility at Nazi G.H.Q. And still we in France did not see. That is to say, we saw a heroic Stoicism in mute resignation or sullen indifference; we saw the firmly set jaw of the resolve to go through with it this time in the rebellious scowl of those who were telling themselves and one another that they would not stick it much longer; we saw silent self-disregarding discipline in the morose inward-turning of those who wondered where *they* got off. In his retrospective summing up, published in the October 1940 issue of a New York popular magazine, Mr. Somerset Maugham speaks of those little straws which should have aroused his suspicions as to the way the wind was blowing, but to which he, like everybody else in France, refused to pay attention. He then goes on to relate how everybody, soldiers and civilians, told him that after the losses of the last war the French nation could not afford to lose men and must above all be careful of human lives; and he adds that he should have asked himself how it was possible to win a war if that was an important consideration. Nothing could be more to the point, but to my mind all that talk about winning the war without sacrificing lives — to which I, too, listened every time I sat down for a drink in a café or had my car serviced in a garage — today suggests an oak uprooted by the storm rather than a straw in the wind. Now, if we did not notice oak trees lying across the road, how should we have heeded mere straws?

Yet the air was full of them. It was as early as January, for instance, that I noticed that travelers in the crowded wartime trains had developed a sudden and startling sensitiveness to the smell of brier pipes. Now your average Frenchman is distinguished among all compartment mates in the world by his complete indifference to what is going on around him. Englishmen are more helpful and also chattier, and they will have told you all about their sons at school and about last summer's holiday in Cornwall or Yorkshire before your Frenchman has as much as grunted; but the Englishman is also jealous of his rights and takes up space, whereas the French co-traveler shrinks into his own minimum, and as long as you don't put your feet into his pockets will object to nothing. Well, for the first time in fifteen years' experience of French trains I was asked one day last January, by a fat man in a beret who exuded consistency in unchanged linen, rather unusual in first class, to put out my pipe because its strong smell annoyed the ladies. He said this politely enough, and yet with a sort of subdued leer in his voice, and I muttered something about being anxious to please and stepped into the corridor, wondering what I had done to offend the fat man, for I was certain that my pipe did not smell of anything but expensive Turkish tobacco. No fanatic of the Anti-smokers' League can loathe the odor of pipe filth more than I do, and I change my pipes daily and clean the one used and put it away for three weeks' rest. So I thought the man was a crank, but the same thing happened again and again when I took the train to Bordeaux and back, which I did frequently; and what was more curious still, if there was a Frenchman in the compartment smoking a pipe, nothing was said; and yet the pipes of Frenchmen . . . I came to the conclusion eventually that it was not my pipe they objected to, but the combination of my pipe and my blatantly English clothes. Only that "eventually" was a few days ago, here in New York, when I was searching the past for what Mr. Somerset Maugham now calls straws.

I found quite a few, good hefty ones; and the wind had begun to blow them about months before the outbreak of the war. I remember now that when in May 1939, or maybe early in June, our ex-valet Dante came to spend ten days' leave with us at Mougins, he related that there was much dissatisfaction in his regiment of artillery at Clermont-Ferrand, because the food was both unpalatable and insufficient; that the soldiers were particularly indignant over the black and moldy bread, and were enraged when they discovered that the Spanish Red prisoners interned in a near-by concentration camp, having refused to eat the same bread, were being supplied with fine white loaves, through the good offices of Communist aldermen. He also said that the officers of the commissariat were piling up money by providing inferior and scanty meals, and even by selling supplies to tradesmen in town. This may have been true, or it may not; the significant thing was that the soldiers believed it. Now I knew that soldiers all over the world, and French soldiers more than any other, are given to grumbling over their food, and things in general; had not the grenadiers of Napoleon's Guard been called *grognards*, a word that explains itself by its sound and need not be translated? But our Dante was an exceptionally intelligent and also an exceptionally decent boy, and I questioned him closely and decided that he was hardly exaggerating; and I told him to shut up and stop spreading disaffection. After the outbreak of the war, toward the end of October, he visited us on another leave, at Pyla, and said that he was now eating excellent food, prepared by himself; it appeared that his colonel, having discovered that his mother was a *cordon bleu* cook (no other than our own Emily), and evidently believing in heredity and the influence of early environment, had made him *chef* to the officers' mess. But he added that the soldiers were more disgruntled than ever, and with reason. He came again on Christmas Eve, looking sleek and well-nourished, but he showed us his boots which lacked soles, and said that he had been promised another pair weeks ago, but nothing happened; so Emily his mother bought him a fine pair at Arcachon, and also some woolen blankets, for he said that they were only supplied with thin cotton ones, and his regiment was now encamped high up in the mountains. Here were some pretty visible straws blowing about; but I saw none. And this was toward the end of December, when the war had been on for four months but had not yet begun.

We were hearing similar stories, and worse, from some very intelligent and decent working women who lived at Arcachon, and whose husbands were noncommissioned officers in the army of Africa. The chief complaints of these husbands, middle-aged men who in civilian life had held responsible jobs and were not apt to talk wildly for the sake of talking, was that their water supply was absurdly ill-organized and inadequate, and that the clothes they were issued were the same as those of the troops up North, and not at all suited to the African heat, whereas during the chilly desert nights they froze for lack of blankets. Now I realized that such stories might be matched by tales that reached the folks back home from enthusiastic and victorious armies; but the note of grievance was too persistent and unrelieved, and the women's reports usually ended by their saying that Pierre, or Louis, had written that they all loathed this war and had ceased to care. We told these women that their husbands were lonesome, and we implored them not to talk too much in this defeatist vein. They replied that they were as patriotic Frenchwomen as any, and their husbands were patriotic too, but what was the use? So I said, Don't worry, everything will come out all right, Gamelin knows his job; and I went my way and thought quickly of du Guesclin and Condé and the Maréchal de Saxe and Ney and Foch and all the rest, and was thrilled to the marrow when I caught, on the radio, strains of the "Chant du Départ," which the soldiers had sung who in the wars of the Revolution chased the armies of the whole world, or of "Sidi-Brahim," which was the march of the African riflemen, or of the "March of Turenne." And I promptly forgot all that the women had told me, and I see now that one of my troubles was that I knew too much French history. I was so full of grand old tags like *"A moi, Auvergne!"* which to the American reader cannot mean anything, but which will send a lump rising in the throat of any Frenchman who ever sees this page, that I never stopped to ask myself why, in all those months at Arcachon, I never saw an officer or a soldier who smiled. (I might as well explain that tag, for it is a great story. When young d'Assas, on outpost duty, found himself surrounded by an enemy company, he was told to keep quiet if he wished to live; but he shouted, "*À moi, Auvergne!*" — that is, "Rally to me!" — Auvergne being the name of his regiment; and he fell pierced by twenty bayonets. And it is sad to think that today it is Laval, the multimillionaire *Gauleiter* from Châteldon, who shouts, at Clermont-Ferrand, "*À moi, l'Auvergne*"; but in his mouth those words only mean, "This whole province of Auvergne belongs to me," which is unfortunately the truth.)

But perhaps the most significant of all the straws that I did not heed in those Arcachon days and months were the straws that the wind blew my way from Stuttgart and Cologne and Saarbrücken. Practically every day somebody, a woman in a shop, in front or behind the counter, or a garage hand, or the waiter in a café, or an old fisherman on the beach, told me, or Emily our cook, or Madeleine our maid, that his or her neighbor had just listened to the broadcast of Ferdonnet, the "traitor of Stuttgart," and just what this French mouthpiece of Dr. Goebbels had said. The person who reported this always added that he, of course, did not believe a word of it; but when I met him next time he would again quote his landlady, or the grocer's wife, quoting Ferdonnet once more.

Now I often listened to Ferdonnet myself, especially in the early days, when the whole business seemed much less serious; and I was struck by the devilish cleverness of the man, but said to myself, what does it matter, the French are the most intelligent people in the world and will see through his lying harangues. But later on I was not so sure, and I was amazed at the inconsistency and short-sightedness of the Rightist papers like *Gringoire* and the *Action Française*, which in the same breath minimized the effect of Ferdonnet's activity and demanded that the death sentence should be pronounced on him *in contumaciam*, and dug up unsavory stories from his past and called him names, but did not seem to recognize him for the evil genius that he was. These usually so clearheaded and keen-eyed people made, as far as I could judge, the fatal mistake of regarding Ferdonnet as a more vicious and slightly more dangerous edition of Lord Haw-Haw. Now the English oracle of Dr. Goebbels was a mere fourflusher and animated gramophone record, one of the few major mistakes of that superb master of the art of propaganda. His bloomers, unmistakably translated from the German of experts guilty of all the stock Teutonic misconceptions about British psychology, often made me guffaw; as far as I know he was never regarded in England as anything but a comic turn, and the music-hall revue based on his lucubrations was a sweeping success. But you could not have based a music-hall revue on Ferdonnet. He made no bloomers. He spoke, not the fantastic pseudo-Oxford, pseudo-highbrow, pseudo-sarcastic, and altogether half-witted jargon of the man Joyce, but good common sense, and was careful to mix at least fifty-one per cent of fact with his distortions and inventions. He was a sham only in the sense in which the whole Nazi ideology is a monstrous, blasphemous, satanic distortion of truth and reality. His lines were obviously not translated from the German, but thought in French for Frenchmen. He was, in a word, no cheapjack and no liability to his employers, but a serious traitor in a big way, a capable and embittered man with a thorough knowledge of the mentality of the French lower and middle classes, a flair for those weak spots of the Allies which a French audience would recognize as weak spots once they were pointed out, and an oily, underbred, but effectual enough delivery.

I realized after a while that he was a very dangerous man; but I had no reason to think that the French Government knew less about these things than a foreigner in a villa at Pyla-sur-Mer, and what could *I* have done about it anyway? There was no doubt in my mind that he knew and did his job infinitely better than the stuffed shirts and superannuated baritones and somebody's cousins of the French official propaganda knew and did theirs; but I did not think that this would make much difference in the long run, for wars were not won by talk but by armies, and I was convinced that the French army could win any war with one arm tied behind its back.

I see now perfectly clearly that as far back as January half the population of Arcachon swore by what Ferdonnet told them, though they reproduced his views without the credit line, referring to him mostly as the cousin of a general or senator whom a friend of theirs had recently met in Paris. And if this was so it was not so much because Ferdonnet was such a prodigy as because the men who were supposed to render him innocuous were such inept fools. Ferdonnet's stuff sank in by sheer gravity, as air will fill a vacuumized bottle once the stopper has been removed. His insidious half-truths seeped into the mental void created by the fantastic inanities and criminal reticences of the French official propaganda. I only saw this happen at Arcachon, or rather I realize that this *must* have happened at Arcachon, if certain things that I saw but did not take in properly are to be accounted for; but the situation could not have been very different in other regions. What went on was not a whispering campaign (though something of that sort was going on too, come to think of it), for everybody spoke quite loudly and openly of what the butcher had been told by the wife of the chauffeur of the senator's niece. And everybody protested that he did not believe it, and everybody went on repeating what he did not believe. The only person who ever told us that she actually believed what she reported, instead of merely mentioning it as a curiosity, was an Englishwoman who sometimes came to tea; and she believed what she told us because she had heard it from Mme. So-and-so, the wife of the respected advocate, or M. Such-and-such, the prominent army contractor, in the strictest confidence. And I made a test and asked her if she ever listened to Ferdonnet, and she said, Yes, I do, sometimes, but of course I don't believe a word he says, he is a traitor. But she was quoting him sixth hand all the time without suspecting it.

And so it came about that although Ferdonnet was a traitor and nobody at Arcachon took any stock in what he said, nevertheless, and after all, and you know that where there is smoke there is fire, and I always say that you never can tell, and perhaps there was something in what people said, that the Jews egged on the English to egg on the French to fight the Germans for the Jews' sake, and that chickens were so absurdly expensive because the English soldiers in the North ate nothing but; and that President Roosevelt was a tool of Wall Street and was supposed to be the son of a Jew named Rosenfeld, though this has not been proved; and that — *this was the meat, the rest was only fixings* — the Nazis were really Socialists, and the only true Socialists in the world, and Hitler was the poor man's truest friend, and that was why the rich international Jews were making war on him. Mind you, people did not *believe* all this; they merely were beginning to ask themselves whether there might not be something in it. And that was quite enough, according to the specifications of Dr. Goebbels, who most of the time knows his job.

There may be people right here in New York, exiled Frenchmen of importance, and American correspondents back from Paris, to tell me that I have exaggerated Ferdonnet's influence and his share in the collapse of the French *moral;* and also that I am now trying to appear clever, and pretend that I had known everything all along, and six months before it happened. My answer would be as follows: People who were busy with big things in Paris had not my opportunities and my leisure to watch small things at Arcachon. They were interviewing generals and cabinet ministers in the Rue St. Dominique and Quai d'Orsay, and rushing to dine in the Maginot Line or to inspect some naval dock at Brest or to have a glimpse at patrol skirmishing in the Saar, and they were worrying about what the Paul Faure wing of the S.F.I.O. would do next day in the Chamber. I had no such important and exciting occupations and preoccupations. I was only talking to the crossing sweeper at Moulleau, and to the old fellow who kept the oyster stall at Eyrac, and to the man who was washing his car; and I used to sit under a pine on the sand cliff of Les Abatilles and listen to what the schoolchildren said. Above all, I had plenty of time to discuss things with Emily our cook and with Madeleine our maid. And you could do worse than discuss things with your cook if you wanted to know which way public opinion was going in a village like Pyla. And France was full of Arcachons and Pylas; you can go and count them in a gazetteer if you like. As to my being very clever now, why, I am only trying to say what a fool I was then, seeing that I heard all that I heard and saw all that I saw and could not put two and two together.

Yet another unrecognized portent that I have dug up lately from the debris of my unheeded war memories is a conversation I had in Paris early in February, with a high official of one of the Ministries, — but not the Ministry of Information, — whom I had known for years and who spoke his mind freely to me. I told this personage about my interview with the nice man at the Hôtel Continental, and said that as soon as my all-in non-army-zone road permit arrived, I would do that survey of the home front which, published in the form of a pamphlet, was to tell the United States how every man, woman, and child in France was doing his or her bit in the sacred war to save civilization. My friend said, "An excellent idea. Just what we need. You know, you ought to go to Toulouse first. The *moral* there is very bad, and so it is in all Languedoc and in the southern regions of the Center, and in part of Gascony. The women, we hear, are particularly restive. We must do something to reassure the American correspondents. You, of course, will know what to see, what to forget, and what to do, for you are not after a scoop but want to serve France."

There was, large as life, the handwriting on the wall, but I could not read it. I thought that my friend probably exaggerated and also I was glad that he suggested something definite for me to do; and what was all that anyway to my unshakable faith in the invincibility and eternal destiny of France?

6

Of those five weeks which wiped the high achievement and higher hope of forty centuries off the continent of Europe, and pushed the fair realm of France back into the jungle which it had been before Caesar's conquest put a period to the incursions of the yellow-haired gorillas — of the unspeakable and unbearable agony of those five weeks from May 10 to June 15, I shall say very little;

for that story has been told more than once, and better than I could hope to tell it. What I want to record here are two lesser details or accompanying overtones of the greater events, which I have so far not seen referred to in print, clearly because the men who recorded those events for their distant contemporaries, as also for posterity, were kept far too busy to take notice of them. And I also want to tell of one particular event which has already been recorded, but which could be observed more closely and more intimately from my sidelines at Arcachon than from the center of things in Paris. What I called accompanying overtones (and I chose the metaphor purposely) were first, the "Marseillaise of Ghosts," and second, the two speeches that M. Reynaud, the Prime Minister of France, made in the course of a single night, that of June 13; though all the newspapers of the world only reported one such speech. And the event which had brushed past the observers of mightier things in Paris, but which we at Arcachon got, if I be pardoned for using such a vulgar locution, in the neck, good and hard, was the Belgian invasion; by which I do not mean the German invasion of Belgium, but its sequel, the Belgian invasion of Southwestern France.

But first it behooves to explain that word "agony," as I used it in the context above; for it might be misconstrued. I used it because I meant it: agony, neither less nor more. Our feelings in those days, when we daily died a hundred deaths between the official French broadcast at 9 A.M. and the official British one at 12:45 P.M., were mingled of pain and grief and horror; but there was in that blend no trace of fear for our own safety, nor yet despair of the ultimate triumph of France. For even after the Germans had begun their southward sweep from Boulogne, far from giving up hope as everybody in Paris had by then, we were telling ourselves that even if Paris were to fall, Weygand would stop them on the Loire; and that, of course, would be the prelude to the great reversal, and to the routing of the invaders whom Weygand would chase as far as the Vistula at least. "Weygand will stop them on the Loire" had become the cure-all which had been "Gamelin knows what he is doing" until the day he was cashiered for incompetence. I see now that what we were, not hoping for, but *expecting*, was a miracle; not the miracle of President Roosevelt's air squadrons, for we had not much faith in that, but the miracle of a new Marne on the Loire.

In the last days of May, Madeleine our cook, as brave and loyal a person as I have ever known, and with a mind which, though wholly untrained, was quick, and sharp as a razor, came to us with tears streaming down her cheeks, and told us how Mme. So-and-so's husband, a lieutenant, had just arrived at Arcachon, having lost his regiment a fortnight earlier on the Meuse, and having staggered across France with a dozen of his men, sleepless and hungry, begging a train ride here and a lift on a lorry there. Having told his story he now lay dazed in his bed, remembering nothing, like a man who had been hit over the head. We heard how the French infantry at first had pitted their own bodies against the tanks, charging the steel walls with bayonets, but were now just fleeing, running, running, anywhere, but away from the places where the sky was black with German planes — for these stories of the great disaster were being brought to Arcachon every day by the men who had run, though the papers and the radio all but refused to admit that there had been a disaster in those days. We had to dose that abstemious French peasant woman who was Madeleine with brandy, to enable her to cook some sort of meal. The women of Pyla stood on the street corners weeping. *And we still believed that France would conquer in the end.*

I believe now that I *knew* that all was lost on the morning when Reynaud's voice, — that voice of an intelligent and high-minded raven which we had come to dread a thousand times more than the sound of the air-raid sirens of La Teste, for it never rose but to announce disaster, — when Premier Reynaud's voice announced on the wireless the surrender of Leopold of Belgium. But I did not admit that I knew it; I did not want to know it; I was fooling myself obstinately, and also I thought it was my duty to prop up the *moral* of the one or two neighbors that we saw, and of people like Madeleine. And, though this seems incredible to me now, I actually went on working, not regularly but by sprints and spasms, on the book that was to demand the Rhine as the eastern frontier of France.

And I only put this work aside, knowing that its end had come, on the day when the Germans took Evreux, and I do not remember the exact date, but it must have been three days before they took Paris. Why the fall of Evreux, which is a not very important town in Normandy, should have been the event that bowled me over I could not fully explain; it was probably because I remembered an afternoon in the spring of 1938, when I had driven with my wife from Rouen to Orléans, by way of Evreux, Dreux, and Chartres, a delicious afternoon but unexciting, of which I had guarded few images; but the spires of Evreux were among the few, and had become a symbol of all that was lost.

7

And that brings me to the "Marseillaise of Ghosts."

When I started out to compose this chapter I thought that would be a grand symbol, and a good story to tell. I am not so sure now. It is almost certain that insofar as the story may be said to carry hidden and sinister implications, there is, as the saying goes, nothing in it. We were seeing ghosts, that's all. But then, this story *is* about ghosts. And whether my interpretation of it, which I have never seriously believed, is true or not, — and I should say the odds are ten thousand against, — the symbol remains.

From the earliest weeks of the war (I am not even sure that the custom had not originated before) each broadcast of the official French "Radio-Journal" was introduced by two bars of the "Marseillaise," repeated five or six times, or as often as the studio conditions of the particular broadcast required. It was just one of those phonetic signatures that all European broadcasting stations used to have — the chimes of Bow Bells for London and so on; I do not know what they are called technically, nor whether they have the same sort of thing in America, for I have never been a radio fan. Now these two bars were broadcast as played by a carillon, and I gathered, though I am not sure about this, that it was not the actual carillon that went on the air, but a gramophone record of it. Nobody paid much attention to the thing, except when the announcer was late, which happened often, and the bars were repeated a dozen times, or fifteen; and in such cases the listeners-in swore.

I don't know exactly when this carillon was taken off, and the same two bars of the "Marseillaise," but played by clarions, substituted as a signature and stopgap. I cannot imagine why the change was made at all; it occurred, I believe, toward the end of April or early in May, but at any rate some time before the invasion of France. Now I, for one, did not like the innovation at all; I thought that the particular tone of the clarion, the brass wind instrument of the French infantry, was at once too high-pitched and too hollow for the purpose; but it was none of my business.

Of course, once more it was not the real clarions that sounded the tune, but a gramophone reproduction. And we noticed after a while that the record used was out of tune and off pitch. We thought this was due, possibly, to the use of a disk of inferior material, enforced by the war. The thing went from bad to worse, and it was not very many days before those stirring notes of the most stirring national anthem in the world began to sound ghastly. In the literal sense of the word.

For a day or two, when we first had become aware of the thing, we thought that our own radio set had developed tonsillitis or the mumps, and we called in an expert to verify it. He said the set was O.K. So we supposed something had gone wrong at the studio end, in the technical sense, not in respect of patriotism or *moral;* and we hoped they would notice the awful effect and set right whatever had caused it. But they did nothing of the sort. Those two bars of the "Marseillaise" now sounded as if they were coming from beyond the grave, hollow and weird and unspeakably discouraging. It reminded me of the strands of the same tune that are sounded off stage in the Wagram scene of Rostand's *Eaglet,* when Napoleon's son, musing on that old battlefield at dawn, hears the shrieks of the wounded who have been dead for a generation. It also reminded me of the cock's crow in the "Danse Macabre" of Saint-Saëns. So my wife and I called the thing the "Marseillaise of Ghosts," and wondered just how demoralizing it was for the crowds who listened to it a dozen times a day.

I am quite sure now that it must have been demoralizing; for it gave *us* the creeps, and I do not think there were many couples in France in the early days of June who had preserved a better *moral* than we.

When all was over, and I began to rehearse in my mind what had happened, I thought of the "Marseillaise of Ghosts," and asked myself just how far that going out of tune and off pitch of a record that had been played perhaps sixty times could have been owing to some accident or to poor material, and if it was, why the defect was not repaired or the worn record replaced at once. Even if all the disks available for recording were of the poorest quality, there must have been still a few dozen left in France. I asked that question of a friend, one of the best-informed American correspondents in Paris, here in New York the other day. I hoped to use his answer in this chapter. But he could not give me any; he said he did not know.

What we *do* know is that Dr. Goebbels has a way of thinking of everything.

8

In one of the official French broadcasts early on June 13, the day the Germans took possession of Paris, it was announced that Premier Reynaud would address the French nation that evening at 7:45. At 7:45 it was stated that he would speak at eight; at eight, that he would speak at nine; then, at 10:30, and finally at eleven. We tuned in at 11 P.M., but for a long time nothing happened; all that came through were some whispers, and the shuffling of feet in the studio, or wherever the French Government broadcast from those days.

Those hours of waiting, with their implication of some new disaster, had been pretty ghastly; they were nothing compared with the effect of the speech, when M. Reynaud actually made it. He began to speak at 11:30, and spoke for about twenty or twenty-five minutes. I do not remember in detail what he said; but it had something to do with President Roosevelt. I think it was what M. Reynaud himself called his last appeal to the head of the United States Government; and there was something about "clouds of aeroplanes" in it. I believe that this speech is now referred to as the Tours broadcast.

It was not the matter of the speech that I remember now as the most terrible experience of those terrible weeks, but its manner. Reynaud was obviously beside himself. His voice, never pleasing or confident, always carrying a note of Cassandra in it, had cracked, and he was not master of it; we expected him to burst into tears or screams at any moment. And when I say "we," I mean ten or twenty million people in France. We believed at the time that the broadcast had been postponed half a dozen times because M. Reynaud was not in a fit condition to make it, and we also believed that the studio noises we had heard before the address betokened a last desperate attempt on somebody's part to keep him from speaking. That will probably never be known for certain. What we know is that several members of the cabinet did try to dissuade M. Reynaud from making that speech that evening at Tours.

We did not sleep a wink that night. Before 7 A.M. I was tuning in on the Government wave length. The "Marseillaise of Ghosts" sounded; then the announcer's voice, "We shall now broadcast a record of M. Reynaud's address to the nation last night."

The rebroadcasting was usual. What was unusual was that the speech to which I listened during the next twenty-five minutes was not the speech that I had heard the night before. That is to say, the lines were the same, and it was M. Reynaud's voice. But it was not the same M. Reynaud's voice. It was not a cheerful or confidence-rousing or courage-stirring voice, but Reynaud's voice had never been that. It was just his normal voice of an extremely intelligent schoolmaster who had bad news to impart but who would stand for no hysterics. Compared with his voice of the night before, it sounded like chirping.

It was evident that they had made him, or he had made himself, read that address a second time; and it says much for the man's mastery of himself that he could do it, and do it with a difference.

That day I asked some of my neighbors if they had noticed that the speech had been made twice. They had, and added, A good thing too; for that first speech ought never to have been allowed on the air.

Later, on board the *Manhattan,* I put the same question to my American correspondent friends. No one had listened to M. Reynaud a second time, and no one seemed to know that the rebroadcast had not been a rebroadcast at all, but a second and different reading of the original address. Newspaper correspondents have no leisure to listen to last night's warmed-up speech on the morning after, especially if the day before happened to be the one on which the capital where they reside was captured by the enemy. And, as far as I know, the story of the two voices of M. Paul Reynaud is told here in English print for the first time.

9

Now for the Belgian invasion; the curtain raiser to the end of our cosy little wartime world at Pyla-sur-Mer.

I believe Ambassador Bullitt's strongly worded notice advising American citizens to leave France at the earliest possible moment appeared in the Paris edition of the *New York Herald Tribune* on the morning of Thursday, May 30; for I am sure that I read it on Friday about 11 A.M., just after the Arcachon bus had dropped it at the *bistro* at Moulleau. For I remember that my reaction to it was to go to the American Consulate at Bordeaux, to find out whether the Ambassador's recommendation was a recommendation or an order. It was inconvenient for me to rush to Bordeaux that day, and it would have been inconvenient for the Consul if I had rushed in next day, which was Saturday. I was not in as much of a hurry as all that. Monday would do.

Now I wanted to ascertain just how far Mr. Bullitt's advice carried sanctions such as a new invalidation of our passports (since the third of September, 1939, when the United States first took up its early wartime position under the bed, the passports of American residents in Europe had been invalidated, revalidated, and rein-validated, more times than I could remember) because I was con-fronted with a momentous dilemma. To leave France or not to leave France? Not a bit of it. To sign a new six months' lease, or not to sign a new six months' lease, of our house at Pyla. Our house was comfortable but dear. Removals were a bother, and a waste of time. There was a charming villa to be rented at Taussat, on the far shore of the lagoon, where we had friends; not quite so perfectly equipped as our *Toki-Eder* (villas in our region had a weakness for sporting unaccountable Basque names) but good enough, and much cheaper. And we *might*, after all, try Ascain or some other place in that heavenly Pyrenees country, just beyond Biarritz, which we had been longing to see.

Such were the worries that occupied our minds on the day of the Sacred Heart of Jesus, more commonly designated as Friday, May 31, when the Embassy of the United States of America had already advised American residents to scram. We had not the least intention of scramming. The Allies were evacuating Dunkirk. The Germans were trying to stop them, and were also trying at the same time to mop up Normandy and so forth. It was terrible. But if the worst came to the worst Weygand would stop them on the Loire, and then hit back, and chase them across the Meuse and as far as Berlin at the very least. I knew this because I was telling it to Madeleine our cook six times a day, to keep her going, and also at least once a day to our village policeman and the real-estate man or his wife and the barber and the district nurse at Moulleau, because I knew that they would go and tell everybody what the American monsieur who was a *savant* and a great political and military expert had said. This pastime was known as keeping up the *moral* of Pyla-sur-Mer. I also used to say that if Italy moved Turkey would certainly do something, because the Turks were like that. But I was also careful to explain on all occasions that though America loved France and wished her to win, and would send her planes and supplies to the limit, she had no army and not much of a navy, and could not declare war. On *this* point at least my conscience is clear.

On Monday, June 3, I went to see one of the Consuls in Bordeaux, who told me that there was nothing compulsory about Mr. Bullitt's notice; those who had reason to stay and wanted to stay could suit themselves. He also told me that the *Washington* was to sail sometime that week. I told him about my lease problems. He said that life was complex. I agreed.

On the way to Bordeaux I had observed an unusual number of southbound cars. They all bore Belgian number plates; but some Belgian refugees had been filtering in ere this, and I said to myself, here are some more. There were a good many Belgian cars in Bordeaux too, causing jams. They were all resplendent American makes, Packards and Buicks and Chryslers, with a sprinkling of Cadillacs. Many had trailers. All were loaded to the brim with luggage and household goods.

The Bordeaux–Arcachon road is very straight and fairly wide, and wartime traffic on it used to be negligible. Outside villages, my usual sustained speed on it was sixty-five miles an hour; I don't as a rule care for going so fast, but this particular road bored me stiff. That evening I had to drive at fifteen. For the road looked like Fifth Avenue on a rainy afternoon, minus the intersections. All the cars were southbound; all were Belgians. Social activities in Arcachon and Pyla, I said to myself, were in for a bit of jazzing up.

Within the next twenty-four hours all prices (supposed to have been fixed by Government decree long ago, and unraisable, but we were after all in France) were up twenty per cent at Arcachon and Pyla. Within the next three days there was not a hotel or boardinghouse room, and not a furnished or unfurnished dwelling below the rank of château, and not an apartment of any sort or description, available on the shores of the lagoon. Arcachon had brimmed over to Taussat, Arès, Andernos, and the rest of those pleasant little places. The conquest of the Department of the Gironde by the Belgians was complete.

Now I know that in the war of 1914–1918 there were many poor Belgian refugees; I had seen them in London, and been more than once taken for one. But in this war of 1940 the only Belgian refugees I saw were very rich refugees indeed. They would arrive in a brand-new LaSalle sedan, sometimes followed by a Chevrolet station wagon full of luggage, and stop in front of a villa that displayed a "To Let" sign, or no sign at all; and then the mother refugee would go across the street and buy up half the shop, and the father refugee would walk right into the house and say "How much?" and pay the price named, and ask no questions. They paid cash, too. Their breast pockets bulged with wallets that burst with banknotes. The Germans had been good customers, while it lasted.

I heard of cases where such a poor Belgian refugee, on being told in some Gironde village, or in the Basque country, that the house that had taken his fancy was not to let, offered to buy it on the spot, and to pay cash for it. I heard of a case where a poor Belgian refugee, on being told that the house he coveted rented at 15,000 francs, handed over 45,000 francs for three months' rent to an owner who had quoted the 15,000 for the whole season. I heard of cases where poor Belgian refugees doubled or trebled the offers that regular Parisian summer visitors had just made, and signed leases before the outbidden bidders had left the premises.

Not only did the invaders take up every vacant square inch of housing space at fantastic rates, but they also made things hopeless for people like ourselves who were actually in possession but had to renew leases, or for Parisians who had been renting the same houses for the summer season for the past ten or fifteen years. I am on safe ground if I say that the rentals quoted at Arcachon and Pyla and Andernos were, for the larger and more luxurious sort of house, three times, and for more modest accommodation five or six times, on say June 7, 1940, what they had been on June 7, 1939. For days, queues of those expensive American cars, twenty or thirty deep, were lined up in front of every single realtor's office in every village of the Department of the Gironde, the largest in

France. In the restaurants you could not get a table; in the shops where you had traded for months they had no time to serve you; for the first time since the war had begun there was a real shortage of gasoline, and you had to hand over your ration coupons for the amount bought, instead of waving them and pocketing them with a wink, as before.

The truth is that the Belgians who had come into our region were an elite. Their majority consisted of the top rank of war profiteers; and a top-rank war profiteer, being the sort of person who had known how to get in on the ground floor, was also the sort of person who knew exactly when to cut and run. The *real* poor Belgian refugees never got as far as Arcachon, for they traveled, not in Packards, but on horse carts, bicycles, and on foot; and they died on the road by the hundred under the machine-gun volleys and bombs of the German aeroplanes, and those who survived were shunted by the French authorities into crowded encampments in Maine and in Poitou. Arcachon only received the best kind, the kind that would leave its limousine parked in the center of the main street, and that, when the Arcachon policeman politely murmured something about rules, would bark at him, "Get to hell out of here, don't you see that I am a Belgian refugee?" I know, for I have witnessed scenes like that. I did not witness the fights; I was only told about them. They occurred in cafés daily when a poor Belgian refugee, waving a wad of thousand-franc bills, would run down France and proclaim that the Germans were very fine people who paid cash for everything, kept the working classes in their place, and were going to win anyway.

Within a week the Arcachonnais hated the Belgians more than they hated the Germans; which was no wonder, seeing that the Belgians were on the spot. But a good many Arcachonnais made a lot of money out of these hated Belgians; though the money they made was not going to do them much good. For within a fortnight of the Belgian invasion of the Gironde Maréchal Pétain, the hero of Verdun, and M. Laval, the little multimillionaire sub-dictator from Châteldon in Auvergne, had turned over France to the Germans whom our Belgian guests loved so much; and within another fortnight Arcachon was to receive that other, bigger and better, invasion.

10

The descent of the Belgians put us on the spot in respect of the housing situation. A week before the arrival of the swarm we might easily have secured a renewal of our lease at the figure we were paying, until the end of the year. Now the lady who owned the house calmly announced that she would not relet at all, but was going to move in herself as soon as she was rid of us; but we suspected that this was not true; our village intelligence service, usually reliable, reported that she was planning to let at a rental which she knew we would refuse even to consider. What was worse, there were now no alternatives. We spent the next ten days touring the region, knowing Arcachon and Pyla to be hopeless, but the realtors on the far shore of the lagoon only laughed at our inquiries. Half a dozen villagers enlisted in our house-hunting campaign, the busiest of these volunteer scouts being no other than my friend the policeman. But it was no use; the Belgians were too many, and had been thorough.

The *Washington* sailed on June 8. On Monday the tenth I went to Bordeaux to consult a lawyer to whom I had been directed by our friend, the manager of the bank at Arcachon through which we had been drawing our money from London. The lawyer was no ordinary man of legal business, but a prominent *avocat* or barrister who lived in a small palace and handled our trifling case out of consideration for our sponsor. We had been told that under the French wartime decrees my wife, being English and an ally, could not be evicted, just as if she had been French, if she could show that there was no other house for her to rent. This would have been easy, but the snag was my American nationality; the law securing the rights of tenants did not apply to non-ally foreigners. The attorney said he would look into the matter; would I come back on Saturday the fifteenth? I drove back to Pyla, in time to listen to Mussolini's fiery bragging about having finally sold the soul of Italy to the Devil.

On Thursday Paris fell; everybody had expected it, and the population remained calm. That is to say, there was plenty of emotion both in the village and at Arcachon; but not on account of the Germans marching down the Champs Elysées. That morning notices had been posted to the effect that all inhabitants who were not occupying their own premises and who had arrived in the region since the outbreak of the war were liable to be turned out at twenty-four hours' notice. The Government had left Paris and was rapidly drifting toward Bordeaux; the Ministry of Air had arrived and was actually housed in the leading hotel at Pyla; the villas were needed for the families of the officials. I consulted my friends at the police station; they advised me to see the mayor's secretary at La Teste. He told me not to worry; they would see to it that we were left alone; anyway our villa was small and the Government was primarily interested in large properties. Just the same I would not take chances, and started to pack our suitcases as soon as I had returned from the *mairie*, much to the annoyance of my wife, who said that I was a pessimist. Today we agree that if it had not been for that timely requisitioning order we should have been obliged to run for our lives, five days later, in the clothes we stood up in, with perhaps a couple of toothbrushes in our pockets, like so many of our friends who left their packing until it was too late. As it was, we were able to save the best part of our mobile belongings, with the exception of my beloved library.

On Saturday, June 15, I drove to Bordeaux once more to see our lawyer. He advised us to do nothing; let *Madame la propriétaire* go to court if she liked; even if she won her case it would be months before she could dispossess us, and realizing this she might prefer to strike a bargain. So far, so good. Next, I called at the Consulate, kidnaped my friend Gannett from the midst of a horde of visa seekers, and took him to lunch at the Hôtel Splendide. He is — at least to outward appearances — the most phlegmatic of men, and I could read nothing in his cherubic face as I confronted him across the table over a dry Martini. He said, "You'd better get ready to quit." I said, "What on earth do you mean?" He told me. The game was up. Capitulation might be a matter of a few days. The sooner we got across the Spanish frontier the better, especially as my wife was not even an American citizen, but British. It was Saturday, and there was not much I could do. Apart from obtaining the required documents, we had done nothing about her American visa; we had told ourselves, there is plenty of time, a visa costs ten dollars and is good only for four months; why not wait until the last minute? The last minute had passed. And all those documents were in Paris; so were the Germans. It was an emergency within the meaning of the act, all right. Gannett suggested that we should return on Monday and take steps about our Spanish and Portuguese visas too; for I had told my friend M. Mendes, the Portuguese Consul, after my interview at the Ministry of Information in February, that we had decided to stay in France for the time being; he said, Never mind, come back whenever you need the visas, they will be waiting for you.

I drove home very fast. For the first time in this particular war, I was frightened; but not much. I said to myself, and on my arrival at Pyla to my wife, that we had better take Gannett's advice and get ready for emergencies. As to quitting our house and France — why, we were in no hurry. The Spanish frontier was only 150 miles distant; an afternoon's drive.

Sunday we spent packing. About 5 P.M. I drove to the garage I used to deal with, to fill up the tank. Mme. Dupuy was very angry, because she had been doing excellent business that afternoon. "These Bordelais ought to be ashamed of themselves; this is no time for joy-riding." The boulevard that connects Arcachon with the wilderness that begins at the great sand cliff known as the Grande Dune was black with cars, like the Merritt Parkway on a Sunday. In the evening we took the back seat out of the car, and loaded her up; as we had done, nine months before, at Mougins. Twenty-six pieces of luggage. We did not believe for a moment that all this was, strictly speaking, necessary, but after all it was better to be prepared for all contingencies, and not very difficult. Two large cases, containing my six hundred books, a smaller case containing manuscripts and notes, and two wardrobe trunks were to be left behind, as well as an assortment of household effects — reading lamps, cocktail shakers, and the like. The idea was that we should go to Bordeaux in the morning and come back in the evening and then make arrangements for either storing or forwarding all those possessions in case we were compelled to leave later in the week.

We went to bed. It was the last night we were to spend under our own roof in Europe, though we did not know it. It was also the last night of the 2000-year-old Roman and Christian civilization of the continent of Europe; for France was to surrender next day to the Barbarians. But we could not know that either.

At this point I shall cede the floor to the only diary that I have ever begun that was to progress beyond the first entry. It was on the Sunday that we spent at Burgos, in Spain, exactly one week after we had gone to bed for the last time at Pyla, that I jotted down a few notes, in the form of captions that would not have meant anything to anybody, but that to me were a kind of mental shorthand or condensed picture writing. I continued the practice until we had embarked in the *Manhattan;* but I actually wrote up the diary in three sittings, a week or ten days after our landing in New York. And I include here this account of our flight across France, Spain, and Portugal not so much because of its intrinsic thrills, as to which opinions may differ, but because I believe that even a few years hence it will have become a historic document of the first importance: an album of snapshots of Europe in dissolution.

V. The Road to Lisbon

MONDAY, *June 17*. We had intended to leave early, but what with one thing and another it was 9:30 by the time we said good-by to Madeleine. We said we should be back for dinner; we meant it. First, to the bank, at Arcachon. We had between us six hundred francs, about fourteen dollars at the prevailing rate; the visas alone, we figured, would cost a thousand. M. Dupin, the manager, said that the fifty pounds for which we had cabled to London ten days ago had not arrived. M. Dupin was a peach. He said that in ordinary circumstances he would gladly let us have the money, or advance what we needed on our July credit; but nobody knew when the communications with England might be cut. It was as bad as that. Still, he cashed a check for ten pounds — 1750 francs. We knew that he did not know whether he would be able to collect. We thanked him.

We set out for Bordeaux at 10:30. The road was not abnormally crowded. The center of the town was Bedlam; I had never seen so many cars in so small a space. A policeman waved us off as we tried to enter the Rue Vital-Carles; it was closed; the Government was in session. (We did not know it, but they were discussing the surrender of French freedom.) By the time we reached the American Consulate it was 12:30. The lobby was black with people, mostly foreigners hoping against hope for visas. Gannett said he would join us at lunch at the Splendide as soon as he could make it. On the terrace of the hotel we ran into the William Henry Chamberlins; they had arrived from Tours the day before. We sat down for an *apéritif;* Percy Philip, of the *New York Times,* detached himself from the crowd, told a funny story without sitting down, and vanished. Booking a table was not easy, but a consular visiting card did the trick. We were surrounded by what used to be called *tout Paris.* For months we had been meaning to go to Paris for a visit; now Paris had come down to see us. At every table there was a cabinet minister's wife, a foreign ambassador, a movie star, or a prominent war profiteer, and party. Gannett appeared, accompanied by a young Dutchman who explained he had begged a lift on a French army truck at Orléans. Halfway through the meal a terrific storm broke. The first thunderbolt struck a tree in the Place des Quinconces, fifty yards from where we sat. It looked and sounded exactly like a bomb. Everybody went on eating.

Back to the Consulate. My wife's application had been typed out when it appeared that her medical certificate was months old. We had to get another. In a couple of hours we had it. The Consul was on the point of entering the visa when he noticed that the passport expired that very day. To the British Consulate across the square, double quick. A hundred people outside, most of them British subjects, but not English — Maltese, Cypriotes, French or Greek wives of sailors, all hoping to get away on the boat that was to leave next day. What with the heat, the fatigue, and the worry, my wife fainted on the sidewalk. A blessing in disguise: a kindly Englishwoman brought her a glass of water; she was the wife of one of the officials; she took the passport and brought it back, duly renewed, in five minutes; but for the contretemps we should have had to wait for hours.

At 7:30 my wife had her American visa. It was Gannett's last official act that day. He would not hear of our returning to Pyla. The danger was that the French might close down all road traffic; we might not be able to return to Bordeaux next day. We went to dine together at the Auberge Basque — an excellent dinner. Later, having parked my wife in Gannett's care at the Café de Bordeaux, I drove with Hans, the Dutchman, to the Ministry of Information, in search of American correspondents; we wanted to find out what was going on. The Ministry of Information was housed in the Labor Exchange, one of those Egypto-Assyrian monuments of Socialist fatuousness on which the Blum Government had spent millions, instead of buying aeroplanes and tanks. The building was pitch-dark; some soldiers at the door said if we wanted information we'd better come back in the morning. We went back to the café. At 11 P.M. Gannett and Hans went to their respective rooms. We hadn't any, and no hope to find one; just as a matter of form I tried the Splendide, the Bordeaux, and the Royal Gascogne; nothing doing. About 11:30 we settled down in the front seat of our car for an uneasy night's rest. We had parked in the vast Place des Quinconces, reputedly the largest public square in the world, with the atrocious gimcracks monument of the Girondins, the Kerensky party of the French Revolution, in the middle. Hundreds of people, mostly from Paris and the North, were spending the night in their cars around us. We dozed.

Suddenly all the lights in the square went out. (They were called "opaline" lights; with their conical caps and minimized glare they were supposed to be invisible from above.) I glanced at my wrist watch — 12:23. Now that was odd. Had it been midnight, or one o'clock, I should have attributed the dousing of the lights to municipal economy. But why 12:23? I got out and talked to a French aviation cadet who happened to pass by; he said a whole company of them, from the North, were encamped in the far end of the square; as to the lights, he thought they were supposed to go out at midnight, and a *fonctionnaire* had been unpunctual. I resumed my uncomfortable seat.

And then we heard them — the bombs. We counted eight, in quick succession; far away to the northwest, in the Gironde estuary, I reckoned. Then the sirens began to shrill, far away too, then nearer and nearer. The popping of the antiaircraft guns followed. We got out, my wife carrying Tosca and I an attaché case with our most important papers. I locked the car. Some soldiers were running toward the Allées de Tourny; we joined them. There was an elaborate dugout, a zigzag of sandbags reinforced with logs driven into the ground and forming a wall about eight feet high; but there was no roof. Absolutely futile, a British officer in a helmet, whom we found inside, commented. There were about a hundred of us, French infantrymen and aviators, four or five British officers, a few English civilians with their women, the rest French and Belgian refugees. Some wore raincoats over their pyjamas, having been rooted out of their beds. We talked; an old Russian couple, Paris shopkeepers, told about having been machine-gunned on the way down. The antiaircraft artillery was hard at work for the next hour and a half. My wife lit a cigarette, and was booed. "Put out that match!" Then the all-clear sounded. The lights came back. We returned to the car.

Tuesday, June 18. At 6 A.M. I drove the car to the big square in front of the Hôtel de Bordeaux, about a quarter-mile from where we spent the night. We found Hans standing there, with his jacket buttoned over his bare chest. He said he could not sleep, he was scared stiff; the Germans were sure to reach Bordeaux today, and would get him. He did not like the idea of a concentration camp. A French captain of colonial infantry was reading a paper. I asked him what the news was. He said there had been no news in this whole God-damned war. "But we have heard some very beautiful speeches," he added. "Daladier, Reynaud, now Pétain. And your Mr. Roosevelt, too. Very fine speeches." He said he wanted a cup of coffee and was off.

At seven we had breakfast in the hotel lobby, afterwards a bath. At nine we met Publio, Gannett's Spanish valet. He had obtained for us numbers in the line waiting at the Spanish Consulate — 75 and 76. We waited. Half an hour convinced us that at this rate our turn would come in about forty-eight hours. We went to the American Consulate and secured letters to the Spanish and Portuguese Consuls. Returning to the Spanish Consulate, I was admitted at once. The Consul was polite but firm. "It is absolutely impossible for me to give you a visa unless you have your Portuguese visa first. Go get it, and I'll give orders that you should be admitted immediately." I thanked him; I thought that was easy enough. I did not reckon with topography. The line at the Spanish Consulate formed in the street; I could present my letter by walking up to the policeman at the door. The line at the Portuguese Consulate formed up a narrow staircase. The office was on the third floor. The only way to present my letter of introduction would have been to mow down the occupants of the staircase with a machine gun. I had no machine gun. I got into the line and waited.

But not for long. The thing was hopeless. There was no admission by numbers; the two or three policemen present limited themselves to umpiring occasional fisticuffs. Publio went to telephone the Consul. He came back to report that the Portuguese officials had taken off the receiver and were not answering calls. That was that.

At one o'clock we met Gannett and the Chamberlins at the Splendide. A table had been reserved, proof of the immense prestige of the United States Foreign Service. Chamberlin said the situation reminded him of the early days of the Russian Revolution — the overcrowding, the uncertainty, the fast-progressing disintegration of all routine. We had cocktails and ordered food. Ed Taylor turned up with his Swiss wife. We sat, eight at a table for four, more or less on one another's laps. Hans reported that a fellow Dutchman knew a Portuguese who would induce another Portuguese to come out of the beleaguered Consulate, take our passports, and return them visaed. This seemed the only possible solution. At 2:30 the headwaiter said he was very sorry but there was no lunch left. "Just like Russia," said Chamberlin. I spoke to the proprietor. In another fifteen minutes there arrived the thickest and juiciest French equivalent of an American planked steak for eight that I had ever seen. It was perfect. Unfortunately Hans and I were to meet our Dutch benefactor at the American Consulate at three. We wolfed our steak and ran for it. The Dutch interventionist proved a washout. We first had to drive across town to some sort of convalescent home in a garden. Negotiations with Portuguese No. 1 went on for half an hour. Then we drove to the Portuguese Consulate. Portuguese No. 2 did not come out. We waited in line for a couple of hours. I stood on the staircase in front of a window between stories. The window opened. Behind it stood the Portuguese Consul. "But my dear Mr. Bagger, what a delicious surprise! I shall see you in three minutes." The window closed. The pushing and elbowing on the staircase grew more and more desperate. At seven o'clock I gave it up.

Gannett was more emphatic than ever that we must not go back to Pyla. Nobody knew just where the Germans were; we might be machine-gunned on the road, or stopped by motorcycle scouts. Bordeaux was not exactly safe, but still. We hated the idea of another night in the car. Somebody had told us about the American Red Cross shelter in the Rue Gobineau. My wife went upstairs and booked two cots. But they would not have dogs. Gannett agreed with me that leaving Tosca locked up in the car, what with the prospect of another air raid, was not to be thought of. I said I would park at the entrance of the Red Cross shelter, and stay with Tosca in the car; if there was a raid my wife would join us and we'd all be together. Gannett proposed that we should go and sleep in his room; he would take one of the cots. This we could not accept. In the end we compromised: my wife, Tosca, and I would share Gannett's bed and he would sleep on a mattress on the floor.

We had a drink in a café with Mrs. Taylor, who said one of her two Scottish terriers had been lost; this was not their first trouble — their car had been stolen a couple of nights ago, with most of their baggage. Ed was working. We were to meet for dinner at the Auberge Basque. But the Taylors never turned up. At 9:30 I went up to the Agence Radio, the improvised news-service bureau where all the American correspondents did their work. I was told by Handler of the United Press that the Taylors had left Bordeaux. How, he could not say. I went to get our car from in front of the American Consulate, and drove it up to Gannett's hotel in a thunder-storm. The crowds, the rain, the lightning, the hundreds of cars moving without lights in the darkened streets, the groups of helmeted soldiers, merged into a Dantesque fantasy. We spent a quiet night in Gannett's room; he did not after all sleep on the floor but shared a room with Publio, whose roommate had left.

2

Wednesday, June 19. At 9 A.M. there was a mob of four hundred in front of the Portuguese Consulate. Half a dozen soldiers, with steel helmets and fixed bayonets, struggled to maintain a kind of order. I waited in line till eleven o'clock. No use. I returned to the American Consulate, hoping for I did not know what miracle to happen; short of a miracle we should not get our Portuguese visa within a week. I was standing in the Consulate lobby when in came an English friend, Enid W., very smart in her American ambulance driver's uniform, but, for once in a lifetime, flustered and out of breath. "We were bombed at Angoulême last night, and machine-gunned on the road. A boat leaves Le Verdon for England at noon. Tell Esther she must come along, with five days' provisions. She must not stay here, the Germans will be here tomorrow. Hurry." She wanted some one of the Consulate to take over her automobile, but they could not do it. I was in a terrible dilemma. If there was immediate danger of German occupation my wife had better sail in the British boat; but I hated the idea of letting her go at five minutes' notice. The dilemma was resolved for me by the clock. It was already too late. Downstairs I met Huot; he said another English boat was to leave that afternoon at five. We ran to the Splendide to see the man in charge of bookings, and were told he had gone over to the British Consulate. We went to the Consulate; the man was not there. There was only one thing to do: go back to the Splendide and have a drink.

We sat down on the terrace. Our *Amer Picon* did not arrive. I stepped into the café to find the waiter. There, at a table, sat the Portuguese Consul, having an *apéritif* with a friend. He hailed me. "But my dear Mr. Bagger, I am desolate about yesterday — the heat — the crowds — overwork — " "Why not give me a visa here and now?" "But certainly, my dear friend, but certainly." He whipped out a fountain pen, scribbled something in our passports. "Here you are. All you have to do now is to go back to the Consulate and have them stamped." I said nothing. There was nothing to say.

It was then that the miracle happened. A distinguished-looking man approached, in his hand half a dozen passports. "My dear M. Skalski, with the greatest pleasure," said the Consul. "M.

Skalski — Mr. Bagger." He signed the passports. M. Skalski said, "You want your passports stamped? Come along." I went. M. Skalski explained. He was the Polish Consul at Arcachon. He had been honorary Portuguese Consul in Poland. He had his credentials with him. At the Consulate the luncheon recess had thinned the crowd somewhat. M. Skalski cut through it as a knife cuts through butter. The steel-helmeted corporal, overawed by M. Skalski's diplomatic passport, saluted and let him pass. Five minutes later M. Skalski handed me our two passports, duly stamped. On the way back to the Splendide everything was arranged. We were to meet at Arcachon, in front of M. Skalski's house, at five o'clock. We were to travel together in convoy. M. Skalski would secure our Spanish visas at Bayonne. I had just seen him at work. Our troubles were over.

It was almost three o'clock. No time for lunch. We drove back to Pyla, at seventy miles an hour. We passed a number of huge trucks belonging to the French air force; headed south, they were parked at the roadside, their crews smoking cigarettes; they did not seem to be in a hurry. At Arcachon we said good-by to M. Dupin and to his teller, M. Martin. We all had tears in our eyes. They were good men and good Frenchmen. We rushed out to Pyla. I stopped at the police station, to shake hands with my friends the *commissaire* and the *agent*. They agreed that the only thing for us was to leave. The *commissaire* said most of the remaining French aeroplanes were leaving for Africa. "When you get back to the States, work for us!" At the house we asked Madeleine to give us something to eat. We had bought some *croissants;* there was nothing in the refrigerator but a tin of *confit de canard,* duck cooked and preserved in its own fat, an expensive delicacy; we had been saving it for a special occasion. Here was the special occasion. We ate a little cold duck and drank a glass of wine. Then I told Madeleine to burn, at once, the small caseful of manuscript. Six years' work. My heart ached, but those papers were dangerous; I could not risk their falling into the hands of the Germans while we were still in France. We also gave her instructions about turning the house over to the proprietress, and about some small bills we owed. She promised to take good care of my library, which was packed for shipment, but was too bulky to be taken in the car; and of our two wardrobe trunks. Esther kissed her. She was a fine person, the best type of intelligent, hard-working French countrywoman; we told her we hoped to see her again, and meant it. Off we went.

At five we pulled up in front of M. Skalski's elegant villa in one of the fashionable streets of Arcachon, on top of the hill behind Notre-Dame. M. Skalski's chauffeur was rigging up hammocks in a huge Packard limousine. "For the babies." There were also a LaSalle sedan with a small black trailer looking like a coffin, an elderly medium-sized Renault, and a small brand-new Renault. The latter was to be driven by a tall and bulky Polish blonde who hadn't had much motoring experience; she was now driving around the block, to get her hand in. In the house several Polish families, members of the convoy, were having a meal. That reminded me that we had no food in our car. I said to M. Skalski I had better drive downtown, a matter of five minutes, to buy provisions. "Don't do that, my dear boy. We shall leave in ten minutes, and we must stick together. Come in and have some sandwiches and fruit and wine." The hammocks were now rigged up in the Packard; the babies had been fed and were being stowed away for the journey. The chauffeur was building a kind of skyscraper out of suitcases on the top of the Packard. When he had finished he took them down again and rearranged them on the luggage grid. At seven o'clock the Polish families went back into the house and had some sandwiches and tea. I slipped downtown and bought two dozen bananas, some crackers, and three bottles of mineral water. I could not get any chocolate. At eight o'clock the Polish families went into the house and had some sandwiches and coffee. Then the baggage was rebuilt once more. At a quarter to nine we were off, only three hours and forty-five minutes behind schedule. The convoy was led by M. Skalski's chauffeur in the old Renault; he knew the short cut to the Biarritz road across the Landes. Mme. Skalski drove the Packard; our Ford came next, followed by the LaSalle, which belonged to M. Ostrowski, the famous Polish sculptor; it was driven by a military-looking

Polish chauffeur who could not speak a word of French. The baby Renault with the inexperienced blonde at the wheel brought up the rear.

Very soon we left the road and were driving along a narrow lane. We stopped at a cottage. M. Skalski's chauffeur got out and collected two gallon tins of gasoline. Then somebody recalled a forgotten waterproof and made a detour to pick it up. Then the Packard had carburetor trouble. In half an hour we had done five miles. Our car was stopping in front of a cottage. I spoke to some French people in the garden; they said they had just heard that the Germans were a few miles north of Bordeaux. The Polish cars caught up with us. I said to M. Skalski, "For heaven's sake let's get a move on, the Germans are at Bordeaux." I drove off. Five miles further I stopped. There were no Polish cars in sight. The chauffeur arrived in the battered Renault. "Where are the others?" "Oh, they are holding a council of war. They want to go back." "What the hell do you mean?" "They say it's no use, the Germans are at Bordeaux, they'll get us anyway."

At this moment a small black Citroën pulled up smartly. A lady in black stepped out, with a "Good evening" in English. It was Mme. L., our Franco-Polish landlady. Our feud was forgotten. She was an extremely capable person, just the sort to have around in an emergency. From this moment on we were friends and allies. I explained the situation. She drove back to fetch the convoy. In a few minutes she returned and said it was all right. They were coming on; if they lost us we all were to meet at the Hôtel Moderne at St. Jean-de-Luz, at 2 A.M.

By this time it was dark. We had come less than fifteen miles in seventy-five minutes. This would never do. We waited for the headlights of the Polish cars to appear over the rise of the road, then made off, with Mme. L. in the lead; she knew the road and I did not. She was an excellent driver. She had her daughter and an English friend, Miss S., with her. We drove at about 45 miles an hour, along a good but very narrow road. There was no traffic. It was a lovely night, with the full moon high above the pine-woods; the breeze wafted the smell of freshly mown grass into our faces. We drove through some sleeping hamlets. It was all very peaceful. Yet we were fleeing for our life before the Barbarian hordes.

Some twenty miles farther on we took a sharp bend to the left. Another five miles, and we waited. There was no sound of engines behind; no gleam of headlights. What happened to the convoy? Mme. L. drove back. She returned to report that the others must have missed the bend and gone straight on. We could only hope that they would reach St. Jean somehow.

So far we had hardly met a car. At Labouheyre, just before we hit the main Biarritz road, we ran into a jam. Some two hundred cars were thronging the main square, all southbound, refugee cars with mattresses and perambulators and bicycles tied to the roofs and the bumpers. Steel-helmeted soldiers with fixed bayonets. Officers, with electric torches, demanding papers. French officers, thank God! One glanced at our passports and waved us on. We lost Mme. L. She must have driven on ahead. We arrived at a roadhouse. A dozen cars were parked in front. We bought six gallons of gasoline and had some ham sandwiches and wine. We also ordered some coffee but it never came. I wandered into the bar. A young Frenchman inquired if I knew the latest news. I said the Germans had been reported that morning to have crossed the Loire at Nevers. I had also heard that they were at Angoulême; there were rumors that they had reached Bordeaux. "Bunk," said the Frenchman. "They never crossed the Loire. *I* crossed the Loire at Nevers. Half an hour later the bridge was blown up." I hoped he was right.

We drove on. This was the main Biarritz road, wide and straight but undulating like a Siberian railway at a fair, with a small ridge to cross every five or six miles. It was full of southbound cars driving close behind one another, but there was no up traffic, so it was easy to overtake. We drove with dipped headlights. Two or three times we were stopped by soldiers who cursed us. "Douse your lights, you fools, the Italians are overhead." However, we heard no planes, and preferred the remote risk of being bombed to the certainty of driving into the ditch. St. Jean-de-Luz was ninety miles to the south. In half an hour we had left most of the traffic behind. It began to rain. About fifteen miles north of St. Jean I spotted a Citroën parked under some trees. It was Mme. L.'s car; she was asleep over the wheel. We gave her some brandy and bananas. She told us we had overtaken her soon after the jam at Labouheyre; she must have passed us while we were having sandwiches at the roadhouse.

At Bayonne gendarmes asked for our papers; they were very polite, as in normal times. We reached St. Jean in a downpour. It was exactly 2 A.M. when we stopped in front of the Hôtel Moderne; the agreed place at the agreed time. There were no Polish cars in sight. A sleepy porter said there were no rooms. Miss S. knew the proprietors of the Hôtel de la Poste. They had no rooms either, but they let us sleep in armchairs in the dining room.

Thursday, June 20. At 8:30, after a bath and an excellent breakfast of coffee and fresh rolls, I sallied forth to look for our Polish friends. At the Hôtel Moderne they had never heard of them. I returned to the hotel and smoked a pipe. About ten, I went out again. There, in front of a small café, stood the unmistakable La-Salle with the trailer, and the baby Renault. I entered the café. The whole party were having breakfast; Mme. Skalski was feeding the babies. It appeared that after having missed the sharp left-hand turning the Packard broke down. The chauffeur had returned to Arcachon; the LaSalle had gone too far ahead. The limousine had to be abandoned. I never quite understood how the babies had been transported to St. Jean; something was said about the baby Renault's having maintained an all-night shuttle service, driven alternately by Mme. Skalski and the now expert blonde. "And you? Have you only just arrived?" "Oh no, we got here last night." "Ah, how marvelous! What efficiency! Ah, these Americans!"

We had to drive back to Bayonne to get our Spanish visas. The Consulate was surrounded by a mob of six hundred. Even M. Skalski's diplomatic passport was no help. We were talking things over on the corner when the deluge came. In two minutes we were drenched to the skin. I had never seen such a thunderstorm in

Europe. The rain came down in blinding black masses, like a waterspout. A continuous barrage of forked lightning interlaced with the flying buttresses of the Cathedral in a kind of infernal counterpoint. In the midst of it all our old friend M. Mendes, the Portuguese Consul from Bordeaux, rushed out of the Portuguese Consulate, pursued by a mob waving passports. He held his head between his hands and screamed, "Go away! No more visas!" He jumped into a car. The car reversed into the writhing mass of visa seekers and shot down the hill, pursued by curses, the hiss of rain, and the roll of thunder.

M. Skalski said we must go to Hendaye for our Spanish visas. In the low-lying streets of Bayonne we drove through a flood; the water came above the hubcaps. At St. Jean-de-Luz we lunched at the Hôtel de Paris with M. Ostrowski, his daughter, and his granddaughter. M. Skalski lunched at the Moderne. I was watching the LaSalle like a lynx; M. Skalski had ridden in it that morning and I assumed that he would continue using it. At four o'clock I glimpsed M. Ostrowski. "Where is M. Skalski?" "He drove to Hendaye in a taxi an hour ago. His family is still here, he is coming back." My wife and I jumped into the Ford and drove off in pursuit. There was a traffic jam on the bridge. A lieutenant of *gendarmerie* asked for our papers. "You have no military permit. You can't go to Hendaye." "But we were told that Americans and British people need no permit." "Sorry, a new order came half an hour ago. You must go back to the prefecture at Bayonne."

We were stalemated. We drove back to the Moderne. Mme. L. had just returned from Bayonne; she said that a thousand people were fighting in front of the prefecture; they all wanted permits. It was hopeless. I left my wife at the Moderne and hired a horse cab; I was determined that we should sleep in a bed that night. We called at nine hotels; there were no rooms. We stopped at a tenth, an attractive one that we had already passed up as sure to be full. "Of course you have no rooms." "On the contrary, we have a very nice room with private bath. One hundred francs." I paid the hundred francs and said we'd be back later. Outside I met Bill Bird, of the *New York Sun;* I had been hunting him at Bordeaux and had not found him. He too was looking for a room. My cabby was very proud of himself; had he not found the last room with private bath to be had at St. Jean? I tipped him twenty francs. In front of the Moderne my wife and M. Ostrowski, seated on a bench, were engaged in deep conversation. It appeared M. Ostrowski had been a lifelong friend of Joseph Conrad. My wife and he had been talking Conrad for the last hour and a half, forgetting about wars and visas and special military permits. M. Ostrowski was a very charming man; he was probably the only member of the party to remain unruffled during those hectic days. I sat down and discussed Aristotle with M. Ostrowski. We had just got to Saint Thomas Aquinas when out of a side street emerged William Henry Chamberlin and his wife; a porter followed, carrying suitcases. They had just arrived from Bordeaux by train; they were finding refugee existence increasingly difficult, on account of not having a car. It was now seven o'clock. M. Skalski arrived on a truck which he had just bought. "We start for Hendaye in ten minutes. Come along. Mr. and Mrs. Chamberlin may ride on the truck if they want to." "How about the military permit?" "You come along. I'll see you through." I was not so sure. It also occurred to me that the French closed all road traffic after dark. If there was a hitch we must sleep in the car. We said good-by to M. Skalski. Off he went in his truck, followed by a Renaultful of babies in hammocks.

We dined at the Bar Basque, with the Chamberlins. Bill and Sally Bird were there too. So was the whole American colony of the Left Bank. I had meant to take my wife to the Café Flore, in St. Germain-des-Prés. Now the Café Flore had come down to St. Jean-de-Luz. It was our last dinner in France; it tasted good. The Birds told us about the big air raid on Bordeaux, eight hours after we had left. Two hundred people had been killed. Mrs. Chamberlin, a lifelong teetotaler, tried a glass of champagne and did not like it. By a miracle both the Birds and the Chamberlins had found rooms. At 9:30 the restaurant closed, under police regulations. Those of us who had beds went to bed.

3

Friday, June 21. At 7 A.M. I drove to the police commissariat and asked to see the chief. "He is not here." "Where is he?" "Out there on the bridge, directing traffic." There he was, a young man with a mustache like Hitler's, in a gray suit, wearing a beret. "I am an American writer. I have been working for France. Here are my credentials." "What do you want?" "I want to go to the frontier. I *don't* want to go back to Bayonne, to fight for a permit." "You don't have to. All Americans and British may pass. A new order came last night." I hurried back to the hotel, collected Esther and Tosca, and drove off without pausing for breakfast. I was taking no chances; the military authorities might change their minds once more.

Ten lovely winding miles among the green foothills of the Pyrenees. There was no traffic; all cars carrying other than American or British subjects and diplomats were turned back. There was peace among the hills; the only sign of anything amiss was a log barricade athwart the road every three miles or so, leaving just room enough for a single car to zigzag across. We reached Hendaye at nine, and were directed by a policeman to the Spanish Consulate at the far end of the town.

At the Consulate sixty or seventy people were waiting, Czechs, Poles, Belgians, a handful of English, five or six Americans. A smartly dressed American woman was distributing bits of numbered cardboard. "I am doing this on my own; unless we have some sort of order we'll stay here a week." People thought she was an official and lined up meekly. At ten o'clock a clerk came out and distributed authentic numbers. I happened to stand near the door and was given No. 43, to which I was not at all entitled in the order of my arrival. I did not protest. Somebody said the Consulate had not yet started work. The door opened and out came M. Mendes, the Portuguese Consul from Bordeaux. Immediately he was surrounded by howling applicants waving passports. He ran to his car, holding his head between his hands, and was whisked off. My wife and I were talking to a jolly-looking tall Englishman in a tweed jacket. He told us that he had blown up the ammunition works which he had been managing for the French somewhere near Tours; then he helped the French sappers to blow up bridges across the Loire. He was very casual about it. He was going to Portugal where he had a sister living. The waiting was not too bad, there was shade and the people were orderly enough; but we had had no breakfast, and every ten minutes or so somebody came up with a diplomatic passport of some sort and was admitted out of turn, amidst booing. At twelve o'clock my wife and I went in with a batch of ten; they then locked the doors. We had to wait another hour, sitting in the lobby in cane chairs. The English-man who had been blowing up bridges settled down to a com-fortable snooze. There was a Brazilian couple who had come down from Paris on a tandem bicycle; they had lost all their luggage. A Polish manufacturer, whom I had known by sight at Arcachon, was holding forth in loud tones; he knew everything better than anybody else and did not make a secret of it. A charming gentle-manly tall Chinese was explaining the intricacies of currency regu-lations to my wife. A Belgian boy of eighteen was sobbing softly; he thought, for some reason or other, that his parents were in Spain; he was afraid that if the Germans caught him he would be made to fight against the Allies.

At one o'clock we were admitted into the inner office. An hour later we came out; but out of the ten of us only five had been granted visas. The Belgian boy was turned down because he was Belgian and of military age. The omniscient Pole was turned down because his passport, which he claimed was a diplomatic one, lacked some stamp or other. At first he blustered; then he wept; in the end he was thrown out, almost, if not quite, literally. The Chinese took it differently. The consular official (he had a thin dark cruel face like one of the valets in an El Greco painting) said to him, "The Chinese Government has not recognized General Franco. As far as Spain is concerned China does not exist. We do not grant visas to the nationals of a nonexistent country." The

Chinese said, "A boat sails from Bilbao for Shanghai in a few days. All I want is to sail in it." The official said, "China does not exist." The Chinese pulled himself up to his full five feet ten and said gently, "There are three thousand Spaniards in Shanghai today, making money. Ask them whether China exists or not. Also, when *you* had your troubles, England and France opened their gates wide to your refugees. Of both sides. Good morning." He walked out, head erect. He had won the round. It was difficult not to applaud.

Two-fifteen. We drove back to the frontier end of the town in quest of lunch. We tried one restaurant after the other; we drove back into the center; we were turned off at eleven different places ("We haven't got as much as a roll") until I glimpsed the Grand Hotel, the best in town. No, there was no lunch left; but the *patronne* could give us a little ham and bread. Before the ham (and cheese and delicious apple jelly) arrived I drank a whole bottle of sweet dark red wine, dipping bread into it. Who says that wine isn't food?

When we left the hotel I had to drive up onto the sidewalk, to avoid a big car parked in the middle of the street. It was full of people. I shouted, "*Imbécile!*" The driver leaned out and grinned. It was M. Mendes, our old friend the Portuguese Consul at Bordeaux. It was the last we saw of him.

It was past 4 P.M. when we joined the mile-long line of cars that stretched from the railroad station down the hill to the international bridge across the Bidassoa. There were two files, one for ordinary mortals like ourselves, on the right; another in the middle, for cars with the magic plate C.D. (*corps diplomatique*). A third lane, on the left, was kept open for northbound traffic coming from Spain. I had an altercation with one of the French soldiers who had let a Belgian car pass ahead of ours. The driver claimed he was an official. A little later the soldier came back and apologized: he had not slept for forty-eight hours; he was worrying himself sick over his family, and over the fate of France. We had a long talk; another steel-helmeted soldier joined in. They leaned

against the door of the car; they told us about their families — one
was a Bordelais, the other a Morvandiau from near Avallon; we
talked about their bits of country which we knew so well. We
talked about France, and how we had been cheated and deceived,
and how we hoped that France would rise again and be free and
great as of old. One of the soldiers leaned into the car and put his
arm around my shoulder, and we wept over France as brothers
weep at the bier of their mother.

From time to time the line of cars moved on a little. The cars
on our left, those with the C.D. plates, moved much faster. Some
of them were Dutch, a few Belgians, the majority were Polish. I
had never imagined there could be so many diplomats on so small
a planet. A huge Dutch lorry, carrying diplomatic baggage, skidded
into a ditch and lay down on its side, blocking not only the diplomatic lane but also that of the up traffic. The baggage had to be
removed piece by piece; this caused much merriment among the
spectators, and more cursing among those who did the removing.

By a quarter to seven we had moved down the mile. Our car
was now the second behind the barrier separating France from the
no man's land on the Bidassoa bridge. In front of us was a Chevrolet
with a Belgian number plate but flying the Stars and Stripes from
its radiator. It belonged to Mr. M. C. Troper, chairman of the
American Jewish Relief Organization, and contained beside him
three members of his staff and as much of his papers and equipment as they could salvage. We made friends; we hoped to get
across and sleep at Irún that night. At seven o'clock sharp the
French gendarmes announced that the Spaniards had just closed
the frontier, and were not to open it until nine in the morning.

Most of the refugees, including the Troper crew and ourselves,
took the announcement apathetically enough, but there were two
rebels. One was a stalwart American lady in a leather jerkin and
an aviator's helmet. She attacked the gendarme in charge in a fluent
and vigorous French, explaining that she simply *had* to reach Bilbao
to stop a cargo of American relief supplies which otherwise might
go to Bordeaux and be seized by the Germans. Her onslaught

swept the officials off their feet and she was the last person to drive
a car across that day. I met her later on board the *Manhattan;* she
was Miss Therese Bonney, the photographer.

The other protestant was less successful. He was a tall elderly
man with a stoop and a Mongolian cast of countenance, looking
yellow and ill; he was extremely well dressed in a dark blue over-
coat and suit and a gray Homburg that bespoke St. James's Street.
He was talking in rapid French and I could not hear what he said,
but something about him struck a chord and I stepped nearer to
have a look. Sure enough it was Titulesco, ex-Rumanian Foreign
Minister, ex-ambassador, ex-President of the League of Nations;
and he admitted it. In fact, he proclaimed it in an indignant treble;
it was an unheard-of outrage that he should be held up like this.
"You don't seem to realize that I am Titulesco." An officer of
gendarmerie was called, then another still higher up; they decided
that *M. le Président* might walk across the bridge into Spain.

Half an hour later *M. le Président* came back, more incensed than
ever; those Spaniards, he cried, shaking with anger, had taken away
his passport and then told him to walk back. "They did not realize
that I am Titulesco," he added. A gendarme behind me murmured, "Or maybe they realized that he is Titulesco." The ex-
President of the League of Nations was not a popular personage in
Franquist Spain.

We decided it was inadvisable to leave our cars overnight; it
was also useless, as finding rooms or even a meal was out of the
question. So the two girls of the Relief staff and I walked up into
town on a foraging expedition. All we could rake up was two
small tins of *pâté* and three bottles of Evian water. The Tropers,
however, had reserves. They generously gave us some tomato
juice, cheese, and bread; Mr. Troper had a bottle of Scotch, I had
a flask of brandy; we did not fare so badly. The mists descended
on the hills of Spain; from the head of the bridge we could see the
lights of Irún and, farther toward the sea, Fuenterrabia. What a
picnic, this mile-long double column of stationary refugee cars,
for German dive bombers and machine-gunning sadists! What a
harvest for a column of motorcycle troops sweeping down the

bridge! They did not come; our last night on the soil of France was peaceful.

The Relief people curled up in their Chevrolet and went to sleep. My wife tried to do the same, with Tosca on her lap. All along the sidewalks, with their heads propped against suitcases or the wall, refugees were snoring. I stayed up late, talking to two customs guards; we smoked our pipes and cursed the swine who had betrayed France. After midnight a column of large black Renaults glided down the bridge along the third, or northbound, lane; they made very little noise and had all their lights out; the gendarmes opened the barrier and they drove across into Spain. I did not need to be told who they were; I had seen those Renault limousines in front of the Splendide at Bordeaux only a few nights back. They were Government cars. One of the customs guards spat. "I'll bet those cars are lined with gold." About 2 A.M. I sat down behind the steering wheel and pretended to rest.

4

Saturday, June 22. I must have dozed, for glancing at my watch I found it was five o'clock. By 7:15, having stood in line nearly two hours, I had our two passports stamped. There were still the customs to clear; the French examined the cars carefully, looking for currency and gold. I went into the customs office and showed my papers; the only favor I asked for was to have my car searched at once, so as to be able to cross over at the word Go. The official said, "When you get back to the United States you will work for us. We aren't going to search your car." We shook hands. My wife and I were entitled to take 10,000 francs out of France. We only had 4200 francs between us.

The frontier opened at 8:45. Two minutes later our car was parked on Spanish soil, behind Troper's Chevrolet. We had hoped for breakfast; we were disappointed. The next three hours we were kept busy. Contrasted with the congenital muddle and the fast-increasing official disintegration, tempered by occasional friendliness, on the French side, the cold-blooded efficiency of the Spaniards, with its Prussian flavor, was almost frightening. We had to have our passports stamped; we had to see three different officials about our car, two more about currency, one about baggage, and when all this was done we had to go to the Military Command and get a permit to enter Spain! Eight separate moves, in all. There was waiting, but there was no confusion. Each motorist was given a young soldier for an escort; mine was a friendly fellow, and extremely courteous. He took me from one cubbyhole to the next, apologizing profusely when we had to wait, but never releasing his firm grip on our passports and other papers. I witnessed one incident. A Belgian woman, just ahead of me in the passport queue, was told she had to go back to France; her Portuguese visa was not properly stamped. Her husband, whose papers were in order, said the Portuguese official at Bayonne must have made a mistake. The Spaniard was adamant; the woman had to go back. "But I can't go back! They won't let me enter!" she cried. "I'll have to stay on the bridge!" The official shrugged. The woman threw herself on the ground, screamed and kicked; her husband and two soldiers carried her into a room; a doctor was called. The American girl next to me wept; we never knew how the affair ended.

We had one pleasant surprise — nobody bothered about our baggage. At the Military Command our passports were marked with an itinerary: Burgos–Valladolid–Salamanca–Portuguese frontier; we had to stick to it or face arrest. We had every intention of sticking to it. At twelve o'clock we were free to proceed. The Tropers waited for us; we set off together. In half an hour we reached San Sebastián and were directed to the Andia restaurant, a luxurious establishment on the fifth floor with a grand view of the harbor. We had a magnificent lunch, the first square meal since St. Jean two days ago. Having heard a good deal about food shortage in Spain, the quality and variety of the food, and even more the enormous portions, astonished us; but the prices were three to four times those charged in France.

I proposed that we should spend the afternoon and night in San Sebastián, but was overruled by the Tropers, who were in a hurry; we decided to go at least as far as Burgos. We tried to get some maps and road information at the Automobile Club, but the office was closed until 4 P.M. This was Spain. We waived the maps. My wife had stayed in the car; she reported she had had a conversation with some Basque workmen who spoke French and were pro-Ally; they warned her that most Spaniards were rabidly anti-English. We left a little before four. Half an hour later I decided I could not go on; I could hardly keep my eyes open. I overtook and stopped the Tropers and arranged a rendez-vous in Burgos. They drove off. We were never to see them again.

I tried to rest over the wheel, but there were too many flies. We went on. The road spiraled skyward; magnificent vistas opened on all sides, tier behind tier of forest-clad mountain, reminding us of the Cévennes above St. André-de-Valborgne; but driving was a terrific strain and all I could do was to keep the car from going over the precipice. I don't know how I managed to reach Alsasua, a little town in Navarra, down in the valley on the far side. We stopped at an inn and had some coffee. I rented a room and lay down in my clothes on an extremely hard but very clean bed. I slept, it seemed for an eternity. I was awakened by the roar of cannon. So the Germans were shelling Arcachon! I rushed to the window. There was a flash of lightning, and another roll of thunder; down below, in the sleepy little square, a company of Spanish infantry stood at ease. At that moment the rain came down. There was a tremendous shout of *"Arriba España!"* as the soldiers scattered for shelter into the surrounding houses. I glanced at my watch; I had been asleep for thirty minutes.

But now I felt completely rested. We drove on in the downpour. Soon the skies cleared. We were now in the province of Álava; the mountains of Guipúzcoa were behind us; others rose on our right in an indigo mist, far up in the north; the road was very bad, narrow, excessively cambered, and full of potholes, but straight enough. Or so I thought. We were going at fifty when, emerging from a slight curve, we found ourselves in a wholly unannounced S-bend that dipped under a railroad trestle on our right. The surface was smooth, for a change; it was also wet, and banked the wrong way. Braking was out of the question; at our speed a disaster seemed inevitable. The car skidded across to the left; I swerved her away from a wall with an inch to spare; she skidded back onto the right and shot through the opening under the bridge. Right ahead there was a black heap in the road. I stopped the car about six inches behind it.

"By God, you were lucky! I expected you to crash into us," said a voice in French. A man stood beside what had been left of the Peugeot; his face was covered with blood. "Ten minutes ago we had done what you did just now; only we did not stop as you did." The car had crashed into a poplar; it was now a mass of twisted scrap iron; the road was littered with suitcases. Miraculously, the driver only had his face cut, and his wife and child were unhurt. We gave him some brandy, and disinfectant to bathe his cuts with; he asked us to send help from Vitoria, only a few miles ahead. At that moment a big Buick issued from the bend, with the leisurely wisdom of local knowledge; the two Spaniards in it took charge of the situation. On we went.

About seven o'clock we crossed the border of Old Castile; the country was just as I had always imagined it: rocky gorges lined with crags tufted by a solitary pine, rather like the Esterel; then beautifully molded hills, light green or tawny yellow like the backs of reposing lions. The villages seemed incredibly poor. We reached Burgos at nine. We passed the Hotel Condestable which we had heard was the best; it looked pretentious; we inquired for the Maria Isabel, also recommended, found it, booked a comfortable enough room, and sat down to a tasty and copious dinner. After the meal I talked to the proprietor, a handsome dark Basque from Guipúzcoa who spoke French well. He told us that the Condestable was German-owned and full of Germans, many of them officers; we were glad to have given it a miss. Here the atmosphere was entirely friendly; the concierge was a Frenchman from Bordeaux, though he had lived in Spain for forty years. I asked him to call up all the hotels and inquire about the Tropers. Nobody had heard of them; they must have gone through.

At Irún we had only been allowed to change one thousand French francs — five hundred per person. What with the terrific price of gasoline and the two long cables I had sent from San Sebastián we had only one hundred pesetas left, not enough to pay our bill, let alone to keep us in gasoline as far as Salamanca. The proprietor said he could not change any money; it was strictly forbidden. The Banca de España, the only one authorized to change, was closed until Monday. This meant not only the loss of a whole day but also an additional hundred pesetas for the room and food, money which we could ill spare. In different circumstances a Sunday in Burgos would have delighted us; as it was, we cursed our luck. It would have been better to stay in San Sebastián. We went into the drawing room in time to listen to the fag end of a French broadcast announcing the armistice; it came through very badly and we could not make head or tail of it.

Sunday, June 23. At ten I went to High Mass in the cathedral. I marveled no end at the beautiful Latin elocution of the priest; somehow it was the most *natural* Latin I had ever heard — it sounded as if it were his native language and as if he never spoke any other. It was very lovely. The light in the cathedral was a warm golden brown, very different from the bluish and purplish grays that fill up the French cathedrals I knew. Coming out I met M. Ostrowski, who was admiring the wonderful Gothic sculpture of the porch. In the afternoon my wife and I and Tosca walked to the Café de Viena, reputedly the center of social life in the town; at that hour it was tenanted only by a few officers and some Belgian refugees, freshly arrived. We ordered some vanilla ice cream, which came in an enormous heap, the size of a small mountain, and looked excellent, but tasted like a particularly horrid cheap scented soap. They charged half a dollar for it. There was a fair in progress along the riverbank; the din was unbelievable, with a dozen loudspeakers going at full tilt at the same time; the crowds were enormous, and everybody smelled of musk. What surprised me was the amount of food displayed in the tents —

prawns, hams, sausages, olives, pickles, pastries, candy. I had been told in France that Spain was starving; Gannett had told me that when he had visited San Sebastián in January he had to leave after two days because he did not get enough to eat. I asked the hotel proprietor what was the truth of the matter; he said he did not know about San Sebastián, but Burgos was the capital of a comparatively fertile self-supporting district and things were not bad. "But you just wait until you penetrate farther into New Castile," he warned.

5

Monday, June 24. It took me an hour and a half to change one thousand French francs — they would not take more — and two pound notes at the Banca de España. We left Burgos at 10:30 and had already gone ten miles when we discovered that the hotel people had forgotten to provide the sandwiches I had ordered. This seemed unfortunate; just how unfortunate it was we did not know at the time. We reached Valladolid at 1 P.M. I had had visions of a good lunch and of a visit to the cathedral, where I believed, rightly or wrongly, Columbus was buried. Vain dreams! There was a barrier across the road. A rascally-looking young man, in shirt sleeves, jumped on the running board and said he would guide us through the town. His cronies, similarly dressed and unshaven, swung the barrier aside. I explained, in my best Castilian, that I needed no guide, that I had no money, and would he please let us go on? His face fell, but evidently he felt that, having assumed official airs, he could not draw back now; he muttered the Spanish equivalent of "That will be all right" and motioned me on. The crossing of the town was unexpectedly short; we were out of it on the far side before we realized it. The pilot jumped off; my wife gave him some French cigarettes, at which his face lit up and he said something like "Come again." We knew by now that there was a tobacco famine in Spain, and cigarettes were the most valued form of tip or bribe. He ran back into town, to look for the next carload of refugees who had no money, only cigarettes. We cursed him and all his works; he had cheated us out of our lunch; but I would not consider going back into town.

We were running short of gas. The day before yesterday, in Guipúzcoa and Álava, the villages were comparatively close together and all had refueling stations. Now we were in the darkest New Castile; the villages were few and far between, and we had a good thirty miles' run before we found a garage that could sell us some *gasolina*. We filled up and, mostly by pantomime, inquired about victuals. "At the inn opposite the bridge, the last house on the left." We stopped at the last house on the left and I went in. An old man dozed in the dark passage. I said, "*Pan, chorizo.*" He said, "*Sí, sí,*" and shouted for his wife. An old woman with a limp appeared; she had a face exactly like a villainous-looking horse, except that she also had a drooping black mustache. The old man looked at me as if to say, "Make your speech." I said "*Pan, chorizo, comprar.*" The old woman said, "*Nada.*" Meaning, nothing doing, nix, or scram. That was that. I said to my wife, "In the next village, perhaps."

There was no next village. The country through which we drove now was a hundred per cent deadly desert. For the next fifteen miles the only live beings we saw were some starved-looking crows. It was very hot and close; it was also getting on to three o'clock and we had breakfasted at eight on coffee and two tiny bran rolls each. I began to feel giddy. I said, "See that clump of trees?" It was the first clump of trees to be seen for miles. "We'll stop there and rest a little."

We did not reach that clump of trees, for within the next fifty yards the car gave a sickening lurch and there came a grinding and groaning sound from the rear. In a word, a puncture. We stopped. We had no more brandy left. I hauled out the jack. I said, "*That* jack will never lift *this* load." I had never spoken more truthfully in my life.

I don't like crawling under cars and fixing jacks under back axles at the best of times. This was not the best of times. About a hundred and fifty yards back we had passed a road mender's hut. I walked back to it and knocked on the door. No answer. I opened the door. On a low stool sat a nanny goat and grinned at me. I shouted, "*Hey! Hola! Monsieur le patron! Hombre!*" There was a wooden structure in the back of the hut, like the upper berths in a forecastle. It contained hay. The hay parted, and a face appeared. "Good afternoon, sir. What can I do for you?" said the face. Castilian courtesy is perfect in *any* circumstances. The face climbed down. It was an intelligent, friendly face. I explained my trouble, combining the Spanish word *coche*, meaning car, with a pantomime expressing utter despair. The man understood; we went back to the *coche*. The nanny goat came too.

The man had never jacked up a car, but he was remarkably intelligent. The first thing he said was that *this* jack would never lift *that* load. He was right. We worked, or rather *he* worked; I instructed, hoped, and prayed. Three times the car rose — almost; three times it collapsed. This went on for half an hour. The rain, which had been toying with the idea for some time, decided to make a good job of it, and came down in sheets. The man said, "Wait a minute." He ran back to the house and returned draped in several layers of burlap sacking. We worked on, with approximately the same division of labor as before. The man said, "I suppose we shall have to unload the car. Let's wait until the rain stops." "Let's wait by all means," I seconded fervently. Three cars whizzed by. Belgian cars. I waved. They whizzed on. Two more cars. Polish cars. I waved. They stepped on the gas. The road mender said, "I have an idea." He ran back to the house and returned wearing a visored khaki cap, like that of a gendarme.

"I am an official," he said simply. A big gray Packard approached. The road mender stood in the middle of the road and held up his hand. The Packard stopped. It had a Paris number plate. I explained my plight. The driver alighted and dug out a fine big jack from his dickey. In another five minutes we had changed the wheel. In the meantime my wife spoke to the lady in the Packard and discovered that our benefactors were English, ex-residents of Paris. My wife said we had been unable to buy any

food. The lady gave us some cheese and bread. We restored the
jack and the Packard departed.

The road mender was collecting his burlap sacks; his wife, who
had arrived at an early stage and had been an interested spectator,
began to wring them out. This gave me an idea. I took off my old
burberry, and braced myself for a speech. In Castilian. I said, "No
pesetas. Refugee. Many coats. Fine coats. From London. Water
does not go through. Please have one."

The road mender looked at me, then at the burberry. He said,
"Do you mean that you want to give *this* to *me?*" I said, "Yes." The
road mender's wife said, "And is it true that the water does not
go through?" I said, "Look." The cloudburst had only stopped
ten minutes ago; the water was running from the coat; I showed
them the inside; it was dry. The wife's face beamed. The road
mender said, "Many thanks, *señor*." He was dignified and re-
strained to the last; but I could see that for some time to come he
was to be the happiest road mender in the province of Zamora. We
shook hands, and they trotted off, road mender, road mender's
wife, and road mender's nanny goat.

It was half past four. We had meant to reach the frontier that
afternoon; it was only another hundred and ten miles, but we had
no spare tire and we were on the verge of collapse from hunger
and heat. Salamanca was only forty miles away. Salamanca for
us.

We arrived, without further mishap, a little before six. We were
pretty dead to the world by then, but the beauty of Salamanca
revived us. There cannot be many places left in the world as
lovely as Salamanca. Oxford, Ghent, Bruges . . . if they are still
left . . . A thought not good to dwell on. The Hotel de Salamanca gave us a comfortable room, and we hurried back to the
Plaza Mayor and sat under the arcades in a café and had sandwiches and beer. Then we walked up to the cathedral, but it was
closed for the night. I went into the church of the Jesuits, pure,
austere baroque reminiscent of the best in Vienna. . . . The dinner consisted of one dish only, a measure of social welfare copied
from Nazi Germany. It was not a very good dish and they charged

the same price for it as we had paid at Burgos for first-rate meals. After dinner, in the hall, we glimpsed our rescuer and his wife, them of the gray Packard. They pretended not to see us. Some English people are like that, though, I am happy to say, not many; the trouble is they give the rest a bad name. The man had rendered us a service, and his wife had fed us, so I ought not to cavil; but their subsequent lack of elementary civility, which is Latin for civilization, calls for recording the fact that the man spoke with a cigar hanging out of the corner of his mouth, in an Englishman the infallible sign of a bounder; and his wife had a council-school accent, which is nothing to be ashamed of, except in the eyes of people of just their sort. . . .

The wireless was blaring out news in Spanish, a bulletin from Rome announcing that the Italians had sunk half the British fleet; we had heard this particular news so often that it did not trouble us. One of the men grouped around the set spoke French; he proved to be an Italian who had been living in Salamanca for the past year, member of an official mission; he discoursed blandly on the advantages, for Italians, of traveling from Ventimiglia to Port-Bou without having to bother about passports and customs — that is to say, from the Italian to the Spanish frontier along the Mediterranean coast. This was the first news I had of the dismemberment of France, and it would have given me great satisfaction to knock the man down, for gloating over it; but it would have been an expensive satisfaction and I forewent it, regretfully. He also said that the Portuguese hate the English, which I did not believe at the time, and which the very next day I knew to be a dirty lie.

6

Tuesday, June 25. We left Salamanca at 9:30; the coffee at the hotel was the worst we ever tasted. We had only seventy miles to drive to the frontier; but what seventy miles! As far as Ciudad Rodrigo it was not worse than the bumpy ill-cambered Spanish roads of the last few days. Ciudad Rodrigo looked exciting on its mountain-top; we were sorry not to be able to explore it. Just beyond the town we saw the first signpost marked LISBOA. Then and there began thirty miles across some of the more hopeless stretches of Dante's Inferno. I had never imagined that such desolation could exist anywhere in Europe. A country made entirely of stone, sickly yellow or dingy gray, with here and there a single clump of some dwarfed bush, juniper or lentisk, just to emphasize the absence of life all around. A few leprous-looking sheep guarded by a man in rags who looked like a wax model of inbred degeneracy. The road a mere lane, excavated rather than made, only in a few places wide enough for two cars to pass; luckily in all the thirty miles we did not meet a single vehicle. This lane now dipped steeply to what appeared to be the rim of the world, now corkscrewed up to some meaningless summit, only to corkscrew down again on the far side. We traversed two or three villages, or what counted for villages in these parts; we had thought the hamlets of the provinces of Valladolid and Zamora poor, but they had been centers of fashion and prosperous commerce compared with these troglodytes' nests shallowly scratched into the rock, without water, without vegetation, without any visible means of or excuse for subsistence. The worst of it was that we could not be sure that we were on the right road, and had no means of ascertaining it; on the one hand it seemed impossible that this should be one of the two or three main routes from Spain into Portugal; on the other hand we *knew* that we had missed no turning, there being none to miss. The thing appeared as pointless and vague as a nightmare, only it lasted much longer than any nightmare I had ever known; there seemed to be no end to it. There were no signposts, and after the first ten or fifteen miles there was not even a lonely scarecrow of a shepherd to nod a toothless, wordless answer to our halfhearted query. At last a battered board, dangling in the hot wind, informed us that we were about to enter Fuente de Oñoro. We were to remember it as the worthy capital of the land of the damned.

After half an hour's waiting in line along the meanest of village streets our car was shepherded into the square in front of the rail-road station and customs office. There were about fifteen to eighteen cars arranged along the four sides of the square, and they moved up as the two or three cars, tortured at a time by the executioners of the *Dogana,* were released and dispatched to the frontier. It appeared that the Spaniards turned every car inside out, ransacked every piece of baggage, and searched all occupants — all this, to prevent them from taking pesetas out of Spain. Why anybody should want to take pesetas out of Spain was not explained. The importation of pesetas into Spain being pro-hibited, people who somehow or other entered Portugal with Spanish banknotes in their possession found it well-nigh impossible to get rid of them, once they had left the station on the Portuguese side. Possibly the Spaniards were on the lookout for gold or jewelry being smuggled out of the land; though how, where, and when foreigners and strangers, who were given two or at most three days to cross the country along a predetermined route, were to pick up gold or jewelry remained another unsolved mystery. To my mind the real explanation of what was going on was that it was psychopathological, a kind of politically tinged sadism. I hasten to add that as far at least as my own experience went the manners of the Spanish officials were impeccable throughout. They managed to combine a devilish malice with smooth courtesy, a feat of which the average American or Englishman would be incapable.

We waited for over six hours in that station square, under a blazing African sun. By this time I had only eight pesetas left out of the seven hundred that we had spent in three days, two thirds of them on gasoline; there was a squalid little restaurant, but not having the price of two hot meals I did not find out whether they served any. I managed to buy a small piece of cheese and a slice of sausage, for five pesetas. Bread was a more difficult propo-sition; the station restaurant had none, and after a prolonged search a kindly *carabinero,* one of the fellows in the pea-green uniforms and the funny rimless shiny hats, virtually confiscated half a small and soggy bran loaf from a peasant woman who was supposed to sell it but seemed reluctant to do so. This cost another peseta.

My wife and I would have loved a cup of coffee or glass of wine, but I suspected that I should need my remaining two pesetas for tips; a suspicion that was to prove well-founded. We still had a bottle of tepid mineral water. There was no shade; there was a scorching hot wind, and smoke from the occasional trains.

Our fellow refugees, or most of them, were not of the sort to make an unpleasant day less unpleasant. There were three large Buicks with Belgian number plates, filled by what seemed a single family with their retinue — four or five young boys and girls, very unfriendly and ill-mannered, and as many secretaries and servants. One of the secretaries was a Portuguese; he appeared to make a series of attempts to beat the game and get the cars through out of turn; I am glad to say he did not succeed. It was only late that evening, after we had crossed the frontier, that I learned it was the family of M. Pierlot, the ex-Premier of Belgium. There were also some fat purse-proud Czechs and Poles with over-dressed wives from Paris, in sumptuous American cars; they looked like, and undoubtedly were, successful war profiteers whose last *coup* had been to cut and run in good time. There was also a nice quiet Belgian couple, a doctor and his M.D. wife; he told me he was born in Belgium of Swiss parents, so under Belgian law he was Belgian and under Swiss law he was Swiss, and this double nationality came in very handy at a moment when in France the Belgians were treated as allies and outside France there were no more Belgian Consuls left; just now he was traveling under the Swiss flag.

Incongruous-looking among the Packards and Buicks was a tiny 5 H.P. Fiat, entirely filled up by an elderly fat Frenchwoman in a cotton print dress, some bedding and kitchen utensils, and two dogs. Her husband, apparently crowded out, was a small, very dark Portuguese with a fortnight's stubble on his chin. He was a nice little man who had traveled all over the world and spoke all languages, including the Chinese — or so he said. They had been living on their farm in Touraine, and were now returning to another they owned in the province of Minho, in the north of Portugal; "and mighty glad I am to be back home," he added in good American. The woman got out of the car and walked her dogs. One was a little nondescript near-Pomeranian; the other a fat oversize mongrel fox terrier. I noticed that the latter had a half-healed flesh wound in his chest. I asked the woman where he had got it. "He got it saving my life," was the answer. They had been in a jam of refugee cars near Orléans. There were German planes overhead, dropping bombs. The din of the motors and the explosions drove the dog frantic; she was hugging him to her breast, to calm him. One of the Germans dived and machine-gunned the cars from the height of a few feet. A bullet hit the dog in the chest. "In on one side, out on the other," said the woman. "He is all right now, and he saved my life."

At 6 P.M. our turn came. Two boys took every piece of luggage — there were twenty-six of them — out of the car, and carried them into the customs office. A couple of *carabineros* poked under the seats and the floor carpets, rummaged in the pockets, emptied the tool compartment, looked under the bonnet. In the office I was asked to open everything; four officers ran their hands through the suitcases and bags; they were tremendously intrigued by my twenty-four pipes and by several reams of typing paper. They were very thorough, and handled everything with extreme care, folding back meticulously the clothes they had disturbed. Then, at a sign from the boss, an officer asked me to turn out my pockets. The three more pipes that thus came to light created a sensation. He ran his hands over my body; it was a perfunctory search, but it was a search. Also, it was a farce. For they never examined my big laundry bag; had I had any currency to smuggle I should have put it just there.

These proceedings took over half an hour. It took another fifteen minutes to put everything back into the car. The two boys worked like experts. They, as also the customs officers, had ample opportunity to collect souvenirs; when I later examined our possessions nothing was missing. I gave the boys my last two pesetas, and half of a two-ounce tin of Craven Mixture. The tobacco made them dance with joy. It was past seven o'clock when the squad of four cars — ours, two Belgians, and the Fiat with the heroic dog

— were expedited to the frontier in charge of a *carabinero* who helped himself to a seat in a Belgian Packard.

We crossed the village, and presently we drove along a straight road rising gently in open country. There was a chain stretched across the road; behind it stood a low whitewashed building, half a dozen cars parked in line, and a group of gray-clad soldiers with Swiss-looking képis. There was also a large sky-blue sign with white lettering. PORTUGAL.

We stopped on the Spanish side of the chain. It was a great moment; our troubles seemed to have come to an at least temporary end. For Spain had been enemy country; we had not actually been ill-treated, but the hostility was there just the same, in the newspapers and the broadcasts, in the eyes and the attitudes of practically everyone we had met, save the Basque people at the hotel in Burgos, one road mender, and a priest or two. The very air of Spain oppressed us; we had expected a Fascist atmosphere but what we found seemed more Nazi than Fascist. It was a great pity, for during the civil war we had been ardent Franquists, refusing to be duped by the Communist eyewash that represented the Red assassins as champions of democracy; and to this day we believe General Franco to be a good man who, as a fervent Catholic, is fighting a losing battle to save his country from being engulfed by Nazi barbarism.

Two Portuguese frontier guards, with rifles flung across their backs, came walking down the line of cars. When they saw our number plate they stopped, all wrapped up in smiles. *"Inglés?"* *"Americano e inglesa."* *"Aliados!"* We shook hands. It was a new world, a world of friends. The country was grand, a vast upland horizon reminding us of the Causse of Larzac in Southern France, between Millau and Lodève, rising gently toward the blue line of the mountains of Beira. A delicious fresh breeze attested that we were three thousand feet up. The sullen dingy square of Fuente de Oñoro, only a couple of miles back, seemed to belong to another planet.

About 7:30 a group approached from the direction of Vilar Formoso: men in black, with grave kindly Latin faces; little rotund smiling ladies in gay summer clothes. The mayor, the judge, the doctor, all the official world of the frontier village, and their wives. They walked down the line, accompanied by soldiers. The soldiers carried large open bags and held them out to the refugees. Round golden-brown loaves of freshly baked Portuguese bread, still warm from the oven; the best white bread in the world, as we were to find. Tins of delicious large sardines. Bars of chocolate. The ladies distributed sweet crackers and tins of condensed milk for the children. As long as we live we shall not forget the Portuguese officials of Vilar Formoso.

There was a tall dark young man in a tweed jacket, with an armlet bearing the letters B.E.C. He looked very English. I walked up to him. "Good evening. My name is Wall. Can I do anything for you?" Two other young men with armlets arrived, one tall, the other short; both fair and freckled. "Mr. Yeatman. Mr. Holroyd."

We only learned next day exactly what B.E.C. stood for: British Emergency Committee. But we learned within the next ten minutes what B.E.C. *did.* They introduced us to the officer of the frontier guards, a tall smiling fair man looking more Swedish than Iberian, very smart in his blue-gray tunic. "Lieutenant Antonio Julio." The lieutenant spoke French; he was very apologetic: it was a very modest house, his house in the square, and a very modest bedroom; but it was his best, and all he had to offer. Would we honor him by accepting it for the night? *Would* we accept!

That solved the question of quarters. Next we were guided to the customs office in the village square; they stamped our car papers. An official said, in French: "Awfully sorry to trouble you, but would you mind opening one of your suitcases? No matter which one. It is the law." I lifted a suitcase from the car. The official put on a pair of clean white gloves. I opened the suitcase. The official took off his gloves. "That will be all. *Merci, monsieur.*" The whole customs procedure took less than ten minutes.

Next, "Come and have some supper." It was Mr. Yeatman speaking. We went to a large barn up the village street. Inside there were tables and chairs and packing cases to sit on; a few cots; there were straw-covered demijohns, by the dozen, and cases of beer. Two young Englishmen were cutting sandwiches; another was making coffee; two others were serving. "What will you have?" They gave us bowls of soup; they gave us delicious roast-beef sandwiches, salad, cheese, cake, fruit. They offered us tea and coffee; they offered us beer and whisky; they gave Tosca a luscious slice of roast beef and a dishful of water. We sat around a low table, with candles stuck into empty bottles in front of us; we ate and drank and smoked and talked. We had been through a nightmare; it seemed very unreal; this was a good dream, but it was also true.

Somebody entered, a tall Englishman in a tweed jacket, and came to our table. "Jack!" "Dick, old boy!" It was our friend M., he of the Spanish Consulate at Hendaye; he who had blown up bridges on the Loire. He and some of our hosts were old friends; they had not met for years. They sat down and swapped yarns. After a while Jack said, "There is one thing that bothers me. I have lost my wife and children."

Murmurs of subdued consternation. "How, when, where?" Jack explained that when the end of the world came his wife and babies had been at a port in Normandy; he had not heard from them and did not know what had become of them. We all hoped for the best.

"Let's have some port," said Dick. "I have brought along a little." Somebody murmured into my ear: "Now you are going to taste *something*. Dick's father's firm handles what is absolutely the best port in the world." Dick came back, carrying a straw-plaited gallon. He poured out. My neighbor had not overstated the case. I had drunk, in my day, some first-class port back in England; but it had been nothing like this. *This* had bouquet; it had aroma; it had body; it had fire; it had, in a word, everything, and then some. A drink for gods, drunk out of thick heavy teacups and tin mugs in a disused stable by candlelight, three thousand feet up in the highlands of Beira Alta.

Mr. Wall seemed worried. He turned to me. "Are you all right about money?" I said I had 2200 French francs and 13 shillings of English silver. "No escudos?" "Not a one. We expect there's money waiting for us at Lisbon." "Don't change your French francs now. You won't get anything for them. You may do better in a few days' time. In the meantime you must have money. I am, treasurer. I cannot lend you any; we are only supposed to lend to British people. So I'll let your wife have some. Say seven hundred escudos. That will see you to Lisbon. Tell me if you need more." I said that was awfully good of him, but he did not know me from Adam and I had no security to offer. "Your wife has a British passport. You will pay back the loan at the British Consulate either at Porto or at Lisbon — whichever is convenient. Or else you can pay me. Here is my card."

Such were the methods of the B.E.C. at the frontier station of Vilar Formoso. British Emergency Committee. A group of young and prosperous businessmen from Oporto. They had driven up in their cars, the hundred difficult miles along narrow mountain roads; they also had a couple of trucks for provisions. They hired the empty barn and fitted it out as a canteen. They slept on the cots, taking turns, if and when they had a chance. In three days they distributed 2000 kilos of bread, 5000 eggs, and two bullocks in the form of roast-beef sandwiches, not to mention other victuals. They provided canned milk for the babies. They found rooms for people. They financed the whole thing out of their own pockets, with a small subsidy from His Majesty's Consul at Oporto. They fed all comers, regardless of nationality; those who had money paid what they chose to; most refugees had no money, and paid nothing. Loans of cash, beer, and whisky were reserved for English customers, and, as I had reason to know, for at least one American; Dick's port was reserved to celebrate the return of Jack M., who had helped to blow up the Loire bridges and had lost his family in a Norman port. (A fortnight later we ran into him at Lisbon; he had heard from his wife, who, with the babies, was safe in England.)

My wife, Tosca, and I slept that night in the best bedroom of Tenente Antonio Julio. In the morning his wife fed us on fragrant coffee, white cheese, home-baked bread, and homemade cherry jam; while we ate she showed us the doctor's diploma of their son, and a cherished edition of *Os Lusiades,* the great national epic of Camoens. And among the things that we shall never forget is that little room, with its red silk hangings, over the elms of the main square of Vilar Formoso, in the house that belonged to the lieutenant of the frontier guards and his little smiling dark wife.

7

Here ends the log of our flight, jotted down in two or three brief entries a day in a little Burns, Oates, and Washbourne pocket diary. It had taken us eight days, including the two and a half spent in Bordeaux, to reach, from our home at Pyla, the Portuguese frontier, and safety. But it took us another fortnight to reach Lisbon from the frontier; and although in the story of a lifetime such delays do not count for much, and although on the day when I write this, ten weeks later more or less, we have lived down what was annoying and fatiguing in the course of our Portuguese adventure, and remember only the great kindness and charm of the Portuguese people and the loveliness of the Portuguese countryside, it seems a great pity that those brief eighteen days in a land with which we fell in love at sight should have been poisoned by the fantastic ineptitude of the Portuguese police. It is true that they were up against an unprecedented situation, the influx of many thousand refugees, hundreds of them of doubtful status, and not a few outright dangerous, the disguised vanguard of the Northern marauders whose official uniformed troops were encamped at Hendaye a week after we had crossed that Bridge of Sighs into Spain. It is true that the hordes of fugitives had to be sifted and sorted, and the sheep separated from the goats; and it is also true that the coincidence, with this tidal wave of homeless and frightened men and women and children and dogs, of the eighth centenary of Portuguese nationhood and the contingent displays and festivities had filled the hotels of Lisbon and of the near-by re-

sorts with native thousands before a single refugee set foot on
that great Avenida da Libertad which is probably the most impressive land approach to any great city in the whole world.

The problems created by this convergence of two vast crowds
on a capital crowded even in normal times were probably incapable
of a perfectly satisfactory solution; but what human problem isn't?
The fact remains that the Portuguese police had hit on the one
way of tackling its task that could not fail to result in the maxi-
mum of hardship and irritation for all parties concerned, including
the police officials themselves. They took away, at the frontier,
everybody's passport, and spent the next three weeks finding the
passports for given travelers and finding the owners of given passports. The complications resulting from this almost incredible bureaucratic *gaffe* were multiplied in our case by the fact that my
passport was American and that of my wife British — an anomaly
which sent the officials who had to deal with it pretty nearly out of
their minds. We had to chase those passports from one end of the
country to the other, and my wife's was actually sent by ship to
England and had to be retrieved by air mail at the last moment; on
the day before the originally scheduled sailing of the *Manhattan*
it was a toss-up whether we should be able to recover it at all.
Both the British and the American Consuls at Oporto had to be
enlisted to fight this battle for us, and they fought it nobly and
well; but it is only fair to record, in contrast to the helpfulness
and charming manner of those officials, the high-and-mighty inefficacy of the young ass at the British Consulate at Lisbon who
did not consider that the inability of the Lisbon police to find my
wife's passport on the very eve of our embarkation constituted an
emergency within the meaning of the act, and who saw fit to lec-
ture me, of all people, the grateful guest of Lieutenant Antonio
Julio, the admirer of the great Salazar, the fanatic of Mediterranean and Roman culture, and the disciple of Latin philosophers,
on the advisability of treating the Portuguese as my equals.

But all that is past, done with, and shall be forgotten. What we
will retain of those days are images like those of that first afternoon's drive from Vilar Formoso to Curia, when the beauty of the

Portuguese North, with its haunting unearthly note like that of
Aeolian harps heard in a dream, puzzled and disturbed us until
we realized that in all our travels from north to south, in France
and Switzerland and Austria and England, the mountain ranges cut
across our path, running mostly from east to west, while here for
the first time in our experience the main trend of the mountains
was parallel to our route. And though we had to climb and to
cross many a saddle, and to descend into many a gorge, taken by
and large we traveled along a ridge, and looked across a valley
at another; and for a while, just after we had entered the province
of Coimbra, our ridge was the middle one of three, and as the
white mists of the approaching evening filled the two valleys to
the right and left, it was as if we had been sailing down the central channel of a tremendous river, of which the two crests which
formed our horizon were the distant banks, one glowing in the
amber and crimson of the setting sun, and the other melting into
an infinitely tender amethystine sky.

There is a painting by Claude Lorrain in the National Gallery
in London, representing a porticoed classical quay-side with a
sheet of water and a sail or two at sunset, that for some unaccountable and probably deeply personal reason has fixed itself in my
memory as one of the most beautiful sights of this world. All my
life, ever since I first saw it, as little more than a boy in 1913, I
have been looking for its counterpart in reality, and in those July
days, a day or two before I left the Old World, I found it. For
that great arcaded square by the sea which is perhaps the noblest
of the many noble views of Lisbon suggested to me the very mood
and ambiance of Claude's canvas, though I was aware that a checking of detail with detail would quickly destroy that impression of
identity. I can best suggest the note or element that in my mind
at least was common to two pictures that the camera, or even the
unpreoccupied eye of another observer, would at once reveal as
wholly different as a finality of satisfactoriness, the feeling that one
need not quest any further, the freedom that is born from the
death of desire. Another phrase that would express the same notion is the happiness of pure contemplation, and if I put it that

way I realize that I am merely describing the painting of Claude, and the composition of that great baroque architect of old Lisbon whose name I cannot now recall, as great art. For it is precisely this sense of release from the burden of willing that all great art gives us; and pictorial art, which is static and a projection of being, gives it to a far greater degree than music, which is dynamic and a summary representation of becoming; and becoming already implies what the German mystic called *ent-werden*, or becoming on the wane, or unrolled the wrong way — that is, the irresistible merging of all life into death.

But I have wandered a long way from the city of that eighteenth-century skeptic, the Marquis of Pombal, to the medieval cloisters of Master Ekkehard; and the point I wanted to make, and missed by chasing after another, was only that all the beauty of the Portuguese landscape, — Guarda on its tall mountain; and Coimbra with its terraced heights above the green Mondego River; and the sleepy grandeur of Batalha with its tremendous Gothic abbey, a southern edition of Lincoln Cathedral; and that astounding walled town and vast castle of Óbidos, that from the distance at least seemed to me to fulfill the promise of an unrestored and unspoilt Carcassonne; and the glamour of Lisbon itself, — that all this has, or seemed to me to have, an *unreal* note, the spontaneity of poetry rather than of life, the finality of achieved art rather than the elastic imperfection of a self-renewing nature. And having got thus far I become aware that I started out to speak of the Portuguese landscape, and yet every instance of it that I named is composed around the work of man. And this is probably what those who love Portugal less than I do, and are less prepared to drop into the mood proper to appreciating what she has to offer, mean when they speak of the preponderance of the artificial over art in that country, but what I prefer to relate to that echo of the unearthly and ethereal and dreamlike which delighted us so much on the road from the frontier to Coimbra.

We spent three very crowded, very hot and uncomfortable, and yet not unhappy days in Lisbon, and were greatly pleased to meet again our good friend Taylor Gannett, him of the Consulate at Bordeaux, who had actually reached Lisbon two days ahead of us, though he had left much later than we and we had no idea that he was following. He was as busy, as calm, and as smiling as ever; and we were delighted that we could at least deliver his messages to his young wife and his parents in Long Island, in return for all his unruffled helpfulness. And then the *Manhattan* sailed, and I was spared the pain of looking at the coast of Europe for the last time, knowing that it was the last, for I was busy trying to make my dog comfortable in those primitive and over-crowded kennels on the sun deck, which I was later to describe as an open-air variety of the Black Hole of Calcutta. We met on board many old friends, including the Birds and the Chamberlins, who had followed us by train from St. Jean-de-Luz; yet the crossing was not pleasant, though it might have been, for most of the stewards of this ship of the United States Lines were German-born Nazis, and did not make a secret of it.

Then we landed in New York, and in the first chapter of this book. But the end of the story of our flight came only when, a few days after our arrival, my little terrier Tosca, who was sixteen years old, who had thrown in her lot with me fifteen years ago in Vienna, and from whom I had never been separated since, collapsed in Central Park, overcome by the heat and the accumulated fatigue of the month that had passed; and she died three days later in the hospital where my wife had rushed her. We drove her limp body twenty-five miles into Westchester in the blackness of a thunderstorm; we have now a little copper box, containing her ashes. A few weeks before we left Pyla our neighbor Commandant Monbed, a famous veterinary, back on leave from the army, had told me that given the care and the scientific feeding to which she was accustomed, she might live another five years. But the Germans wanted *Lebensraum*, and Hitler got it for them by driving us, and ten or twenty or forty millions like us, from our homes. So Tosca had to die.

And here I shall break a rule of my own which I believe I have consistently followed so far, and shall speak, for once, of my emotions; though the reader will see that what I have to say about them will rapidly turn into reasoned argument. I will confess that the death of my dog has shaken me as much as anything that ever happened to me; though in a sense it was not unexpected, for I knew that at sixteen she could not hope to survive very much longer. And if some people will call me silly and sentimental for this confession, I have only to think of what so many people love and prize — roisterous parties, vulgar races with their neighbors in ostentation, inane shows that would make my stomach turn — and their condemnation or derision means nothing to me. I will also confess that on the subject of dogs I cherish certain views that I am afraid the Church might frown upon. I believe, for instance, that dogs are good; good not in the sense opposed to naughty, but in the sense opposed to evil. I see, of course, that they cannot be good in the sense in which men may and must strive to be good, for they have no faculty of choice, except in an extremely limited way; but it is a fact that very few dogs will kill once they have satisfied their hunger, which is more than can be said of mankind; and that generally dogs do not claim more than their proper share, and a very small share it is, considering the work many of them do, and the help they render to their masters. They fulfill the functions which are assigned to them extremely well, and are content with their place in the scheme of things; they are faithful, and full of gratitude. And there is no malice in them, ever; and they readily forgive their enemies.

Now I ask the reader, in all reason, if all that is not goodness, even though of a certain closely circumscribed kind, what is? I will say that they are good, not by a moral effort, of which they are incapable, but because they are *born* good, in their narrow modest way, because God has made them so. I have discovered that the ancient Persians felt about these things exactly as I do, and their religion even calls the dog the noblest of all the creatures of Light; and their penal code punished very severely maltreatment of dogs, and feeding them on bones from which the meat has been scraped, or giving them their food too hot. I cannot help feeling that this appreciation of the great virtues of dogs, which are loyalty, gratitude, and the total freedom from malice, hangs somehow together with the reputation of those Zoroastrians, which they enjoyed among the Greeks who were their bitter enemies, for being the most truthful of men, and among the most pious; and I feel that on the whole I should have got on very well with the ancient Persians. I will even go to the extent of believing that dogs have souls, though of course I use the word "soul" here only to denote something which is not a soul in the human sense, *per analogiam;* let us say that they have little humble steerage souls, not first-class ones.

And holding these views, I am also convinced that we owe a definite duty to dogs (as we do also, though to a lesser extent, to all domestic animals; for they did not ask to be domesticated by us, and would probably have preferred to go on living on their own). In a textbook of ethics which is among the books that I have left behind at Arcachon, and which is by Father John Rickaby, S.J., it is asserted that we owe no duty, and not even kindness, to animals, though we owe it to ourselves and also to God to be decent to all created beings. This attitude used to trouble me very much and I wondered to what extent it was official and compulsory; and one day I asked my stepson Martin to make inquiries on the point among his learned clerical friends at Oxford. He did this, and reported that an eminent Dominican assured him that the matter was by no means clear-cut, and that Catholics were allowed a certain latitude in forming their own views on the subject.

Be that as it may, I feel the loss of my dog as a very great loss, and I am sure that I shall go on feeling this. I am also convinced, strictly on reasoned grounds, that we owe a certain debt to all beings that we have loved, and even, on a lower plane, to the lifeless things that have served us; and I have always felt that to throw even an old coat, which has done its duty for years, on the dust heap is an indecent thing to do. I feel that I owe this debt to a great degree to the memory of my dog, not because she loved me but because I loved her; and I feel generally that there is not much to the man who will not, every now and then, light, figuratively speaking, little candles at the stations that line the road of his past. I call this not sentimentality, as would most foolish and coarse-grained people, but by the Roman name of *pietas,* which is not exactly the same as piety, for the latter word is mostly applied to religious sentiment and practice in a narrow sense; while *pietas*, though it includes piety, means more. And I shall wind up this emotional outburst by saying that there was at least one Englishman who would understand all I said about dogs, and would approve of it; and his name was Thomas Hardy.

VI. The Flag on the Mountain

ALTHOUGH this autobiography has not only begun some sixty-five or seventy thousand words ago, but has also reached its conclusion with my arrival in New York on the eighteenth of July, 1940, the fact of my birth, indirectly attested by the goings-on registered in the preceding pages, has not so far been stated in as many words. This omission is herewith rectified. I was born on the twenty-first of March, in the year 1892, in a modest but not comfortless middle-class apartment at Budapest, Hungary. My father was an attorney of the kind called family solicitor in England. He was the son of a peasant who was also a Jew. There existed thousands of such in the old Hungary, people whose ancestors had lived in and on the land for more centuries than anybody could remember, often intermarrying with their Christian neighbors, and practically undistinguishable from them to the outsider's eye and ear. At the age of ten I was, like most boys of my social kind, sent to a State gymnasium, which in Hungary meant, and I hope still means, not a place where tired businessmen ride rumps of artificial horses and acquire athlete's foot, but an eight-year combination of prep school, high school, and college. Throughout those eight years I was at the head of my class, a distinction which I have not ceased to regret and to pay for ever since. For my eminence was not the reward of work, but was the unearned increment of quick perception and a prodigious memory. My easy triumphs at school put the fatal notion into my head that all life would be like that.

I was the particular pet of one of our Latin masters, a tall handsome man with a soft voice, velvety brown eyes, and a heavy drooping mustache in the English military fashion of the early century. He wrote poetry in his spare time, and used to ask me to tea at his flat and to tell me about two or three summers that he had spent at Oxford. I worshiped him; and the fact that he was a literary person, with many English experiences and associations, was to bear on my whole life.

The subjects I shone in were Latin and history, but the one I was most interested in was religion. Only it was not the religion under which I was matriculated, but that of the boy with whom I shared a desk for years; he was a Roman Catholic. My home was wholly, I will not say irreligious, but unreligious. My father was a liberal agnostic, and a true one, for he manifested an indifference to religious matters entirely untinged by hostility; few agnostics, self-styled, are like that. When I, at the age of twelve, told him that I wanted to join the Catholic Church, he said, "Go ahead; that is your business; you cannot do it, under the law, until you are eighteen; but we shall see what we can do about it." My mother used to tell us children that there was a God who would punish us if we were naughty and reward us if we were good; and she told us something about guardian angels when we were very small, chiefly by way of explaining a colored print of one of Raphael's that hung on the wall of our bedroom. This was all the religion I had received in my early years. My mother, as I see her now, had a certain amount of religious feeling; I believe she used to pray, in an improvised manner; but she was also inarticulate and the most easy-going and volatile person I have ever known, and I realize now that if she never spoke to us about religion it was not because she disapproved of it, but because it was no more likely a subject for her than the differential calculus. She was of Jewish origin, too, but both her brothers were Christians, and moved in Gentile circles. One of them had his two daughters brought up in a convent; when I last heard about my cousins, some three years ago, they were both on the point of entering a religious order. I mention this by way of suggesting a background that has now become, as far as Central Europe is concerned, something as remotely historical as powdered periwigs; and yet my childhood lies only a single generation back.

My early leanings toward the Church had, however, nothing to

do with the militantly Catholic family of my uncle. They were produced, principally, by a kind of instinctive protest against two
somethings that I could not have named in those days, but that I
see now were, first, the Jewish conception of religion, and second,
the fact that one was supposed to belong to a religion simply because it was marked on one's birth certificate as that of the parents.
In our home the Jewish religion was no more a perceptible factor
than was Shintoism. But I received religious instruction at the gymnasium; it was compulsory for all denominations, and the teachers
were paid by the State, but appointed by the various religious com-
munities themselves. Now religious instruction for Jewish boys
consisted of three strands, running parallel throughout the cur-
riculum: Jewish history; a perfunctory reading of Hebrew texts;
and a vague throwing about of ethical maxims. I thought that the
whole thing was a terrible bore, and very soon I began to wonder
what it all had to do with religion and with God. For I found the
stories of massacres and battles in the Old Testament detestable,
pointless, and also incredible. In his ethical and theorizing moments
the teacher discounted miracles as related by the New Testament,
and urged a strictly rationalistic attitude toward such things, but
in the historical section we were told of Joshua's stopping the
sun, and the tumbling of the walls of Jericho, and so forth, as of
uncontestable and never-contested facts.

I have always had a passion for languages, and had an attempt
been made to teach us Hebrew properly I should probably have
liked it; but we were given a text, the master translated it, we had
to memorize the translation, and that was that. I thought the proceeding idiotic. But what estranged me most was the ethical aspect
of our tuition. We were told to be honorable, to pay our debts,
not to tell lies, to give honest measure (I wondered particularly
what that had to do with me; I never saw myself as a merchant), to
fulfill our obligations, and so forth. I said to myself (I must have
been a frightful little prig, precocious and smug) that all that was
excellent advice and worthy of following, but perfectly self-
evident and hardly worth mentioning; and why should God be
dragged into it when He was not dragged into the multiplication

table? One maxim revolted me: I refused to love my neighbors. I did not see why I should; I thought most of the other boys stupid and unpleasant.

I was, on the whole, easily bored in those days; it was an early sign of what I believe to be my worst vice, intellectual pride. I found that one of the worst things about going to school was that the masters went on explaining the same things for hours after they had made them perfectly clear. I sought refuge and diversion in reading books under the desk. It was in this way that I first got hold of the religious textbooks of my Catholic neighbor; later I borrowed them and took them home.

2

Those textbooks opened up a new world to me, and the most grandiose and most fascinating of all the new worlds which my twelve- or thirteen-year-old imagination was discovering all around. There were the stories of the Gospels, both their substance and their manner; this was something different, I told myself, from how a bunch of nasty Jews ambushed and murdered a bunch of nasty Amalekites. There was Church history, with all its splendors. In the Jewish textbooks the Pope Innocent III was described as one of the greatest criminals that ever lived, because of the measures he had enacted against the Jews. Here I read of some other things that he had done. I asked myself why we were not told by the Jewish teacher about all the marvelous achievements of the thirteenth-century Church. And it occurred to me that, if such a great man as the Pope Innocent III did not like the Jews, it was perhaps because the Jews had some faults.

The three things that impressed me most, however, were the Incarnation, the Passion, and a little textbook of Catholic apologetics. It seemed to me that the Incarnation was much the most important thing that ever happened, and I thought it was a pretty dirty trick that Jewish boys were not told about it. It also seemed to me that if God wanted to prove to men that He existed, He certainly had chosen the best form of proof when He became man and mingled among men, and that in view of this well-attested fact any denial of or doubt about His existence was stupid and wicked. Also, I could see that if God loved men so much that He died for them, there was a good reason why we should love our neighbors and even our enemies; it seemed to me that the Jewish religion missed here a very strong point in favor of a proposition not easily defended on any other ground. I went on arguing to myself that since Christ was God, the Crucifixion had been the greatest and most abominable crime ever committed, and that the Jews had fully deserved their subsequent sufferings; and I thought it a low dodge in the Jewish textbooks to whine about the punishment without referring to the crime upon which it was visited. What I could not see at the time was that everything depended on whether the Incarnation was true or not. Today I realize that while my judgment of the doctrinal aspects of the two religions was sound, my critical attitude to the Jewish version of Jewish history leaned over backward, as the saying goes. Anti-Semitism is not a problem that admits of a simplicist solution, and in any case the cruelties to which the Jews have been subjected throughout the centuries cannot be excused on any ground. But I will admit that I have little patience with those Jews who make philo-Semitism the test of anybody's intellectual level and moral worth, and who repudiate all attempt at a critical objectivity as anti-Semitic.

What I, however, found most exciting in Catholicism was apologetics — that is, the systematic defense of the tenets of the Church on purely intellectual and rational grounds. Here was a specific way — one that suited my instincts, my craving for the thrill of downing an opponent by showing myself cleverer than he — to deal with a subject that I considered extremely important. I suppose that is as good a way as any of describing the kick I got out of a small textbook of Catholic apologetics at the age of fifteen. For the better part of the next thirty years I was to forget about those early thrills. Today, on the threshold of fifty, I have returned to appreciating them; and I think that the most fascinat-

ing, as well as the most worth-while, pastime in the world is a
good theological argument. But then, as the girl at Castelnaudary
said in an earlier chapter in connection with the respective merits
of potted duck and potted goose, there is no accounting for tastes.

What finally made me "take the plunge," as the Anglican phrase
has it, was not theology at all, but a purely historical argument,
put forward not by a priest but by a Latin master. He pointed out
that European civilization was entirely of Christian origin and
rested on Christian foundations, and was on the whole the work
of the Catholic Church; and that, this being so, it was not altogether decent to claim to belong to that civilization, and to share
in its benefits, and yet at the same time to deny its foundations.
This seemed to me absolutely unanswerable. After thirty-three
years, it still does. It was at that time that I was introduced, by a
boy who called himself a Socialist and an agnostic, but who prided
himself on recognizing good literature when he saw it even if he
disagreed with it, to the writings of G. K. Chesterton. (And we
were sixteen. Our incredible priggishness, as I see it now, makes
me almost approve of the English method of education that treats
the intellect as if it did not exist.) Now, the Latin master's argument chimed in admirably with Chesterton's saying, somewhere in
Heretics I believe, that in European civilization everything is of
Christian origin, including the denial of Christianity and even outright atheism. Chesterton puts this much better; but that is the
gist of what he says, and it is the incontrovertible truth. It seemed
to me, when I first read that passage, that in a way it was defensible
for a man to be an agnostic if he had been a Christian previously;
but that it was unworthy of an intelligent person to reject the
Christian doctrine without carefully examining it first. As I have
already mentioned, I was a ghastly little prig in those days. Also,
I was right; at least I still think so.

And so it came about that I was, at the age of seventeen years
and three months, baptized as a Catholic and a member of the
Roman Communion. Theoretically, my baptism was illegal, for
under the Hungarian law no minor could change his religion unless

his parents changed theirs at the same time, up to the age of eighteen, when he could do it on his own. My father, however, who was a lawyer, pointed out to me that if he did not stop me from doing what I did nobody could; and that he did not stop me, not because he thought that the Catholic religion was true, but because he was not convinced that it was false; and because he thought that the thing was for me to decide, and that it was his duty to help me in doing what I thought was right. My father, as I see him now, had his plentiful share of human failings, and my relations with him were not always satisfactory in the last years of his life; but he was a just man.

I had been wanting, then, to become a Catholic, for years. Now I was one. Within the next five or six months I lost all interest in the Church and in religion; and went forth in quest of new gods whose prophet, I confess regretfully, was Dr. Sigmund Freud, of Vienna.

But though I thus ceased to be a Catholic, except in the sense in which nobody who has been baptized in the Church ever can cease to be one, those early convictions and emotional upheavals, and those early contacts with two or three priests of the Church, did not pass without leaving their mark; and I take great satisfaction today in being able to say this. For even after my apostasy, which was not by any express act of repudiation but by indifference and neglect, and the holding of views incompatible with Christian teaching, three things have never left me. Firstly, I retained a certain intellectual respect, mingled with vague nostalgic sentiment, for the Church; and I may say with a good conscience that I have never, in my subsequent years as a writer, put on paper a line to attack or belittle the Church, nor yet a line in direct and purposeful controversy with any of her teachings. Secondly, I have never for a moment dropped, let alone repudiated, my conviction that our civilization is founded on the Christian teaching, and by this I mean, and have always meant, the theological doctrine of the Church, and not merely the ethics of charity and neighborly love and good will; and if I became an agnostic, and remained one for years, it was because I regarded my kind of agnosticism as a legitimate development of the original Christian position. I know very well that in the eyes of the Church this does not in any way mitigate my falling away. But I do value consistency as an intellectual virtue, and it seems to me that being consistent even in error is at least less ridiculous than flopping about mentally, like a seal on the rocks of a zoo. And thirdly, I preserved, from those early contacts, a wholehearted admiration for the priesthood as an institution, and for the priests of the Church as individuals, an admiration in which there was an element of nostalgic affection. For the priests with whom I had dealings in those early years were good men, of high intellectual striving and accomplishment, content with poor living, and kindly and helpful to a degree surpassed by no other men within my experience. And I have met no priest in the course of the thirty intervening years who gave me cause to revise my early opinion of his order. I must admit that even in the years when I was most completely indifferent to religion, meeting a man who heaped hate and scorn on the priesthood, just because some priests in fifteenth-century Spain did this and other priests in sixteenth-century Rome that, never failed to make me angry, and seldom failed to make me lose my temper, which is a very stupid thing to do at any time, but most particularly so in matters of religious controversy.

And that, for the next chapter or two, is all that I have to say about religion, and my early playing with it; and as regards my childhood there is only one more thing I want to say, one that is not irrelevant, since it goes to explain how I ever came to write this book in English. From my very earliest years I had somehow a special love and admiration for England and things English; I have no idea why and how this came about, but I know that at the time of the Boer War, when I was seven years old, I was often beaten by my contemporaries because I was pro-English and they were pro-Boer; but if you asked me what had made me pro-English I could not say, to save my life. It was just one of those things that happen to and in a child, like preferring strawberries to raspberries or vice versa.

Then one of my mother's brothers, who was a famous actor, went to spend a holiday in London, and was entertained by Sir Henry Irving and Beerbohm Tree and I do not know what other celebrities, and brought back signed photographs and resplendent leather kits and riding boots and pipes and pouches, and for me particularly a folder containing very good photographic views of London; and I believe it was this folder that was responsible for all that followed, and hence indirectly for this book. He also had a lovely library, in four or five languages, for he was, apart from being a great comedian, a very cultivated and even learned man, and my earliest idol and high example of what a man should be. He had in this library a fine edition of the plays of Shakespeare, in the Hungarian translation; I used to read them, as also his other books, on Sunday afternoons in the cosy flat which he shared with my grandmother and two maiden aunts. And I bothered the life out of my father, begging him to buy me that same Hungarian edition of Shakespeare; he said, however, that he would do nothing of the sort, but that he would buy me a complete edition of Shakespeare in English as soon as I knew enough English to read it. Being a little beast, I thought that that was a cheap way out of it; and so I worried my father to hire me an English governess; which he did, though I regret to say the one he hired was an American woman of German parentage, and I realize quite clearly today that her accent was one of the less lovely varieties of English as spoken at Milwaukee; but that meant nothing to me in those days.

Anyway, in a year's time I claimed that English edition of Shakespeare, and my father bought me a beautiful one, printed on India paper and bound in limp dark red leather, and published by the Oxford University Press. I settled down to read it with great gusto, but found to my surprise that I only understood every fifth or sixth word; this, considering that I had only had lessons in English conversation and grammar for a year, and was only about eleven or twelve years old, surprises me less today than it did then. But somehow I got hold of a copy of Macaulay's *History of England* in the original, and also of a full translation published by the Hungarian Academy of Sciences, I sat down and read both of them side by side, and by the time I was through I could read most English books without a dictionary; and I read as many of them as I could grab, by hook or by crook. One of the first I read was *Henry Esmond*, which I thought was a very beautiful book; I still think so. Only in those days, having just been dosed by Macaulay, I believed all the nasty things said about the great Duke of Marlborough, and also against the Tories; and I proudly called myself a good Whig, which was really something very funny and even grotesque for a Hungarian boy of fourteen or so to do. I have not altogether given up doings things that I afterwards recognize to have been funny, in the above sense; but I have been cured completely of calling myself a Whig.

I was not yet eighteen when, having passed, with flying colors and without having done a stroke of work for it, the examination which in France is called *baccalauréat* and which was the terminus of the eight-year course of the gymnasium, I became an undergraduate in the University of Budapest and selected Germanic philology and the history and theory of the fine arts as my subjects; the latter because I liked it, and the former because my best friend chose it too. I shall say no more about my career in the university, and saying no more is the best thing I can do, for it was a complete flop. After the brilliant promise of my early school years I flickered and went out like a match thrown into a puddle of beer on a café table; and I choose the simile advisedly. I attended lectures if I found them amusing, but not otherwise; and after three years of it I left the university without so much as trying for a degree; which was just as well, though I might have bluffed my way to one that I did not deserve. I should explain that the undergraduates in a Hungarian university were left entirely to their own devices, and if they played truant for weeks on end and did not make any personal contact with the professors and lecturers, it was their funeral. But I must say that all the while I lived this unworthy and wasteful, but not, in the narrow sense of the word, debauched, life of the undergraduate cafés, I went on reading books and maintained my interest in the things of the mind, which by this time were represented to me chiefly by Freudian psychoanalysis and the possibility of its application to literature. You see, I had not given up my early dream of becoming a scholar and a writer; only I thought the way to realize that dream was to sit in cafés till sunrise and talk about it. In this, as in many other respects, I manifested a very high degree of unoriginality.

I was nineteen when one evening my father had a stroke, and died within ten minutes; I was not present when he died, for I had rushed out to fetch one of my uncles. He was only fifty-three years old, but had aged a great deal in latter years and was a very depressed and even sad man; partly, as I know now, because his business had drifted away from him to more enterprising younger men, and partly because he suffered from a grave kidney trouble of which he refused to take proper care, on grounds of economy. It was soon found that he did not leave a penny to his widow and four children; he was not even insured. And we had been used to a comfortable, and even, in a small way, luxurious life, because he had spent every penny he made, and this meant a very decent income up to those last two or three years, on giving his family a good time; but he did not think he could afford life insurance. All this was very Hungarian. He looked very Hungarian, and I remember him best not as he was in his last years, but as he had been when I was about ten or eleven, with his jaunty black mustache, smartly dressed always in a light gray check suit of old-fashioned cut, with a black stock tie, looking rather like a major of infantry in mufti. In those last years he used to shut himself up, day after day, in that office of his where no clients came any more; he sat, not at his desk, but in the big armchair where the clients should have sat, and read: Sir Walter Scott, the elder Dumas, Jules Verne — volume after volume, day after day, week after week, smoking numberless cigars. I could not understand why he should read such old-fashioned romantic stuff and nothing else; I understand it now.

And so, at the age of nineteen, I had to go out and make a living, which is something that happens to a good many young men of nineteen, but not to very many who were brought up so softly, and so carelessly as far as money is concerned, as I. It so happened that I had a friend of my own age, a very decent youth who was the only son of a millionaire ironmaster who amused himself by buying a newspaper and becoming a publisher and editor-in-chief, a kind of Hungarian Mr. Munsey. I had first met him years before when he spent a summer with his father, as we did with ours, at a luxurious hotel which they could afford and we could not. A few months after my father's death I met this boy in the street by chance, and told him about our trouble; and he said, Come along, why not become a journalist, Dad will give you a job. So he took me to his home, and his father drove him and me to a very smart restaurant in what was the Bois de Boulogne of Budapest, and stood us a grand dinner; and after dinner the old man drove me to the editorial office of his newspaper and introduced me to his managing editor, and said to him, Mr. So-and-so, I want you to give this boy a job.

And that is the way I became a newspaperman in the first place, and it sounds, in the telling of it, like a fairy story; which is just what it was. They gave me at first things to translate from the English and French newspapers; then they let me write little half-literary news stories, the kind Continental newspapers used to publish, sometimes signed, sometimes not; after a while they took away the translations from me and made me write longer stories, of the same kind, and let me sign them with my name. They also doubled my salary, and then raised it again, and in about a year's time they said, here is a very promising young man, and they took me to their clubs and parties and even introduced me to Mr. Ferenc Molnár, the celebrated playwright, who sat enthroned in the Café Abbazia every night, year in, year out, when he was not in Paris or on the Riviera. And then one day I said to myself, Why, all this looks very bad, it looks as if I were making a success of it. So I promptly resigned my job and took a train to Copenhagen, Denmark. For I was the sort of person who knew a good thing when he saw it, and would run away from it instantly.

It seems to me that I have said a good deal more about my early years than had been my intention, but this, I suppose, happens quite frequently to authors who set out to compose impersonal autobiographies. It has amused me to do so, and I hope it did not bore the reader more than other things in this book; so what's the odds?

3

Now at this point it might well be asked, by a reader whose interest in this narrative has been sufficiently aroused to make him wonder about this and that, what hit this foolish young man who would throw up a good job and better prospects to take a train to Copenhagen, Denmark, of all places? Now if it had been Paris or London, not to say New York . . . ! Well, a full answer to that perfectly reasonable question is not required here, since most of it would have no part in such organic unity as my story possesses; and I see this unity, not in the advance of my personal fortunes, but in the development of certain ideas, which might have taken place in anybody but happened to take place in me, within a historic constellation that was full of foolish young men just like myself. So I will only plead such commonplace, but wholly truthful, reasons as that I was foolish and young, and restless, and full of curiosity about things and places and hungry for the nourishment called experience. Also, and in this too I was a very ordinary young man of the cleverer sort, I had been, in that odd sort of way which the Freudian jargon calls unconscious but which is not really unconscious at all, only inarticulate and unconfessed, scared by too close a prospect of success; that is to say, frightened by a self-set level of achievement which I should be expected to maintain by unrelenting effort. And I mention this kink in me only because it was a common enough mark of my generation and kind.

But I had also another kink in me which was more special, and which was one of the two fundamental factors that fixed my choice on Copenhagen. At the age of fifteen I had conceived a great interest in the plays of Ibsen, and this interest was not unusual either but was shared by all the budding young geniuses who were my friends, though it would have been unusual in an English or American boy of the same age. The kink I speak of consisted in this, that I was not content to read Ibsen in the available Hungarian and German translations, but set my heart on reading him in the original Norwegian. I made inquiries, and found that Ibsen did not write in Norwegian at all, but in pure Danish spelled and pronounced in a different way; and why this should have been so has nothing to do with my story. So I went and bought an edition of the complete works of Ibsen in Danish, and a Danish grammar and Danish-German dictionary, and after a while I could read my Ibsen to my heart's content. It occurs to me, as I write this down, to ask myself what became of that complete edition of Ibsen which seemed so important to me at the age of fifteen. The answer is that I took it with me to Copenhagen, and left it there when, my time being up, I went away, never to return; and this means that the Germans have it now, just as they have my six hundred books that I was obliged to leave at Arcachon twenty-seven years later. And this fact may seem, but is not, irrelevant to my story; which is the story of how the Germans got hold of everything that anybody else had in Europe, and why.

So my interest in Scandinavian literature was one of the two principal factors that made me fix my choice on such an unlikely stage of youthful extravagance as the staid old capital of Denmark. The other factor, a much more important one, was that it stood written somewhere that I, being the sort of person I was, should do just what I did; but we won't go into that.

I will also say that my fifteen months at Copenhagen were not really a detour from the main itinerary of my life, a kind of impasse that led nowhere, but rather a station of the road; for the train that took me to Copenhagen also took me to London, on my first short visit there, when I could see the originals of all the photographs in the folder given me by my uncle when I was seven years old, and also the Strand, just as it was to be seen on the cover of the old *Strand Magazine*, with the policeman and the girl and the red buses and St. Clement Danes in the middle of the road, or it may be St. Mary-le-Strand, I am not sure which; and this was also a picture that had etched itself into my memory when I was a boy, for I read some of the Sherlock Holmes stories in that review, as they came out. That train also took me to Ireland, on an even shorter visit which was to remain the only one, in September 1913, when from my window in Jury's Hotel I saw the lancers charge Jim Larkin's strikers in College Green, and saw Phoenix Park, which I still think the finest of its kind in the world; and, for a day or two, Belfast, which I hated like hell. But much the most important of the places to which that train for Copenhagen, which I had boarded in my native city of Budapest on the thirteenth of August in the year 1913, was to take me was New York.

And if that is not all that I have to say about my fifteen months in Copenhagen, from August 14, 1913, to January 28, 1915, it is almost all. For the fact that Copenhagen was a lovely city, and the people there good and kind, and the life very pleasant, about as pleasant as it had been anywhere in that comfortable, cultured, easy-going, secure, and extremely blind nineteenth century which was the Antonine age of the modern world, and which came to an end, not on August 1, 1914, as we used to think, but on the day in January 1933 when Adolf Hitler became the Chancellor of the German Reich — all that formed part of my life, but does not necessarily form part of my story. And yet it seems to me that I ought not to pass over those months in Copenhagen without saying at least a word or two about its mellow beauty: about the Langelinje with its white-globed lights, and the white sails of pleasure craft on the steel-blue Sound, and the lights of the fort, that tragic useless fort, of Trekroner coming out flickering in the twilight; about those noble Renaissance palaces of red brick, mirroring themselves in the dark green waters of the silent canals; about the bright green of the hundred copper spires and domes which form the skyline of Copenhagen; about that other bright green, that of the great beech forests north of the city, the beech being the tree of Denmark, as the olive is that of Provence; and about my favorite walk along the lakes within the city, with Queen Louise's Bridge, and the flashing gulls, and the squat gray square tower of Frue Kirke melting into the winter dusk on the opposite shore. And this is a commonplace enough description, and it will not mean much to the

reader; but to me it means something that is rather like the respectful lowering of a flag. For the Copenhagen that I knew is no more;
it, too, has been swallowed up in the German *Lebensraum*, which
is but the pseudo-learned Nazi word for a stable.

4

It occurs to me, however, just as I am on the point of boarding
the good ship *Hellig Olav* on my way to New York — I mean, of
course, across the ocean of memory, for all this was a quarter of a
century ago — that I have so far dismissed this Copenhagen interlude too lightly, without allotting to those fifteen months (of
which three were actually spent on two short visits to England
and a flying trip to Ireland) the share that was theirs in the process
of turning a very silly young man into a less silly and less young
one; which after all is the personal theme of this impersonal book,
and may contain a lesson for others. Copenhagen was an interlude,
and in a sense the end of a branch line in my life; but it was an important interlude for two reasons. And the first of these was that at
Copenhagen I made my first contact with something that till then I
had only known in books, but never seen in real life, and that I have
never ceased to respect and to love since, though it is only of late
years that I have come to comprehend it fully. This something was
Tradition.

For in my own home, and in my native city, I had not met with
Tradition as the framework and illumination of everyday life. And
yet Hungary was one of the most conservative countries of Europe,
and the life of certain layers or sections of Hungarian society was
firmly rooted in and deeply attached to the old inherited ways.
But it so happened that none of these layers or sections supplied
the background of my childhood. They consisted of the classes
that lived on and by the land: the titled nobility, though this was
less Magyar and rather more international than the other groups
in this category, being intermarried with its equals in other coun-

tries, and spending much of its time in Vienna and other foreign places; the untitled, very important, but slowly disintegrating squirearchy; and the peasants. The most conservative of all was a small town-dwelling middle class, in Budapest and certain cities principally in northern Hungary, old families of lesser merchants and prosperous artisans and so forth, mostly descendants of a German "plantation" of centuries ago, partly still German in language, but very Hungarian in feeling; and these lived a life wholly isolated from modern progress in beautiful old houses smelling of the lavender of linen cupboards and generally of the eighteenth and early nineteenth century. I had been inside one or two of these houses, because I had one or two casual friends who came from such families; but I had no constant traffic with them.

Now the particular subdivision of the bourgeoisie of Budapest from which I sprang, and which was in the economic sense determined by its living on, and beyond, middling or small incomes as they were earned in business or the professions, but not inherited — this particular group, I say, held nothing in common with any of those old-fashioned sections except the Magyar language. Provincial in manners and in outlook, these families, of which my own was one, were yet imbued with that international liberal spirit to which they owed their very existence. For most of them were Jews, or what are today, in the half-witted Nazi gibberish, called non-Aryan Christians. And the legal enfranchisement of the Jews, which gave birth to this particular class as a social entity, had only taken place in 1867, less than a generation before the year in which I was born. It was a new class, and it possessed the chief virtue of new classes, which is intellectual eagerness; and also their chief and obvious fault, which is lack of tradition and failure to understand tradition. But to blame this class for having dropped the old Hebrew ways without fully digesting and assimilating the ways of that tiny Gentile bourgeoisie to which I referred above, within the span of thirty years, would be about as intelligent and as fair as to contemn a New York Negro bootblack in the same breath for not practising the crocodile religion of Nigeria in Columbus Circle, and for not speaking Harvard English.

The fact remains, however, that as a boy I lived, like most of the boys I knew, a life ordered by the immediately preceding generation according to their lights and tastes and financial resources, but without any reference to fixed standards derived from the past. Moreover, to my class tradition meant not simply something strange, but also something hostile and to be abhorred; for it was the mark of political reaction, whereas our families were Left-minded, partisans of an ideology which I now recognize as the exact counterpart of that of the French Radical Socialists, the party of Daladier. This political coloring, ranging from a kind of timid pink to a bright red, characterized the mode of life of even those of my friends who were of full-blooded Gentile, and Christian, background, but who had adopted liberal or radical views.

Now I, as an ardent admirer of G. K. Chesterton, knew a little more about tradition than most of the other boys who were my friends, and I did not think that tradition was just bunk and something that intelligent men can have no truck with. But Chesterton was not my only prophet now. Another was Mr. George Bernard Shaw; a third, Mr. H. G. Wells. I had been introduced to these latter by the same socialist–anarchist–syndicalist–atheist–agnostic–esthete–hard-boiled–proletarian boy who had lent me *The Man Who Was Thursday* and *Heretics*. And I saw nothing incongruous in not only loving, but also believing, Chesterton, Shaw, and Wells all at the same time, for they were, all three of them, very marvelous literature; and I made no attempt to reconcile or integrate their conflicting preaching, but got along being a Traditionalist two days and a Progressive one day — though by and by this came to be the other way. In all fairness to ourselves I must say that my friend and I were not quite so abominably priggish and book-wormish as would appear from the things I have related. For after all we were boys aged fifteen or sixteen; and so in the school recess, when we did not discuss the Fabians or Dostoevski or Georges Sorel, we organized cavalry battles in the courtyard, with half the boys acting as cavaliers and the other half as mounts. On these occasions the highbrow boy was my horse. But ball games we detested and despised, for they were compulsory, though very little time was given up to them. The last I heard of my horse, in 1926 or '27, he was doctor to a mining village in Chihuahua, and a naturalized Mexican. We young unathletic Budapest bookworms did get about; almost as much as the strong silent public schoolboys from Winchester and Eton and Marlborough.

When I arrived in Copenhagen, which was early in the fall of 1913, it was as if the curtain had risen on yet another new and fascinating world; but, though it was my first experience of a foreign land, the strangeness and the beauty came out of history rather than geography. It so happened, which was my good fortune, that I was taken in by some very fine people and treated not as a stranger but as a friend. Most of these people belonged to the professional classes — doctors, lawyers, professors, journalists, and so forth; but the man I have special reason to remember with respect and affection was a landowner from the island of Laaland, a very old man but tall and straight and with fire yet in his very blue eyes. He looked exactly like the old Viking that he was, though his immediate forbears had been farmers like himself, or Lutheran preachers, for centuries; and he was very kind to me, I don't know why.

The loveliest thing in this very agreeable milieu in the midst of which I had landed was that it lived by its past. For the first time in my life I was with people who ate off silver and heavy linen tablecloths and slept in beds and read books bound in old leather or vellum that had all belonged to their great-grandfathers, and who remembered, and quoted, what Cousin this and Uncle that had said, and then explained to me, who was a stranger, that Cousin this and Uncle that had been dead these hundred years, and had been bishops or generals when alive, and played important parts in the destinies of their country. But the strangest part of it all was that these people called themselves not conservatives, and not even liberals, but radicals, and were all for universal suffrage and disarmament and imposing heavy taxes on the rich to build model houses for the poor, and so forth, and in intellectual matters followed the leadership of that prophet of Radicalism and free thought, Georg Brandes, who was a Dane and also a Jew; and they never went to church. All of which would have been unthinkable in Budapest, where such political and intellectual views were at home in the literary cafés, and in apartments that, though comfortable and often luxurious, had been furnished the day before yesterday from the shop around the corner; whereas the counterparts of the homes and the general atmosphere that I have just described belonged to people who were strict Catholics or Calvinists and voted invariably for the extreme Right.

But I must make exception, from that general account, for the old man from Laaland, who was a conservative and went to church on Sundays; and I am glad to know that he died in 1920, and was thus spared the terrible tragedy which befell his beautiful and noble old country of Denmark in our own days. It is only today that I can see the fatality that was to lead from the radical and pacifist views of my Danish friends to that tragedy; but we won't go into that now. But I will here add to those memories of Copenhagen that are still with me, and that I tried to suggest on an earlier page, evenings spent in those old homes where the walls were lined with old books and the candlelight shone on polished walnut, and where there were flowers in every corner, in tall vases of silver or crystal glass, or in those lovely blue-gray bowls of Copenhagen china; and all this has now been stolen by the Germans.

5

The second permanently important thing that happened to me in Copenhagen, between the fall of 1913 and Christmas in the first year of the first World War, was that I discovered my native country, Hungary. Now I shall not go off into an abstract discourse to explain why I had to go to Denmark to discover the land where I was born, for the more intelligent of my readers will see the thing at a glance, and the less intelligent will have ceased to read this book ere they reached this particular passage, judging it

too heavy going over all kinds of outlandish terrain, from Cnossus
to New York and then to Provence and back to Hungary and then
to Denmark and again New York and then back to Cnossus again;
though such, of course, is the way of the very world in which we
live — from one Cnossus to the next, in four thousand years or so;
but not everybody sees it like that. Suffice it to say that while back
in Hungary I had prided myself on my progressive and Western
outlook, I had not been in Copenhagen very long before I saw
that though it may have been progressive it was certainly not
Western. For the thing that most struck the Western critic of
Hungarian politics — and other aspects of Hungarian life did not
interest Westerners — was that here was an almost exclusively agricultural country in which nine million Magyars and ten million
non-Magyars — Slovaks, Croats, Serbs, Rumanians, Ruthenians,
and also a small number of Germans — were ruled by three thousand Magyar nobles who owned half the land, while fifteen million
peasants, who owned the other half, lived near the starvation line,
and had no rights to speak of. Further, this political and economic
despotism of the great Magyar landowners was sold by them to all
the lesser Magyars who owned little land or none, as the God-
ordained supremacy of the Magyar race. This unjust and in the
long run untenable state of things was not only bad for the people
of Hungary, including the Magyars and excluding only the three
thousand landowning bosses, but also a source of danger for the
whole of Europe, for it created the explosive nuisance of all sorts
of discontent and thereby forced the not too unwilling Magyar
ruling group to secure itself by an alliance with Prussian militarism.

Now there had been a small group of intellectual radicals in
Hungary, not half-baked pseudo-literary youngsters like myself
and my friends but serious scholars and thinkers of a more mature
age, who recognized this evil and preached against it by a very
excellent monthly review and by lectures, though to say too much
about the military implications was dangerous; and the leader of
these men was no other than my friend Professor Oscar Jászi, now
of Oberlin College, to whom I have already referred. I had met
him in those early days but would hardly dare call myself a friend

of his, for he was a great *savant* and I a rather ignorant boy, and though I see now that I was also a rather impudent one, my impudence had its limits. Anyway, though I fancied that I belonged to that progressive wing of which Professor Jászi's Sociological Society formed the serious core (and we even called ourselves "Westerners" after a quite bright but as I see now over-literary and precious review which announced its program by captioning itself *The West*), I had not taken in the political aspects and implications of our Westernism, being like so many young fools of the literary-esthetic persuasion easily bored with politics.

And so it was only when I had already spent some time in Copenhagen that I became, for the first time, aware of Hungarian politics and began to suspect the larger issues inherent in the so-called "problem of nationalities," by which were meant the non-Magyars. It so happened that the Scandinavian public was particularly exercised by this thing, for the famous Norwegian poet and playwright Björnson had published some pamphlets and articles and whatnot against what he called the Magyar tyranny. I do not want to go into the rights and wrongs of this wretched question now; I hate the sight and the sound of the whole business, for to me the half-witted enmity between the Magyars on the one hand and the Rumanians and Slavs on the other is one of the symbols of that general European lunacy that made Hitler the master of Europe and put European civilization on the spot. All I want to say here is that I embraced wholeheartedly the preaching of Björnson on this tiresome subject, and began to read with enthusiasm the far more learned works on the same subject of the gentleman who called himself Scotus Viator, and who was a Scots professor in London by the name of Seton-Watson, and whose voice rang even more mightily than that of the old Norwegian dramatist; and I used to see, from these Copenhagen days onward and for the next fifteen or twenty years, in this Professor Seton-Watson one of the great engineers of the new Europe. But now I can see very clearly that all that he and the like of him engineered was a coffin.

Yet I ought not to speak ill of this Dr. Seton-Watson, for the truth of the matter is that he probably saved my life, though he did not know it, and when I met him many years later in London I forgot to tell him. Here are the facts of this rescue: The outbreak of the first World War found me in London; I had gone there just at that moment because toward the middle of July everybody in Denmark expected the civil war to break out in Ulster, and, having spent a week in Dublin and two days in Belfast in the preceding year, I not only considered myself a great expert on the Ulster trouble but also persuaded the editor of a great Danish newspaper that I was one. So I sailed across the North Sea with a credential of that newspaper in my pocket, but I did not sail across the Irish Sea too, for in the meantime the greater war had begun and the Ulstermen woke up. And on the evening of August 4, 1914, I stood in Whitehall as a member of the enormous crowd that cheered Asquith and Lord Kitchener as they drove out of Downing Street. Though born in Hungary, I cheered too, because by this time I was firmly convinced that Germany and Austria-Hungary were wrong and the Entente was right, and that this conviction did not betray the country where I was born, because Germany was her mortal enemy too, as she was of the whole world.

And I shall say this with a certain amount of pride: that from the day in 1914 when the Germans invaded Belgium I have hated and despised them with a hatred and a contempt that did not abate but grew as I became older and less ignorant of history; and this is more than a good many Englishmen and Americans and even Frenchmen can say for themselves who have reached high positions and earned much money as experts on European politics, and who between 1919 and 1938, that is to say between Versailles and Munich, fuddled the world with their hokum about the Germans being very good people but ill-treated. But we know today that history will curse these men for the fools that they were.

Now the way in which Dr. Seton-Watson saved my life, without meaning to do so, was this: that it was principally under the influence of his writings that I had come to condemn the politics of the Austro-Hungarian Empire, and had made up my mind, in those early August days of 1914, that I would not return to Hungary and join the army, as I was bound to do under the law —

and it would have been easy enough in the first week to slip out of England. I should certainly have returned to fight if I had thought it was the right thing to do, for though I was but a young pseudo-literary ass I was not altogether a rotter. But the idea that I might be accused of being one bothered me, so I wrote to the British War Office, enclosing with my letter one from an important English journalist I knew, and asked if they would take me as a volunteer in the British army. They declined with thanks, and so did the French Consul in Bedford Square whom I went to see, and also the Belgian Consul whose address I forget; but the Belgian Consul was charming about it and did not conceal that he was moved to see a young nincompoop like me, five foot five and hardly athletic-looking, inquire if he were allowed to fight for Belgium, just because he thought that it was the right thing to do. For years I guarded my correspondence with the British War Office as my one and only war souvenir, but in the end I lost it. And if Dr. Seton-Watson had not convinced me before the war that Austria-Hungary was all wrong and Serbia was all right, I should certainly have gone back to Hungary and joined the regiment of garrison artillery to which I had been assigned before I went, on leave as it were, to Copenhagen, and the chances are that I should have got myself killed in the first World War, like so many of my childhood friends, including the good youth whose father gave me my first newspaper job. I was much shaken when I heard, after the war, that he had fallen in battle as a cavalry officer, fighting against the Russians, but now I rather think that it was clever of him; for he was a gallant youth and also a non-Aryan Catholic, and that is not a very good combination in that Hungary of today which has become yet another protectorate of the Fiend.

The long and short of it is that when I saw that the Entente Powers did not particularly want me to fight for them I returned to Copenhagen, leaving London on September 15, 1914, just when they began to douse the street lights because of the Zeppelins, and when they had begun to intern the nationals of the enemy countries. They did not intern me because the official of the War Office who intimated that Kitchener could do without me was

convinced of my good faith and told somebody in the Home
Office about me; and the Home Office let me go, after I had given
my word that I would not join the Austro-Hungarian army; which
I did with pleasure. I was glad to sail for Copenhagen, past the
west coast of Scotland and north of the Shetlands and south by
the coast of Norway, in that small Danish tramp steamer called
Nidaros; for by then I had no money left and could not get any
from Copenhagen, and for the last ten days or so in London I had
been living on bananas. The captain and the chief steward of that
little ship were very good to me and let me travel first class for a
third-class fare, because the first night of the five days' voyage,
which I spent in the forecastle, had made me very sick; they gave
me excellent and plentiful food and beer, and the steward even
lent me ten shillings when he heard I would not have a penny left
when I had bought my railroad ticket from Aarhus to Copenhagen.
And yet I was nothing but a young foreigner whom he did not
know from Adam.

I have already said that the Danes are a very good people; and the
only fault I could find with them when I lived among them, at the
age of twenty-one, was one that I could not put my finger on,
or find an accurate name for, but that I tried to express by saying
to my friends that whereas they did all the small near-by things
exceedingly well they let the big things go, on the ground that it
was no use. Today I know exactly what that fault was, if it was a
fault and not a misfortune. They were an old people, a very
civilized people, and a very tired people; and they waited for the
blow that would fall when it was written that it should. In this
they were like the people of Cnossus, and the people of Egypt in the
days of the terrible lament known as the Admonition of Ipuwer —
about 2500 B.C., that is, just before the Shardana and the Tulsha and
the other Sea Peoples landed; and also like the Romans in the years
that stretched from Alaric to Odoacer; and also like the French in
the days of Daladier, Reynaud, and Pétain. In the last accounting it
was more of a fault than of a misfortune; for people grow tired only
when they lose their faith, and God has given men their reason to
warn them of the danger that lies in the loss of faith, and to guide

them back to the faith which would make them strong again. But this function of the human reason, which I indicate according to the Catholic authorities, is not evident to those who are not Catholics, so I shan't say any more about it.

6

After my return to Copenhagen I wrote several newspaper articles, one or two about my impressions of wartime London, and two or three stating why I, as a Hungarian, thought that the Entente was right and the Central Powers were wrong; and I predicted with much verve that the Allies would win the war and that the whole world would live happily ever after, for, I said, this was a war to end war and to make the world safe for democracy. I even advocated self-determination for the Czechs, Slovaks, Rumanians, and so on, of Austria-Hungary, within a Danubian Confederacy to be established by the Allied victory. We all know by heart that sort of talk now, and also the catastrophe that was to result from it; but in those days it seemed just grand and very advanced; at any rate I had a good three years' start of President Wilson in boosting that fateful fraud. I wrote those articles in English and good people translated them into Danish; and they were printed in the dailies called *Social-Demokraten* (for by this time I was a confirmed and enthusiastic socialist) and in *Politiken*. One of my articles that appeared in the latter in November 1914 made the local Austro-Hungarian Legation quite angry and I was beginning to receive devious messages about the awful things that were going to happen to me if I did not hold my tongue.

It was not, however, the wrath of the Central Empires that eventually made me decide to leave Denmark and try my luck in the United States, but the fact that the war stopped such modest income as I had been earning by freelance work for two Budapest dailies and two or three highbrow magazines. The former would not and the latter dared not publish my pro-Ally stuff, and that was that, and the end for all times of my career as a writer in my native country. There had been moments, in the course of those fifteen months, when I toyed with the idea of settling permanently in Denmark and trying to make good in some line or other; for I loved the country and the life, and the people were very kind. But I realized that the notion was hopeless, because Denmark was not only small but also overcrowded, and sent out swarms of her clever young men all over the world, from Siam to the Argentine. Also, though I now understood the language perfectly, I found speaking it beyond me on account of its tricky pronunciation that makes the difficulties which English heaps on the foreigner seem like child's play; for it is not a question of mere discrepancy between spelling and speech, but of certain very soft guttural consonants that are breathed rather than spoken, and of a frequent curious halt or hesitation between two sounds that makes Danish talk resemble a kind of fluent stuttering, and that no person not Danish born and bred has ever fully mastered. Though later on in America, where I had occasion to practise it, I learned to speak Danish quite well, and can to this day carry on a conversation in it, that particular phonetic stunt has always beaten me, and my Danish sounds like that of a Swede, hard and clear instead of soft and blurred as it should sound.

Yet even had there been no war I should not have returned to Hungary, for my old restlessness had grown on me and my appetite for the exotic was not appeased, but only whetted, by this Danish interlude. There was in my yearning for new empires to conquer more than the usual adventurousness and ambition of youth. What I craved was not so much the thrill of battle or the rewards of success as a wholly new life, and more even than that — a new personality or character in that new life, created by myself not out of or according to my given circumstances but in spite of them. I wanted to be a self-made man, but not in the stereotyped sense of the American success stories, in which a barefoot newsboy comes to own the newspaper that he once peddled, but has remained in all his magnificence the same barefoot newsboy with the same mind, the same outlook, and the same values. I wanted to change, not my fortunes, but myself. I shall, however, explain this crazy notion more fully later on, in the chapter which is to relate how, though failing to write the biography of Stendhal, I succeeded in reliving his life. But I will say right here that though at this time my dream was to be reborn, what I yearned to enter was the kingdom of *this* world, which I considered mine by birthright; and that there was, in my plan to remake myself in my own image, an element of nothing less than blasphemy that was not to remain unavenged.

But for the war — that first World War of 1914 upon which we of 1940 look back almost with nostalgia as upon a better world — I should have remade myself in England, thus realizing the pyrotechnic dream of my childhood that was set off by my uncle's folder of London views; and I should have become an English writer and not only a writer of English. That was out of the question now, and by November 1914 I was preparing for my invasion and conquest of the United States of America. I did this by reading Lord Bryce's *American Commonwealth*, Henry George's *Progress and Poverty*, a volume by Professor Woodrow Wilson entitled *Mere Literature*, and *Roderick Hudson* and *The Princess Casamassima* by Henry James. As a boy of twelve or thirteen I had read *Huckleberry Finn*, *Tom Sawyer*, *A Connecticut Yankee*, *Hiawatha*, *Evangeline*, and the stories of Fenimore Cooper; at sixteen and seventeen I had read Emerson's *Representative Men*, Thoreau's *Walden*, Whitman's *Leaves of Grass*, Motley's *Dutch Republic*, Prescott's *Conquest of Peru*, and Charles Dickens' *American Notes*. I also knew several poems of Edgar Allan Poe by heart; but what made me more pleased with myself than anything else, in this domain of American culture, was that at the age of nineteen I had made, from the psychoanalytical point of view and with the apostolic blessing of Dr. Alexander Ferenczi, a special study of all the stories of the same author, and thought that I had discovered, in the story entitled "The Pit and the Pendulum," the Freudian key to all his secrets. So I thought now that taken all in all I had given myself as thorough a grounding in American ideas and American ways as I could wish, and I faced the future with confidence.

In those last two or three months in Copenhagen I made friends with a group of Russian refugees from Germany who before the war had lived there in exile. Most of them belonged to the Social Revolutionary Party, the one Kerensky was to make famous later on; but a few were said to adhere to another Marxistic school of thought of which I did not catch the name, for I was not particularly interested in the niceties of those Russian ideologies. But I noted that while the Social Revolutionaries that I knew were cultivated and charming people, anxious to make a good impression, those others were gloomy and brusque and looked as if they hated and despised the world; and I was inclined to put this down to their bad digestion and worse breeding. One of my S.R. friends, an accomplished essayist who wrote and published in Russian, German, and Yiddish, seemed anxious that I should meet some man of this second group who he said was a very remarkable person and one of whom the world would yet hear. My friend tried to arrange a meeting, but something always cropped up to interfere — either the man walked out by the front door of the café as I came in by a side entrance, or else I missed a party owing to being invited out of town over the week end, and all that sort of thing. So I never came to meet this man. I confess that I did not try very hard; I thought my friend might have exaggerated his remarkableness, and I disliked most of these Russians who talked, as the Viennese say, holes into your stomach and asked personal questions and poked your ribs with their index fingers when they wanted to emphasize a point. The man's name, by the way, was Leon Trotsky.

But another man who was to make history I did meet toward the end of my Copenhagen days, at a dinner party in the house of a Swedish nobleman who was my friend. This man was tall and handsome and looked extremely smart in his evening clothes, and was introduced to me as a Russian general, but he had what sounded like a German name, though it turned out to be Swedish. We spoke of the war, and I was shocked no end to hear a high officer of the Tsar express confidence in a German victory. He seemed shocked even more to hear a young Hungarian contradict him and toast the victory of England and France; and he explained that he was a Finn and the Russians had oppressed his people for the past century, so he was naturally for the Germans; whereupon I explained that the Germans had oppressed *my* people for the past four centuries, so I was just as naturally for the Allies. But while I could see his point I had the impression that he could not see mine — not because he was slow, for he seemed a very remarkable man, but because he had other things on his mind while he talked, and had the air of one who was forever pondering a plan. He spoke Swedish to me which I understood but could not speak, and I answered him in German; and the reader has probably guessed by now that my neighbor at that dinner party was no other than Baron Mannerheim, who was later to free Finland from the Russian yoke, and still later to lead one of the most famous campaigns in the annals of mankind, the story of which would be remembered with that of Leonidas and his Lacedaemonians; and he was certainly the greatest hero and the greatest gentleman with whom I was ever privileged to share a meal. But at the time I could not know this.

And so, a few weeks after this dinner party, which I instantly forgot but was to remember in 1918 when Mannerheim chased the Asiatics out of Finland, I came to eat the last mouthful of the bread which, so the Turks say, or maybe the Arabs, God deposits for each man in each place through which he is to pass on his pilgrimage to the grave; and once his allotted store in a certain place is consumed he has no choice but must move on to the next. On January 28, 1915, I embarked on the Danish steamer *Hellig Olav*, which was to take me to the conquest of America; and now that the moment had come I was sorry to leave, and frightened of arriving. I had not then seen my native city of Budapest for over a year, my last visit having been a short one at Christmas time in 1913. I have not been back to Hungary since, and it looks very much now as if I were never to tread her soil again, never to see the embankment of the Danube with its acacia trees, and the hills and palaces on the opposite shore, with the old citadel on top of Mount St. Gerald which in Hungarian is called Gellérthegy. I remember this as one of the most beautiful sights in the whole world. Nor do I want to set foot on the continent of Europe as long as Hitler and his hordes desecrate its ground; unless it be as a member of an American Expeditionary Force.

I only remember of that, my first, crossing to America one incident, which occurred on the second day. The *Hellig Olav* berthed at the quay at Oslo, which was then called Christiania, early in the morning, and we were allowed to go on shore; but Christiania was not an interesting town, so I took a cab or a tram, I don't remember which, to the mountain beyond the city called Holmenkollen, and had lunch there by myself in a kind of chalet, and was greatly taken by the calm beauty of that wintry landscape. I especially remember the beautiful blood-red flag of Norway, flown from a mast on top of the hill, against a background of snow and firs. The sun was setting behind the low mountains as our ship steamed out of the winding Christiania Fjord, and on the deck a group of Norwegian emigrants stood with bared heads around a Norwegian flag and sang their national anthem; the words of this are by Björnson and are very fine, and the tune is slow and of a majestic swell; I have always thought that it is the most inspired of all national airs in the world, next to the "Marseillaise." But there is a reference, in the first stanza, to that last great night that will sink on our earth at the end of time; and it has always seemed to me that that was not a happy note for a national anthem to strike.

The flag that is flown today from that mast on Holmenkollen is still blood-red; only the charge on it is not the beautiful blue and white cross of Saint George, but the black swastika of Hitler, that devilish parody and desecration of a cross that has grown claws. And the great night has descended on Norway, and on Europe.

VII. Another "Life of Stendhal"

I LANDED in New York, or more accurately in Hoboken, about four o'clock in the afternoon on February 9, 1915. By five o'clock I was installed in a modest little room in the Chelsea district. At nine o'clock that evening I had a job as a newspaper writer. My next move toward the annexation, with indemnities, of the United States was to take out my first citizenship papers. This I did within a week. When in May 1920 I was handed my naturalization certificate the clerk of the court congratulated me on having done the thing in record time.

Securing a job in my own line of work within five hours of my arrival in the New World was undoubtedly a piece of good luck, but not quite the miracle that it might seem. For I called at that dingy little office of a Hungarian Socialist newspaper, somewhere below Astor Place, in my quality of a Hungarian Socialist journalist who had arrived from Europe that very day; and whatever class I might have been in as a newspaperman, I was certainly in the first class as news, being probably the only Hungarian male of military age to have crossed the Atlantic since the outbreak of the war six months earlier. Had I been a lawyer, a businessman, or a singing waiter, the paper would have splashed an interview with me across its front page the next morning. As I was a newspaperman, they let me interview myself and write it up; they did this partly because they were decent people, willing to help a newcomer, and partly because they were short of help. So I was engaged as associate editor, foreign editor, and special columnist, all in one, at the munificent salary of twelve dollars a week. What pleased me most, since it fulfilled my hopes, was that many Hungarian Socialists in the United States, and also a section of those Hungarians who were not Socialists, shared my pro-Ally views, detested the Germans and all their works, and feared a German victory from the point of view of world democracy in general, and from that of the true interests of Hungary in particular. So I could now let myself go, and I did.

About a year after this start another Hungarian newspaper, which we in our Socialist jargon called bourgeois, and which had a much larger circulation, offered me a job at triple the salary I had been earning. I argued to myself, and to my colleagues, that if a bourgeois publisher was willing to feed a Socialist who would go on writing the truth as he saw it, the cause would gain and not lose, especially as the bourgeois paper would bring those Socialist views before a much larger public, one that an avowedly Socialist publication could not hope to reach. I see now that I argued thus because I was not really a Socialist at all, but a democratic liberal, and because I did not give a hoot for Marxism but was solely interested in doing pro-Ally propaganda among American Hungarians. So I wrote to the publisher in question and said that I would accept his offer on condition that I was allowed to express my views freely in his newspaper, under my signature. To my surprise, he engaged me on these terms; so I moved to Cleveland, Ohio, where that newspaper was published, and lived there from January 1916 until September 1918. My job consisted of writing a daily signed column, more or less about everything; in this I was allowed to say what I thought about the war, as long as I made it clear that I spoke for myself only and not for the newspaper, which was fair enough. After a while I secured a part-time reportorial job on the *Plain Dealer.*

I had worked on the Hungarian newspaper for about eighteen months when one day my employers decided that I was throwing my weight about too much, and sacked me. I immediately obtained a job on the *Cleveland Press,* and now my dream had come true and I was an American newspaperman in the strict sense of the word and on full time. At first I did sundry reportorial assignments, which I detested; I regarded the whole dogma and ritual of "scoops" as a humbug and a bore. After a while I was promoted, or perhaps demoted, to a desk job, and made state editor, in charge of all the newborn triplets and two-headed calves in Ohio. Then an exclusive interview which I secured from Professor Masaryk, at this time president of the Czechoslovak National Council, on his arrival from Siberia in May 1918, and two or three articles published in the *New Republic*, established me as a sort of expert on European politics, and I joined the ranks of those who clamored for the breaking up of the Habsburg Empire in the name of national self-determination. The egg laid by the books of Dr. Seton-Watson three years earlier had hatched, and the chicken had come home to roost. I was the chicken.

In September 1918 I decided to go the way of all Midwestern newspaper flesh and to try my luck in New York. A day or two after the Armistice I was engaged by the then managing editor, Mr. Garet Garrett, on the staff of the *New York Tribune*. I was soon made editor of the Sunday foreign news section, and editorial writer; and for the next two years and a half I held down as pleasant a job as anyone may wish, though it was hardly overpaid; but I was young, and pleased as Punch with the kudos and responsibility of my position. Then the managing editor who had replaced Mr. Garrett, Mr. George D. Smith, died, and one of the first things his successor did was to fire me. He did this without rancor, and without even any particular cause; it is the way of new managing editors to begin their reign by reducing the payroll.

One incident of those *Tribune* years stands out. I had to write an editorial that had something to do with the Zuider Zee, and I inquired aloud, of the universe at large, where the hell can I get information about Holland. Whereupon one of the men with whom I shared a room said I did not need to go quite as far as that, since there was a chap right in the *Tribune* building, working in the office of a Dutch firm of exporters, who knew all about Holland; why didn't I go to see him? I went, and sure enough found a great big chap who not only told me what I wanted to know, but also invited me to lunch at Haan's Rathskeller. And that is the way I first met Hendrik Willem Van Loon, though I had already known his name from the columns of the *New Republic* and the *Nation*. He was to be my best friend during the three years that followed, before I drifted to Europe, and he drifted to fame and riches with the aid of the cunning little pictures that he was already drawing when I first met him, and the little stories he was telling, about how big things were done in the old days; it was a trade and a literary genre that he had invented himself, and I cannot easily think of another man who has done as much as he to make Americans, whose minds are oriented toward the future, take interest in the past, whence the future emerges. But in those days we were both poor and without fame. We had nevertheless a very good time, playing chess in Greenwich Village, and talking about both the past and the future, and eating dinners according to the money we happened to have in our pockets; and he played, on the violin or the gramophone, the music of Bach, which we both preferred to any other. It is good to look back on the brightness of those days from a present much less bright. We made a funny pair to look at, for he is very tall and I am short and stocky; rather like Mutt and Jeff.

2

The months that followed the loss of my *Tribune* job are registered in my memory as a kind of professional and intellectual twilight, lit up in patches by a concert or two that I went to hear at Carnegie Hall, performances of the music especially of Bach and of Sibelius, and by a sort of steady glow in the background, which was the friendship of Hendrik Van Loon and also of William Seabrook and his wife Katie. William Seabrook was at this time a very disgruntled newspaperman during the day, and a very pleasant partner of chess games and high intellectual disputation in the evening, these occurring in a kind of cosy private café in Waverly Place, kept by Katie for the benefit of their friends; the custom of strangers was tolerated but not encouraged. I had many a savory dinner there, cooked in the authentic style of Katie Seabrook's native South; and when I had not the cash to pay for them, which happened not infrequently, nothing further was said about it, and I believe that I was not her only customer of this expensive sort. And it just strikes me, as I write this, that though it would be difficult to line up three men as different in almost every respect save a respect for the things of the mind and a love of music, which all three of us shared, as Hendrik Willem Van Loon, William Seabrook, and myself, there was something in the mood of each of us in those days that the other two had also, and that set us apart from most people, and especially from the happy-go-lucky newspapermen who were Seabrook's colleagues at this time and had been mine but recently. I can best describe this something as an ever-nagging discontent that is closely akin to what people of the world call ambition, but is at once more and less than ambition, for it sets its aim both higher and lower; and that drives those who are cursed with it, or maybe blessed, to spend many days loafing and brooding or fretting over small unimportant things, and then again their nights in furious concentrated work; and that makes them impatient with what most people call amusement. Willie Seabrook had this thing, which some would call the divine fire and others a highbrow itch, to a remarkable degree in those old Greenwich Village days; so I was not surprised when five years later, in Europe, I heard that he was now celebrated and prosperous as the author of books that not only sold but were also worth buying. But the same something only made me bury myself in a garden in Provence; for I was probably much more impatient than those two, and was therefore condemned to wait.

Goethe says somewhere that a person's life may be divided into progressive and regressive periods, and that the latter are marked by an overwhelming preoccupation with the past. I have never in a lifetime, during which the past always meant to me more than to most people, been so exclusively concerned with a rehearsal of bygone days as in these last six weeks, writing this pseudo-auto-biography that now begins to look not so pseudo as all that; but I am not sure now that I would agree with Goethe in calling these six weeks regressive, for I have made my way to the understanding of many things that puzzled me in my own life; and he who proceeds to understand anything cannot be said to yield ground. But this again is rambling, for all I meant to say in the first place was that those months in and around Waverly Place were, though on the whole the source of pleasing memories, also, on the whole, a "down" period.

The next "up" chapter of my life opened one day in the first quarter of 1922, though I could not come nearer than that to fixing it to save myself from a firing squad. A friend, an older man well-versed in the ways of this world, came to me on that day and said, why not write a book? I said why not indeed, but what sort of book, and who would publish a book written by a nonentity like myself? My friend said, "I shall tell you." And he did. So a few days later I not only signed a contract with a publisher, for a first book of which not one line was written, but also pocketed a very decent advance against royalties, which I needed badly. That was how I made my first contact with George Palmer Putnam, and for the next five years he was my best friend, though not in the sense in which I have already assigned that role to Hendrik Van Loon, for the period that is now drawing to a close in these pages as I approach my first return to Europe; that is to say, in the sense of smoking numberless pipes together till dawn and playing chess and putting a record of Bach's Concerto for two violins on the gramophone while the bacon is sizzling in the kitchenette, and the cat upsets the glass of beer; and that to my mind is as good a description of what happens when one man is the best friend of another as any I have ever seen. But there exists another sense of the same term, and this I will apply to George Palmer Putnam, in the five years from 1922 to 1927. He believed that I would be a really good writer one day, and he proved his belief by his actions; and as that day seemed to recede rather than approach, he did not lose his faith but did what he could to make me live up to it. He also saved me from feeling, in later years, like a fool, by rejecting a very silly novel of mine which I sent him in manuscript from France, in 1928. He helped me in every way in which a publisher can help a young tyro of an author; and he was patient with me far longer than I should have been with him had our positions been reversed. So if that is not a best friend, in this second professional, as distinguished from the first personal, sense, what is?

My book was a collection of ten short biographical essays on Continental personages then in the limelight. I wrote the greater part of it in Baltimore, where I spent five or six pleasant months and made some friends. I came back to New York in the fall of 1922, and it was then that I had my first taste of being really hard-up in America; I had a nice enough room and had paid my rent in advance for a month, but meals were a great problem, and some were destined not to advance beyond the problem stage. Yet my situation was anything but hopeless, for my book was in the press and I was to get another sum of money down the day it was out. That day came, and I was paid the sum of money, and before I had had time to spend it (though these things don't take much time with me) I found that I was a success. Not a very great, spectacular, Deck-A sort of success, just a little, homely, tourist-class one, that ran, in time, to three editions; but it was just the same the fated preliminary to all the grandeur and all the misery that followed. The critics, above all Elmer Davis and F.P.A., were very kind to me and overpraised my book: they said that it was an honest book, which was true, for I believed in the truth of what I wrote and in the rightness of writing it; they also said that it was a clever book, and this was true too, but today I am no longer proud of having written a book labeled clever. For cleverness is the curse of those who have a sort of mind but do not know what minds are for. And my cleverness in that book was something without focus and purpose, drifting from one wisecrack to the next for its own unimportant sake. Yet in those days I was very pleased, and it would have been strange had I not been; for I was no more a newspaperman out of a job, but an Author.

A few months later, in March 1923 to be exact, I went to Vienna with an assignment from a newspaper syndicate. In October I was back in New York, but by January I was once more on my way to Europe, having secured a roving commission from the *Sunday Magazine* of the *New York Times*. My program was to obtain a series of interviews with prominent British and Continental scientists, scholars, and other public figures, to whom I proposed to submit a list of questions concerning the state and prospects of Western civilization. I had framed my questionnaire under the influence of Spengler's *Decline of the West*, which I had read in Vienna; at this time I thought Spengler a very great prophet, and though I have since arrived at a more accurate estimate of his worth, I still recognize that I owe him a great deal, for it was his book that first aroused my interest in the philosophy of history. My interviews were to be published in the *New York Times Sunday Magazine* by Lester Markel, and were later to be reprinted in a book. I thought this a grand scheme, and on my arrival in London I set about its execution with gusto: I sent my questionnaire to some eighteen or twenty shining lights of English culture, and got what I wanted from about seven or eight, among them Bertrand (now Earl) Russell, Dr. (now Sir) Alfred Zimmern, Sir Charles Oman, and others whose names I forget; their replies made excellent reading, and were duly published by Mr. Markel. The others declined politely, either on the ground that they disapproved of the trend of my questions, which I see now was not a difficult thing to do, or else with the no less reasonable excuse that they were accustomed to write their own articles. But one correspondent was extremely abrupt in turning down my very courteous and well-meant request; his note was to the effect that he preferred not to give interviews to American newspapermen, and as far as I knew this was not even true, for this scholar, whose haughty un-Christian tone surprised me, was no other than Dean Inge. But the kindest and most understanding of those with whom I had to deal on this occasion was Professor Zimmern.

As the shrewd reader may already have noticed, I had a way of getting tired of my own excellent ideas and laudable departures before I had given them, and myself, a chance; and my grand project of a synthetic Spengleriad came to nothing. By May I had convinced Mr. George Palmer Putnam that the one and only task for which I was predestined was to write the first biography, not only in English but in any language to date, of the last but one Emperor of Austria and King of Hungary, Francis Joseph. So I returned to Vienna and set to work with greater gusto than ever, and it took me exactly three years to write a book that I see now I could easily have completed in eighteen months.

At the risk of disappointing the reader, who for whatever reason might like to hear about them, I shall give no account here of those three Vienna years, for two reasons. First, I lack the space; and second, I feel that I should disappoint him far more by giving him the only sort of account that I could truthfully give than by a tactful and economical reticence. For most American, and also English, people who carry in their minds or souls images of foreign places have a very special corner reserved in that gallery for Vienna, a corner lighted by a radiance that is hardly of this world, but issues from dreams in which mingle strains of Mozart, Beethoven, Schubert, and Johann Strauss, couplets from Hofmannsthal, and pages from Arthur Schnitzler and Peter Altenberg, with the glamour of first nights at Reinhardt's, with the luminous eighteenth-century vistas of Canaletto, with the lively images of the Opernring at dusk, the great Square of Heroes in front of the Hofburg and that small square behind it; baroque palaces and churches, and the cool green silence of the Wienerwald. But even to a great many Americans and English people who have never heard of those things, the name of Vienna is a banner, and a symbol of something distant and lovely — of gay color and rollicking dance tunes and a carefree life of wine and song in cafés where the bill is never presented, and in White Horse Inns where every waitress is a soprano in a short skirt and tight-fitting bodice, and every bouncer a tenor, and of all the rest of that musical-comedy heaven sold by Herr Lehar and other members of the trade in millions of copies at a cut rate, on the basis of small profit, large turnover.

Now if I were to tell the reader, whom I suppose to belong to the former and not to the latter degree of the Universal Grand Order of Vienna-lovers, all that I think of Vienna, he would say that I have robbed him of something valuable and valued. So I shall say nothing, except that I, too, carried with me that image to a Vienna which I had never seen until, at the age of thirty-one, I arrived there from London via New York, although I had been born in a city only five hours distant by rail, but as the son of a people which, though historically and politically associated with Austria for centuries, was as different from the people of Austria as it was from that of Denmark or Portugal, in its mode of life and temperament and outlook. I *lived* that dream during those three years in which I wrote a book that I might have written in one; and my study of Austrian history even served to broaden and deepen the dream, and if I did not learn a great deal in that period I learned at least three things. First, that the armies of Prince Eugene and of Salm and Starhemberg had been no less Austrian than the army of intellectuals which now filled the cafés of the Ring and the Herrengasse, and that the tragedies and odes and diptychs of Grillparzer, and the comedies of Nestroy, were rather more representative of the genius of Vienna than the modern best-sellers of Herr Felix Salten. Second, I learned that the best thing about a great city was that it was a place from which you could escape into the country. I loved Vienna, but I loved even more the Austrian countryside, to which I ran away every time I had a chance in those three years; and I know in retrospect that the life in Vienna, with its spaciousness and leisure, suited my temper better than did ever the life of Paris, where the tables that touched one another in the restaurants were a symbol, and where everybody was in a hurry and bumped into you at every turn. But the third thing I learned was this: that the Vienna of the dream was a dream, and that the Viennese of the twentieth century were not like the Viennese of the dream at all. Some day I shall perhaps say more about this subject, but not now.

3

At or about six o'clock on the morning of April 27, in the year 1927, an observer who happened to be on the spot and had nothing better to observe might have seen a thick-set, clean-shaven young man in well-cut gray flannels, accompanied by a small white wire-haired female fox terrier, step off the Geneva–Nice express of the

P.L.M. railroad onto the platform of the station of St. Raphaël, in the Department of the Var which used to form part of the province of Provence, in Southern France. About eight o'clock of an evening in early October, in the year 1932, another observer, situate as the first, might have seen the same thick-set clean-shaven young man, now slightly less young, in the same gray flannels, slightly the worse for wear, climb, accompanied by three small white wire-haired female fox terriers, from the same station platform onto the fast train for Paris. Those who know the good people of St. Raphaël would add that it was probably the same observer.

It occurs to me that it might save my time and that of the reader if I admitted without further hedging that the young (and respectively the rather less young) man in question was myself. I might add that the excess of two small white wire-haired fox-terrier bitches represented the total increase of my worldly fortunes in the course of those five years and five months, which had come and gone without my particularly noticing that they had.

To give a consistent chronological account of those years and months, in the manner in which I have already given such account of earlier periods, and also of later ones, of my life, would be for me entirely impossible; it would also be entirely superfluous. The outstanding fact about my return, for all that time, to a kind of vegetative form of existence is that it was unintentional and unplanned. Rip van Winkle had never been Rip van Winkle by a deliberate and purposeful act of his will. What had happened was this: About April 15, 1927, I had dispatched the last chapters of my life of Francis Joseph to a long-suffering George Palmer Putnam in New York. The proofs of same had to be sent to some address. I had decided that after all those labors in Vienna, of about four or five hours a day five or four days a week, I needed a rest, and also a change from the somewhat top-heavy Austrian style of cooking string beans and other vegetables with a generous seasoning of pork fat and flour. I had also decided that the best stage for such a rest would be the South of France, partly because I liked the South of France, having got acquainted with it on two short winter holidays from the same labors in Vienna, and partly because many other important writers used to recover from their important exertions in the South of France.

Two or three days after my arrival at St. Raphaël, lunching at my modest but comfortable hotel, I was addressed by a tall gentleman with a drooping white mustache, who occupied the next table and looked every inch the retired British colonel that he was, with the query whether I cared to go for a drive in his car that afternoon. I said that I would do so with great pleasure. He drove me to a little village, or rather resort, on the coast, fifteen miles east of St. Raphaël, called Le Trayas. A year before, hiking along the same coast, I had noticed, in the same locality, a charming and cosy-looking little house built in the Provençal style, surrounded by tall pines, and I had said to myself it would be just lovely to live in that house; so I rang the bell and was told by a courteous French-Swiss gentleman that the villa, of which he was tenant, was neither for sale nor to let, but that he would be pleased to show me over it anyway.

On the afternoon when Colonel Wickham drove me to Le Trayas the house was still there; what was more, it was to let, or for sale. So, proper arrangements having been made, I moved into that house, thinking that I would correct the proofs of my book there as they arrived from America, and that when the book was published in the fall, and had sold its first thirty thousand copies, I would return to New York and hold levees in my suite at the Waldorf-Astoria and would allow frantic publishers and kow-towing magazine editors and persuasive syndicate presidents to force lucrative contracts on me, and would live happily ever after in places of my choice. The proofs arrived, were corrected and returned; the book was published, and in the course of time was purchased by some 3500 or 4000 curious and well-intentioned people, and was then duly and completely forgotten by them and everybody else. It was, as I see it now, a much better book than my first, which had sold better; it was more mature, less given to wisecracks, and far more seriously conceived and executed, and it presented a quite good panoramic view of eighty years of European history. These merits were duly acknowledged by a number of reviewers; but at the same time the book was longer than it should have been, and more loosely knit; and its publication coincided with that of a biography of Kaiser Wilhelm, a much more spectacular and better-publicized personage than his Austrian friend and ally who had loathed and despised him; and this biography had been manufactured by that great and famous Henry Ford of the biographical industry, Herr Emil Ludwig, and may have been, for aught I know, a much better book than mine. I never read it.

The upshot of it all was that the New York publishers preserved, in respect to me, a remarkable *sang-froid*, instead of going off their heads with admiration and hope; and there were no suites for me at the Waldorf-Astoria, and no levees, and no fat contracts. It was very disappointing, but it did not break my heart; for although I was, as the shrewd reader may already have guessed, an easy mark for my own schemes of grandeur in those days, I had sense enough to realize that such awakenings were all in the day's work. So once more I cut my losses, and sat down and wrote, in three weeks, a play about certain imaginary personages in a make-believe kingdom of Southeastern Europe; and a friend showed this play to a producer in Paris, who was kind enough to accept it, and unscrupulous enough to go bust before the famous French playwright, who was supposed to translate it into French and to adapt it to the Paris stage, had a chance to do his job. By this time I was a champion loss-cutter, and without giving the Paris fiasco more than one or two thoughts I sent my play to various agents in London and New York who wrote me optimistic letters at first, and then no letters, and then went and lost my typescript, in several copies, and forgot all about it. But I understand that these things will happen. In the meantime I had converted the plot of this play into a novel, which I finished in six weeks, and had returned in three by George Palmer Putnam with the advice to think again.

These goings-on occupied me for part of the year 1928. After the untimely death of my innocent young novel I decided that I was no author and locked up my typewriter; but I went on using my fountain pen, more or less daily, making notes about the books I read, and putting on paper what I thought were my thoughts. But apart from such vague preparations for an unspecified battle to come I did not write anything between the years 1927 and 1933, with the exception of three articles, on topics that had arisen from my life in France; these were published in *Harper's Magazine*, and it took me six months to turn out each. A friend who watched me at these creative labors remarked that they did not seem a very profitable way of employing time, an assertion which I found difficult to contradict. And that is as fair a précis of my professional activities during those five years and five months at Le Trayas as could be expected by any friend of mine who wondered then, and may still wonder, whether my grave in some remote part of the world is properly tended.

In an earlier chapter of this book I related how I had driven, in the early days of the present war, from Castelnaudary in Languedoc to Pau in Béarn, in so exhausted and highly strung a frame of mind that I now remember nothing of that trip except a few place names, and for the rest an emerald haze. I might say the same of the five years that I spent at Le Trayas; except that the reason for their images getting blurred in my mind was not fatigue, but the lax, undisciplined, purpose-free, and generally goofy quality of my mind in that whole period. I saw and took in and thought a good deal but retained very little, though I see now that I had retained more than I was aware of having done at the time. For the sake of accuracy I ought also to add that this haze which has come to crowd out of my mind more articulate memories of my Le Trayas years is not colored emerald, like that Pyrenean afterglow, but changes its hue according to the season and even the time of the day upon which I happen to focus the spyglass of recollection. And I see the blinding white of summer noons, the mellow gold of October, the luminous and tender greens and mauves of the eastern sky after sundown, reflected in a mirror-smooth nacreous sea; and, in the days when I would wander away from my coast, that roseate limpidity which is peculiar to all Provence, and which the traveler who comes from the North first notes as he leaves behind Montélimar on the left bank of the Rhône, or Serres or Gap in the Alps, but which he will hail much sooner, for a reason which I have not been able to fathom, on the slopes of Vivarais, if he comes from the northwest to descend on the right bank of the Rhône above Viviers. But I see what is perhaps the most glorious of all these images of a past that now seems to contain a great range of illumination and no shadows at all when I think of certain dawns in March; of dawns when, after sitting up all night with Bergson or Kant or Dorothy Sayers, I would step to my window to find the universe filled by a light that cannot be described, since it had neither color, pitch, nor any other namable quality, but was just light, light *in et per se*, essential light, pure evenly diffused luminousness. Day after day, for I liked those all-night sessions, I would see, in the same sector of the southeastern horizon, a wall of massive cloud, towering in fantastic rugged indigo shapes outlined in gold against flame-red; and I had seen this vision six or seven times, much puzzled why the same cloud should appear in the same place and in the same shape day after day, before I realized that what I saw was no cloud at all but the mountains of Corsica. For that great island, a little over a hundred miles distant, could be seen from my home in the hillside of Le Trayas only for a few minutes before the sun emerged from behind its serrated summits, but disappeared immediately after that; and only in the month of March, and only on mornings when the mistral had swept the skies clear of even the tiniest specks of cloud. And four or five times in those years I saw, on such occasions, not one crimson sun but two, one dipping into the sea in front of the island as the other slipped out above and extinguished the whole apparition; an illusion which I leave to learned opticians and meteorologists to account for.

But let the external happenings of those six years rest in the blessed peace of those multicolored and glamorous mists. I will only refer, for they have an integral part in my impersonal story, to my travels in my little car, when I first explored Provence, thoroughly enough yet not nearly as thoroughly as I might wish, and also the strip of the lower Languedoc which stretches from St. Gilles on the Rhône to Carcassonne, and includes Nimes and the Pont du Gard. I also went further afield, and visited Perpignan and the Eastern Pyrenees as far as Mont-Louis and Font-Romeu in Cerdagne; Dijon and Beaune in Burgundy; the Vosges of Lorraine and Alsace, and that lovely French city of Strasbourg which today is French no more. Also Aurillac in upper Auvergne, and Mende in Gevaudan, and the great gorges of the river Tarn, and all the Cévennes country beloved by Robert Louis Stevenson; and Besançon in Franche-Comté, where Victor Hugo was born, and where Julien Sorel, the hero of Stendhal's great novel, had been to school; and parts of the Jura, when I visited Geneva on two occasions which involved crossing the high passes of the Alps on my way home. And thus it was in the winter of 1927 that I first got to know Paris, though I had been there before three or four times, but only for a day or two; in the course of my six Le Trayas years I visited Paris about twice yearly, and stayed a few weeks each time. Two other cities of France that I became familiar with in those days were Toulon and Grenoble: Toulon, because an old friend lived in the town, or near it, of which more anon; and Grenoble, because it was the town of Stendhal. But of this, too, I shall have more to say by and by.

There are also, emerging from the haze of those years, the faces of friends. New ones that I made in the South, like Colonel Wickham, to whom I have already referred. He was seventy when I first met him, but his age did not stop him from driving his car, all alone, from London to St. Raphaël every December, and back again in June; he was happy only when he could do little good turns to others, like taking carless visitors for excursions, or teaching young folk to drive. I tried to make him talk of his experiences as a soldier, but found this rather difficult. I had known him a year before he let slip that he had been in the siege of Ladysmith in the Boer War, when the small British garrison of that fortress earned great fame by its heroism; and I had known him three years before a casual remark of his led to a cross-examination in the course of which he reluctantly admitted that he had marched with Younghusband to Lhasa, the forbidden capital of Thibet. English soldiers are like that.

But the most intimate new friend, and of all those new friends the one who was to play the most important part in my life, was Ludwig Lewisohn, whom I had first met in the old Vienna days and then again in Paris, and who came to stay with me later on at Le Trayas three or four times. I admired his immense erudition and his prompt and forceful way of marshaling and expressing his thoughts, but in many matters he and I did not see eye to eye at all; and yet that did not prevent me from being happy in, and greatly stimulated by, his company. I was very sorry to lose him when he returned to America in 1933; and I hoped that his *Expression in America*, a good part of which he had written under my eyes, as it were, would be recognized as the masterpiece of penetrating imaginative scholarship that it is.

There were other faces too, faces that came out of the past, only to return much too soon whence they had come. One was a large, generously molded Nordic face; its owner, Hendrik Willem Van Loon, had the from my point of view objectionable habit of coming to Paris only on flying visits, and of refusing to come South at all, though I had asked him to more than once. Another was the face of a great serious tomcat who wore his hair *en brosse*, as the French say, though in American that style is called, I believe, pompadour. And this face delighted me more than any other in those days, for William Seabrook, who now was no more a grumbling newspaperman in Greenwich Village, but an opulent author of international fame, loved Provence as much as I did, and we not only passed many an agreeable day and evening together in Paris, but he also came to stay with me at Le Trayas, or else I went to stay with him at his house at Bandol near Toulon, or at Toulon itself, where he spent some weeks from time to time in the studio on the quay that belonged to that great lover of Provence, Ford Madox Ford. And I will say this of William Seabrook here, that he differs from most people I know by dint of a certain intellectual modesty; for most people will pretend that they know a good deal more than they really do, but William Seabrook, I found, used to hide his light under a bushel, and tried to appear an average intelligent reader of subjects in which he possessed special knowledge.

I see finally, just as that haze curtain of the past is about to drop, faces of which I shall say but little; they were little fuzzy faithful faces, the faces of my dogs. I had many of them, for at one moment I fooled myself by thinking it would be fun to breed wire-haired terriers; but it was not long before I knew better, when they fell ill, or when I had to give away or sell a litter because it was impossible to keep them all. And it is the source of much regret to me that I only know of four where they lie buried. But one little copper box I have with me, and shall keep.

4

What remains with me of those six years, in front of that curtain which I do not intend to raise again in these pages, is the smell of pines; and the books I read. As to the first, I have never been, and shall never be, able to enter a pinewood, especially in the vibrant heat of summer, without having the images of my life of Le Trayas flash past my inner eyes with the speed of light. As to the books, I do not think that their number in those six years was particularly large; not one eighth, probably, of what I had read between the years of twelve and eighteen. Books were not easy to get, for my means were limited and did not run to subscriptions to those marvelous but expensive English lending libraries, the London Library and the *Times* Book Club. There was a small but surprisingly good English circulating library in Cannes, kept on a commercial basis by an Australian couple; its stock was constantly renewed, and I borrowed there what was available, and bought what I could afford to buy. Incidentally, this difficulty of obtaining books contributed to my decision, taken after the failure of my *Francis Joseph* to run into a third edition, to leave the biographical industry alone. For in those days I thought that one had to read biographies if one wanted to write other biographies. Today I realize that the libraries of Nice and Aix-en-Provence, within easy reach, not to mention others, contained more unpublished material for fascinating biographical research than I could hope to exhaust in a lifetime. And it is not only a fact, but also a fact of which I was fully aware at the time, that one of the reasons that prompted me to take up a systematic, more or less, study of philosophy was that it could be pursued by means of a comparatively small number of books, most of which I was in the position to purchase secondhand from Foyle's or from Vienna.

It occurs to me that I have forgotten to explain why, after my brief but unprofitable excursion into the fields of fiction and the drama in 1928, I did not do the only businesslike thing that was there for me to do, namely, return to the United States. Well, that is just how it was. I had forgotten to return, and this is a fact. Every now and then I realized, with a pang, that I had forgotten to do something extremely important, and with a little anamnesis, which is the scientific term for prodding one's own goofiness, I even managed to recall that something — it was buying a ticket to New York. Of course I knew enough psychology to realize that this forgetfulness was not the mere spontaneous fading-out of a purpose, but the purposeful obliteration of a purpose. In plain English, it was due to wounded vanity and frustrated pride, and to the hope of mending what had gone wrong within the next six months. Then the six months passed, and I was still where I had been; and then I ceased to count the months, and then the years.

I set out to study philosophy by having sent to me, from a Vienna bookstore kept by friends, Windelband's introduction to philosophy, and also his two histories of philosophy — the one a general textbook covering the whole field, the other a collection of monographs in two volumes. I selected Windelband because I thought, rightly, that he was more colorless than the alternatives I had in mind, Cassirer and other adherents of the Marburg school. Only at the time I called this preferred lack of character objectivity. If today I were asked by an adult possessor of a university education and an average intelligence how to approach the study of philosophy, I should unhesitatingly tell him to read, first, the works of Plato, without footnotes, from cover to cover, and second, a good annotated edition of Aristotle; he would then be in the position to proceed on his own. This is what I ought to have done, but did not know enough to do. Also, I see now that given my psychological approach to the theory of knowledge, and my initial anti-Freudian and anti-rationalist conviction that the mind of man changes its scales of importance in the course of history, I ought to have turned to Max Scheler at a very early stage; had I done so, I should have saved myself three or four years of blind groping. As it was, the first philosopher whom I tried to read after I had gone through my long-distance apprenticeship under that painstaking and reliable, but wholly uncreative Heidelberg professor was A. N. Whitehead; which was just like my foolhardy attack, at the age of twelve, on Beethoven's most difficult sonata. I read *Science and the Modern World* with great enthusiasm, but without understanding more than isolated sentences.

It is, however, not my purpose to take the reader through either a preliminary or an advanced course in philosophy, nor yet to sketch the stages of my own progress in that fundamental department of knowledge, which to most outsiders seems to bristle with unsurmountable difficulties, but which in reality, once the first steps have been overcome and the idiom has been mastered, is no more abstruse than any other pursuit that engages the cogwheels of the brain, if the brain has cogwheels, which does not seem likely. At any rate I found philosophy a good deal easier than bridge, in which noble mental exercise the good Colonel Wickham gave me, at this time, a few lessons, until one day he declared that he would prefer as a pupil one of his Indian army mules. I told him that his preference was reasonable enough.

It was in this period that I discovered a form of relaxation to which I was to remain addicted during thirteen years, and more accurately until midnight, May 9, 1940. Two or three days after my arrival at St. Raphaël, toward the end of April, 1927, I found myself at a loose end and was looking for something to play with, when in the drawing room of my little hotel I discovered an English book, sporting a gaudy jacket with a corpse and revolver, evidently the relic (I mean the book, not the corpse) of an English visitor before my day. I turned up my nose at it, for, although as a boy I had been an enthusiastic follower of the great S. Holmes, and also of the still greater Father Brown, in later years I shared the highbrow abhorrence of what was lumped together under the heading "that sort of stuff." There being no alternative I took the book to my bedroom, and resigned myself to my inclement fate. Having read about twenty pages I realized with surprise that what I was reading was literature; and I did not put down that volume until, several hours later, I had finished it. That was my introduction to the modern English detective story, and it was an auspicious one, for the book I had picked up by chance was no other than *Trent's Last Case*, by E. C. Bentley, generally rated as the unsurpassed masterpiece of its kind.

From that moment my consumption of the best type of detective story was limited only by the available supply; and by the best type I mean stories with a sustained psychological and intellectual interest with as little "lurve," a wholly extraneous and cheapening element in any good detective or mystery plot, in it as possible, and written in as careful an English as is expected of the best of the current "highbrow" novels. There are or were before the war far more books of this kind published yearly on both sides of the Atlantic than is suspected by the esthetes and the snobs, and I do not hesitate to say that some of the best fiction that has appeared in the English language within the past ten years belongs to this class. Later I tried to analyze my passion for detective stories in contrast to my complete inability to read most contemporary "legitimate" novels, and concluded that it is due to the fact that the sound and well-constructed detective story and mystery thriller constitute the only type of fiction in our day which relegates the emotions to their proper place and recognizes unreservedly the primacy of the intellect over the will and the passions. It is also the only type of novel, apart from those written by Catholic authors and an occasional freak (from this particular point of view) like H. M. Tomlinson's unforgettable *Gallions Reach*, which in opposition to the prevalent Shelleyan and esthetizing mushiness and anarchistic blah-blah recognizes the elemental fact that human life without respect for the Law (by which I mean the law of nature and the law of God, and of which the penal code is a particular instance) ceases to be human, and very rapidly ceases to be life.

Having thus reduced what at first glance appeared a mere taste in recreation and a personal idiosyncrasy to a reasoned philosophical conviction, I made it a rule to forget about philosophy at 7:30 P.M. and to limit my after-dinner reading to those despised "thrillers," and I kept this up for thirteen years until the news of the invasion of Holland and Belgium put an abrupt end to my habit, as it did to most other habits the aggregate of which makes up the routine of civilized existence. Needless to say, although my wife, in charge of this important department of our daily life, exercised the greatest care in separating, with the aid of the "Literary Supplement" of the London *Times* and the book reviews of the *Observer*, the wheat from the chaff, mistakes were inevitably made, and not all the detective stories from London, that in latter years we used to await, in France and Switzerland, with the suspense that precedes the draw of a lottery came up to specifications. Many were duds, and more fair to middling; and yet I owe some of my greatest intellectual and artistic joys of the last few years to books like Paul McGuire's *The Spanish Steps*, a psychological thriller that by virtue of its distinguished workmanship and scintillating English, and the haunting beauty of its descriptions of Roman vistas and of bits of Campagna landscape, would rank as one of the best English novels of our decade if it had a dull instead of a supremely exciting plot. I call it a psychological thriller by way of separating its genre from another and only slightly inferior type, in which the suspense is determined by a brilliant treatment of atmosphere and of extravagant situations; this latter might be termed the "atmospheric" brand, and I am thinking of two American novels, Mignon Eberhart's *The White Cockatoo* and Carter Dickson's *The Unicorn Murders*, a fantasy of almost Chestertonian exuberance, as its outstanding examples.

And while I am on this subject I would note, without claiming originality for my remark, the sad fact that the public, and even many reviewers, often judge books as if they were cigars, by the band showing the maker's name; I was reminded of this only a few months ago by yet another psychological mystery story, not properly speaking a detective novel, Eric Ambler's *The Mask of Dimitrios*. Now I yield to no one in my admiration of Mr. Somerset Maugham, whom I consider one of the three greatest living masters of English prose, my other two choices being Mr. Hilaire Belloc and Professor Santayana; so the reader will perceive that I intend no disrespect for the author of *Of Human Bondage* when I say that Mr. Ambler's story is superior, within the "secret service" genre, to *Ashenden,* by dint of its much more closely knit plot and the resulting crescendo of tension, and its subtly prepared climax; and I believe that had Mr. Maugham's name appeared on its title page *The Mask of Dimitrios* would have been recognized as the superb piece of narrative art that it is, instead of being patted on the back as a good specimen of a literary form hardly deserving serious consideration.

5

On rereading the preceding sub-chapter I find that in a way it falsifies the picture of my life at Le Trayas, for it suggests an intense and well-ordered intellectual activity moving toward a definite purpose; and such activity simply was not there. The impression of neatness and purposiveness comes from my injecting into the narrative elements of a later date, such as my analysis of the philosophical background of detective stories, which is of 1934, when one day, in London, I developed those ideas in a chat with Mr. Charles Williams, the author. The truth is that in the second half of the year 1927, and in the years 1928, '29, '30, and until the fall of 1931, I led, at Le Trayas, a tiny village of the Provençal coast, the life of a more or less animated vegetable. I read some books on philosophy between 7 A.M. and 7 P.M., and a number of detective stories between 8:30 P.M. and midnight; I took my dogs for walks in the Esterel; and from the end of April to mid-

November I swam a couple of miles, or more, every day, in the little bay known as the Calanque de Notre-Dame. But then even a non-animated vegetable has to do things if it wants to keep alive; and I wanted very much to keep alive. For I was, in a sense that I had not known before, enjoying life. I enjoyed, not doing this or that, nor looking forward to some petty, or not so petty, gain or advancement, nor yet enhancing my self-conceit by shining in intellectual repartee or by overcoming difficulties and worsting rivals and catching the eye of this publisher or that editor — but sheer existence, which I thought at this time had itself for its supreme purpose.

It was much later, in London, that I read a line in Chesterton's short biography of Saint Thomas Aquinas that expressed better what I am trying to convey than might any phrase of my own coining. That fat and brooding Dominican, who was also the greatest philosopher of the Church, and in the view of some the greatest philosopher *tout court*, loved, says Chesterton, the blaze of being. It is that blaze of being that I saw for the first time in my life as I sat smoking my pipe in that little overgrown and untidy Provençal garden, gazing at that Provençal sea which was also the sea of the Greeks and the Romans. And though I did not know it at the time, something that had not been there before was growing in my mind: the knowledge that the truly great and important things in life are the things that never change, that are what they are, and endure in being from the beginning of time to time's end, and beyond; and that although men love, and cannot help loving, the things that change and pass, there is in their love for these things always an element of distrust and fear; but the eternal need not be feared. Yet, at this time, I still feared the eternal, I still distrusted sheer being, *ipsum esse subsistens*, though I had already begun to learn to love it. For my mind, such as it was, was still enmeshed in that unconscious philosophy which I had absorbed in the course of my American years — the philosophy of pragmatism, which is one of becoming, not of being, and which teaches men to conquer and to direct becoming, and not to accept and be grateful for Being. It is a Northern philosophy, the philosophy that is born at the fireside while out of doors the storm rages in the dark of a Northern night; and men who were born in the North and have the North in their blood must forever ponder how to make things better than they are, how to keep out the cold and the storm, and so they become pragmatists. . . . But I was now beginning to abandon myself to that way of the South which was in *my* blood, to that Southern mode of thinking which does not want to improve things, but only to accept what is, to live, and to thank God for the gift of life. And it was at this time that I began to see through Spengler, who, succeeding Freud, had till then been the greatest of my minor prophets. For Spengler preached the Faustian glory of unrest and subdual, and despised antique, that is Greek and Roman, or Mediterranean, acceptance and contentment, which he, like the beastly German he was, mistook for resignation and sluggishness. It occurred to me, in those days, that it was a great pity for all mankind that the leadership of the white world had passed, at the end of the sixteenth century, from the peoples of the Mediterranean to those of the Northwestern Atlantic fringe.

Not that my then life was all acceptance and contentment. I thought of myself as one who had reached an impasse, and stagnated. Except for rare moments, there was always in my enjoyment of the present an undercurrent of regret and remorse: regret over the several lives, which had looked like lives of advancement and success, that I had, at the age of thirty-five, thrown away; remorse over not doing anything to recapture what I had lost. There was also fear — fear that what I had and loved could not last, and was to come to an end some day; and I remember that when I was walking with my dogs in the gorges of the Mal Infernet, or along that glorious cornice path of the Mont de l'Ours, there was always at the back of my mind the blighting notion that one day all that soul-satisfying loveliness would be nothing but a memory. I thought then that that haunting apprehension was peculiar to my situation and my character, but I see now that it was only something that is proper to man, and to all men; or at least to all men who think, whatever their situation.

And I began to ask myself after a while (and not such a long while at that) why I was not *doing* anything, doing in the good old American, pragmatist, Calvinist sense (for pragmatism is a kind of Calvinism minus God, holding as it does that truth is always on the winning side, just as Calvin taught that the big men of this world were the elect for the next). Blaze of being, I said to myself, though not in those words, is all very well, but it will not pay my creditors. Why the devil didn't I *write* something, anything, and sell it? I had, to a modest extent, learnt the tricks of the trade; I had twenty-four hours to write things in, and the whole world to choose my subjects from. I had even better than that — I had that little world of the French South, which had then just begun to be a sort of frontier for American writers and artists; one could imagine some highbrow Horace Greeley, 1928 model, telling his visitor, Go East, young man; meaning by East, France, and her South. The Mediterranean coast had been discovered, but it had not yet been exhausted; the new prospectors, wearing the brick-red linen trousers and canary scarves of St. Tropez, and the horn-rimmed glasses of Kansas City and Washington Square, were arriving daily in their new Chevrolets and old Buicks, or by train, and were staking out claims. Whereas I had had a year or two's start, and was now an old squatter. And there were, in those early days, still two or three people in New York, among editors and publishers, who would have given me a leg-up if I had shown a sign of wanting and deserving it. Ten years later those same men, if they thought of me at all, which they had no reason whatever to do, could only think that I had died long ago in Vienna or Zanzibar or Valparaiso; and had I suggested that I was still alive might have intimated that they were not interested in *revenants.*

Well, I was asking myself why I did not write books or at least articles, and sell them to such as were willing to buy; for after the crash of 1929 a return to New York in quest of a job was out of the question. So I spent a year or two in asking myself why I did not write, and the next two or three years in inventing fine, profound, and cogent answers to that question. Yet for one thing I must give myself credit. I was, in most business matters, almost incredibly stupid then, and though I see this clearly now I am not sure that I have become much cleverer. But I was never stupid enough to think that I, or anybody else, could write stuff for sale, and despise the stuff; and also those who bought and read it, for mugs and dupes. The thing cannot be done. No author can "write down" to a public and yet expect sales; at least not consistently and for long, and this was something I knew.

I used to meet a man in the old Brevoort days, an intelligent and well-bred New Englander who wrote adventure stories and such for a string of popular magazines, three thousand words a day five days a week, at so much per word, and he had regular customers and made a comfortable if hardly rich living out of them. He used to tell me, and others, that he thought his stories were rubbish, and the editors who bought them had for their only excuse the fact that the readers were bigger fools still; and he also said that he despised himself for condescending to live by such a fraud. Well, it seemed possible to me that this man had conceived, many years ago, a different picture of himself as a man of letters, and of the career ahead of him; but I never believed all he said about seeing his own potboilers for what they were. He probably told himself — what author doesn't? — that he could turn out better stuff if he tried *really* hard, and if he were not compelled to work so fast and so regularly to make ends meet. At the same time he was probably as glad when he hit on a phrase that seemed to him particularly well turned, or made a character of his say just the right thing, as Henry James had been in corresponding circumstances; and I am certain that he was secretly proud of doing well and with ease what was expected of him. He was, and this is the point I am trying to make, doing his best, such as it was, most of, if not all, the time.

I remembered this man in Le Trayas, and his memory kept me from doing such idiotic things as trying to write articles for what I regarded as the "cheap" magazines in the hope of selling them for five hundred dollars, when I felt incapable of writing the real thing for the *Atlantic Monthly* at a hundred and fifty dollars a throw. And if there is one conviction that I hold in respect of my craft, it is this: that Pollyanna represents the top level of her author, as Jude the Obscure represents the top level of his.

I was, in short, determined to do, and give, my best, not because I was particularly honest, but because I was intelligent enough to see that I should not stand a chance if I tried to cheat. The trouble was that I did not seem to be able to do my best, and soon I came to doubt if I had a best to give, and even if I had anything to give at all. For it seemed to me that short of such freak topics as the journey of the man who would climb the Andes walking backward or cross the Pacific in a single-paddle canoe, there was nothing left in the world to write about, for there were already books about everything, and books several layers deep about anything whatso-ever. And it was not only that there were not enough new subjects left, but there were also too many points of view about all subjects, new or old, and all had already been expressed some time or other; and besides, since one point of view was as valid, or as invalid, as the other, what difference on earth did it make if somebody, say Eugene Bagger, of La Casita, Le Trayas, Var, France, added the expression of his point of view to ten million others, or else with-held it?

It seemed to me that there was a good case, on general principles, for withholding it. I was at this time, as I had been before and am still, greatly interested in literary criticism. But it seemed to me that if one man had written a book, say, about what Mount Everest seemed to him, and then three other men got up and wrote a book each about what he thought about what the first man's book about what he personally thought Mount Everest was like, nobody was much forra'der, and we had one secondhand and three thirdhand versions of the appearance of Mount Everest, and could not be at all sure what Mount Everest really was like, but only got some glimpses of what Mr. A, the original author, and Messrs. B, C, and D, the critics, thought about mountains that none of them had climbed or could climb. And, not to put too fine an edge on it, *who the hell cared?* And that is only a very crude and studiedly child-like, but by no means inaccurate or unfair account of the state of literary criticism in Western Europe and America at the time of which I am writing.

Being, or fancying myself, in the comparatively lucky position of not having to worry about tomorrow's dinner even if I did not write and sell anything today, I had come to ask myself why I should write anything at all, since I knew that what I might write would probably be dull rubbish. And I had attained this knowledge, I regret to say, by studying what other men who were more or less like myself, only less scrupulous or more brave and business-like (it comes to the same thing), had written and were writing all around me. I had, in other words, got thoroughly sick of that individualism which was the literary creed (I thought at this time, *only* the literary creed) of my own generation. Now, since everybody was not only an individual, but also an individualist, they all looked startlingly alike to me, and so did their books; and I shuddered to think that I too probably looked exactly like them, and so would my books look exactly like theirs, if I brought myself to write them. It occurred to me that if some dictator (though there were no dictators to speak of in those days, except in that paradise of Red freedom, Soviet Russia) decreed overnight that the first-person singular was henceforth to be signified in writing by a lower case *i*, instead of a capital *I*, everybody who wrote would realize that he looked exactly like Don Marquis' famous archie, and this might have happy effects on English and American literature, as it could not fail to stop many of the more intelligent individualists from writing at all. But I see now that in assuming this I was an optimist, for after all French literature was not better off in this respect than English, and yet in French not even that ultra-arch-super-de-luxe Individualist, M. Romain Rolland, spelled his ego with a capital *Moi* or *Je*.

There was also the amazing thing, perhaps the most amazing of all in this particular sphere, that men who wrote criticism expected to be taken seriously by those who read them although they did not know what they wanted to say, and admitted it. They admitted it by changing their point of view, and their standard of values, every five pages or so in any given book, offering such fickleness or volatility as proof of their breadth of vision and their tolerant frame of mind. Now I asked myself how can we judge anything if we have nothing to judge it by; for I can only measure the length of a rope or a road or a speech by the Senator who advocates unpreparedness as the best defense for the United States by comparing it to a yardstick. Now if I declare that yardsticks are outmoded, and that I ought to measure a length of rope by comparing it successively to itself, the Queensborough Bridge, a small bottle of attar of roses, a green apple pie à la mode, the left arm of the Venus of Milo, and the right eyebrow of M. Paul Valéry, I may fill a book with what might be described as the conceptual representation of an unnecessary type of wind, but I should certainly not arrive at telling the reader exactly how long the original rope was. And I came to see an infallible mark of the prevalent type of individualist in this, that while he looked exactly like any other individualist at any one moment, he never looked like himself for two consecutive moments; but all individualists looked like a herd of trained chameleons all changing their color in unison.

I was also revolted by the prominence that so many contemporary writers accorded in their writings, in the field of both fiction and nonfiction, to matters of sex. Now I was, and am, anything but a prude; those Le Trayas days of which I write followed my Vienna period in which a good deal of the time I should have spent on my work was devoted to an intensive cultivation of wild oats and other kindred grasses and vegetables; though by the time I went to France I had decided that this agricultural game was hardly worth the candle, and had stopped playing. What made me impatient with the current oversexed literature was not that it was indecent but that it was dull. I held in those days that there was a place for everything, and that the place for that sort of thing was not between the covers of a book. And I call the books I have in mind oversexed, but I am aware, and was aware in those days, that their authors were probably the other way round, for a virile man does not need to "abreact," as the disgusting Freudian phrase has it, his virility in partnership with a portable typewriter. Ever since my days of adolescence it has seemed to me that whatever may be said of, for, and against sex in other respects, as a subject of conversation and literary presentation it is not much more interesting than the peristaltic movement of one's intestines, another vitally important matter in its unattractive way. And if this way of thinking seems abnormal to you, dear critic, make the most of it and call me names, and I shall call you back names that have each two syllables more, for I, too, have browsed in the Freudian pastures, herded by a shepherd no less distinguished than the great Dr. Ferenczi himself, and this at a time when you, dear critic, still thought that a lollipop meant a piece of candy on a stick, and nothing else.

I would also say while we are on the subject of lollipops and so forth that I have always thought D. H. Lawrence the dullest of all the authors to whom the word "genius" was ever misapplied; I base this opinion on his idiotic preoccupation with sex; and I have always thought that what Professor Joad (at least I believe it was he) called D. H. Lawrence's philosophy of abdominalism was the philosophy of a nasty schoolboy who had grown articulate without having grown up, professed for the benefit of other ungrown-up schoolboys of all ages and divers sexes. And yet I recognize that there are passages in his novels, especially his descriptions of exotic landscape in *The Plumed Serpent* and *Kangaroo*, where he soars to the heights of genius.

But what, in those Le Trayas days, irritated me more than anything else, in my oscillating capacity as a writer who was too proud to write and an onlooker who ached to throw off his coat and to launch a good one on the point of somebody's jaw, was the antics of those who proclaimed that the English language was an obsolete instrument, and one unfit to re-present the only thing that mattered nowadays, which was the peristaltic movement of what they chose to call their Subconscious and/or Unconscious. Now I could easily see even then the several fallacies involved in what might be called the Work in Regress racket; for it did not take any special perspicacity to see them, but only a moderate knowledge of Freudian psychoanalysis and a small amount of intellectual honesty. I could not, and did not, claim the rank of an expert psychoanalyst, but I knew enough Freudian lore to realize that the gentlemen who gave out that they were dragging the messy contents of their subconscious and so forth minds into the daylight did nothing of the sort, but were faking the whole works. It would be easy for me to demonstrate this, only the procedure would be too technical to interest the reader; but I will do this demonstration on request, if a stamped and addressed envelope is enclosed.

One of the fallacies to which I refer needed no special knowledge to expose it, but mere common sense. The authors who were engaged in inventing their unconscious processes presented their findings in a language, or in languages, of their own concocting, since English was not good enough for them; and this language or these languages were intelligible to no one but their inventors, and one or two intimate friends who were let in on the secret. Now, language means communication — namely, the conveying from one man to other men that which they have, or are capable of having, in common. Once the communication-purpose of language is denied, and intelligibility is kicked overboard, writing comes to possess no more significance than is proper to the noise made by a child's rattle, and the alternative to not writing at all for publication becomes a comfortable padded cell, where the rattle would annoy no neighbors. But I am flogging a very dead horse, and I refer to the poor beast at all only because it forms part of the picture of an epoch.

Having thus drawn up a particularized indictment of the literature of the day, as an excuse for and even glorification of my failure to make an honest living by contributing to it, I promptly quashed that indictment and declared it a psychopathological evasion device. For it was clear to me, to substitute short words for long ones, that my aversion was that of the fox from sour grapes, and a matter of being too lazy to fetch a ladder and do a bit of clambering. Nothing, I said at this second stage, was wrong with contemporary literature; but everything was wrong with me. I was just incompetent and intellectually impotent, and that was all there was to it. And I was much more sure of this second and personal diagnosis than I could be of the first and impersonal one.

For who was I to lay down the eternally valid laws of literature? Even granting that the holes and flaws in its contemporary context were real holes and real flaws, I could offer nothing to fill and to repair them; granting that the criticism of the day lacked reliable standards, so did I, and it was the mote in my own eye which I perceived and magnified into the beam in the eyes of others. In condemning the world I did only what many disappointed men, in circumstances similar to mine, had done and did every day. But in condemning myself I was not merely rationalizing my sense of failure, and endowing it with a halo of humility and self-knowledge, though sometimes I told myself that I was doing just that; I was carrying on a proper scientific job that I knew how to do.

For whether I knew anything about literature or not, I did know a good deal about psychology. The one lasting benefit that I derived from those half-squandered Vienna years was my apprenticeship under, and friendship with, that great scientist, great healer, and great man, Alfred Adler, the founder of individual psychology. Out of the kindness of his heart, which was perhaps seconded by his relentless intellectual curiosity, he had taken a fancy to me and encouraged my idea of applying his doctrine to biographical reconstruction (which is indeed what I attempted, though only in a superficial way as I see now, in my life of Francis Joseph); and I was privileged to spend whole afternoons, and an evening or two a week, during the last twenty months of my stay in Austria, in his company, at his flat in the Dominikanerbastei or in that favorite café of his on the embankment of the Danube Canal where he presided over a *Stammtisch* of his friends, in the manner of an Athenian philosopher in some wineshop in the shadow of the Acropolis. We organized picnics together, in that improbably delicious country of the Wienerwald, and in the summer of 1926 we had a very pleasant week-end party which lasted about ten days, at a château near Salzburg, where Elizabeth Duncan, the sister of the great Isadora, carried on a school of dancing. But I am losing myself once more among the dear shadows of a past which now seems as remote as the days when Socrates conversed in the Agora. What I meant to say was merely that I had absorbed

Adler's teachings until they were transmuted, from a mere external discipline like any other branch of science, into a part of my personal context, a kind of organic spectacles through which I viewed the world, and myself. And now I turned this special knowledge of the workings of the mind which I had assimilated against myself and my life, seeking to subdue by its means my diffidence, and yet realizing that in so doing I was merely re-entrenching, as well as getting a new kick out of, the very evil that I was trying to destroy — to wit, my laziness.

Now I think I ought to say here that laziness is not simply the negative thing, mere animal inactivity, for which most people who have never looked at it properly take it, but a reckless form of expending power, and therefore highly pleasurable, like all unstinted spending. Therein lies its fatal attraction; for to an intelligent man laziness serves as proof that he can do anything, since he cannot fail in the deeds that he does not attempt; and thus laziness is a kind of omnipotence — not omnipotence in the act, for of that man is incapable, but omnipotence, as the schoolmen might say, in potentiality. This is why laziness is recognized, by competent authorities, as a deadly sin, and the antechamber to presumption and blasphemy. And this interpretation of laziness as the most seductive substitute for power known to man may be read in the books of Alfred Adler, though not expressed in the same words, for Adler, who did not believe in a transcendent God, could not believe in the reality of sin; but the substance is there all the same. And that substance may be read also among the sayings of a Frenchman who lived in the seventeenth century and was not a scientist or savant at all, but a man of the world and courtier, and who may yet be regarded as the first psychologist in the modern purposeful and observant sense, if we do not count one who lived much earlier and was the greatest of them all, Saint Augustine of Hippo. The fifty-fourth of the "Suppressed Maxims" of the Duke de la Rochefoucauld reads: "Of all the passions, the one which is least known to ourselves, is laziness; it is the most ardent and the most malignant of them all, though its violence be insensible, and though the damages it causes remain deeply hidden. . . . To give a veritable idea of this passion, one should say that laziness is like unto a beatitude of the soul, which consoles it for all its losses, and fulfils the place of all its possessions."

The perspicacious reader will at this point interrupt me with a remark for which I was, as it were, asking: to the effect that I had better stop spinning words and get down to brass tacks and call a spade a spade, and myself a neurotic; which is all that my carefully prepared and documented diagnosis amounted to, *in summa summarum*. And it is true that I was just coming to that very point. But I will add, in fairness to myself, that I regarded, at the time, neither the fact of my being a neurotic nor my discovery of it as anything original or extraordinary. For as to the discovery, any intelligent man or woman who knew not one fiftieth of what I knew of psychopathology could have told me just by glancing at me and my way of life that I was a neurotic; and if I remember rightly about two or three dozen of them did tell me, in the course of those years, and received in reply a polite "You are another."

As to the fact of my being a neurotic, why, there were about three, four, five, or six thousand men and women of my age, or under, or slightly over, who were writing, or meant or tried to write, books in English in that period, who were neurotics too, and who knew it, and were complaining and boasting of it in the same breath, thereby furnishing proof of their condition; for one of the marks of the true neurotic is that he is doing contradictory things most of the time, being unable to choose the one and to leave the other alone. All these people, in whose ranks were found most of, though not all, my friends, were in a way better off than I, and in another way worse. For almost all of them, having more courage than I had, and also less faith in financial miracles such as the self-perpetuation, by fission, of a very small bank balance, contrived somehow to adjust their neurotic craving for grandeur and their neurotic consciousness of futility to the exactions of their everyday lives, and performed during the day more or less useful and more or less lucrative tasks that enabled them to pay for the drinks over which they discussed their complexes and so forth during the better part of the night.

I, for my part, had let the little leaking pleasure-boat of my life drift off its proper course for far too long to seize the rudder and make for even an emergency port just from one minute to the next; also, the one Gospel saying that I had never, not even in my least Christian days, lost out of mind was the one concerning the lilies in the field, and their reasonable attitude to tailor's bills and such; and I was willing to pay for the freedom to employ my time, and such mental powers as I had, in a disinterested and unprofitable pondering of abstract problems, by putting up with a financial and general instability which most other people might have found intolerable.

And it was precisely in respect of this dearly bought freedom that I was better off than the wiser people who were careful to feather the nests in which to do their neurotic brooding. For while thinking to them meant rehearsing and recombining the same thoughts over and over again, and writing meant composing variations on their own old themes, and sometimes even variations, after the fashion of Brahms, on a theme of some Haydn or other, to me, who had the leisure, the opportunity, the pleasing urge, and finally the fateful and relentless compulsion, to think everything *à fond*, thinking came to mean examining the validity of my own old thoughts and finding them invalid, and refounding the whole world and my whole life on better substantiated bases. Which is only another way of wording the old platitude that you may obtain almost anything in this life if you are willing to pay the price. God knows that I have paid a heavy enough price for my ten or twelve years' freedom to think, a price which I have not yet done paying, for my arrival in New York as an all but penniless refugee three months before the date of this writing was an installment on it. And yet I know that in the final accounting I have chosen the better part, and would choose it again. There is also what one of my favorite authors has said about all things working together for the good of certain people, among whom I now definitely count myself.

But now I am running too fast ahead, for a change. We are still at Le Trayas, or this narrative is; the date is September 1931, or thereabouts; and I am still a neurotic wanting to snap out of it, and not daring to. Now on the one hand it is very difficult for me to realize that everybody is not as familiar with the Adlerian interpretation of neurosis as I am; and on the other hand this is not a treatise of morbid psychology but a book already overcharged with miscellaneous and not too easily assimilated matter. Thus I am afraid both of not saying enough and of saying too much on the subject, but in any case a few explanatory words are indispensable to the understanding of both what has gone before and what is to follow. So I will say that the neurotic is a fellow who thinks too much and too little of himself at the same time, but the one thing he is incapable of is seeing himself as he is, and valuing himself for what he is worth; and since he also loves himself above all things, or rather is incapable of loving anything or anybody but himself, his being of two minds about this all-important subject will cause him to look at and appraise everything else in the world in the same undecided or oscillating manner. For instance, if he has set his heart on marrying a certain girl, he will tell himself at one moment, "I am a genius, the greatest man that ever lived, if unappreciated, and she is not good enough for me," and at the next, "I am a little squirt, and my virility is not what it should be, and how can I ever hope to win the hand of such a Queen?" And this will go on until the girl gets sick of it and marries the handsome soda clerk round the corner, or a maharajah. Another way of describing the neurotic (who, as all readers will agree, is essentially a goop) is to say that he is so greedy that he wants not only everything, but also the opposite of everything, and, not being able to make up his mind what to choose and what to renounce, ends usually by getting nothing at all.

This incapacity for decision determined by too much love of self is the core of the neurotic character; and the wisdom which the English language has accumulated in the course of the ages expresses itself in a large number of idioms which described the neurotic type or the neurotic way long before the word "neurotic" was coined by some professor or other in Vienna. Thus the man who falls between two stools is a neurotic, and so is he who wants to eat his cake and have it too, and the chap who grabs too much and seizes nothing, and the other who cuts off his nose to spite his face. But perhaps the two best popular images of the neurotic are the everyday one of the child that is told to share the candy with the others, and refuses to play; and that contained in the medieval story of Professor Buridan's ass, which could not make up its mind between two luscious bundles of hay suspended on its right and left, and starved to death.

It is easy enough to see how this conception of the neurotic self-destroying shilly-shallier applied to me at Le Trayas, and I shall not labor the point. But I will add that according to the Adlerian theory the neurotic, when he finds that he cannot have his own way in everything, on no better ground than that he wants it, will turn his back on the wicked world and will retire into a private world of his own where he can think both that he is a greater man than Shakespeare and no one will laugh at him, and that he is just a poor nincompoop, without fear of being stepped on. That is to say, it is of the essence of the neurotic that he will run away from all tests, even as I ran away to Le Trayas in the year 1927. Now Adler tells us that the neurotic's excessively low opinion of himself (which in everyday parlance is now called inferiority complex) is the result either of some organic flaw like short sight, lameness, and so on, or of unreasonable treatment experienced as a child, — too much severity or too much pampering, the latter working by making the child too thin-skinned, — or both the organic and the environmental causes working together; and that those who suffer from this sense of inferiority will make their lives bearable by running to the opposite extreme and fancying themselves great and above the common ruck and the common law; and this is called "overcompensation." Finally, Adler also says that "neurotic" and "normal" are not clear-cut contrasting terms like black and white, but gradations between two limit-cases along a single scale; everybody in modern society has a bit of the neurotic in him, and every neurotic has certain normal traits, and it is only a question of more or less, how to classify any person.

I am sorry that I had to try the reader's patience by these textbook explanations, but as I have already said they are necessary in the ensuing context; and had I shoved them into a footnote the reader might have liked them still less, and might have cursed this book for a learned monograph or some such highbrow horror that it is anything but. Be that as it may, by the fall of 1931 it was clear to me that nothing but Adlerian psychology could deliver me from Le Trayas. Now I did not yearn to be delivered from Le Trayas because I hated the place. On the contrary, I loved it to the last, and love it still; and if things in the world were different and I had enough money, I should return there and buy up half the village and acquire a dozen dogs, and spend my remaining years among the pines and the mimosa in the shadow of the Pic d'Aurèle; and I would rather do this tomorrow than the day after. But the moment had come when I understood that sometimes in this life we must part with what we love most, if life is to have a meaning at all; and I believe that it was in that very moment that I had left my youth behind me and entered upon middle age. And so I wanted to be delivered from Le Trayas against my will; and I thought often of that grand sentence in Tacitus which says exactly in three words that Titus sent Berenice away, although he did not want her to go, and she did not want to leave; but the thing was necessary. *Dimisit invitus invitam.* And yet I expected to be delivered, and to be delivered by psychology, and said so to myself and to one or two friends. But when I said that, I already suspected that I meant, not psychology, but something bigger; what was in my mind was something that I was to read later in a certain book by an author called John. For by then it had begun to dawn on me that there is only one thing that can make men free, the thing called Truth.

6

The idea of writing a biography of Stendhal, and of thereby resolving both my inner and my outer deadlock, occurred to me some time in the early fall of 1931. It grew out of conversations I had at this time with Ludwig Lewisohn, who was spending a few days with me at La Casita on his way to, or from (I forget which), three weeks' holiday in Nice. We discussed the relation of neurosis to creative work, a problem which was in the forefront of interest in that heyday of the Freudian or quasi-Freudian literary biography; and we agreed that it was a problem that could not be solved by the approach and methods of Freudian psychoanalysis. There we rested the case; but when he had left I sat down to puzzle it out; and for the next fifteen months I had once more a purpose in life, and a self-set and self-bossed job.

The problem formulated itself as follows. That there was an obvious and yet profound connection between the creative activity of the writer and other artists on the one hand, and the neurotic state or character on the other, had been by this time recognized as axiomatic. A number of biographies and critical studies had been written and published with that recognition either for their central, or at least for their subsidiary, thesis. But as far as I could see none of the authors who dealt with this problem had advanced beyond stating it. To say that these biographers and essayists started with the implicit or explicit assumption that all geniuses were neurotics, and that neurosis could be therefore regarded as the source or matrix of artistic creation, and then wound up with the discovery that their chosen instance, the hero and subject of their particular inquiry, was a genius who was a neurotic, and also a neurotic who was a genius, would be a somewhat crude and yet by no means unfair way of summarizing the current procedure. It seemed to me an entirely unsatisfactory procedure, as easy as conjuring a rabbit out of the hat in which it had been previously concealed, and also as pointless. The questions that this method left unanswered were these: Granting that all geniuses are neurotics, why are not all neurotics geniuses? Just when, how, and why does the neurotic called Smith turn into a creative artist, while millions of other neurotics called Jones, Robinson, Durand, and Schwarz remain neurotics?

Now it seemed to me that attempts to find an answer to these questions by means of Freudian psychoanalysis were doomed to failure, and betrayed an insufficient acquaintance on the part of practitioners with the writings of the Master. For it was true that Freud, too, had started out to explain the work of art as a product of the sublimation of repressed sexual wishes; but Freud had come to the conclusion, long before the time of which I write, that the theory of sublimation did not supply the required explanation, and was probably unable ever to supply it. With the intellectual honesty of the true scientist, Freud admitted just that in the last pages of his fascinating if wrongheaded essay on Leonardo. The theory of sublimation does not explain *what* sublimates the repressed sexual wish; nor does it explain why in some cases the repressed wish issues in some form of sublimation (artistic creation being one, but by no means the only one, of these forms) and in other cases breaks out in homosexuality, or impotence, or fetishism, or the compulsion to walk along the curb, or in any of the numerous other forms of neurotic behavior.

Some months after I had left Le Trayas I resumed pondering this business of sublimation, and arrived at constructing what I called a theory of inverted Freudism. I asked myself why we should accept, just on the word of an angry and narrow-minded latter-day Jewish prophet, the sexual desire as the fundamental and irreducible urge of the human soul. It should be possible, I argued, to assume that there is in every man a *creative* urge which seeks outlets by hook or by crook. In certain rare cases this urge manages to overcome inner and environmental obstacles and issues in its original purity in the form of artistic, literary, religious, philosophical, or scientific masterpieces. But in the case of the average man this basic urge has no such luck, and has to content itself with mere procreation as a pale substitute for creation. But if this is so, the work of art is not the product of the sublimation of repressed sex, but, on the contrary, the sexual wish is a messy *Ersatz* for thwarted religion or thwarted art, and so on. I toyed with these ideas rather than worked them out, and even added the corollary that probably both the inverted Freudism and the original Freudism were true, and that you could pay your money and take your choice, according to the sort of man you were. But, be that

as it may, the theory of sublimation as a key to the secret of creative art seemed to me a washout long before I attempted to find
one that fitted better.

I attempted to find it by way of Adler's individual psychology.
To be sure, Adler, unlike Freud, was not particularly interested in
the problem of artistic creation. His attitude to that problem may
be summed up — once more crudely but not unfairly — in the statement that he regards the creative artist as an escaped neurotic. Now,
I said to myself, this is obviously true as far as it goes, but it does
not seem to go very far. But then I turned to the Adlerian account
of neurosis. I have already summed up this account on a previous
page, but I will now state the same idea in different words. According to Adler neurosis results from the frustration, not of the sexual
impulse, but of the power-impulse — that is, the will. Repressed
sex, that maid-of-all-work of the inner household according to the
Freudian census, is, in terms of Adlerism, merely an aspect of the
repressed Self. Everything in a man, and in a man's life, is determined, Adler holds, by this paramount power-motive. It sets itself
a purpose which Adler's English translators have dubbed person-
ality-ideal, but which I prefer to call self-conceit or self-image;
it is the inner picture, not of what I am or appear to others, but of
what I seem to myself when my imagination has a field day. The
normal person is he who tones down his self-conceit to the possibilities of its realization; who, in other words, wills what he can;
who adjusts his ambition and his dreams to social reality. Now the
neurotic is precisely he who fails in this self-adjustment. He therefore retreats from an unacceptable public reality into a private
world of his own, into his "inner life," where his self-image, released from all checks of public verification, reigns supreme in a
cloud palace of fictions. These fictions are the neurotic symptoms.

It is evident that this Adlerian description of the neurotic fits
the artist like a well-made glove. For the artist, too, is one who,
finding the world of reality unacceptable, retires into an inner
world consisting of fictions. Only, unlike the neurotic, the artist
does not stop there. The glove needs a little stretching. The artist
reissues from his inner world, and brings back with him some of

those fictions which he then imposes on the world of public reality in the form of a work of art. It is evident that the difference between the genius and the neurotic is that the former *does* something where the latter merely mopes; that genius performs an act of the will of which the neurotic remains forever incapable. It was by this act of will that genius transmuted the burden of lead which had weighted down his neurotic self into shining gold. And I recalled those lines of Richard Crashaw's, among the most beautiful in all English poetry: —

> Tears take comfort, and turn to gems,
> And wrongs repent to diadems.

I had now a kind of preliminary formula: "The creative artist is an ex-neurotic who has turned his private fictions into public truth by an act of his will." I tried out this formula by a cursory review of what I knew of Stendhal, Joseph Conrad, Thomas Hardy, Proust, and Henry James; and I saw at once that I had discovered something that my master Alfred Adler had missed because he never looked for it.

But I also saw that something all-important was still lacking. For granted that my formula was true — what was there in it to explain when, how, and why certain neurotics called Stendhal, Conrad, Hardy, Proust, and James came to perform that supreme act of will which millions of other neurotics could never perform? Thus my "act of will" revealed itself as the Adlerian counterpart of Freud's "sublimation," with this important difference: that whereas we do not know in the least what sublimation is, we do know what an act of the will is; at least we may, by correlating definitions taken from various schools of psychology and philosophy, arrive at a working hypothesis concerning the meaning of the term "an act of the will." To this extent my explanation of the work of art as the product of an act of the will whereby a certain neurotic saves himself from remaining a neurotic represented a marked advance over the Freudian account. And yet it was clear that I had failed to penetrate to the core of the problem, because

I was unable to answer the question about the how and why and when of that act of the will.

I spent the next fifteen months trying to find an answer to that question; and in the end I found it. But by that time the whole problem of the genesis of artistic creation had been relegated, in my mind, to a secondary place, and my attention was claimed by a much larger problem to which my original inquiry was preliminary and subsidiary. So, having read everything that Stendhal had ever written, and almost everything that had ever been written about him in French and English, and having examined his manuscripts and other relics in the municipal library at Grenoble, and visited the house where he was born in that city, and other places which had loomed large in his life, in Grenoble and elsewhere, and having thus eaten and drunk and breathed and dreamed Stendhalian lore for many years, I did not, after all, write my great and conclusive Life of Stendhal. What I did write was an essay of 8500 words which I called "The Riddle of Stendhal"; and I packed into that one short essay not only the labors and the thought of those fifteen months, but a good deal more; thus bearing out the remark of my friend that at the rate at which I wrote articles for highbrow magazines I was not likely to keep myself alive as a freelance contributor to same. But I believed, and still believe, that in that article I solved not only the riddle of Stendhal, but also that larger riddle of how some other miserable despised all-round failures like him have risen, at the very moment when all seemed lost, from the defeat of their poor self-duped selves to the deathless triumph of Genius.

I also believe that by and by it will be discovered that in that essay on Stendhal I discovered, in the year 1934, the one thing that matters about the secret of artistic creation, and also proposed a test whereby the work of authentic genius may be separated from that of — well, I won't name names, but will say, merely, very clever writers who know their business. But these things take time; hadn't it been thirty-five years before Taine discovered the very novel of Stendhal upon which I was to base my discovery another eighty years later? So, as long as there is still an R.A.F., I despair of nothing. But there were at least two men who judged at the time that my solution of the riddles that I had set myself was worthy of attention. One was Mr. Ellery Sedgwick, to whom I sent my essay in June 1934, from London, and who published it, under the title "The First of the Moderns," in the *Atlantic Monthly* for October 1934; and he intimated that he published it rather to his own surprise, for my paper was heavy going, and had a recondite subject. The other was Professor Denis Saurat, of the University of Lille, the philosopher, and director of the "Institut Français" in London, who read my manuscript and told me afterwards that the problem of Stendhal was now solved. And it was a problem that had worried French critics and savants for at least two generations, and had caused them to fill a small library with books all trying to answer the question posed originally by no less a man than Sainte-Beuve. For it was that dean of the art of criticism who wrote way back in the sixties that Stendhal "was not meant to become such a great man." And *that* was the problem of Stendhal that I attempted to solve. How does a man who was not meant to become great become great? How does one of the last become one of the first?

Professor Saurat recommended, at the time, that I should have my study published in France too. But the translation would have cost me five pounds, payable at once. I hadn't got five pounds. That was that.

Now that larger problem, to the consideration of which I was eventually led by my general inquiry into the relation between genius and neurosis, and by my special study of that relation in terms of the life and works of Stendhal, was the problem of Reality; and I bumped into this problem in the following way. I had been pondering Alfred Adler's definition of the neurotic as the person who fails to adapt himself to the demands of reality. The moment came when it occurred to me to ask myself why the devil should anyone bother to adapt himself to the sort of reality that we saw all around us and that was the only reality we knew; and what right this reality had to expect that everybody should conform to it. It struck me that, if some people refused or were unable to adapt themselves to this twentieth-century reality, an accurate reporting of which in the best daily newspapers constituted the worst kind of libel and caricature imaginable, perhaps those people were extremely sensible and worthy of all consideration and praise, and that the people who voted them abnormal (for it was clear to me by then that the standard of normality was established by a majority vote) were fools. From that I went on inevitably to the last question that may be asked in this particular sphere of ideas: What *is* this Reality that we hear, and talk, so much about?

It was at the moment when I asked this last question, and by asking it arranged into a meaningful pattern the other questions by which it had been preceded, that I ceased to be primarily interested in the problem of creative art and in my biography of Stendhal. It was also at that moment that I ceased to be a student of philosophy and became, by dint of running up against that very question in the course of my day's work, and by dint of having to hold up that work until I found an answer to it, a philosopher. And I shall treat of these things in the two remaining chapters of this autobiography of a fool who tried, in obedience to the injunction of the ancient Stoics, to shed his foolishness by using his reason. Here I will only add that had I been working on my biography of Stendhal in New York instead of trying to do the job in that small village of the Provençal coast, a thousand miles from nowhere, I should have probably finished it in six or eight months, and should have answered my own question (had it ever occurred to me to ask it), "What is Reality?" by telling myself, Why, everybody knows that; and should have answered those other questions that preceded it, about reality's right to exact adaptation and so forth, by sundry wisecracks; and my biography of Stendhal would have been published in due course, and it might even have sold 32,563 copies, and would then have been forgotten by everybody except myself, and I should have remembered it only to ask myself in later years why I had ever written it.

But in that small village called Le Trayas I had plenty of time

to ask myself questions and to try to answer them, though I never
had time enough to finish the books that I had begun to write.

7

One day in May 1934, when Le Trayas had become the memory
which all things we love in this life are destined to become sooner
or later, I was standing at the window of my bedroom in one of
the less fashionable streets of Chelsea (London, not New York),
when I saw one of those street singers whose livelihood consists in making it more difficult for others to earn one. This man
caught my eye because he did not look tough, but rather like an
old actor who had seen much better days; his clothes were very
old and threadbare but unmistakably of good quality, and he had
a narrow sensitive face that reminded me of Lord Buckmaster,
who had been Lord Chancellor of England. But what struck me
most about him was his hat, a gray Homburg, like his clothes very
old, and battered; but one which had cost twenty dollars when
new, and I would have taken my oath on this, being a judge of
sorts in matters of felts and such things. As a rule I object strongly
to street musicians who ply their trade in residential streets, and I
refuse to pay their mild form of blackmail. But for this old fellow
I felt sorry, and yet I could do nothing for him, being broke myself at the moment. It was that wreck of a fine hat of his, symbol
of bitter failure, that set me off thinking of Stendhal, and of the
failure he had been most of, though not all, his life; and of failures
nearer home, such as that unachieved biography, for which I had
collected enough material to fill two of the suitcases in that very
room. I thought of the young men who go out into life, not to
make a living and marry and beget children and live in a decent
little house in Yonkers or Tooting, but to conquer the world,
and of what happens to most of them; and I thought that "overcompensation for an infantile inferiority-situation" was rather a
mild way of putting their predicament.

Then I thought of myself when very young, and of the essay on Stendhal that I had written at the age of thirteen, fresh from the reading of *Le Rouge et le Noir*, which I somehow recognized at once as the unsurpassed masterpiece that it was. Our Hungarian master had set what was called a free theme, under the general caption "Thoughts in a Library"; each boy was expected to go to a library and to think what he could, and set it on paper. I remember nothing of that childish outpouring except that it dealt with Stendhal, and that it contained a lie; for I made much of describing a portrait of my subject that gazed down on me from the wall of the library as I wrote. But there was no such portrait and there was no such library, and I was not to see a likeness of Stendhal until some thirty years later. In those thirty years, I reflected, Stendhal had never ceased to be the author whose life and character and work intrigued me more than that of any other; and while my interests and preoccupations were changing all the time, to Stendhal I remained faithful.

I wondered now why this should have been so; and then all of a sudden I *saw*; and I understood many things in my own life that till then had been obscure. My mind returned once more to that unfinished biography which I had once expected to make me great and famous. But now the sting of self-reproach had gone out of my thoughts, and I stepped into the next room, which served me as a study, and sat down to my desk, and three weeks later that essay of 8500 words which was to be my monument to the memory of Stendhal, and which was in the fall of that year to appear in the *Atlantic Monthly*, was in the mails. And I have reflected since that battered old felt hats that hailed from a shop, well-known to all Londoners, behind the Burlington Arcade, and also my silly flair for identifying them as such, may have unexpected uses in the universal scheme.

In that essay I told, among other things, about the early youth of him who was later to call himself Stendhal; how his childhood was embittered by what he was to describe as the bottomless gloom of his Catholic and royalist home in the days of the Revolution, and how he reacted against his background by turning, at the age of nine, into an ardent republican, freethinker, and hater of priests.

Routed by an overwhelming hostile reality, the boy finds refuge in a tremendous discovery: he has a Mind, an Inner Life, where he is free and safe, and where he can picture himself as being better, stronger, cleverer, more brilliant, more powerful, than anybody he knows. . . . At the age of fourteen he has an inspiration: he himself calls it a stroke of genius: "Mathematics will deliver me from Grenoble." He means: if he wins a prize in mathematics at school, "they" will send him to Paris — the gateway of freedom, greatness, happiness, conquest. A very young general of artillery was just then leading the armies of the Republic from victory to victory. . . . And this young general, Bonaparte by name, had also started out as a student of mathematics. . . .

Two years later the boy won his prize, and was sent by his father to the École Polytechnique in Paris, the nursery of those artillery generals one of whom had just made himself the dictator of France. There was an entrance examination to pass. When the morning came, the boy stayed in bed. For the boy was a neurotic, and the neurotic dreads failure, but he dreads success more than he dreads failure. For he knows that for the likes of him achievement is a mere prelude to being found out.

Being ploughed would have meant an unbearable blow to Henri Beyle's self-conceit as a great mathematician; still he could always comfort himself with the thought that he was a great poet. But being passed would have imposed on him the unbearable strain of having to act like any normal young man; and acting like a normal young man was precisely what he knew he could not do. Defeat could be explained away; but victory must be followed up. He solved his dilemma by shirking it. He stayed in bed.

Having thus disposed of the riddle of that arch-dereliction which had baffled all his biographers, who, unlike me, were not disciples of Alfred Adler, I went on to trace the same pattern throughout Stendhal's life, in the succession of his abortive careers as clerk to the War Department, cavalry officer in Italy, and grocer's assistant in Marseille — the last being his idea of training for the career of a get-rich-quick financier. But the moment came when success thrust itself on an unwilling but delighted Henri Beyle. His cousin, the great Count Daru, one of Napoleon's "organizers of victory," secured him an appointment in the Imperial War Commissariat; and for eight years he had his share of authority, responsibility, adventure, luxury, of all the good things of this world that he craved. He surprised his benefactor, his family, and most of all himself, by distinguishing himself through unusual competency, devotion to duty, and cool unflinching courage in danger. He was promoted, and promoted again.

But this steady advance along a single track proves, in the long run, too much for him; for he is a Superior Person, and a superior person must be Free — free to dream himself supreme. So he is positively relieved when the Napoleonic power house of cards collapses and his career is over. His comment is magnificently curt: "In 1814 I fell with Napoleon." What a narrow escape from the humdrum prospect of becoming a Prefect or Ambassador!

The next six years are the happiest of his life. A decade and a half earlier, as a youthful lieutenant of dragoons, he was garrisoned at Milan; and Milan has become, in retrospect, the Golden Age of his dreams. He now returns, and a miracle happens: the dream comes true. A miracle? Not really; rather, an exceptionally favorable constellation for the blossoming out of the neurotic pattern. All his life Beyle had been dragged down to the depths of misery by his exaggerated notion of his own importance which "the world" — that is, his native environment — persistently tested and rejected. *But in Milan there were no more tests;* Milan accepted him at his face value fixed by himself simply because he was a stranger whose claims were not important enough to call for verification. When in 1814 he was charged with organizing the defense of his native Grenoble against the Austrians, he signed a poster as *de* Beyle. The usurped particle of nobility set the whole town laughing: "Fancy the son of old Lawyer Beyle giving himself airs!" Milan knew nothing of old Lawyer Beyle. In Milan, as M. Léon Blum brilliantly puts it, he could acquire the habit of not being judged. He was docketed, for the asking, as "M. de Beyle, a distinguished retired high official of the Empire." The dream that had come true was the dream of all neurotics: the dream of Greatness without Effort. What Beyle discovered in Milan was the psychological trick of turning the status of outsider into a device of Superiority, the sleight-of-mind substituting "above" for "apart from" in his relation to his environment. In a word, at Milan Henri Beyle, the first neurotic, became the first Expatriate.

But I have quoted myself enough to make my point. In writing that essay on Henri-Marie Beyle, better known to posterity by the name of Stendhal, I was writing my first autobiography. It was only a short essay, destined to find a dusty haven in the files of a magazine; but by it I proved to myself, to my satisfaction, that although I had failed to write the Life of Stendhal which I had originally planned, I had succeeded in reliving it. America had been my Paris; my years on the *Tribune*, the early abortive success of my first book, and its sequel, had been my Imperial War Commissariat; in those three reckless and happy years in Vienna I had been the important and admired high panjandrum of the French Army of Occupation that Stendhal had been at Brunswick. Above all, Le Trayas had been my Milan. And that was not the end of my story, any more than it had been the end of Stendhal's. For here I was, in London, an unsuccessful *littérateur* and ex-anything that I had ever been, wondering where my next meal would come from; as Stendhal had wondered, strolling along the banks of the Seine, or rambling in the Luxembourg Garden, eight or nine years after his return from that Milan which had been his Trayas; until one day he shut himself up in his hotel garret and wrote in three months *Le Rouge et le Noir*, to be recognized fifty years later as the greatest of novels.

Well, here the parallel breaks down. For I did not write then, and have not written since, any *Le Rouge et le Noir*. And yet it is a true parallel, and I could elaborate it down to minute personal details that would not interest anybody. But the most important point in respect of which my life has doubled Stendhal's is one that on the surface suggests the most important divergence. Henri Beyle, the son of the Catholic ultramontane lawyer of Grenoble, turned atheist and Jacobin at the age of nine; and he was to remain

an atheist, though not a Jacobin, for the rest of his life. I, the son
of a Jewish liberal lawyer of Budapest, turned Catholic, and a
lover of the old ways, at the age of seventeen; and although I fell
away from my new faith and my new love soon afterwards, today
I have returned to them; and I may exclaim here, with the greatest
of those who first saw the light in their mature years, "*Sero te
amavi, pulchritudo tam antiqua et tam nova.*" "Late have I loved
thee, O Beauty so ancient and yet ever-young."

Now that dispensation of Man the Sovereign, which had
launched itself in the twin movements of the sixteenth century
known as Renaissance and Reformation, reached the stage of its
final triumph in the French Revolution, at the time of Stendhal's
birth; and he embraced that victorious creed, discerning its implications more clearly than anybody else in his day, with all the
ardor of which his passionate soul was capable. But I was born at
what the great Russian thinker Berdyaev was to call the End of
Our Time; and it is only today, when I am almost fifty, that those
of us who have eyes to see may perceive just how final, in a sense
not intended a hundred and fifty years ago, has been the triumph
of that Renaissance religion which saw in man the autonomous
master of his destiny, and his own supreme and absolute end. And
so I have returned to the old faith, and to my love of the old ways;
and I believe that in doing so I have not, as my agnostic friends
say, slipped backwards, but have advanced along the path of history. But Saint Augustine too had lived at the end of *his* time,
and tells us all about it in his *Confessions.*

Earlier in these pages I recorded my ambition, of which I had
first become aware in my Copenhagen days, at the age of twenty-
one, to achieve, not mere success in the everyday sense, but a new
life; to remake myself, according to my own specifications, not
out of the materials provided by my birth and early environment,
but in spite of them, as it were. That had been the ambition of that
Henri-Marie Beyle, too, whom the world remembers as Stendhal; and the latter name in itself bears witness to his success.
Whether I have succeeded in mine, it is for the reader of these
chapters to judge; but I believe that I am on safe ground when I

say that had some whimsical visionary traced the external course of my life in advance, on the day of my birth, a bookmaker would have offered pretty heavy odds against his prophecy ever being fulfilled. Yet when I say this, I know that remaking the external course of one's life is not very difficult for anyone who has more imagination then staying power, and who is always prepared to side with that better which the French say is the enemy of good. Also, I know that remaking one's self in the sense in which I aimed at remaking mine at the age of twenty-one, and for many years after that, does not matter much one way or the other. For today I know that there is another way for a man to be reborn, and it is the one way that counts.

VIII. *The Birth of a Mind*

EVERY author who deals with a philosophical, and indeed with any other abstract subject knows and has to fight the temptation to squeeze his whole book into his preface, which is usually written not first, as the layman might suppose, but last of all. It is the same kind of temptation that I have to overcome if the two remaining chapters of this book are not to be turned into a preface to the next. For in the room where I write this there is a large chesterfield, on which recline, dressed in elegant *chemises* or shirts, as the French call folders, of all colors, — orange, gray, blue, red, green, purple, and yellow, — no less than 400,000 words of my "Philosophy of Freedom," the fruit of seven years' labor, or of fourteen, if one looks at it that way; but no publisher will look at it at all, until I have reduced it to less than half that length. Which is what I intend to do next; but I have served the reader with generous samples of what that other book is all about. And that reminds me that my unproductiveness, as it has been called, during those seven years, or rather fourteen, has turned this book into a sort of bargain counter, where the reader could pick up for the price of one book the contents of half a dozen that I started but did not finish in that time; and I believe that these contents did not spoil for having been kept in the wood, as it were. And it is perhaps not for me to say, but it might be a good idea for Congress to pass a law making it a punishable offense for any writer to publish more than one book every five years. But I hope that no such law will be passed within the next twenty-four months, in which period I intend to publish at least three books, but possibly four. After that I mean to take a rest, and let Congress do its worst; it probably will.

Now I am not going to make these two chapters a summary of

that next book, for it would be bad for the reader, who might succumb to an attack of mental indigestion; and that can hardly be my purpose. And yet I cannot help dealing, from now on to the end of this book, with ideas that will go into the making of the other. For these ideas germinated in the first five months of my stay in Paris in the fall and winter of 1932 and in the spring of 1933; and it is to this year in Paris that this chapter has been allotted in the scheme of this book. And I may say that in a sense I have been living, for the past seven years, on the compound interest of the intellectual capital which I laid in during those five months, in the form of about eight or ten basic notions which I worked into the first outline of my "Philosophy of Freedom," though it was called by a different name in those days. That outline, which I have been sensible enough to save, seems to me, on the whole, naïve and ignorant now, and rather analogous to my attempt to play the Hammerclavier Sonata at the age of twelve, and after three years of piano lessons. And yet the germs of everything that was to follow, including this book, were contained in that typescript of about 35,000 words; and there must have been some glimmer of something in it, since Mr. Jonathan Cape gave me a contract to make an honest book of it, and Mr. Jonathan Cape knows his business. So, for that matter, did his reader, who advised him to advise me to put my outline into the drawer of my desk and "sleep on it." Well, I have followed their joint advice, haven't I? Four years later, when I saw definitely that it would take me yet another three or four to live up to that contract, I returned to Mr. Cape the cash advance which I had received from him upon signing it; thus making him, for five minutes or so, probably the most astonished publisher that ever lived.

I spent those five months (after a brief experiment with a studio in the Rue Delambre, behind the Dôme in Montparnasse, in a building well known to all Paris Americans) in a tiny ground-floor flat of the Rue Cassini, opposite the Observatoire. I did my writing there, but I did most of my thinking in the Jardin du Luxembourg, that loveliest of all city parks in the world, where I took my three dogs to exercise twice a day. There, in those avenues and groves and open spaces, I experienced some of the unforgettable thrills that are the by-product of the hidden chemical process which takes place (so the naturalists say) when something vague and soft and blurred called a dream turns into something hard and clear and luminous, called an idea. Some of the happiest moments of my life I lived in those gardens, of a life with perhaps more than its strict share of happy moments. And speaking of strict shares, it occurs to me that the Luxembourg Gardens probably hold the world's record as the scene of thrills such as I have just described; for the spirit of young France used to roam those spaces for a century and a half; so that in thinking new thoughts on those walks I merely followed an old tradition.

With the coming of spring, and open windows and gramophones and street musicians, my little flat in the Rue Cassini had become uninhabitable, and I moved from its frying pan into the fire of a studio building in Passy, full of young American girls, budding Lily Ponses and Grace Moores. So my thinking went on with a little less *brio* than before; and in a sense it was now not so much a matter of thinking as writing a book for which I held a contract, and of making a lot of money by it; and I thought more of the book than of the thoughts that were to go into it. I meant to finish this book in six months, and that is why I never finished it at all; for had I been less eager for royalties and fame, and given myself four years to do the job in, I should probably have finished it in three. As it was, I was always to do the thing in the next six months, and life was just one damned six months after another.

Then, as the film captions used to say in the old days, came summer; and having been spoilt, for the rest of my life, by my six years at Le Trayas, I found, and still find, life in any great city hardly bearable even in winter for longer than a fortnight at a time. I simply could not face the prospect of a summer in Paris, so I rented, for myself and my three dogs, a cottage in a tiny village called Chamant, near Senlis and Chantilly, about an hour's ride north of Paris. It was a very pleasant cottage, and a charming village, and lovely country to walk in, and I spent the next three months there, but I was not particularly contented, being homesick for my South. Also, I was very ill, for the first and to date the only time in my life, and was saved by the devotion of the same American friend whose company had been my comfort and greatest stimulus in Paris, and to whose pitiless analysis of my situation I owed my escape from Le Trayas; for that analysis had made it clear to me, and that in the eleventh hour, that the beauty of the place and my easy contentment would have destroyed me in the long run, and a not so very long run at that.

2

It was, I believe, on one of those gray November walks in the Luxembourg Gardens, perhaps while I was gazing at the very bust of Stendhal, by David d'Angers, that I asked myself that fundamental question of all philosophy, "What is Reality?"

I was meditating upon Adler's definition of the neurotic as a person who has failed to adjust himself to reality; and it struck me, all of a sudden, as odd that such people had to be *cured*. For I reflected that, after all, a tribe of monkeys in a banana grove, and a flattened-out fish with a phosphorescent something-or-other ten thousand feet below ocean level, were adjusted to *their* reality far more perfectly than any human beings were to theirs; and yet nobody proposed to cure the human race by exhorting it to take its cue from those monkeys, or from the esoteric pals of Mr. William Beebe. If the ancestors of man had succeeded in self-adaptation to a degree equaling that of apes, or, as some people with a queer taste in family trees would have it, of other apes, they would have remained just another species of apes, and I should not have been walking at that moment in the sixth *arrondissement* of Paris, trying to puzzle out problems about neurotics and their insufficient self-adjustment to a reality which — well, what was this reality anyway?

Yet there I was, walking on my hind legs, thinking away for dear life, while my three dogs, who had to all intents and purposes done a far better job of self-adaptation than I could ever hope to, were walking on all four, and were, as far as the best authorities on these subjects knew, not thinking at all. But was it *better* to walk on one's hind legs? Was the capacity for thinking, which was evidently some sort of compensation for a shortage of corporeal adaptability, a premium or a penalty? This opened up another problem, that of the value, as distinguished from the mere fact, of the failure in self-adjustment. Evidently there was something to be said for a failure in anything that produced such unexpected results as "Hamlet" or the Cathedral of Notre-Dame. On the other hand, if there were any intrinsic merit in adapting oneself to the demands of one's environment, then a healthy full-grown baboon, or a naked pygmy in the Congo jungle, represented a far higher state of evolution than Nietzsche, whose maladjustment to the exigencies of his life ended in insanity. I asked myself a second question. Why should we be *expected* to adjust ourselves to a reality which we have not even properly defined? Why should extreme failure in self-adjustment be punished by a life term in a lunatic asylum?

Now I realized that my master Alfred Adler had never answered these questions, because it had never occurred to him to ask them. When he said "reality" he meant something that "everybody knows" — something that the overwhelming majority of people agree to regard as reality. For his purpose, which was to help miserable people to snap out of their self-inflicted misery and to live like other human beings, this implicit conception of reality was, of course, serviceable enough. And yet it struck me that by not inquiring into the nature of this reality Adler did more than merely accept it as something ineluctable: he endorsed it. For he set out, not to change reality, but to change the wretch who did not see reality as *he* did. And I remembered a passage from Professor Eddington's *The Nature of the Physical World*, where he speaks of those who use the word *reality* "to evoke sentiment," as a "grand word in a peroration." Adler's reality was thus not "just plain reality," but what Eddington, in that passage, calls "Reality (loud cheers)." When I got home I looked up the passage in question, and transcribed it. "The illustrious psychopathologist then went on to say that while neurotics, artists, madmen, saints, and criminals entrenched themselves behind a network of dreams and fictions, the distinguishing mark of the good citizen was that, like a man, he faced and accepted Reality (loud cheers)."

Today it seems odd to reflect that that little joke (for which I then and there entered due mental apologies to my friend and teacher Alfred Adler) represented a turning point in my whole life. For it was by discovering what I then called the smugness and the socialistic bias, but what I would today call the ideological partiality or regionalism of Adler's reality-concept that I came to ask my next question: Granting that the neurotic is he who fails to adjust himself to reality — why blame the neurotic? And Adler does blame him; for he calls him a neurotic, and offers to heal him. *Why not blame reality?* This question implied the next. In what way could reality be blamed for producing numberless cases of individual maladjustment?

Adler works out the formula, "The neurotic is he who responds to social reality with maladjustment," by examining the individual disposition which does the responding. It occurred to me that it should be possible to isolate the particular features of social reality which evoke, from a large number of given individual dispositions, the reactions called neurotic.

Now the very first thing that this line of inquiry revealed was that Adler's system, like that of Freud, ignores history. Granting that he was right, I said to myself, in deriving neurosis from the frustration, by social reality, of individual striving, what right or reason have we to assume that this social reality is a constant, something that is the same in all climes and remains the same throughout the ages? I answered this question without a moment's hesitation. *No right and no reason whatsoever.* On the contrary, it was clear that Adler's implicit assumption was wrong, and that the way men look at the world, and sum up what they see in the form of a given *Weltanschauung*, differs from age to age, and from one region of the globe to another. It was equally self-evident that with the constitution of this social reality varies not only the resistance encountered by the striving individual, but also the nature of his striving: his conception of self-fulfillment. Now what could be more obvious than that the terms "social resistance" and "individual striving" or "self-fulfillment" could not have the same meaning in the Athens of the third century B.C., in thirteenth-century Florence, in twentieth-century New York, and in twentieth-century Lhasa? Yet, I reflected, this was a point not only that Alfred Adler has missed — and after all he was neither a historian nor a sociologist, but a physician — but that no contemporary historian ever raised; it seemed to be an axiom of modern English and American historiography that in all ages and all climes men want the same things, to wit, the things that *we* happen to want, and that the main difference between Dante and Mr. Henry Ford was that Mr. Henry Ford got what he wanted and Dante did not get what Mr. Henry Ford wanted. Was it possible to believe, once the point was raised, that Saint Joan of Arc or Buddha or Sophocles wanted the same things, conceived the purpose of life in the same terms, as Dr. Sigmund Freud, Aimee Semple McPherson, Babe Ruth, John D. Rockefeller Jr., King Lobengula of the Zulus, and an Andaman islander? To me this belief, of which the chief adherents were all kinds of liberals and progressives on the one hand, and psychoanalytic practitioners on the other, seemed puerile, a relic of that most naïve of philosophic schools, eighteenth-century rationalism.

Having reached this point in my reflections I asked myself whether it was not possible to regard all human history as a succession of psychological stages, each with its distinctive conception of what I at this time called social reality. What these changing reality-concepts contained, how they arose, how they were validated, and so on, were not clear to me, but I assumed that they had something to do with what man wants in and from life and what he can attain — that is, with human desire and human limitation; thus each of these successive stages centered round some question or point of right, in the sense of title or warrant, a question of what is technically called *quid juris*. It also occurred to me that it might be possible to discover some sort of law or pattern according to which these stages changed from one to the next.

This idea of a traceable psychological articulation of human history, an articulation determined by changing notions of what is *right* for human beings to expect, to will, and to do, was destined to be the central thesis of my "Philosophy of Freedom." My great trouble at this time was that knowing little history, less philosophy, still less science, and no theology whatsoever, I saw my problem in far too simple terms. I thought, for instance, that I could fit my pattern of historic articulation into Auguste Comte's well-known tripartite scheme, according to which history may be divided into a theological, a metaphysical, and a positive stage; and the first outline of my system actually incorporated this Comtean plan. It is in contexts such as this that the advantages of being a failure in life become apparent. Had I been at this time say a successful novelist, I should have had sufficient self-confidence to overrule my qualms and my scruples, should have gone ahead and written my "Suicide of Freedom," as the book for which I had contracted with Mr. Jonathan Cape was provisionally called, and should thus have committed a kind of intellectual hara-kiri which might have passed unnoticed, since most people knew even less about these matters than I did, and which would have been indemnified to an extent by an increase of my bank balance. Now Mr. H. G. Wells *was* a successful novelist when he wrote and even published his *Outline of History*, a book which pleased many contemporaries and sold many copies and established its author as an authority on the history of mankind and so on; but a book which will make future generations, if any, — that depends, at this moment, mainly on the R.A.F., — wonder about the mental capacity and equipment of an age that could take Mr. H. G. Wells's *Outline of History* seriously.

My promising — as I see it now — start in the field of the philosophy of history thus soon hit the snag of an ignorance which stopped short of mistaking itself for knowledge. And yet I had even at this early stage a few quite intelligent notions to play with. For instance, I find incorporated in the outline that pleased Mr. Jonathan Cape the following passage: —

Social reality . . . plays a double role in determining maladjustment — that is, in producing neurosis. Negatively, it limits or vetoes undue individual expectancy. But positively it shapes — it may inflate or divert — such expectancy. It seems to me that a social reality which has defined strictly, and *a priori*, the limits of individual expectancy or aspiration would have fewer occasions to veto such expectancy or aspiration once it has come to be formed, and consequently such a social reality would produce fewer neurotics than one that leaves the limits of individual expectancy vague, and calls Halt! only when it is, psychologically, too late.

That feature of social reality which evokes the neurotic response thus assumes contour as the discrepancy between what the individual is led to expect from life and what life is willing to grant him; as the margin between individual expectancy and the social possibilities of its realization. This margin may be called the margin of disappointment. It would follow that the wider the margin of disappointment is in a given society, the more neurotic individuals that society will produce. But this suggests the possibility of a whole society becoming neurotic: which would occur where all individuals are encouraged to believe that there is no limit to their potential achievement, and where the margin of disappointment thus becomes, so to speak, infinite.

After seven years spent in pondering the same problem, and its kith and kin, I would amend that passage today only in one respect: I would point out that "social reality" does not necessarily coincide with *real* reality — that is, the true state of things in the universe — but may constitute a distorted and partial version of the latter. The philosophically trained reader will see at once what this amendment implies. In those early days I still thought of *all* reality as something made and unmade by a collective interpreting effort of human minds, and I conceived of human limitations as being imposed (apart from the resistance of matter) by social existence alone. That is to say, when I wrote that passage I was a pragmatist. But today I know that reality exists independently of human cognition and desire, and I recognize that the ultimate limitations of human striving are laid down in the nature of the universe and by the command of God. In other words, today I am an Aristotelian Realist. I consider that I did not waste those seven years.

But the above passage already introduced one of the most important theses that I was later to work out in my "Philosophy of Freedom," to wit, that Modern civilization represents a limit-case of the gamut of mankind's psychological development. For the aim that Western mankind set itself at the end of the sixteenth century was nothing less than Omnipotence; and that aim-setting, being vetoed not only by the express command of God, but also by the things that comprise the order of Nature, was bound to land our civilization sooner or later in an orgy of self-destruction. And I marveled, in those early days of 1933, at the stupidity and ignorance of the publicists and other wiseacres who were grandiloquently tracing the advent of Hitler to the clauses of the Treaty of Versailles. For it was clear to me even then that Hitler was implicit in Luther's *sola fides*, in Bacon's *Novum Organum* and in Descartes's *Meditationes*, not to mention other manifestoes of Man the Sovereign. European man had spent four centuries playing at God, until one came to show him how to play that game in earnest; and so we reached the End of Our Time.

My preoccupation with the question about the rightfulness or *quid juris* of human striving had arisen from my recognition that the real subject of all psychopathology was the problem of Sin. Only at this time I did not call it Sin; I called it guilt, which is the equivalent of sin in a Godless universe. Freudism is of course full of references to man's sense of guilt, and to psychoanalytical healing as the scientific equivalent of and successor to the Catholic Confessional. But although I had had my doubts for a long time about the validity of a good many pretensions of psychoanalysis, it was only at this juncture that the peculiarity of Freud's attitude to man's sense of sin dawned on me. To quote my outline of February 1933 once more: —

What Psychoanalysis undertakes is not a sacramental remission of sin, but a medico-moral casuistic interpretation of the individual difficulty to the effect that there is no sin involved. . . . The Freudian theory does not postulate atonement in the form of contrition plus reparation commensurate to the delict. The Freudian theory sets out to prove that there is no delict at all; that the guilt is only imagined — that is, a superstition. . . . The Oedipus complex . . . is not a formula for the sense of sin, but a substitute for it. It is a medicineman's bogey whose only *raison d'être* is to be bowled over. For the point of the guilt of Oedipus is that it *does not exist*. It is, in each individual instance, merely "imagined," and thus capable of being dispelled, or "cured," by the rationalist argument to which the Freudian treatment may be reduced. The Oedipus complex, far from being that revelation of the deepest secret of the human soul which it purports to be, is a stupendous lawyer's trick, the most colossal *ignoratio elenchi* in history: a monster of the fallacy which consists in the attempt to disprove something by substituting something else and disproving *that*. Adam, accused before his Maker of the arch delict whose punishment is death, has at last found his cleverest advocate. "This man is charged with a capital crime. I move his acquittal on the ground that he is a very good son: he loved his mother."

It was also at this time that the notion first occurred to me that the Adlerian "inferiority complex" is nothing but the pragmatistic interpretation of Sin; and it seemed to me that the obvious philosophical superiority of Adlerian individual psychology to Freudian psychoanalysis rests on the fact that the former recognizes the reality of Sin, even though it does not call it by that name, whereas Freudism tries to explain Sin away, and thus starts out with a basically false assumption about that human soul whose secrets it claims to expose. As a matter of fact I have realized since that Adler does not recognize the *reality* of Sin, but bases his theory and practice on the maxim, "Men being what they are, we must act *as if* Sin were real." For Adler's philosophy, of which he was aware but about which he was never specially articulate, was a Vaihingerian version of pragmatism; and pragmatism implies a Pelagian theology — the notion that man is born without sin. But even Vaihingerian pragmatism is preferable, as a philosophic basis, to the almost incredibly shallow Freudian position, compounded of eighteenth-century French rationalism at its thinnest and of Talmudistic casuistry, a position that culminates in the assertion that Sin is *Schmonzes*, this latter being the Viennese-Yiddish jar-

gon term for buncombe. To do justice to Freud, however, I ought
to add that in his old age he abandoned this early attitude; for in
what is much the profoundest of all his writings, the late essay entitled *Jenseits des Lustprinzips* (in English, "Beyond the Pleasure
Principle"), he reaches the Buddhistic conclusion that all existence
is evil, a kind of cosmic disturbance forming a prelude to that only
Good which is Death. Now this position, though entirely wrongheaded, has at least dignity and even a certain grandeur, in contrast to the merry chatter of those popularizers of psychoanalysis
who advise themselves and their clients, "Sin away, my boy and/or
girl, for after all who the hell is Oedipus?" I have always thought
that one of the worst things about the current type of Freudian is
that he has not read Freud, or else, if he has read a little Freud, has
probably misconstrued him; this being one of the few points on
which I may claim being in accord with Freud himself.

My interest in the problem of Sin (and I am afraid that it may
be necessary for me to explain that by Sin I do *not* mean mere
sexual whoopee) was, however, aroused at this time more by my
reading of Schopenhauer than by anything else. Now I did not at
this time agree with the fundamental dogmas of this philosopher
any more than I agree with them today; but my disapproval did
not, and does not, prevent me from recognizing his greatness, insofar as greatness is compatible with divergence from basic Truth.
He towers above the facile if often obscure spinners of polysyllabic
trash who in the nineteenth century passed for philosophers as
Mount Everest would tower above the artificial cliffs and peaks
in an open-air zoo; his style is, though rather heavier, fully as brilliant as that of Nietzsche, and his thought cuts much deeper. And
yet Nietzsche exercised a profound influence on the late nineteenth-century ideologies as well as on the external destinies of
Europe and the world, being in many ways a precursor of Hitlerism; whereas Schopenhauer always remained the prophet of a very
small esoteric cult. In 1933 I was puzzled by this contrast, but today I understand it only too well. Schopenhauer's theology was
Buddhistic, for he regarded all existence as evil, and Not-being as
the only good. Nietzsche's theology was Manichean, for he con-

ceived existence as a battle between the principle of Good, as championed by an over-life-size athletic edition of Nietzsche, called the Superman, and the principle of Evil, championed by those who considered that viewed as a Superman Nietzsche was somewhat of an anemic prawn. Now Buddhism is the religion of wrongheaded and discouraged saints, but of saints just the same. Whereas Manicheism is the religion of the Gadarene Swine. And today Nietzsche's Superman reigns supreme over the destinies of the white world, in the guise of the man with the Charlie Chaplin mustache and the voice of a syphilitic drunkard.

I have no doubt that were Nietzsche alive today he would unhesitatingly repudiate Hitler and all his works, and come out strong on the right side; for Nietzsche was, when off duty as trainer of the Blond Beast, a civilized European, among other things, and a respecter of that *bourgeois* law and order, heir to the Apollinian tradition, in the midst of which it was comparatively easy and safe to write ecstatic Dionysian propaganda; and however pleased he was with himself in the role of a kind of Alan Breck of the mind, and with his ivory tower as a kind of roundhouse on the deck of a corrupt and foundering European civilization manned by pygmies and cowards, he was at heart an old-fashioned intellectual, and Himmler would clap him into a concentration camp in no time. So Dr. Suchandsuchsky need not write an angry letter to the *Times Book Review* defending him against my charge of crypto-Naziism, and vindicating him for the non-Aryan cause. Nietzsche did not *will* Hitler any more than Mazzini had willed Mussolini; yet Nietzsche is the spiritual father of Hitler, even as Mazzini is the spiritual father of Mussolini. One cannot be too careful in these matters.

But I have digressed again, and should fine myself a dollar for it had I a dollar to spare. In the summer of 1934, eighteen months after the period with which I am now dealing, I was thrilled to find that T. E. Hulme, whom I now regard as one of the most important English philosophers, on the strength of a single slender volume containing the notes and fragments of a young man who fell in battle for England — that T. E. Hulme, too, dated the complete change of his world outlook from the moment when he first woke up to the reality and implications of Original Sin.

What I, however, believe was the most important, and as far as my own intellectual development is concerned the most decisive, of all the ideas with which I was playing tag at this time was one suggested by an article by Mr. Aldous Huxley in *Harper's Magazine* for September 1929. I was lugging around this old number because it contained one of my own articles; I regret to say that my notes do not quote the title of Mr. Huxley's essay, and my copy of the magazine now forms part of the German loot of France. But here is the sentence for which I am eternally indebted to Mr. Aldous Huxley, for it inspired what I regard as at once the most significant and the most amusing product of the intellectual boom which I experienced in the quarter of the Observatoire, in the winter of 1932-1933. "To talk about religion except in terms of human psychology is an irrelevance." Thus spake Mr. Aldous Huxley, and he made at least one reader happy by his dictum. For one day, when rereading his piece I came on that sentence, I danced, metaphorically speaking, with joy as I transcribed it into "To talk about human psychology except in terms of religion is an irrelevance." Now this paraphrase was funny, but it was anything but a joke. It opened up new and fascinating vistas into the psychological understructure of atheism and agnosticism; and this was a subject which it had occurred to none of the well-publicized masters of modern psychology to investigate.

Freud has much to tell us about the psychopathological origin of religion, and it had always seemed to me, long before my return to a theistic interpretation of the universe, that his theories about the Old Man of the Tribe and the Prometheus complex and its origin in a peculiar attempt at putting out a forest fire were absolute unmitigated tripe. They have been recognized as such by many ethnologists who have no love for positive religion in general and the Christian religion in particular, but who happen to know something about primitive religiosity. It occurred to me at this time, under the Marx-Brotherish stimulus of Mr. Aldous Huxley's marvelously confident *ipse dixit*, that it might be well worth while to inquire into the psychopathological origins of Freud's hatred of religion and of his nasty little grammar schoolboy's attitude to God. Later I actually undertook this inquiry, but this is not the place to publish either my procedure or my detailed findings. But I will summarize them. The thesis in which the theories not only of Freud but of all the agnostic psychologizers about religion may be summed up runs, "God is a fiction contrived by the human mind in response to one of its own needs." *My* thesis runs, in its briefest form, "The thesis that God is a fiction is a fiction contrived by the human mind in response to one of its own needs, the need for playing at God."

Now it would be possible to show, by means of a purely logical argument, that my thesis is true, and that of Freud and his fellow atheists and agnostics false. But this strictly logical demonstration would not convince those who do not want to be convinced by it, and if they knew enough about these things they might find a way to stalemate me by the simple questions, Who the hell is Aristotle anyway, and why do I think that Aristotelian logic is the only valid logic, when there are other logics just as good and even better? And then I would have to abandon the field of logic and seek to prove my point by other means, and that would take yet another book. However, it is not necessary at all to decide here and now which is true, the Freudian refutation of the existence of God, or my refutation of the Freudian refutation. To my mind the most exhilarating consequence of my turning the tables on the agnostic psychologizers was this: Once I have shown that it is possible to psychoanalyze atheism and agnosticism in the same way and with at least the same validity that Christianity and positive religion in general have already been psychoanalyzed, then I have also shown, without any extra effort, that psychology is not competent to say the last word about religion and the existence of God; and I may respectfully invite the psychologists who claim such competence to take a breather in the park. If I can demonstrate that disbelief in or denial of God is a neurotic fiction prevalent in a small corner of the globe during a few centuries out of sixty, or two hundred, then the ground has been cleared for those who specialize in investigating and demonstrating the existence of God, as distinguished from the Wellses and Huxleys and Bertrand Russells, who claim a hearing for their views on God on the strength of a reputation gained in spheres where they know what they are talking about. Now the men who specialize in investigating the existence of God are the Christian theologians. How about giving the Five Proofs another chance?

The reader might think that when I arrived at this stage in my meditations I felt like Saint Augustine in that garden in Milan, or Saint Paul on the road to Damascus, and that I went to the nearest parish church and made my general confession and lived happily ever after. I wish that I could confirm what the reader might think; but I am afraid that I could not confirm it truthfully. The fact is that when I saw that not only a closely reasoned logical argument but also a strictly scientific demonstration, that of the psychopathological origins of atheism, was driving me back into that Catholic fold from which I had slipped away twenty-four years earlier, I felt extremely depressed. For I did not want to be driven anywhere, and least of all into the Catholic fold. I had the greatest respect for Aristotelian logic, and I was thrilled by my discovery of what I realized was not exactly a new proof of the existence of God, but at any rate a new preamble to proofs already known. I had always preserved a certain nostalgia for the Church, a nostalgia that was not exclusively emotional, but had an intellectual basis; for I suspected dimly that Catholic philosophy offered the most complete and logically most hole-proof explanation of the universe known to the mind of man, and this suspicion grew stronger even in the years when I was least inclined to act on it, and to examine Catholic philosophy from top to bottom.

But the plain truth is that in February 1933 I had no desire to rebecome a Catholic. For I knew enough about Catholicism not to have illusions on one point, and this was the point which at the moment decided the issue for me. I knew that it was far easier, far more comfortable, and in many ways more satisfactory to live as a non-Catholic than as a Catholic. I did not know much about

Catholicism at this time, for my early conversion had been superficial; but I knew enough not to be taken in by the twaddle of
those who spoke of it as a sort of easy cure-all, a spiritual tummy-
warmer and general comforter for the weaker brethren. There
are people who have never read a Catholic book in their lives and
yet denounce Catholicism on the ground that it is based on prejudice; who object to the Church because she is an enemy of knowledge, and who yet know not much more about her than the man
knows about Jews who has only studied them in the columns of
Julius Streicher's *Stürmer*. Such people usually also think that Catholicism is a religion for sob sisters. Well, I knew better than that.
I knew that Catholicism is a man's religion, hard and clear and as
exacting intellectually as it is morally. And at this time I did not
particularly want to live as a man; I preferred the easier existence
of a polished and discreet playboy-de-luxe with a certain amount of
intellectual ambition which was that of the estate that I had begun
to leave behind spiritually, the estate of the twentieth-century
agnostic man of letters.

I remember one evening in February 1933 when I dined early
in a little Chinese restaurant near the Cluny Museum, and walked
back home, up the Boulevard St. Michel and the Avenue de l'Observatoire, to take my dogs out. I was thinking as I walked that
the greatest mistake of my life, one with a higher than average
score of mistakes, had been to leave the Church before I was
eighteen, without giving myself a chance as a Catholic. I thought
of the priests who had been my friends, one of whom had been my
godfather, and who had intimated that they would help me all
they could if I felt a vocation to enter their order; and for a brief
moment I had thought that I might. Now I was not thinking of
what I had missed in terms of advancement and prestige, but in
terms of a great intellectual loss to myself, for by this time it was
evident to me that what I had loved, and was now beginning to
love again, most about Catholicism was its clarity, completeness,
consistency, and uncompromisingness. And I reflected that although
I had many faults that barred me from ever making a good priest,
I had at least one quality that a priest must have; and this was a

certain inelasticity of the intellect, what those who dislike it call a dogmatic turn. By this I mean the refusal to compromise about truth once recognized as such, and the inability to see that perhaps a little less of it might do just as well.

Those who have followed me to this page are in the position to judge whether I may rightfully claim such mental rigidity as one of my traits, though I am aware that most contemporaries, far from wanting to claim it, would rather not touch it, as the saying goes, with a fifty-foot pole; for it is the denial or contradiction of a virtue that they prize above all others, to wit, toleration. Now I too can see the beauty of this virtue, but I also hold that an excess of it is not much better than an excessive love of wine, which also tends to blunt the mind's edge; and I hold that a free man is a slave to nothing, not even to his fear of appearing intolerant in defense of the truth that he knows. But it is true enough that I am by nature and temper an extremist, and I know now that had I entered the Church at all I should not have been content with being a secular priest, but should have become a Dominican, this being the order of Saint Thomas Aquinas, and the one that specializes in philosophic inquiry.

But on that evening in February 1933 of which I write, though in a way I was passing judgment on myself and my past, I was not yet ready to execute the sentence. I had seen the light, but refused to follow it, for the road was uphill and too arduous for one of my easy habits; and I said to myself that evening, not knowing that I was quoting Saint Augustine, "There is yet time." It is the one passage of the *Confessions* that all the world knows by heart, and cites *con amore*.

There are, writes Father D'Arcy, the English philosopher, many doors whereby a man may enter the Catholic Church; but the Church herself prefers the door of the intellect to any other. Well, that door was being held open for me, in February 1933, by Mr. Aldous Huxley, Professor Sigmund Freud, and a few other scholars and gentlemen of their agnostic kind, all working in shifts; and they would have been surprised, though perhaps not flattered, to know what effect their writings had on one particular reader.

But though the door was open, and I liked the illumination within, I still hesitated, for I preferred, for everyday purposes, the vague comfort of the twilight outside. I was eventually pushed in by the lady who said that Puccini was as good a composer as Bach, because *she* thought so, and her opinion was as good as anybody else's; and what was I going to do about it? I did nothing about it, except that I stepped through that door and shut it gently; and found myself sheltered forever from ladies, and others, who claimed for their *obiter dicta* on music, and on any other subject, the infallibility that the Pope only claims for himself when he speaks officially on points of Catholic doctrine.

3

There was a lady from Chicago, thin and dark, who went in for the severe Pre-Raphaelite line in black or white dress, and considered herself a great expert in matters of the mind because she had read Marcel Proust in the original French, and the later James Joyce in the original gibberish, and Pirandello in English translation; and she lived in a flat on Montparnasse. And this lady told a friend of mine, who was also a friend of hers, that this Bagger fellow had quite a good embryonic mind, and that his conversation consisted in a half-baked stammering exposure of quite intelligent ideas. My friend, who reported this conversation to me, was greatly angered by what he called the cattiness of the remark, and said that the Pre-Raphaelite lady had a nerve indeed, and was generally a big fool. But while I could not help smiling at the lady's superior tone, I could also see what she meant by what she had said, and I did not resent it, for I felt that somehow she was right; and I could never, for the life of me, see why anybody should resent truthful criticism, instead of seeking to profit by it. Looking back on this episode, which I have often pondered since, I realize that the Prousto-Pirandellian lady from Illinois not only was right by and large in calling my mind embryonic and my conversation an attempt at one, but hit the nail on the head with great accuracy, and that I owe her a sort of apology for having underrated her intellect in 1933.

For the fact of the matter is that in those days when I was exercising my dogs in the Luxembourg Gardens and discovering great thoughts at the rate of two or three a day, my mind had just woken up from a kind of prenatal sleep and had begun to wriggle; and the lady's feline observation was a wholesome reminder of this fact. Indeed, that summary of hers not only fitted me as I really was at this time, in contrast to what I imagined myself to be, but might be labeled a composite portrait of the philosopher as a young man. For the philosopher is not one who says to himself, "From today onward I shall think seriously about everything," but one who says, "Until today all the thoughts that I have thought have been wrong, and I must begin to think over again." Philosophy, that is to say, is not a mere extension and intensification of the accepted ways of thinking, but a radical re-examination of those ways; philosophy may be described as the systematic debunking of the current and conventional sales talk about the universe that most people regard as an unbiased report, simply because they have never heard any other. Because he wonders about everything that other people take for granted, the novice of philosophy will appear to these others as a kind of newborn babe, no matter what his age; for his old world has crumbled away from him and he has not yet found his bearings in the new world which he is in the process of discovering. Hence people who call his mind embryonic are right, even though they use the adjective with a disparaging intention, oblivious of the well-known fact that the future belongs to the embryo and not to the fossil.

But that lack of self-confidence and of mental finish which the dark lady of Montparnasse noted in me was not a new thing. It was something that I had always felt as a handicap, and suspected of being one of the penalties of my intellectual precocity as a boy, the unsubstantiality and wobbliness which are the price of too rapid growth. Thus it had always seemed to me that in highbrow conversation I was never a match for my fellows, because they expressed their ideas, such as they were, with great verve, accuracy, and promptness, while I expressed mine, such as *they* were, gropingly, with all sorts of halting reservations and qualifications, and only *à peu près*, as the succinct French phrase has it; a phrase which I must try to render into English by the clumsy circumlocution that whatever I said expressed what I meant almost, but not quite. Nor did this self-criticism spring from modesty, for I felt at the same time that when it came to putting my notions into writing I did not do so badly. And I used to comfort myself with a saying of Oliver Goldsmith's; for he, too, had suffered from a tongue-tiedness similar to mine, but turned his admission of it into a boast by remarking that while he lacked small change, he could write a draft for a thousand pounds at any time — which was a very neat way of putting it. In fairness to myself I ought to add that I did not think that I could write a draft for a thousand pounds, but I did think that I could write one for ten; which, as I see it now, was rather overrating the inclination of my bankers to honor an overdraft.

Now I explained this inability of mine to formulate ideas by word of mouth, firstly by the fact that I was not born to the use of English; and secondly by a certain shyness which I, in my capacity of psychologist, diagnosed as the expression of an exaggerated self-conceit undermined by the knowledge that it was not justified by achievement, and by the suspicion that it was not justified by capacity for achievement. But while I could thus account for my own backwardness in intellectual talk, I could not account for the fact that some people who were quite obviously not superior to me in respect either of originality of thought, or of learning, were just as obviously superior to me in respect of facility and cogency of expression.

In retrospect, however, the whole matter has become quite clear. My friends could communicate their ideas readily and accurately because they were absolutely certain that those ideas were true, and derived from sound unassailable premises. They called themselves, for the most part, skeptics, and held that there was always something to be said for the other fellow's point of view. At the same time it never occurred to them to doubt that skepticism was the proper attitude of an intelligent human being; nor did they realize that their lack of doubt on this point gave their philosophy the lie; for to hold that skepticism is the only rational way of looking at things is the same as to cease to be a skeptic, and to profess naïve faith in a gratuitous dogma; the person who is absolutely sure of his skepticism is like one who saws away the branch on which he is perched. Also, when these friends said that they were always prepared to see things from the other fellow's viewpoint, they ignored the not insignificant detail that the viewpoints of most of the other fellows were, in all fundamental matters, exactly like their own. For instance, they were quite prepared to see things from the viewpoint of the man who said that there were two sides to every question; but they were emphatically not prepared to admit the legitimacy of the viewpoint that some viewpoints are absolutely right, and others absolutely wrong. All of which sounds a bit involved, but it is really very simple and straightforward, once you have grasped it.

Now I, for my part, did not share this comfortable certitude that we cannot be certain about anything; and to this extent I was a truer skeptic than my friends who called themselves skeptics, while I did not call myself one. To begin with, it had dawned on me that an intransigent skepticism is incompatible with survival. If we really doubted every proposition offered to our assent, as the ardent skeptic says that we must, we should not be able to perform the most elementary actions that keep us alive, since we should be obliged to tell ourselves that we can never predict with any sort of assurance the results of such actions.

Not to cast our net too wide for instances, a true skeptic would starve himself to death in a few days, since he could never be sure that his food does not contain deadly poison. In order to live man must act, but in order to act he must know in advance what will happen if he acts in such and such a way; he must, for example, be able to rely on a degree of constancy in the properties of matter and of consistency in the reactions of his own body. Moreover, the true skeptic would not even try to survive, since his creed would oblige him to doubt the value of survival. Thus the true skeptic, if he were at all an intelligent person, would have to admit that he is a skeptic only about not immediately vital matters, whereas in respect of things that affect his physical well-being he plots his course in accordance with a non-skeptical philosophy. But this admission would reduce his skepticism, in fact all skepticism, to a kind of intellectual mah-jongg. On the other hand, the skeptic who refuses to make this admission exposes himself to the charge of being a muddleheaded poseur. He might retort to this charge that as a skeptic he doubts the value of consistency and the validity of labels; but I would rejoin that I doubt the necessity of the survival of people who talk trash, and will he kindly put his head into the gas oven? The chances are that he would refuse point-blank to do this, not being in the least skeptical about the fate of people who put their heads into gas ovens; and if I were to apply physical pressure he might even go to the length of shouting for the police, thus demonstrating that he is no skeptic at all, since he believes in the value of life and in the functioning of the machinery of law and order.

There are more ways than one of showing up skepticism as the nonessential and undignified intellectual parlor game that it is; but at the time with which I am dealing I was not concerned with exposing the basic absurdity of the skeptical creed, but only with making sense of some of its implications. For I was, as yet, not prepared to admit that the agnostic position, of which skepticism is but a goofy variant, is untenable as such, though I had already discovered some of its flaws and had begun to wonder just how fatal they were. I was, in other words, hoping that by mending a leaking roof I might make habitable a house that I suspected of being built on quicksand five hundred miles from the nearest food market. Thus I still believed in those days that the willingness to see both sides of a question is the mark of the truly rational person, and I justified my own opinions on the ground that others were entitled to theirs. And yet I had already begun to realize that such broad-mindedness, of which I was as proud as anybody else in my intellectual neighborhood, was apt to lead to conclusions which I could not honestly accept. I shall illustrate what I mean by an example.

From my earliest youth I have always admired the music of Johann Sebastian Bach more than that of any other composer. When I was twenty or twenty-five I *loved* Beethoven more; but even then I felt that Bach had something that Beethoven lacked, though I could not have said what this something was. As I grew older and came to know more music, my tastes broadened in the sense that I could appreciate composers I had been unable to relish before; at the age of thirty, for instance, I found Gustav Mahler unintelligible, while at the age of forty I thought him not only admirable and lovable but also crystal-clear, and came to regard him, in spite of a great unevenness and a certain prolixity, with Sibelius as the greatest of moderns. But in another sense my tastes were narrowing at the same time, and apart from a few latter-day composers whom I appreciated for their individual merits and more or less in spite of the schools or tendencies that they represented, I came to reserve my full enthusiasm and my unqualified intellectual approval for the musicians of the seventeenth and eighteenth centuries, and to prefer, on the whole, old music to anything written after 1800. Moreover, I could now give reasons for these preferences, and this is one of my excuses for discussing my musical tastes at all; for their development was not something independent and isolated, but a direct consequence and integral part of the development of my philosophical ideas. It is my firm conviction that everything in this world hangs together with everything else, and I regard philosophy as the highest form of our knowledge of this world precisely because it explains how and why things hang together.

Now, at the time of my life with which this sub-chapter is concerned I had already arrived at the conclusion that Bach was the greatest composer of all, and I knew enough theory and history of music to state my grounds for this view. The music of Bach gives me a pleasure that no other music can give, with the exception of Gregorian plainchant, and an occasional bit of polyphony from the seventeenth or sixteenth century. But, as I have already pointed out more than once, it has always seemed to me that one's ideas and one's tastes could not be both keen and broad at the same time, and that if you love one thing very much, you are bound, by your human nature, to love other things in the same order less, and even to hate some things. Thus the more I loved Bach and Palestrina and plainsong, the more I came to dislike certain compositions of Beethoven, and among these the Fifth Symphony is one that I positively detest. To me it stands out as one of the arch examples of the most offensive brand of Teutonic bombast, hollow and vulgar in spite of all its superb craftsmanship, the most perfect expression in terms of music of the self-inflation and self-celebration of that poor fish, Man the Sovereign.

In anticipation of the howls of scorn and condemnation that this statement will provoke on the part of the Beethoven fans and the art-for-art's-sakers I will point out that to make a case for it would take another chapter, which I intend to write, but do not intend to incorporate in this book. For the moment suffice it to say that the idea that you can judge a symphony, or any other piece of art or literature, out of its historic context, as an entity governed by its own laws that are unconnected with other fields of human endeavor, is one of those baleful nineteenth-century fallacies which have brought the Western world to its present pass. There are also those who are offended if one suggests that Wagner is the precursor of Naziism in terms of music; but their getting het-up over this self-evident assertion merely proves to me that they know nothing about Naziism and little about Wagner beyond his technical brilliancy and their own emotional reactions to the more aphrodisiac aspects of his music. Now old Papa Haydn, who was himself a musician of sorts, and among other things had been Beethoven's teacher, knew better; for his comment on hearing the "Eroica" was simply, "The man is an atheist"; and nothing could be more to the point.

That brings us to the lady who backed Puccini against Bach. Now the reader will perceive that my digression into my musical tastes was more excusable than most of my other digressions, for it was intended to suggest that while I cannot, among musicians, claim even amateur status, among laymen I have, in the course of forty years, advanced somewhat beyond the position of those who do not know anything about music but know what they like. In justice to the lady aforesaid I ought to state that she did not really rate the composer of *Madama Butterfly* higher than the composer of the "Passion According to St. Matthew." She had a cultivated, if theoretically untutored, interest in music, and a sense of musical values which one could find little to quarrel with. She and I crossed swords on purely abstract grounds, and it was a mere accident that we used as our concrete instances Puccini and Bach, instead of Sir Hugh Walpole and Thomas Hardy, or Sargent and Giorgione. Her point was that individual preference supplies the ultimate basis of any judgment of artistic merit; that not only has everybody a right to his opinion in these matters, but that it is impossible to say that one man's opinion is more authentic and more worthy of general acceptance than another's. All this I denied with more vehemence than articulate cogency. She admitted the existence, and superior claims to be heard, of experts; but according to her the expert was one who, on the strength of his systematic preoccupation with a subject, was in a better position to argue his point than the layman; his expertness did not necessarily mean that his point of view was intrinsically worthier than that of the nonexpert; and the layman could always counter the argument of the adept with an "I do not agree," and that was the end of the discussion. For (and this was the apex, as it had been the base, of this lady's reasoning) everybody has a right to his opinion.

I did not deny the thesis that everybody has a right to his opinion; I pointed out that everybody has the right to make a fool of himself, and this latter right already includes the former. But having the right to hold an opinion is one thing, and claiming public consideration for one's opinion, let alone a status of equality with all other opinions, is something quite different. The validity of an artistic or any other judgment, I went on, is not a mere outflow or reward of personal sincerity. Nobody can be more sincere than the lunatic who maintains that he is Julius Caesar or Donald Duck; and if mere sincerity were the source and warranty of truth, we ought to reorganize society so as to make room for his claim, instead of locking him up in an asylum. There is, I argued, a certain unalterable context in this universe that we must accept as such, and according to which we must think if we want to think truly; and this context contains not only elemental identities — a dog is a dog and a cat is a cat, and so forth — but also immutable relationships between such identities. For instance, no personal opinion could modify the fact, this world being what it is, that Glasgow is north of Liverpool, or that if you burn hydrogen in certain conditions you get water, or that a cake that you eat today cannot serve for tomorrow's tea.

Now this unalterable context, which we may deplore but which we cannot ignore, comprises, also, certain hierarchies or scales of values, one of these being the scale of musical values; and this allows us to determine beyond question that Bach was a greater composer than Puccini, and that a person who asserts the contrary merely proves his ignorance. Whereupon the lady inquired, where did I get all that stuff. I said proudly that I got it from Aristotle. The lady said, well, she had thought it was something of that sort, but why worry about Aristotle, after all he is only an old Greek who has been dead these twenty-five centuries, and how do I know that it was really Aristotle and not somebody else by the same name, just as Shakespeare was really Bacon. And she added that even if it had been Aristotle who invented all those stuffy ideas, they were only his personal opinions and no better than anybody else's. I said she was wrong, and she asked what made me think so. I replied that I just knew it, whereupon she uttered a triumphant yell to the effect that there you are, you base your judgment in the last resort on yourself, just like me and everybody else, and you poke fun at individualists and you are just another. If you run out of reasons you fire off a big capital I, and think that you have settled the point. She wound up her campaign speech boosting subjective idealism by pointing out that anyway far more people agreed with her than with me and my precious Aristotle. "You just try to put the matter to a referendum," she said, "and millions of decent normal taxpayers will vote for everybody's right to his opinion, and it will be only a dozen cranks like yourself who will vote for eternal hierarchies and all that sort of rot, and I'll bet that not one of you has ever sold an article to the *Ladies' Home Journal,* which only goes to show that you are disgruntled and full of envy because you are unsuccessful." And I saw that she had won the argument, but I remained unconvinced just the same.

4

Now this mental joust had taken place some time before the period with which I was dealing in the preceding sub-chapter; but I recalled it on those walks in the Luxembourg Gardens, and also in connection with the Pre-Raphaelite lady's uncomplimentary description of my mind as embryonic, and with the difficulties I experienced at this time in intellectual controversy. And I told myself that the lady who championed Puccini had been sure of her ground, such as it was; whereas I was not so sure of mine, though I believed that it was probably a better ground. For had I been absolutely certain of what I professed, namely, that there exists an order of eternal truths which determine sets of enduring values, I should have realized that such sets of values govern, and may be discovered in, all fields or spheres of human endeavor; and that it would be absurd to maintain that the esthetic order contains a permanent hierarchy of values, while in the ethical order, or in the order of political action, values are "relative" — appointed provisionally by individual preference or sincerity, or by the spirit of the age, or by some other fluctuating and adjustable authority. And yet in that discussion which I have quoted at length it was my opponent, and not I, who saw that the method of determining truth which she defended is either valid in all spheres or isn't valid at all. The lady who championed the right of the man in the street to pit his sentimental preference of Puccini against the expert's documented preference of Bach had realized quite clearly that what was involved in our argument was nothing less than the fundamental postulate of modern democracy: that all truth and all value may be determined by taking a vote. By contrast I had, at the time, believed that in the field of art we must apply permanent standards that are fixed in and by the nature of things and are independent of our will, whereas in the field of politics or ethics "everybody was entitled to his own opinion" — that is, could fix for himself such standards as happened to suit him. In other words, the lady in question knew her own mind, and I did not know mine.

But now I had begun to see more clearly. It struck me, in the first place, that my opponent's reasoning fitted in admirably with certain conclusions which I had reached by an approach that had apparently nothing to do with standards of artistic value. It was by examining the Adlerian theory of the abnormal mental condition called neurosis that I had discovered that in our age the prevailing conception of reality is determined by a majority vote. But this conception of reality, whereby men decide what *is* and what *is not*, what *is so* and what merely *appears so,* already includes standards of truth and value, and is applied to everything that men do and think and feel and dream. It dominates the sphere of art, where it manifests itself in the make-up of the programs of symphony concerts, in the designs of magazine covers, and in the dissertations of critics who see in highbrowized jazz the contemporary equivalent of seventeenth-century polyphony. It dominates the sphere of literature, where it commands publishers to publish the books which tell people what they already know and like to hear, and to reject the books which seek to stir people out of their smug ignorance. It dominates the sphere of politics, where it reduces leadership to a series of frantic attempts on the part of politicians to catch the bus which they pretend to drive, and where it also enables men to believe that they can make things happen by passing laws and resolutions.

Thus under this democratic dispensation knowledge being recognized as a good thing, and ignorance as a bad thing, it is believed that knowledge can be made compulsory by passing laws that send every child to school for a number of years. By the same token, peace being recognized as a good thing, and war as a bad thing, it is believed that war can be abolished by voting for disarmament in our own country, quite regardless of the fact that there exist bad countries that go on arming; or by voting for resolutions which "outlaw" war — which is actually what the Western democracies did in the happy days when Mr. Kellogg was in flower, and the Nazis were only murdering individual Jews at home, instead of exterminating by wholesale methods a dozen nations all over Europe.

Thus I had begun to realize, in the winter of 1932–1933, just how the democratic principle of establishing reality by a referendum worked, and in which direction it was leading the Western world. But I also began to see that the method of defining truth and value by counting heads did not, as it were, stand on its own feet, but was based on yet another, more fundamental principle; on the principle that the source of and authority for all truth and value is the individual — myself, yourself, and the respective selves of Tom, Dick, and Harry. And so in an age which prides itself on being guided by reason, and reason alone, we accept, as the ultimate basis of truth, personal faith; for nobody can be made to state his grounds for thinking *this* rather than *that*, and most people would be unable in most cases to state such grounds even if they wanted to state them. Now faith is a belief which imposes itself in its own right and neither requires nor is capable of demonstration or motivation. But if we accept such individual faith as the fountainhead and criterion of what is true and what is good and desirable, then taking a vote becomes the indispensable method of establishing the rules that direct corporate effort and restrain both individual exuberance and public encroachment.

Several further conclusions emerged from these meditations. One was that contrary to the prevalent belief, according to which individualism is something that is rendered possible by democratic institutions, it was a fundamental individualistic philosophy that has made democracy inevitable as its proper mode of self-realization. Nor could I accept any longer the at once peevish and hopeful notion which I had held in my highbrow days in New York, to the effect that the leveling and standardizing tendencies of democracy represent abuses or excrescences of the democratic principle, a kind of growing pains which will disappear with the gradual rise of the general level of democratic culture. I now recognized that leveling and standardization belong to the very essence of democracy, being the price that democracy has to pay for its internal equilibrium and security. Then, I realized that there exists a fatal contradiction between the underlying theory of democracy, which is individualistic *à outrance*, and the practical necessities of the democratic superstructure, which is bound to develop along anti-individualistic, collectivistic lines if the rights and interests of all individuals are to be safeguarded. From this follows that democracy is by its very nature incapable of fulfilling all the expectations of its component members which the democratic creed rouses.

This realization took me back to the concept of a "margin of disappointment" which I had evolved in the course of my Adlerian reflections; it was clear that in democracy, which encourages the individual in quest of self-fulfillment to believe that the sky is the limit, the margin of disappointment is bound to be wider than under any other form of social organization. Finally, I began to suspect as the most fatal flaw of democracy a certain facile optimism which focuses men's minds on the silver lining and makes them ignore the black cloud; that blinds them to any but the most immediately menacing danger, and engenders the trust that somehow everything will come out all right if they only wait and see.

Next I asked myself how and when had originated this strange idea that the individual has both the right and the capacity to determine all truth and all value out of the depths of his own wisdom and sincerity. I called it a strange idea, since it seemed to me that a week's reading of the newspapers (and this was in 1933) ought to incite doubts as to its tenability, while even a cursory study of mankind's history should suffice to brand it as the fateful absurdity which it is. Now the event that had let this idea loose on the Western world, and had turned it from a topic of highbrow talk in the Parisian salons into the basic principle of the Modern dispensation, was the French Revolution. It was not difficult to see that the proposition, "individual faith is the source and certifying principle of truth," was the translation, into terms of the prevalent theory of knowledge, of Rousseau's thesis about the natural goodness of man. But Rousseau did not invent this thesis; it had been proclaimed fourteen hundred years before him by the British monk Pelagius, who denied Original Sin and asserted man's ability to reach perfection by his own unaided effort, and who therefore may be regarded as the founder of the religion of Progress and the ideology of Liberalism. In his day Pelagius was put into his place by Saint Augustine, whose account of human nature, which differs from that of twentieth-century psychological science mainly in its terminology, was to dominate Western development for the next thousand years. The views of Pelagius were, however, revived, at least by implication, by the thinkers of the Renaissance, and above all by Bacon and Descartes.

It might be objected to this statement that Bacon, at any rate, was not much concerned with the doctrine of the Fall and its consequences for human history; but that is just the point I wish to make. Bacon disposes of the Fall and of Sin by identifying knowledge with the knowledge of cause-effect relations within the natural order. Such knowledge, he says, is power, since it enables man to exploit nature for his own purposes. But this "anticipation," to use a Baconian term, already implies that man need not worry about the divinely appointed purposes of things, being fully capable of determining what things are for, and what is good for him; and it also implies that whatever is good enough for man is good enough for the universe. No less clear is the Pelagian bias of Cartesian philosophy. Descartes taught that an idea is true if it appears clearly and distinctly to our consciousness. Now this definition repudiates the older notion that man's vision is distorted by his selfishness, or by what Christian doctrine calls his fallen nature, Adlerian psychology calls the will-to-power, and pragmatism calls the purposive character of thinking. Thus Jacques Maritain hits the nail on the head when he says that the Cartesian definition of truth assumes that men are angels.

It was, indeed, the philosophy of Descartes that laid down the theoretical foundations of Western civilization for the following

350 years. And his philosophy may be reduced to the principle that truth is a matter of individual preference. For that is just what we imply when we say that any idea is true that presents itself clearly and distinctly to our minds. Bossuet had no illusions as to the way Cartesianism was headed when he wrote, "Under the pretext that we must not accept anything but what we understand — which, within certain limits, is very true — everyone gives himself liberty to say, 'I understand this, and I do not understand that,' and on this sole basis they admit and reject whatever they like."

But the modern conception of truth as personal conviction and an outflow of sincerity has a double, and not a single, ancestry, and this was yet another of the things that I had begun to perceive during that Indian summer of 1932 which was also the Indian summer of Modern civilization. In an earlier chapter of this book I related how a contemplation of the Pont du Gard in Languedoc had started in my mind, back in 1928, a train of ideas which I was eventually to organize into an interpretation of European history as the struggle between two stages of psychological development — the stage of the Builders, represented by the Roman Empire and its heirs, France, England, Italy, Spain, Switzerland, and Holland, and the stage of the Raiders, represented by Germany. I now began to trace this dual strain in the evolution of European philosophy. In the Middle Ages, when the "Two Races" were spiritually united by their common allegiance to the universal Church, European thought formed a whole. But this unity was disrupted by Luther, who captained the revolt of the Teutonic world not only against the Church of Rome, but against Mediterranean civilization in all its aspects and bearings; and the breach thus inflicted on the body of European culture has never been healed. Now the principle whereby Descartes revolutionized the thought of the Roman West in the seventeenth century, the identification of truth with clear and distinct ideas, had been put forward in Germany a century earlier by Luther, in the form of the doctrine of justification by faith alone, and of its philosophical variant, the right of private judgment.

Both these fundamental notions of the Lutheran Reformation

were originally aimed at freeing the individual from the authority
of the Church of Rome; but in the course of time they converged
in repudiating all checks and obligations imposed on the human
mind by the external world. The doctrine of justification by faith
alone, as proposed by Luther, was intended to do away with the
juridical system of rewards and punishments with which the
Church of Rome had surrounded personal salvation. The right of
private judgment, as claimed by Luther, meant the right of every
believer to interpret the word of God in the light of his own
conscience. But by the dawn of the twentieth century, after the
lapse of four hundred years, justification by faith alone had come
to mean, not to Lutherans but to all comers, "Whatever I believe
is true"; and Luther's demand, "Every Christian his own priest,"
had been distorted, by the ineluctable irony of Western thought,
into the thesis, "Every agnostic his own Pope."

For the argument whereby my opponent in that discussion of
1927 sought to prove that Puccini was as great a composer as Bach
if she chose to think so, the proposition "Every man has a right to
his opinion" meant nothing less than everyman's claim to infallibility: an infallibility which enthroned itself above common sense,
above the accumulated wisdom of the ages, above the very laws
of thought; an infallibility which disposed of the claims of logic
by never having heard of them, and of the claims of facts by interpreting facts in the light of the moment's whim. If the twentieth-
century body politic was presided over by a Congress of sovereign
princes called Smith, Jones, and Robinson, the spiritual and intellectual body of Western civilization had come to be governed by a
Council sitting in permanence at a place called Vanity Fair, and
consisting not of mere bishops but of millions of sovereign pontiffs
who bore the names of Tom, Dick, Harry, Herb, Percy, and
Clarence.

It is impossible for me to trace here the evolution of the ideology
of Man the Sovereign, in which converged the two strains of
Western Modernity. On the one hand was the Roman or Renaissance strain represented by Bacon, who preached the subdual of the
physical order by Science; by Descartes, who inaugurated the

conquest of the spiritual order by Idealism; and by Rousseau, who set out to re-create the moral order in his own image. On the other hand was the Teutonic or Reformation strain, represented by Luther and Kant. That evolution makes up the history of the Western world from the early sixteenth century to our own day, when the ideology of Sovereign Man collapsed with a suddenness and finality unparalleled in the annals of mankind, and brought down with it overnight the whole thousand-year-old political edifice of Europe. To describe that evolution in detail, and to account for that collapse, are among the tasks that my "Philosophy of Freedom" has set itself, and that I intend to tackle, with the help of God and under the protection of the R.A.F., as soon as this book is finished.

But I will record here the fact that as far back as the spring of 1933, when I had just begun to outline my philosophy of history, and to analyze the theoretical understructure of Modern civilization, I had no illusions left as to the practical consequences of a philosophy that was based on the claim of every individual to accept as true ideas that he wanted to accept, and to reject as false ideas that did not happen to suit him. I asked myself, what would happen if somewhere on the outskirts of our civilization there arose some unprecedented and incalculable danger, say a new religion capable of fanaticizing the souls of its followers in the same way in which Islam had fanaticized the Arab and Turkish world in the Middle Ages, and that in addition could draw upon the terrific power-plus developed by modern science since the days of the Caliphs. I asked myself, how long would it take to convince the majority in a great democracy that this danger, which was something remote in space and, for the moment, in time; which was, because of the fullness, or as some might say totalitarianism, of its power for evil, something unprecedented in history; and which could not be possibly understood and judged in its roots and bearings by the average elector in Minnesota, or Yorkshire, or Gascony — I asked myself just how long it would take to convince the majority of the peoples of England, France, and the United States that this danger was *real*, and that something had to be done about it in a hurry. For under the democratic dispensation, which assumes that the opinion of the man in the street is as good as that of the greatest of experts, it was necessary to persuade the majority of the electorate before anything was done at all.

I asked myself, also, whether a philosophy which told man that he was the sovereign master of the order of nature, the order of ideas, the order of values, the moral order, the esthetic order, and any other order he could think of; a philosophy which promised man the fullness of life, and the power and the glory of this world; and which, in four hundred years, has brought European mankind to the brink of destruction by bombardment from the air and poison gas — I asked myself whether such a philosophy could be true.

I asked myself these questions in the Rue Cassini, which is in the precinct of the Observatory in the fourteenth ward of Paris, in the month of March in 1933, when Adolf Hitler had been Chancellor of the German Reich for two months, and within a month of the day when the men of Goering set fire to the Reichstag building and thus lighted the beacon that announced to the world the New Age, the age of the Teutonic We-God and of the annihilation of the Other-Race.

In the months that followed I surveyed the origins of that philosophy of Man the Sovereign; and I saw that however widely the views of its four founders may have differed in every other respect, there was one respect in which Luther and Bacon and Descartes and Rousseau were at one — their implacable hostility to the philosophy of Aristotle and of Thomas of Aquino, which is also the philosophy of the Catholic Church.

In a preceding page I quoted the saying of Father D'Arcy, the English philosopher, to the effect that among the many doors which lead into the Church, the Church herself favors the door of the intellect. I said that the moment came when this door was being held open for me by such unexpected ushers as Mr. Aldous Huxley and Dr. Sigmund Freud; and I also said that I was eventually pushed through this door by the lady who backed Puccini against Bach. Well, in a way it is true that it was she who had pushed me; for it was our argument about composers, way back in 1927 or '28, that had set me off to investigate the philosophical foundations of the doctrine according to which every individual is entitled to believe that what he thinks is true just because he thinks it. I should perhaps say that that lady had shoved me, by her reasoning, into the arms of Luther, Bacon, Descartes, and Rousseau. But it was these four giants of the mind, the spiritual founders of the Modern Age, who eventually hustled me through the door of the Church; for it was through the study of their writings that I discovered at last what was wrong with the modern world, and where the remedy of all our evils may be found.

IX. The Fey Years

MOST men past forty-five or so, or at any rate most men of intelligence and imagination, have, I suppose, tucked away in some corner of their minds a picture of the good life, a formula that answers the question, "How would I spend my days if I could spend them the way I want to?" and answers it not with the omnivorous and ignorant greed of youth, but with the selective wisdom distilled from knowledge of self and experience of the world, a wisdom that cuts the dream to the cloth of possible fulfillment. To me that vision centers round a little house with a roof of S-shaped Roman tiles, a house covered with honeysuckle and bougainvillaea, surrounded by pines; an arbor where I would sit in a deck chair and read the *Summa Theologica;* a terraced garden with olive trees and cherry trees and a vegetable patch where I would grow my own tomatoes and green peas and sweet corn; walks in the hills in the company of my wife and my two stepsons and half a dozen terriers; a couple of miles' swim off a clean beach of pebble and rock — and the house would be situated somewhere in the flank of a mountain between Cannes and Toulon.

The dream also includes trips, in the hot months, to Auvergne, to those immense moors which stretch between Clermont-Ferrand and the Mont-Dore, and that vast heath of Charlannes where you may wander for days on end on more or less level ground, but at an altitude of 5000 feet, and gaze on those giants of the Massif Central — the Puy de Sancy in the north, and the Puy Mary and Plomb du Cantal in the south — and on the winding valley of the young Dordogne above St. Sauves. Or to the mountain city of Le Puy, with the Cathedral of Our Lady perched on its tall perpendicular rock, proud symbol of what France was and will be again; or to that Lake of Geneva the shores of which I love better than any land in Europe outside France, save for that northern rim of Exmoor which drops down to the sea between Minehead and Lynmouth, and which to me is the quintessence of the immortal beauty of England. The dream winds up with autumn and Christmastide in New York; and I would call a year so divided a year well-planned. Not the least among the advantages of such a scheme of existence is that it could be lived at half the cost of a year's commuting from Connecticut to Grand Central; but when I say this I speak in terms of that prewar golden age which has been swept away by the unclean flood of the mechanized gorillas from beyond the Rhine.

And that is just the point of my talking about my old dream at all — a dream of maturity, of which I had a foretaste when I was young and when I still believed that it was right to enjoy the reward of exertions not yet made. That dream has been stolen from me. By the Germans. By the same Germans who have also, and at the same time, stolen from over a hundred million Frenchmen, Dutchmen, Belgians, Norwegians, Danes, Poles, Czechs, and Austrians all they possessed and all they loved. But the end is not yet. There is still England. An England whose strength of mind and body has been utterly miscalculated by the gorilla generals and the gorilla psychologists, as also by their jackal helpers who have sold out France. And there is also, towering in her untapped might behind the rampart which is England, this United States of ours, the predestined leader of the English-speaking race of men against the German-speaking race of self-debased sub-men; a United States which is at last waking up to the realization that men cannot keep aloof while other men fight for the survival of humanity against an overwhelming force of prehistoric beasts of prey.

But the people of the United States have only just begun to understand that the war which England has been waging single-handed so far is a war for our freedom just as much as a war for the freedom of England. And there are two or three things that the majority of the American people have not yet begun to understand: that its free traditions and its tolerance are being exploited by those who hate all freedom, all tradition, and all tolerance; that

France was defeated not by the German tanks and aeroplanes, but by her own native-born French Lindberghs and other appeasers; and that America's most dangerous enemies are not Hitler and Goering, but our own native-born American Lavals, who deliberately or unwittingly — it does not matter which — are playing the game of Dr. Goebbels. So there is still plenty to do for men of good will who possess first-hand knowledge of how France lost her freedom and how the cause not only of the old civilization, but of the very survival of the human race, was defeated on the continent of Europe. Among such men I count myself; and for the next few years at any rate I shall have no time to mourn over the dream which the bullet-headed guttural-voiced evil-smelling mongrels from the Eastern marches of Europe, who have stolen from their Danish and Norwegian victims the designation "pure-blooded Nordics," have stolen from me, along with the material possessions that I was obliged to leave behind in France.

2

In October 1933 I migrated from Paris, or more accurately from the village of Chamant near Senlis, to London. I regarded this move as a stage of my return to New York, which it was in a way, though not in the way originally planned. For London was to remain my home for the next three years, while my homeward voyage was to be accomplished by yet another migration which took another three years and a half, and had for its stations Hyères, Montreux, Geneva, Aix-en-Provence, Mougins, Arcachon, and Lisbon. My itinerary can hardly be called a direct one, and there were moments when I reproached myself with playing for and squandering time. But I see now that these delays and procrastinations were not mere drifting, as they may appear from the point of view of a shallow and self-contradictory philosophy according to which we exercise, on the one hand, full mastery over our purposes, but are, on the other hand, obliged to subordinate our purposes to that arch-convention of Modern society which measures achievement in terms of dollars and cents. My "drifting" was the outcome of my own decisions; but the fact that this drifting resulted in my *living* the last seven years of the old European civilization, instead of merely reading about its catastrophic decline in the New York newspapers, was not of my own choosing, but was part of a greater plan. And this plan prescribed, in the historic order, that the End of Our Time was to occur on the seventeenth of June in the year 1940, the day when the pusillanimous gang that had seized the government of France surrendered France to the Barbarians; and the same plan also prescribes, in the psychological order, that each person is what he is, and exercises his faculty of choice within the limits laid down by his being what he is, and not something else. It was, in other words, foreseen that I should be there when Cnossus fell to the Northern invaders, and that I should be one of the messengers who brought the news of its fall to our people across the ocean. And it is really quite funny to think that it will be the very wiseacres who would call my way of life "drifting" who will, in the same breath, accuse me of taking myself too seriously; the wiseacres, that is to say, who measure a man's plodding advance through life according to whether he makes a bigger income in 1940 than he made in 1930. But then this book is not addressed to such as these. I speak to those upon whom it has already dawned that man's faculty to will freely implies the obligation to *think;* and that this obligation is higher than all other obligations.

I spent the first six months of my London stage at Blackheath, a southeastern suburb bordering on Kent that few foreigners know. The choice of this residence was determined by the act of Parliament which imposes six months' quarantine on dogs arriving in England from abroad. On landing at Dover my three dogs were whisked away from me by the might and majesty of English law, disguised as the representative of a firm of forwarding agents, and were taken to the kennels of a veterinary hospital near Shooter's Hill; and I rented a tiny furnished cottage near by, and went to exercise my dogs twice a day for twenty-six weeks, in an enclosed run provided for the purpose. My dogs were not the worse for the experience, and neither was I; for it was due to those quarantine regulations (which are, incidentally, quite unreasonable, three months sufficing, according to authentic veterinary opinion, to safeguard against a delayed outbreak of hydrophobia) that I spent those six months in what is much the most beautiful of London suburbs, what with its rows of Regency mansions, grouped along the edge of the immense Blackheath Common, superior in their unspoiled old-world grace even to the far-famed terraces of Regent's Park; what with, also, the vicinity of Greenwich Park, incomparably the most picturesque of the open spaces of London, with its Observatory, its lovely Naval Hospital, one of Wren's masterpieces, and its high terraces overlooking the soul-stirring grandeur of London River.

Those six months also stand out as the only period of my seventeen years of Europe when I went in for what is called social life — attending cocktail parties and receptions and dinners and all that sort of thing, and meeting new people, mostly writers and artists, every day. This mode of life was alien to my accustomed ways, and my taking it up was due principally to the solicitude of some very kind friends who thought that a change from my seven years of reclusedom in France would do me good. They were probably right, and I owed to their initiative and their hospitality many a cosy and entertaining evening spent in the literary precincts of Chelsea and Campden Hill; but in the end these excursions into an easy-going noncommittal sociability merely served to confirm my suspicion that my six years at Le Trayas had set the pattern of my external existence for the rest of my days, and that at my age (I was forty-one then) a switching over to new ways, even to superior ways, involved an expenditure of psychic energy hardly justified by its results.

The fact is that I have never been interested in people as such, and have always found any company of more than four, myself included, a definite strain. Nor is this aversion from what I might call the free-for-all intellectual badminton game of literary cocktail parties and so forth due, as might be supposed, to self-centeredness, but rather to something which is the very opposite of self-centeredness, namely, my exclusive preoccupation with things, and with those clarified and classified pictures of things which we call ideas. I have been described, by people who intended the description as an insult, as a hopeless case-hardened extrovert; only I took the insult as a compliment, for if I have to choose between being an extrovert or an introvert, I will opt for the former every time, holding that for one introvert called Keats there are ten million introverts who are merely a nuisance to their families and a danger to public safety on the motor roads. Not that I regard my attitude to the stereotyped forms of social intercourse as a virtue; on the contrary, I feel that it is probably due to a flaw in my make-up — let us call it a lack of mental nimbleness. For what I dislike most, and am unable to cope with, at highbrow parties is the constant skipping from subject to subject. Now if I am interested in a subject at all, I want to hear and to talk about it till the cows come home; to touch on it lightly, and then to float gracefully to another, has no more attraction for me than being offered a succession of tempting dishes without a chance to help myself to them. But at the average dinner party in Chelsea or Kensington the desire to exhaust a given subject used to be considered the infallible mark of a bore.

By and by, as I came to recognize that it is difficult to find any one subject that will hold the interest of eight or ten casually assembled people, I gave up attending such casual assemblages, finding this easier than giving up my interests and learning the use of a mental skipping-rope. The people whose conversation I find most worth while are the people who know one subject well, and let themselves go without worrying about the reactions of their audience; and I do not care whether that one subject is epistemology or Dyak head-hunting or the ways of the red mullet or the problems involved in bringing down the sheep from the mountains for the winter; though I am inclined to draw the line at football or stamp collecting or the Russian ballet. In the course of my Provençal years I discovered that the people I best liked to talk to were farmers, fishermen, and artisans; for such people combine the great virtue of expert knowledge with the no less great virtue of being unconscious of possessing it, and unpretentious in discussing it.

I remember a week end I once spent in the wilds of Shropshire, when my hostess warned me at lunch that the village bore threatened to come to tea that afternoon. The bore arrived, and turned out to be a shy little retired solicitor with an appealing look in his eyes. It took me five minutes to find out that his particular fad was Dickens, and another five to make him overcome his fear of being sat upon; but in the end I got him going, and when he left an hour and a half later, during most of which time he never stopped talking, my hostess exclaimed, "But we never knew that Mr. T. is such a *fascinating* man! Why, he knows all there is to be known about Dickens and his characters, and it is just lovely to hear him talk about it!"

Another conversation, of a different nature, shall be recorded here, for the sake of the entirely different lesson that it holds. It was one I had in the winter of 1933 with two prominent figures of literary London, "Beachcomber" and Mr. Edward Shanks, the poet, critic, and novelist. It took place at a Chelsea cocktail party, about three months after my arrival from France, and on this occasion it was I who played the part of the village bore. For I had spent those three months, and also the previous three months at Chamant, absorbing all the original Nazi literature, Hitler and Rosenberg and Möller van den Bruck and Sieburg and the rest, that I could get hold of. Also, as the reader may recall, I had, long before Hitler came into power, begun to develop my theory about European history being a 2000-year-old struggle between the race of Builders and the race of Raiders; my study of Naziism, which I pursued not by reading trashy books and articles by authors who seemed to think that European history had started in 1914, but by tracing the religious and philosophical ancestry of Hitler's doctrines, had confirmed my belief that the last phase of that struggle was upon us; and, not to mince words, I was thoroughly frightened. So I told "Beachcomber," whom I knew to be a disciple of Chesterton, and Mr. Edward Shanks all about it, and told them that the Germans were the born and sworn enemies of the human race, and that we should have to fight them to the death within the next five or six years. I was so full of the importance of my subject that I must have been talking for half an hour before I noticed that Mr. Edward Shanks was not amused. I stopped, and Mr. Edward Shanks said in his most superior Cambridge accents, "Why, it seems to me that you exaggerate. The Germans are the nicest people in the world; my wife and I spent last spring in Bavaria, and all the innkeepers and guides and waiters and villagers were perfectly charming, and they all love us English."

It so happens that I particularly remember this conversation because it was the first time that the conclusions I had drawn from my many years' study of German history and the German character were countered by a grown-up person with the argument that he had spent six weeks in the Bavarian mountains and had found the innkeepers and guides and railway porters perfectly charming. But it was not the last time I heard that argument in England, or some variant of it. And if I had my books here I could quote chapter and verse to show that some of the publicists who later made blatant asses of themselves, and also wrought untold damage, by their books and articles about the Abyssinian crisis, and the destruction of Austria, and the civil war in Spain, had already furnished incontrovertible proof of their stubborn ignorance of the things that matter by the books that they had rushed into print within a few months of Hitler's advent to power; by books that argued that the Germans were very nice people, and that Hitler was the fault of the Allies who had maltreated them at Versailles. I could name, offhand, half a dozen of these gentlemen who today still consider themselves, and are considered, experts on international politics; and it is enough to make one's blood boil to think that they hold down cushy jobs and some of them even sit in Parliament, while it is the young men who have to go out to fight and to pay with their lives for the mistakes made ten and twenty years ago by the Liberal Oh-the-German-people-are-all-righters and the Labourite self-disarmers. But when I say this I had perhaps better add that I have not forgotten those Tories either who gave dinner parties for the man Ribbentrop and whose daughters and wives marched in Strength through Joy and Health through Beauty (or maybe Joy through Strength and Beauty through Health) parades at Nuremberg.

3

By the winter of 1934 it was clear to me that Hitler's advent to power raised the question of the survival of Western civilization.

To say this is not much of a boast, since it merely amounts to stating that I was able to see the Obvious, three inches beyond my nose. Millions of people, about 99.99 per cent of Western Europeans, did not see the Obvious three inches beyond their noses, but that does not make me a superman. It was simply that those who did not see were still wearing the blinkers which I had thrown away: the blinkers of nineteenth-century empiricism. It took a nineteenth-century empiricist not to perceive in 1934 what Hitlerism meant; unfortunately Europe was full of nineteenth-century empiricists, a large percentage of whom were writing and publishing books to prove (1) that Hitler was a product of Versailles, and the Allies had only themselves to blame; (2) that Hitler was a charlatan without importance, and Naziism a short-lived outbreak of mass hysteria; (3) that the best way to get rid of Hitler was to give the Germans what Hitler demanded for them, whereupon the Germans would show their gratitude by kicking Hitler out and electing Mr. Vernon Bartlett Lord Protector of the German Republic.

Now if I, or anybody else, had told these good people that the trouble with them was that they believed in the wrong philosophy, they would have raised their eyebrows four or five inches and would have declared that they had nothing to do with philosophy at all; if pressed to explain themselves, they would have gone on to say that philosophy is nothing but a mass of preconceived notions, that is, of prejudices, whereas *they* were nothing but modest experts on international politics, guided by experience, and by experience alone. And had I countered this by pointing out that their repudiation of philosophy was a kind of philosophy, they would have retorted that I was trying to be funny. Yet empiricism, according to which nothing is true that cannot be verified by experience, is a philosophy which begins to be one by repudiating philosophy; it is the school of thought which prescribes as the first rule of thinking that thought is worthless. According to the empiricist, first principles, which cannot be demonstrated by experience but are true in their own right, are mere prejudices, since you must take nothing for granted, but must trust to experience alone. According to the empiricist you must live by the method of trial and error, and must never attempt to cross a bridge before you get there.

Well, here are a few points that the empiricist ignores. In the first place, far from taking nothing for granted and trusting only to experience, the empiricist takes it for granted that this world is so constructed that he can survive, and become a bigger and better empiricist, by the simple thought-saving process of making a fresh mistake every day, and profiting by it. Now this is not only rank prejudice, but prejudice belied by that very experience to which the empiricist makes his appeal. For the empiricist arch-principle — that the only way to separate life-promoting truth from life-hindering error is to go and try, and if you are wrong go and try something else — assumes with a jolly disregard for the annals of mankind that there is always plenty of time to correct your own mistakes. But if there is one lesson that history teaches us it is this: whenever a nation or a civilization has gone under it was because that nation or civilization took it for granted that there was plenty of time. The Cnossians thought, when they heard of the incorporation of Mycenae and Tiryns in the Achaean *Lebensraum,* that there was plenty of time; anyway, they said, why worry, there is the Aegean, which no enemy has ever crossed, and which therefore no enemy can ever cross. The Cnossians, in other words, were empiricists or positivists, who cheerfully refused to study the principles of the Achaean *Blitzkrieg* by deductive reasoning;

though we only know this from the indirect testimony of their art, a typically modern, optimistic, impressionistic art, the art of a people without metaphysic; and we know their art because Sir Arthur Evans went to the trouble of clearing away the eight-foot debris which had, in the course of thirty centuries, accumulated on top of the final consequences of the Cnossian conviction that what had happened across the water could not happen here. And the Athenians who quarreled among themselves about third terms and high taxes and unemployment relief, while Philip of Macedon was swallowing up one Greek city-republic after another, thought that there was plenty of time; they, too, were empiricists who refused to believe in the real existence of the unprecedented; and they despised the Macedonians as hicks and illiterate backwoodsmen who had no freedom of speech, or bathrooms, and who thus were no match for free-born Athenians. And the Romans, too, thought, A.D. 409, that there was plenty of time, and listened to speeches advocating appeasement of the Goths and the division of Italy into spheres of influence, while Alaric was marching his armies up and down the road, practising the Visigothic version of the goose step; and some Romans told their wives that Visigothic goose step was good for business, while others said that it was too militaristic and too ridiculous for words; and then Alaric stopped marching up and down and put Rome in his pocket.

And the strange thing is that nations and civilizations always put their faith in there being plenty of time when they have already lost their faith in everything else, and when therefore their time is running short. All this you may discover for yourself if you will only study a little history; but the true empiricist is not interested in history and refuses to study it, for he holds, in the first place, that the old peoples were very backward and can teach us progressive moderns nothing; and in the second place that no two situations are ever alike, and there must be a new rule made for each; though these beliefs, which stop the empiricist from knowing history, do not stop him from writing Outlines of history, in which yesterday is re-created in the image of that tomorrow which the empiricist notoriously knows all about.

Well, by 1934 I had begun to see through the great empiricist-positivist-pragmatist racket, called the Empire of Man by the promoter who inaugurated it four hundred years ago with the most eloquent prospectus that ever sold mankind a gold brick, listed in the libraries under the title *Novum Organum*. I had begun to understand that Bacon's first "aphorism," "Man, as the minister and Interpreter of Nature, does and understands as much as his observations on the order of Nature, either with regard to things or the Mind, permit him, and neither knows nor is capable of more" — that this somewhat loose statement, condensed into modern English as "Only that is true which can be verified by observation or experiment," really aims at annulling the Divine Design of the universe, and at replacing it with the little everyday purposes and twopenny halfpenny schemes and self-assertive vanities of Smith, Jones, and Robinson.

I had also begun to see that the empiricist maxim, "Seeing is believing," a sound enough rule if applied legitimately, is interpreted in our day to mean "I will believe anything that I see, and nothing that I don't see"; that the formerly reproachful proverb, "Out of sight, out of mind," has become a respectable political program; that, in other words, the empiricist bias of contemporary society has put a discount on thinking, and a premium on word juggling and dishonest cheapjack salesmanship in every field of endeavor. By the same token, that other empiricist maxim, "Cross your bridges when you get to them," is unexceptionable if taken literally; but it becomes vicious and suicidal nonsense if it is interpreted to mean that you need not think out in advance what you would do if such and such a situation confronted you at such and such a bridge.

Moreover, by the winter of 1934 I had convinced myself that the empiricist-humanist-liberal standpoint that history is a mere narration of unique and contingent events, and contains no regularities and therefore no worth-while lesson for the future — that this standpoint, represented by ninety-seven per cent of contemporary historians, is wholly false. There was, I told myself, at least one kind of recurrence that even Mr. H. A. L. Fisher, that past-grand-master of liberal historiography, could not deny, nor explain away: the periodic decline and fall of civilizations. I had by this time recognized that Spengler's explanation of these recurrences — that civilizations were like plants that germinate, shoot forth, grow, blossom, wither away, and die, and that consequently history was wholly meaningless and moral effort a self-deception — was nonsense; but I had also given the devil his due, and acknowledged that Spengler was the first to see the outstanding historic fact of our age: the fact that our civilization was on the downgrade. And this was something that the wiseacres of Progress, aptly portrayed by the cartoonist Low in the figures of the Eskimo twins Upanupanup and Onanonanon, were congenitally incapable of seeing.

But *why* did civilizations fall, and why did they begin to totter just at the moment when they seemed more secure than ever, when the men who lived within their particular orbits thought that all human problems were on the way to a completely satisfactory solution? Pondering these questions, I was struck by yet another fact: that the civilizations of the past did not succumb to attacks from without, but were destroyed by some mysterious inner malady. The only exception to this rule was the case of the Aztec and Inca civilizations of the American continent, which were wiped out by an unexpected raid while they were still in an early and hopeful stage of material bloom. But the civilizations of the Old World, the archaic cultures of Egypt and Mesopotamia and the Aegean, and the great Antique, Mediterranean civilization of the Roman Empire, did not fall because they were attacked; they were attacked because they were on the point of falling. For centuries Egypt and Crete had repulsed wave after wave of barbarians; the first Teutonic invasion of Rome resulted in the slaughter of a hundred thousand Teutons by Marius; for the next four hundred years Rome not only held her ground, but also carried her conquests deep into the Barbarian hinterland of the North. And then, within fifty years all was over, and the first Nazi, the Herul Odoacer, made himself Führer of the Western Empire. The Chaos that for half a millennium had sought in vain to kill Order took at last possession of the ruins when Order was dead. But what was it that killed Order?

At last I thought that I had found the answer to that question. Civilizations die when their religion dies. Such religion as they happen to possess; it is not necessarily a true religion. For what makes a civilization live is its religion: its unshakable certitude that there is some ideal plan, prescribed by the gods, or by the unalterable texture of the universe, or by the changing but ever-unsated desires of man; a charter or existence that man *must* realize, a blueprint to which he must build up his world. This certitude will *seem* unshakable, and will seem to explain everything in this world and even beyond this world, for a while; but in the course of its self-realization flaws will appear: men will bump into obstacles that stop them from satisfying what they regard as their legitimate wants; or they will discover new wants for which no provision has been made by the blueprint; or they will collide with that eventual barrier which is posited by the disappointment that follows satis-faction. And once their certitude begins to totter, men will say to themselves, and to one another, "Perhaps we were wrong all along. Perhaps we have set our hearts on the unattainable; perhaps on that which is not worth attaining; perhaps on what is both. *We cannot know for certain;* we can know nothing for certain; it would seem that we have been deluded. Perhaps there is something to be said for the other side, for any side but our own. What is the use of it all, anyway?"

But when men begin to say these things, they will cease to act according to a plan; they will cease to make plans, but will live for the moment, from hand to mouth; and in the end they will just sit down and wait. Behind the Great Wall of China; or be-hind the rampart of that Aegean which no enemy has ever crossed; or behind that Roman *limes* which was the Maginot Line of the antique world. And then the Achaeans will arrive; or the Huns; or the Goths.

Or Hitler.

Cnossus fell because the Cnossians had ceased to believe that performing the proper rites at the proper times on the altars of the proper gods would make them the masters of their lives. That was the religion of the Archaic civilization; when it died the Archaic civilization died too.

The Roman Empire fell because its old religion was dead, and its new religion was not yet robust and deep-rooted enough. But that old religion was not the religion of Jupiter and Juno and Minerva; nor yet the religion of Sol and Mithras. It was the great Stoic faith which by the third century had become the universal world-view of the Mediterranean basin, and which shaped the thoughts and actions even of those who sacrificed at the altars of Sol and Mithras and Isis; just as in the nineteenth and the early twentieth century the real weekday religion or "effective creed" of Europe was the faith in scientific progress. Now the Stoic religion had been based on the all-sufficiency of human reason; but for two or three centuries the Skeptics had been attacking the claim of reason to supply certitude. Eventually the Skeptics carried their point; and the Goths carried Rome.

But the Archaic religion of profit-sharing gods, and the Stoic religion of reason and moral restraint, had been false religions. The civilization of the Middle Ages fell too, though not in the sense in which the Minoan and the Roman empires had fallen; there was much strife and destruction in the fifteenth century, but there was no wholesale annihilation. The Medieval civilization ended by being absorbed in that of Modernity; and the latter was carried on by the same peoples. Yet the Middle Ages had built their civilization on the true religion. Did the true religion, too, desert those who had put their trust in it, as had the religion of the hungry gods and the religion of the Stoic sages? Did the Catholic Middle Ages fall because the Catholic religion proved in the end yet another failure? No. Those other religions had been "true" for those who believed in them while they believed in them; once they were disbelieved they ceased to exist. But the true religion remains true even though it be abandoned. For man's finite reason is so constructed that though it is capable of discovering Truth, it is not bound to discover it; nor yet is it bound to adhere to it once it has been discovered. When a false religion is thrown overboard it ceases to be a religion; but when the true religion is denied, men go on living in error. The culture of the Middle Ages was based on the true conception of man's destiny — that which sees the purpose of life in reunion, after life, with God from whom man was separated by his Fall; and this other-worldly purpose endows all the purposes of *this* world with a beauty and wholeness that they lose the moment when that other world is lost sight of. That conception was the true conception; but it neglected that aspect of human nature which craves Mastery. So Luther nailed his theses to the door of that church in Wittenberg; and Bacon issued his glittering manifesto about *Regnum Hominis*. And Western man, freed at last from the authority of the Church on the one hand, and from the shackles of the Divine Design, now declared unknowable and nonexistent, on the other, could proceed to take possession of the universe, and to make himself, with the aid of Science, the master of Creation.

During four hundred years Western man played at being his own God. It was a grand adventure, while it lasted; full of that grandeur and misery of which Pascal speaks. But in the end he made a sorry mess of it; and then came one who said, "I will teach you." He was a house painter from Braunau in Upper Austria, and his name was Adolf Hitler. And he taught them.

4

But I let that last paragraph race ahead of my narrative. The date is December 1934; and I am still in my flat on the tenth floor of that tall apartment building in St. John's Wood, from the windows of which I can see the rooms of one third of London, dominated by that water tower on top of Campden Hill of which Chesterton sang; and in the distance the North Downs of Surrey.

The threat to the survival of Western civilization, as I then saw it, did not reside in the mere existence of Hitler. In those days of far away and long ago the actual military power of Nazi Germany was negligible. If the nations of the West, above all England and France, realized their danger in time and prepared, not to meet it, but to nip it in the bud, Europe could be saved.

But would the nations of the West, would England and France, act while there was still time? I hoped that they were going to; I feared that they might not; and I realized that if they did, it would be by a sort of miracle. For while in those last days of 1934 I still believed in Europe, and above all in the historic destiny and eternal greatness of France, what I believed in was not the civilization of Modernity that since the sixteenth century had shaped the thoughts and feelings and actions of Western man, but a new civilization that was to take its place and salvage the accumulated values not only of those four hundred years, but of the preceding two thousand as well. In those last days of 1934 one fact towered above all other facts that my mind perceived and pondered; and this fact was that *Modern civilization, the civilization of post-Renaissance, post-Reformation Europe, was dead.*

Of course, given a reasonable equilibrium of environmental forces, the external life of a civilization may go on for centuries after its inner energies have been exhausted. We have seen that happen in Egypt, in China, and in India. But in the case of Western Europe such a vegetative continuity was precluded by the rise of Nazi Germany. The alternatives confronting Europe, it seemed to me, were spiritual rebirth on the one hand, and acceptance of the external consequences of inner death on the other. The latter alternative has since become known under the unattractive designation of *Lebensraum.*

The wheels of the external machinery of life were still going round: the moving pictures were still moving, the parliaments were still talking, the newspapers were still printing all the news that was fit to print and some news that wasn't; motorists in a hurry on their way to or from cocktail parties were still killing pedestrians on the roads; surplus food products were still unsalable, and the unemployed were still starving — in a word, the business of Western civilization, so called, was still going on as usual. All that had collapsed was its inner scaffolding: the faith which made all these activities, and the rest of them, seem worth while; which assured men that their chosen ends were right, and their means adequate; which imbued men with the certitude that what they knew was really so, and what they hoped for might be attained.

What had broken down, in a word, was the religion of Modernity. *But this religion was not the Christian religion.* Christianity had never broken down; it could not break down, for it was true in all eternity. But Christianity had been abandoned, and replaced by another religion, though most people did not realize that this had happened. For the new religion did not call itself religion, but Freedom. There were plenty of people who still called themselves Christians, and who were sincere Christians on Sundays, when they went to church or chapel; but most of these people also held that their Christianity was something that had to be kept uncontaminated by contacts with sordid weekday pursuits. Above all these people held that religion and politics had to be kept separate; and the great charge which these sincere Christians leveled against their brethren who had remained faithful to the old dispensation was that "Catholics mix their religion in everything, and carry it even into politics." The long and short of it is that for the past four hundred years the weekday religion of the vast majority of Europeans, as distinguished from their Sunday religion, was not Christianity but something else. And the business of the world was transacted on weekdays.

For this religion, the real, if not the true, religion of Western Modernity, I coined the term "the Doctrine of the Sovereign Self." You have, of course, hardly heard this expression before, but you have heard it said that man is his own law, the master of life, and the measure of all things; and that phrase expresses exactly what I mean when I speak of the doctrine of the Sovereign Self. And one day in December 1934 I sat down and wrote a long letter to my friend Professor Jászi, of the faculty of Oberlin College, a letter which was also the second outline of that system of philosophy upon which I had started to work twenty months earlier. I have already, in the third chapter of this book, quoted a long passage from this outline. Here I shall quote another: —

. . . The psychic dispensation of Modernity is dominated by the Doctrine of the Sovereign Ego, which may be formulated as the self-authorization of the Self as the ultimate ground of certitude. . . . Under the dominance of the Doctrine of the Sovereign Self man seeks to bear out his claim to power and to freedom (that is, acquittal of that sense of guilt or sin which is the psychological price of power and inhibits its use) by acting *as if* he were omnipotent and guiltless. But this doctrine can maintain itself only by re-creating reality as a network of fictions, all of which may be reduced to the arch-fiction, "Man may (can, should) act as if he were God." This re-creation of reality is possible for a time by a redefinition which limits reality to such regions as can be subdued and manipulated by the increase of human power. This redefinition of reality (its identification with the order of nature) is the function of Science. . . . This new "reality" will be believed in as long as the fictions which compose it cohere and work. But once these fictions develop contradictions within themselves and between one another . . . and once the discrepancy between their theoretical promises and their practical results becomes increasingly apparent, men will begin to question its validity. . . . The moment will come when the whole structure of this pseudo-reality collapses, and the truths certified by the Sovereign Self are exposed as claims which have not been proved.

. . . *This moment has arrived.* I submit that the present crisis of Western civilization is due to our increasing awareness that the assumptions upon which this civilization is based and which so far have been either unconsciously surmised or, when occasionally challenged, declared self-evident have ceased to cohere and to work. The psychological structure of Modernity has already broken down, but this fact is not yet realized in its entire scope; to most people the breakdown is apparent only in some of its external effects which then are interpreted as a purely temporary disorder of institutions and processes, while a few perceive that the trouble lies deeper and trace some of its particular aspects to a fundamental inner uncertainty about principles hitherto taken for granted; but even these few have not, so far, integrated these "sectional breakdowns" into a comprehensive *psychological* pattern.

Such obvious "sectional breakdowns" are: the crisis of democracy; the failure of liberalism; the economic crisis; the dissatisfaction with mechanical progress (the feeling that its promises have not been kept, that it tends to make man a slave of the machine; above all the fear

that the military exploitation of its achievements may wipe out civilization itself); the general social tension and unrest, "regimentation" on
the one hand and the rise of lawlessness on the other; individual un-
happiness and aimlessness, a sense of frustration, the feeling that life
has lost dignity and meaning; the decay of literature and the arts into
mass production of counterfeit; the growing disappointment with a
"freedom" which tells man that he may do as he likes but does not tell
him why he should prefer any line of action to any other — with a
"freedom" moreover that has on the one hand destroyed man's inner
equilibrium and has, on the other, resulted in new and unexpected external checks on man's conduct. Such a "sectional breakdown" appears
in that "despair of Mind," that feeling that Reason cannot help us,
that it is indeed a handicap in survival, to which books like J. W.
Krutch's *The Modern Temper* give popular expression and which has
been formulated most pointedly, perhaps, by Theodor Lessing (*Unter-
gang des Lebens durch den Geist*). In the West this mood is, as yet,
merely literary and esoteric, but in Germany it has exerted, mainly
through Spengler and Klages, a powerful influence in preparing the
mental ground for Hitlerism. . . . Hitlerism represents precisely the
German re-solution of the psychic deadlock of which the nations of
the West have not, as yet, achieved an integrated experience but which
in these nations is only sporadically realized in the form of seemingly
unconnected "sectional breakdowns." These sectional breakdowns
may be, indeed, likened to functional symptoms of a psychic disease
not yet diagnosed. Such a functional symptom — one of the less obvious
but perhaps the most disquieting — is the inability, almost unwillingness,
of the Western democracies to organize their defense against the growing power of Nazi Germany.

I went on to point out that a clear diagnosis of our predicament
was being retarded by a number of "protective fictions," accounts
which pretend that things are not as bad as they seem. "Some of
these borrow the psychological pattern of the ostrich. . . . There
persists, particularly in England, a purposeful misunderstanding of
the real nature of Hitlerism and of the issues it raises; a misunderstanding masquerading as the 'judicial attitude' and the demand
for 'fair play' for Germany, and culminating in the suicidal delusion
that it is possible to come to terms with Hitlerism, that the world
can live half Nazi and half free." Another such protective fiction,

I pointed out in a subsequent passage, was the belief that the nations of the West could hope to ally themselves with Soviet Russia against Nazi Germany. I expressed the view that far from there being a fundamental antagonism between Hitlerite Germany and Stalinite Russia, both Naziism and Communism were variants of the same Manichean creed which explains the presence of evil in this world by attributing it to the "others," the not-I, and preaches holy war for the greater glory of the We-God against the You-Devil; only the Bolsheviks of Berlin call the We-God "Nordic Aryan Germans" and the You-Devil Jews, Frenchmen, Anglo-Saxons, and so on, while the Nazis of Moscow call the We-God "proletariat" and the You-Devil "capitalist class." I thus demonstrated, on strictly theological grounds, that both Nazi Germany and Soviet Russia were the mortal enemies of the West. But let us return to the passage quoted: —

I submit that all these "sectional breakdowns," all these symptoms of disintegration, all these forebodings of doom, all these suggested remedies which are but disguised symptoms of the disease itself, have their common origin in the collapse of the doctrine of the Sovereign Ego, in the downfall of the Self as its own ground of ultimate certainty. This doctrine has dominated Western civilization during the last four centuries, and has now destroyed itself by the same dialectic process whereby it once achieved its ascendency. The history of Western man since the Reformation and Renaissance consists in the self-explication of this doctrine, implicitly posited in those twin movements that, so we have been told on their own authority, liberated man from the "tyranny of the Church" and the dead weight of an obsolete authoritarian world-view, and helped him to shed the "blinkers of superstition." From the sixteenth century onward Western man taught himself to regard transcendent sanctions, upholding an other-worldly legal system of rewards and punishments, as unreal, and to concentrate his efforts on improving his lot in *this* world. He taught himself to reinterpret reality in terms of his newly gained and ever-expanding knowledge. This reinterpretation of reality constitutes the theme of all philosophy, literature, and art since the sixteenth century; but its main exponent and instrument is Science. It culminates in the concept of Progress — the proposition that the increase of human power is the same as the increase of human freedom; *the equation of human power with human freedom.* I submit that it is this reinterpretation of reality that has collapsed, that it is this equation that has been disproved. I submit that the reinterpretation of reality by post-Renaissance, post-Reformation philosophy and science has revealed itself as pathological distortion of reality; that the unprecedented increase of human power during the last four centuries has resulted not in an increase, but in the all but complete inhibition, of human freedom, in a *paralysis of the will.*

The present crisis of Western civilization is not a passing unpleasantness but a nervous breakdown of the Western peoples from which they can emerge only by a complete change of mind and heart, by what in theology is called *metanoia* or repentance; by a complete revision of the basic philosophical assumptions embodied in its present existence. The one thing that the Doctrine of the Sovereign Self has proved during the four hundred years of its dominion is its own absurdity.

This passage foreshadows the initial thesis of that revised "Philosophy of Freedom" on which I was to work during the next four years and a half. And if in many ways I diagnosed our predicament more clearly than did most people in those days, there was one respect in which I shared the universal self-delusion, for I told myself that there was plenty of time; and worked away leisurely as if the British postage stamps had still borne the image of the good Queen Victoria. And so 1935 passed, and '36, '37, and '38, and the first half of '39. On the twenty-first of August, 1939, I was still working. But on the twenty-second I opened the morning newspaper and saw that Hitler's Germany and Stalin's Russia were now allies. It did not surprise me; but it did stop my work. On that day I laid off, and became just another of fifty, sixty, or seventy million refugees; I have lost count long since.

5

It was, I believe, Talleyrand who said that those who had not known life under the *ancien régime,* that is, under the old French monarchy which was swept away by the Revolution, never knew how sweet life could be. Men of my own generation used to quote that remark after the first World War, substituting 1914 for 1789 as the boundary which separates the golden from the iron age; I often quoted it myself in the old days, but I see now that I was wrong. For the war of 1914–1918 merely marked a chapter in the history of the old European civilization, the conclusion of the Antonine period of Modernity. It was one of the fruits of our much-vaunted "progress" that the Decline which preceded the Fall was squeezed for us into a mere twenty years; the Romans, who lived at a much more leisurely pace, minding, as it were, the law of entropy of which they had never heard, had managed to carry on for three centuries between the death of Marcus Aurelius and the banishment of the shadow Emperor Romulus Augustulus to the Hôtel du Parc at Vichy — I beg your pardon, to the estate of Lucullanum at Baiae.

The old Europe, political creation of Charlemagne, came to an end on the thirtieth of January in the year 1933, the day when Adolf Hitler, renegade Austrian, renegade Catholic, renegade European, acceded to supreme power in that German Empire which had once styled itself Holy and Roman. For on that day the German nation seceded from Europe and returned to the Teutonic *Urwald,* which means primeval forest in English if we want to be literal and polite, but which should, in this context, be translated jungle if we want to be accurate and historically minded. But Europe was to have a respite of seven years, while the self-made Barbarians, aided by the ideological blindness which had smitten the governments and peoples of the West, gathered strength to deliver their mortal stroke. The lethargy which precedes death turned into the last agony on August 22, 1939, when the two enemies of Christendom, Hitler and Stalin, announced to the world their Unholy Alliance, and their agreement to wipe out Western civilization on a profit-sharing basis. And the agony ended on June 17, 1940, when Marshal Pétain, the hero of Verdun, turned rubber stamp, broke the solemn pledge which had allied the destiny of France to that of England, and delivered the eldest daughter of the

Church into the hands of the advance agent of the Antichrist.

But we who lived through that seven years' grace in Europe did not know that Europe was enjoying life under a suspended sentence of death; for even those of us who saw the relentless approach of the Last Battle were confident that Right would conquer Might. Our existence and our outlook, our daily routine and our plans, our very dreams, were based, in those years, on the axiomatic invincibility of the French army. Even a person like myself, who spent those seven years studying the psychology of declining civilizations and tracing historic parallels to our situation, could believe in a happy ending of all our troubles. For to me the drift of Modern civilization toward physical destruction seemed determined, not by a blind unsurmountable natural necessity, but by the neglect or surrender, by the Western peoples, of that use of Right Reason which instructs the will of man to choose the good in preference to evil, the helpful in preference to the harmful, that which pleases God in preference to that which promotes the designs of the Devil. Yes, I knew throughout those seven years that the End of Our Time had come, that the peoples of the West were staggering toward the brink of the abyss, blindfolded by a false philosophy which did not allow them to distinguish the real from the apparent, the essential from the unimportant, the salutary from the merely pleasant. But I also believed in a last-minute miracle, a miracle, as it were, wrought in the natural order by human reason tearing off its blinkers; the miracle of the peoples of Europe becoming their old selves once more, and rallying to the banners of God with their old-time strength reborn in the new illumination of their minds. I believed, in a word, in the miracle of the Last Stand; the miracle of the Third Marne.

And I also believed that the privilege and the duty, the glory and the responsibility, of leading this last stand of Western Christendom against the rising Pagan power of the North and East were conferred by history on the nation of Saint Joan of Arc. Three times before France had saved Europe: in the first Battle of the Marne, A.D. 451, from becoming Mongol; in the Battle of Poitiers, A.D. 732, from becoming Arab; in the second Battle of the

Marne, A.D. 1914, from becoming Prussian. The danger that now threatened Europe on the part of Nazi Germany and her back-door crony Communist Russia was greater than had been those dangers of the past; for whereas the Huns had been mere casual footpads on the highway of history, and the Arabs of Spain had been comparatively civilized and generous conquerors who imposed taxes but did not extinguish the spiritual freedom of their Christian subjects, in the fourth decade of the twentieth century civilization faced for the first time a totalitarian enemy who vowed complete, final, irrevocable destruction of all human values, indeed of all life not its own. Not being an empiricist, I did not need the experience of 1939 and 1940 to teach me all this; I had read *Mein Kampf* and Rosenberg and Banse and the rest in 1933 and '34; and I did not think that we could dispose of Adolf Hitler by invoking mother fixations and inferiority complexes, or that Germany's hatred and envy of the West were generated by the Treaty of Versailles.

Well, I was wrong about France; and yet today, on the twenty-third of October, 1940, when I write this page, we are witnessing the miracle of the Last Stand of Christendom — the Battle of Britain. The ruler of France, or of what is left of France, successor *de facto* of that François I who exclaimed in defeat, "All is lost save honor," is today a *Gauleiter* of the Third Reich, and dances to the tune of the Pied Piper of Berchtesgaden. But England fights on, strong and free and more resolute than ever. And if those enduring Christian values which agnostic Modernity has inherited from the Middle Ages are to be saved for humanity, they will be saved by England.

But once more I have wandered; for all I started out to say a page or two ago was that I am thankful to Providence for the privilege of having known the sweetness of life in the old civilization of France and England, before the Barbarians came. So I may now look back upon a year of Paris and three years of London, those two great capitals of the Western world, as God made them, as they were before the Barbarians defaced them, and as they never will be again, even though the curse may be lifted from Europe, and our world may be redeemed by the self-immolation of the gallant youth of England. And those three years of London also allowed me to insert a few more pages of abiding beauty into my picture book of memory, for it was during those three years that I first saw, and learned to love, those two English cities which are among the loveliest jewels of the old European culture, Oxford and Bath; and also the English country. For the word England, which until 1934 had in the main meant English books and English history to me, now brings back the tang of the wind that sweeps the Marlborough Downs, and the scent of wood smoke and the rustle of a carpet of leaves of evening walks in Cotswold villages; the hills of the West and South, the Malverns and Mendips and Quantocks; the blue ridge of the Welsh mountains seen from Worcester Beacon; the valleys of the Wye and Severn and Avon, and, most beloved of all, the sights and sounds and smells of Exmoor. To the reader all this may seem a mere list of names out of a gazetteer; to me it is a section of the list of the realities that make life worth living.

6

In January 1937, yet another of my dreams came true, for I was once more in France, on the way to that Provence which I still regarded, and shall never cease to regard, as the country where I ought to have been born. It was more or less by accident that we settled down, for a few months, at Hyères, which up to the Great Crash of 1929 had been one of the *mondain* centers of the idle English rich, but had since reverted to the sleepy little market town that it was meant to be. Its climate, more humid than that of any other section of the South Coast of France, is responsible for its luxuriant vegetation, unmatched elsewhere; and also for its being unsuited for summer residence. It is the gateway to one of the most charming, and least known, bits of Provence, the valley of the Gapeau, a wilderness of cherry blossom in the early spring, leading up to that little oasis of Montrieux, unique with its lush forests in the midst of the arid foothills that herald the desert of limestone through which Marseille is approached from the east.

But for us the chief attraction of the Hyères region was that it is Conrad country. For the little white hotel on the hilltop where we stayed formed part of the hamlet of Almanarre, where Peyrol the Rover was born, and where he came home to die; and in those eight months we traced his itinerary from that building of the Port Authority, flanking the inner harbor of Toulon, where he called to draw his prize money, along the little road which winds by way of Carqueiranne and Salvadour, and the narrow strip of land known as l'Accapte, a kind of natural bridge across the salt marshes, to that lovely peninsula of Giens, perhaps the last unspoiled spot between Marseille and Menton. We found, as Peyrol had, the farm Escampobar, where he spent his few remaining years; in real life it is called Escampobariou, which is Provençal for waste land, and is not a farm but a charming little château belonging to M. Louis Renault, the automobile magnate. We also found the little *calanque* at the foot of the cliff where Peyrol hid his boat, and whence he escaped to his noble death under the English guns. I count those last pages of *The Rover* among the finest passages of English literature; and I don't know whether I love the book so much because I love the Giens country, or whether it is the other way round. But I do know that the grandest sunsets I have ever seen are the sunsets behind Cap Sicié; and they are just as Conrad describes the one that saw Peyrol die.

One of the great joys of those months at Almanarre was that I shared three of them with my two stepsons. I shall never forget (neither will they) that April morning when they arrived at 6 A.M., staggering with sleep after a night in a crowded train compartment, but happy as two kittens with a new ball of wool, at that old-world Hôtel de l'Europe in Avignon where half a century earlier Henry James had stayed. It was their first holiday abroad. A hurried bath and breakfast, and off they went to explore the Palace of the Popes, and the churches and ramparts and other wonders of Avignon; and when that afternoon, after a reverent first inspection of the Pont du Gard, I drove them into Nimes, I had to bend back from my driving seat to shake Joe awake as we passed the Amphitheater. And that was only the beginning. Those three years gave them eight holidays, including two long "summer vacs," on the Continent, and a more thorough first-hand acquaintance with the geography of France than falls to the lot of most Frenchmen. They share my passion for landscape, and in addition they also have a passion for, and expert knowledge of, ecclesiastic architecture. At the close of that first Easter holiday I drove them to Paris by the not exactly direct route of Carcassonne, Albi, Rocamadour, Périgueux, Poitiers, Tours, and Chartres; in the course of the following summer we explored the Cévennes, visiting Mende, the uplands of Velay, Le Puy, and the upper canyon of the Ardèche; crossing the Rhône at Pont-St.-Esprit and looking in on the Orange of the Romans, the Carpentras of M. Daladier, and the Vaucluse of Petrarch. There were other trips to come: the country of Lake Leman, the Valais, the Jura, Dauphiny, Auvergne, Provence again.

The pattern of the day's stage was always the same: arriving in a new town, a rush to the cathedral, or the most interesting church; ten minutes' devotion, then a well-planned *Blitzkrieg* with cameras, discovering points of vantage and comparing vistas; then the best available dinner in town, with sampling of the noteworthy local vintages. They both took to French life as ducks take to water. Martin was seventeen when, on his first visit to Almanarre, he discovered the secret of Provence which it had taken me years to unravel. He said, "It is the best and the worst thing about Provence that it makes you stop wanting things; you just eat and gaze."

After the Easter term of 1938 Martin, having won a scholarship for Brasenose College, Oxford, found himself at a loose end, and adopted with great enthusiasm my suggestion that he should spend the next four months in the University of Grenoble. When he joined us, toward the end of the summer, in Auvergne, he averred that he had spent the happiest four months of his life, which did not surprise me; for Grenoble, city of Stendhal, is much the most attractive of French towns, and also has a long tradition of making foreign students comfortable. I must say that he made the most of his opportunities; and now he can look back on those four months spent in that charming country house of M. and Mme. Bouchayer on the hillside at La Tronche, with its grand view of the snow-clad chain of Belledonne. From the back door of the garden he could start, so to speak, climbing the tremendous mountain of the Grande Chartreuse, which he did more than once, equipped with sandwiches and a hip flask of the agreeable liqueur bearing the same name. Thus he too, and at the age of eighteen, had his fair sample, what with the cafés of the Place Grenette, young company of many nationalities, and tours on foot and on bicycle all over Dauphiny and Savoy, of that *douceur de vivre* of which Talleyrand had spoken; at the moment when I write this, he is probably guarding some crossroad in England in the uniform of a corporal of Royal Engineers.

On those eight trips of exploration across French history and geography the two of them took something like three thousand photographs each. They are keenly aware what this means in the year 1940; it was only the other day that Joe, now once more a scholar at Merton after a long vacation spent in farm work and as a volunteer in the Home Guards, wrote, "Those snapshots of ours are now historic documents."

Here I may be allowed to enter upon this record of a life as poor in achievement as it is rich in promising starts and fascinating detours, the one deed of lasting importance that I can claim to my credit: the conversion of Martin and Joe. Not that I had much converting to do; I just set them off, and they converted themselves, entering the Church by that door of the intellectual approach of which Father D'Arcy speaks. In fact, it all began with Father D'Arcy's little book in Benn's "Sixpenny Library," when Martin was fifteen and Joe fourteen; one day they asked their mother, "What is this Catholicism that Eugene talks about?" They had been brought up in a nonchalantly agnostic milieu, where religion was represented by compulsory, and therefore not much relished, attendance of Anglican chapel at school; extremely intelligent boys that they were, they were eager to explore any new world that offered itself for exploration. Their mother, very wisely, and with a subtlety that it is perhaps not altogether polite to advertise, gave them to read not only Father D'Arcy's *Catholicism*, but also, by way of counterweight, Dean Inge's booklet, published in the same series, on *Protestantism*, with the remark, "Now you can judge for yourselves." Which is just what the boys did. Having had their first taste, they went on reading Catholic literature, of the philosophical type, Chesterton, Belloc, Maritain, Christopher Dawson, Father R. Knox, Father Martindale, and so forth; they bought copies of the Roman Missal, and studied it; when Martin, in the sixth form, won a book prize he startled his headmaster by asking for the *Summa Theologica*.

During all this time I did very little in the matter, beyond suggesting books and answering questions; that very little took the form of adapting to the boys' capacity the philosophical arguments outlined in this book, about the unintended corollaries of private judgment and *sola fides*, and about the rush of Western civilization toward self-destruction, precipitated by the Renaissance doctrine of human sovereignty. These two Harrow schoolboys, it may be truthfully said, were Catholic Realists before they were Catholics. The first thing they did after leaving school, each in his turn, was to go to Father Bevan of the Brompton Oratory, with whom they had already been in touch, and ask to be received in the Church; so that it was as Catholics that they went up to Oxford.

7

In September 1937, my wife and I drove up to Lake Leman, and for the next fifteen months Switzerland was our base. The first twelve we spent at a hotel at Glion, a hamlet situated on a cliff rising sheer two thousand feet above the lake, and accessible from Montreux by a narrow corkscrew road, the gradient of which rises to one in five for the last kilometer. And I wish now that I had yet another chapter or two to go before this book comes to an end; for I should need at least as much space to tell what I feel should be told about Switzerland. It was before the war the most-publicized country in Europe, and one of the least known; for all that publicity was purely commercial, aiming to attract moneyed people to the winter sports and other touristic amenities which were Switzerland's chief source of income. There is nothing wrong with that; to sell holiday facilities to people who want them is as legitimate as selling automobiles or harvesting machinery. But the trouble with the sort of publicity which was so brilliantly organized by the Swiss was that it put a false façade on their country, encouraging the idea that Switzerland was nothing but an agglomerate of skiing hotels de luxe, and that the Swiss regarded it as their historic mission to act as head porters and mountain guides to wealthy and less wealthy Anglo-Saxons.

Now Switzerland is not, and the Swiss are not, like that at all, once you have come to know them. I cannot speak of and for the German-speaking cantons, as I do not know them; but I did learn something of *la Suisse romande*, as the French-speaking states of the Confederacy are called. Most of their population are Calvinists, and the Calvinist temperament and mode of life are alien to me; but in those fifteen months I conceived not merely admiration, but also affection, for those Swiss Protestants. They possess to an eminent degree two of the finest qualities of civilized men, and these happen to be qualities which I particularly prize: a sense of order, based not on a mere external observance, but on a genuine penetration of the meaning of the Law; and a sense of reality. The French-speaking Swiss are realists in the best sense of the word; not in the confused sense of everyday parlance, which applies it indiscriminately to the hard-boiled materialist and cynic, to the gangster of *Realpolitik*, international or private, and to the low time-serving opportunist. The realist, according to the proper signification of the term, is one who is able, and keen, to distinguish the real from the apparent, the true from the false, the genuine from the sham; one who does not believe that we can create facts by hoping for them, and remove facts by wishing them out of the way; one who does not believe that we can change things by changing their names; one who, to put it as briefly as possible, refuses to be taken in by words. Now the Swiss are a people of realists in this very sense; and I shall give two instances of their realism. They know that in a world like ours, a world teeming with evil, the way to maintain democracy and individual liberty is not to make, and listen to, speeches about democracy, but to practise sharpshooting; and beside being the truest democracy in the world, the Swiss are also a people of enthusiastic trained soldiers. And, true lovers of liberty, they know that to grant unrestricted freedom to freedom's enemies is to invite its destruction. So the Swiss were not taken in by the fashionable bunkum about the Communists being the champions of democracy, and being entitled anyway to the privileges that the democratic commonwealth vouchsafes to its citizens; to the noisy claims of their Communists to freedom of speech and association they retorted by inquiring just how much freedom of speech and association is granted to non-Communists in Soviet Russia.

In those fifteen months I came to regard Switzerland as the finest democracy in the world, a democracy based on the effort of hard thinking, on the dignity of hard work, on the beauty of self-imposed discipline. It was the one democracy in Europe that was, on the one hand, truly democratic, and that, on the other hand, *worked*; and this was because, of all European democracies, it had remained most faithful to the Christian origins of our civilization. It was the most advanced of European nations because it was the most conservative. And I also came to regard the Swiss Confederacy as the most perfect illustration, in the real order, of two propositions of the political philosophy which has my allegiance. One of these propositions is to the effect that while democracy is the ideal method of local government, its unrestricted application to the field of international policy is, in a world full of Nazis and Fascists and Communists armed to the teeth, a source of danger to its own survival. For the indispensable condition of healthy politics, as of any other form of human action, is Knowledge; and it follows from this that in order to make democracy work, it is necessary that every member of it should be thoroughly familiar with all the problems with which he is called upon to deal. Now this condition is fulfilled in the local government of small units, on the principle that it is the man wearing the shoe who knows whether it pinches or not, and where it pinches. But the great decisions of international politics, in a world where the aeroplane has abolished distance, require accurate knowledge that is not within the reach of the average voter; that this is so may be deplorable, but it is nevertheless true, and to ignore this truth is the same as to invite the destruction of democracy on a planet half of which has been overpowered by Totalitarian gangsterdom. When the average householder has a severe tummy-ache he calls in an expert to cure it; why he should assume that he is capable of curing, out of the resources of his own inspiration, the mortal political diseases that beset this tottering world of ours is beyond Reason.

The other proposition expresses the same idea in different words: it is to the effect that democracy and decentralization are inseparable; and this means also that democracy and Federation are inseparable, for while local problems may and must be dealt with on a basis of decentralized small units, the problems that concern the whole of the body politic can only be dealt with by the association of those units. Now this is something that most believers in democracy already know, and it would not be necessary to restate the idea at all were it not for the inability of most believers in democracy to see that to demand full scope for individual judgment in the field of international politics is the same as to decentralize international politics. And in a world where a Hitler could conquer Europe in ten months, the notion that international politics should and can be decentralized is no more reasonable than the idea that the second law of thermodynamics should and can be decentralized.

8

During those months of our cliff-dwellers' existence at Glion our contacts with the outside world, apart from receiving mail, consisted chiefly in a trip or two a week to Lausanne, an hour's distance by car. To the conventional seeker of commercialized gaiety Lausanne may seem a dull place, but to those who regard the life of cabarets and night clubs as a form of piecemeal death by boredom it is, or was (the reader must blame Hitler for my recurrent uncertainty in respect of tenses), one of the most agreeable cities of the Continent. I found it particularly interesting because of a subtle anomalous quality of its life which had struck me on our very first visit; but it took me some time to puzzle it out, and to discover that Lausanne marks the cultural frontier between Western and Central Europe.

Now Lausanne is French-speaking like Geneva, but its atmosphere and manners are not French at all, while Geneva is a French city which is also a member of the Helvetic Confederacy. One might say that the Genevese are Frenchmen of Swiss citizenship, but the Vaudois are Swiss who speak a French dialect. You could observe the difference in many little things. For instance, although measured by French standards traffic in Geneva is very well regulated indeed, compared with the automaton-like ruthless efficiency of the Lausanne police the traffic cops of Geneva seem amiable anarchists. Then there is the matter of masculine dress. The Genevese affect somber hues, and don't seem to give a hoot for smartness, being in this respect very French; but the men of Lausanne dress carefully in well-cut tweeds or other smart English materials, as the men of Vienna used to in the old days. This may be due to the prewar presence in Lausanne of a considerable colony of British residents, but other distinctions cannot be accounted for in the same way. Thus the cafés and restaurants of Geneva, apart from those of the big hotels which seem to have come out of the same box all over the world, used to look exactly like the cafés and restaurants of Bordeaux or Tours or Dijon, with every square inch of space utilized, and red plush and gilt and other marks of an older conception of the good life predominating over comfort and ventilation; and yet the general impression was one of cosiness and careless elegance. But the cafés and restaurants of Lausanne are spacious, resplendent with up-to-date gadgets, and also, with one or two exceptions, slightly vulgar, like those of Vienna and Budapest of the pre-Nazi dispensation. But perhaps the most significant of these cultural divergences appeared in the matter of food and drink. In the restaurants of Geneva meat and vegetables were served in separate courses, in the French way; but in Lausanne you got everything together, as you used to in Vienna when Vienna had everything, and as you do in New York. And in Geneva a man who spent an hour or two sitting about in a café would drink coffee or beer or an *apéritif*, as in France; but in the Lausanne cafés they drank wine, which they also did in Belgium and Western Germany; whereas Frenchmen of the upper and middle classes — I am speaking of the days before the deluge — never touched wine between meals, holding, very sensibly in my view, that a good bottle is at its best when accompanied by a good dish, and vice versa.

These are trifling matters; but the surface of culture consists in the infinite variety of such trifling matters. And if the French prefer to drink wine with their meals, but beer at 4:30 P.M., whereas the Germans prefer to drink beer with their meals and wine in between, there is no reason in the world why they should not continue to do so, and there is an excellent reason why they should. And that reason is that these seemingly inconsequential differences have their roots in human freedom. No two persons are exactly alike; but generations of persons who have lived together in the same town or the same valley or on the same side of a river for ten centuries, or twenty, will in the course of time come to exercise their faculty of free choice in a more or less similar way in similar cases; and at the end of ten centuries, or twenty, there will have grown up in the same town or the same valley or on the same side of a river certain strictly defined ways of doing certain things. Such ways are called traditions, and they are corollaries of human freedom as exercised in the course of history, practical expressions of the God-given right of a group of men to resemble one another and to differ from other groups, if they choose so to resemble and so to differ. And to the shallow thinker the fact that a Frenchman will eat his lamb chop first and his spinach afterwards, cooking the leaf whole and smothering the dish in hot butter, whereas the American will crush the leaf and mix cream with it, and will eat chop and spinach off the same plate, while the Greek will cook lamb and spinach together in the oven, and flavor the single dish with olive oil and garlic — to the shallow thinker, I say, these things will appear unworthy of notice, or else merely quaint and amusing. But he who is wont to probe under the surface of what he sees will appraise these culinary variants at their true value as trifling manifestations of the all-important human right to do things in one's own way; and he will know that the attempt to deprive men of their traditional way of cooking lamb and to force on them another man's way may be a prelude to depriving them of their traditional way of worshiping God, and to forcing on them another man's God. Which is exactly what is happening on the continent of Europe today, and may yet happen elsewhere. But to those who are capable of reading the lesson of history properly it is plain that the Frenchmen who think that they can yield to their Nazi oppressors in minor details and adopt lesser Nazi ways, and may yet save the soul of France, are fools or knaves, or both.

It might be inferred from the foregoing dissertation that I spent that Swiss year sitting about in the cafés of Lausanne and Geneva, studying ethnography by the agreeable method of sampling vintages. But the inference would be wrong; for I spent most of that year in the open air, climbing mountains in a mild way, not because I particularly like climbing mountains, but because if you live at Glion-sur-Montreux you cannot even buy a packet of cigarettes without doing a spot of mountaineering. I did not do much work during those Glion months, at least not in the way of writing, for I had by then reached the conclusion that if I ever

wanted to finish my "Philosophy of Freedom" I must stop trying
to finish it "within the next six months," as I used to promise myself, and must let it grow. We went about a little in our car, up
the Rhône Valley to that fine cathedral city of Sion, capital of the
sovereign state of Valais, and to Brigue, at the entrance of the
Simplon tunnel; in the Pays d'Enhaut, which is a sort of table top
or roof behind the northeastern edge of Lake Leman, and which
looks on the map as if you needed a ladder to scale it; in the Jura;
and we also had half a dozen trips in France. But most of the time
we were just walking, exploring the country behind and above
Montreux by paths that sometimes had a gradient of one in two.
And we had once met, in front of the cathedral at Le Puy, an
Englishwoman who said scornfully that Switzerland is just one
damned English tearoom after the other; we wondered where she
may have got her information, for we found that once we strolled
fifty yards from the tracks of the little funicular railway which
climbs its preposterous slopes all the way up to the Rochers de
Naye, we were in country as wild and unspoiled as if it had been
a couple of hundred miles from the nearest post of the Hudson
Bay Company. And that brings me to what was the most important
contribution of that Swiss year to the context of my life: to the
memory of the matchless beauty of Montreux.

Now I have not, in these pages, concealed from the reader the
fact that I am something of a landscape fan. Born and bred in a
great city, dweller in half a dozen other great cities up to the age of
thirty-five, I was thirty-two when I discovered, among the mountains and lakes of Austria, the existence of country as distinguished
from space crossed by trains between cities; but from that moment
onward landscape came to mean something to me that no other
form or manifestation of this-worldly beauty could fully equal or
replace. And in that collection of memorable landscapes which is
about the only asset, as they say *pace* Mr. Fowler, that I have to
show for my seventeen years spent in eight European countries,
the landscape of Montreux occupies quite a special place.

The landscape which corresponds most perfectly to my idea of
what landscape should be, the landscape in which I feel more

completely myself, more unreservedly at peace with my lot and with the world, than in any other, is that of Provence; the region of the Esterel and the Moorish Mountains; that old Comtat-Venaissin of which Avignon is the capital, with its extension across the Rhône, the Uzégeois and the country of Nimes; and that Durance country which stretches north of Aix toward Manosque and Digne. My wife says that one of the reasons why I am such a difficult person to live with is that wherever I am, I want to be somewhere else; but she admits that Provence is the exception to this general rule of my unruliness, for when I am in Provence all I want is to stay put.

But if anybody were to ask, "What is the most beautiful spot that you have ever seen?" I should answer unhesitatingly, "Montreux."

I shall not attempt to describe it; if I did, I should fail. Those who know Montreux, with those terrific 10,000-foot mountains rising sheer behind that narrow strip of houses and gardens along the lake, the terraced cliffs of Glion and Caux forming a sort of prelude to the Rochers de Naye; the green cone of the Cubly, with the taller one of Les Pléïades beyond; the gorges of the Chauderon, with their cascades and meadows and great trees rising as a kind of gigantic staircase up to the fir woods and pastures of Les Avants, with that wall of desolation, the chain of Verreaux, for a background; the pyramid of the Dent de Jaman; the glistening white Dents du Midi shutting off the horizon in the southeast, the placid ridges of the Jura in the far west, and the austere crag of Grammont towering across the blue-green lake — those who have seen all this will know why I agree with Ruskin in calling Montreux the loveliest corner of Europe; and those who have never seen it would not get an adequate picture from whatever I might say.

The lakeside walk from the landing stage of Territet toward the center of Montreux passes through a small tropical wilderness. For in spite of its Northern latitude, those stupendous walls of rock which enclose Montreux on all sides endow it with a climate milder than that of the French Riviera; the abundant rainfall produces in that far-flung reserve of the Mediterranean South a vegetation more luxuriant than that of the South itself; the presence of some Northern trees, willow and larch and fir, enhances the exotic note, while the light reflected from the dark green water creates the illusion of some enchanted garden on the bottom of the sea, or inside a gigantic emerald. And when you, half-dazed, lift your eyes and behold, right above your head and so near that you feel you could touch it with your outstretched hand, the snowy pyramid of the Rochers de Naye, two miles high, rearing its blazing whiteness above the somber bastions of Sonchaud forest, you are tempted to exclaim, "No, all this can't be true!"

Contemplation of too much beauty leaves one with the feeling that it is too much rather than beauty. That perfection in restraint which is the keynote of the Provençal landscape is exhilarating and healing, that is, whole-making, because it restores that harmony between the soul and the world which is the finite reflection, in the highest moments of this mortal life, of the infinite peace of God. But the beauty of that Montreux lakefront has the opposite effect: it crushes and exhausts; it suggests somehow that a limit has been reached, in the sense in which the limit of a sanity which is losing mastery of itself is madness.

The long and short of it is that the lakeside of Montreux, not in spite but because of its beauty, is one of the saddest places in the world. In the fall of 1937, when we climbed or drove down from Glion five or six days a week, we found it practically deserted, except for a nursemaid or two wheeling a baby carriage, or an old fisherman drying his nets on the parapet. Once the all-year-round capital of fashionable idling on the Continent, Montreux is now a dead city, almost as dead as Bruges-la-morte; the English rich have migrated to the South of France, the Russian rich have been murdered, and those great palace hotels stand all but empty during nine months of the year; only the summer brings an influx of middle-class families from German Switzerland. Now I love the solitude of mountain passes and forests and the high valleys of rivers, but the solitude of an overcivilized urban nook has nothing lovely about it; it breathes failure, the vanity of human striving.

The silence of that lakefront always suggested to me that of a luxurious but empty house, the inhabitants of which had gone away for a holiday, leaving everything in perfect order for their return, and then died instead of returning; it suggested the desolation of waiting for one who never came. Territet is haunted by the shade of that tragic Empress Elizabeth of Austria who loved it, and whose statue, marble symbol of frustration and death in exile, adorns the little square next to the English church. Even on a bright spring day there is beneath the green canopy of those lakeside groves a faint scent of decay, half-sweet, half-acrid, a dank autumnal smell like that which wafts from the novels of Turgenev.

I tried, on those walks in the fall of 1937, to analyze this mood, unlike any that I had ever experienced elsewhere; and I decided that it could not be accounted for in terms of that decline of material prosperity which had been induced by changing fashions; for the same process resulted in a change for the better at Hyères, where it caused that little town of fruit growers and market gardeners to reassert its ancient identity. On the other hand, I felt that geography was partly responsible for that sense of having reached the end of something, for Montreux actually stands on the edge of its spatial world; it is the last outpost of Southern nature in the North, and also the last outpost of the French-speaking West, for just beyond lies the bilingual canton of Valais, where for a generation or two the Latin race has been on the defensive against the higher birth rate of the Alemannic Swiss.

But I concluded that the last clue to that strange blend of fascination and abhorrence which made me return day after day to that lakeside walk lay not in geography but in history. Montreux seemed to me the limit of a mode of existence not only in space but also in time; the last outlook tower, perched on the rim of Nothing, of a civilization about to break down under the weight of its own complexity and self-sufficiency; of a civilization that had been, for centuries, so busy improving the circumstances of human life that it had lost sight of the meaning of life, and had begun to wonder whether life had any meaning at all — a civilization so preoccupied with means that it had forgotten all about ends, and was now asking itself, What is the use of anything? And I thought, on those walks from Territet to Les Planches, in those unforgettably glamorous autumn months of 1937, of other civilizations, now dead, that had, like our own, come to regard Beauty as its own end and justification, forgetting that Beauty that declares its independence of Truth reduces itself to a mirage; of civilizations that, like our own, had set out to realize a dream of human grandeur, and ended by discovering that human grandeur is but a dream.

And I used to ponder, on those lakeside walks, two texts that I had found in books in which I had been seeking the solution of that greatest and most tragic riddle of human history, the riddle of the decline and fall of civilizations. One of those texts is now almost two thousand years old; and it runs as follows: —

One day when the sky was serene and clear there was heard in it the sound of a trumpet, so shrill and mournful that it frightened and astonished the whole city. The Tuscan sages said that it portended a new race of man, and a renovation of the world, for they observed that there were eight several kinds of men, all differing in life and manners; that heaven had allotted to each its time, which was limited to the circuit of the Great Year; and that when one race came to a period and another was rising, it was announced by some wonderful sign from either earth or heaven. So that it was evident at one view to those who attended to these things, and were versed in them, that a different sort of men was come into the world, with other manners and customs, and more or less the care of the gods than those who had preceded them. . . . Such was the mythology of the most learned and respectable of the Tuscan soothsayers.

That passage is from Plutarch's life of Sulla, and I had found it quoted in a wise little book by Sir Matthew Flinders Petrie, entitled *Revolutions of Civilisation;* and he explains that the Great Year of the Etruscans, of which the sages spoke, comprised 1100 years, and one had come to an end in 87 B.C., in the time of Sulla. The other text is to be found in another little book, one by Max Scheler, with whose death ten or twelve years ago that great line of German philosophers which began with Leibniz has terminated.

In the passage that I had in mind Scheler quotes Nikolai Hart-
mann: "The higher categories of being and value are *ipso facto*
the weaker ones." Then he goes on: —

That stream of efficacious power which alone can determine essential being and accidental existence, runs, in this world of ours, not from
above downward, but from below upward. In proudest independence
towers the inorganic world, sufficient unto itself in its autonomy, containing at only very few points anything that may be called "life." It
is in an independence still proud, if a little less so, that the plant world
and the animal world confront the world of man; and be it noted that
the animal is far more dependent on the plant than is the plant on the
animal. The fact is that the animal mode of life marks not only a gain,
but also a loss, in comparison with the plant mode, since animals do not
possess that direct contact with the inorganic world whereby the plant
nourishes itself. It is in an analogous independence that the masses confront, in history, the higher forms of human existence. Of rare occurrence and brief duration are the periods of cultural bloom in the annals
of mankind. *Rare and short-lived is Beauty in its tenderness and its
vulnerability.*

The necrology of Cnossus, pronounced in advance by a Cnossian philosopher in 1417 B.C., three years before the landing of the
Nordic Achaeans.

But as I thought over those words of Max Scheler, on those
walks along the Territet lakefront the beauty of which oppressed
me and filled me with despair, I also reflected that Max Scheler,
who as a boy had converted himself to the Catholic faith and
whose philosophy reflects intellectualist and realist elements of the
Catholic tradition, was not a Catholic when he wrote his brilliant
little book on *Man's Place in the Universe.*

The misery of man without God, said Pascal.

And yet Max Scheler is right, in a way. It is, even as he writes
in the same book, a fatal illusion to believe that truth will conquer
falsehood and right will overcome might, just because truth is
higher than falsehood, and right is higher than might. But that
illusion is not shared by Catholics, whose religion teaches that
Works are as necessary to justification as is Faith, and that if you

want God to conquer you must fight for Him. On the contrary; the notion that when we have declared "Right is superior to Might" we have done our share and may attend courses for conscientious objectors to that compulsory military service which the presence of evil in this world imposes on mankind both in a figurative and in a literal sense; the notion that being in the right is the same as making right prevail, was the central theory of nineteenth-century Liberalism; and Western civilization is dying of it today. It is no less a prophet than Benedetto Croce himself who defined the Liberal creed as the identification of the ideal with the real, the desired with the existent; he might have added, the identification of the potentiality with the act. It was the Liberals who wanted to end war by signing documents that outlawed war; the Liberals who only three years ago made speeches against Hitlerism and for disarmament off the same platform, I almost said in the same breath. We know that they meant well; we know that they were genuinely anxious to preserve the Christian values of our civilization. But they were unwilling to pay the price: they willed the end without willing the means; they wanted Christian justice and Christian mercy without Christian doctrine and Christian discipline; they wanted to defeat the armed forces of the worst tyranny that the world has ever seen, without building up armies and navies and air forces stronger than those of tyranny; they wanted to win this very war without fighting in it. And so we have come to the End of Our Time.

Max Scheler is right, too, when he says that the "up" periods of history, the flowering times of culture, are of rare occurrence and brief duration. Between the last fall of Cnossus and the rise of Periclean Athens spread one thousand years — the Great Year of the Etruscan priests. Six hundred years elapsed between the end of the Roman Empire in 476 and that renascence of the European spirit which first took place, not as the Liberal historians would have it, in the studios of Italian painters in the fourteenth century, but in the cells of French monasteries in the eleventh.

Seventeen hundred years between the Antonine age of Rome and the Antonine age of Modern Europe; between the second century and the nineteenth, the only two centuries in recorded history when it was possible to travel unarmed and unharmed from one end of the known world to the other.

But consider: the single structure of history admits of two interpretations.

The interpretation which seems true to the man without God is one of misery and despair. "One thousand years: thirty generations from the fall of one Cnossus to the rise of the next. I am fifty. In twenty years I shall be dead; or maybe in ten, or in five, or maybe next month. One thousand years are a very long time. Human life is short. What is the use of it all?"

Now the Catholic philosopher contemplates the same structure that is visible to the agnostic; but he sees that structure in a different light, because he sees through it to what is beyond the facts; and he will ask, "What are thirty generations as measured against God's Eternity?"

I have spent seven years of my highly problematic threescore and ten counting the generations that separate one Cnossus from the next, and meditating upon the relation of truth and existence, value and efficacy, right and might; upon the very problem that Max Scheler solves in such a despairing spirit. I, too, have reached the conclusion, "Rare and short-lived is Beauty in its tenderness and its vulnerability." I, too, know that mere strength, propelled by the brute Will and unillumined by that light of Reason which is the faint reflection of the Divine intellect in the finite mind of man, is the mortal enemy of truth and of value, of justice and of mercy. During those seven years the field-green masses of the Power of Darkness were gathering on the eastern frontier of our twentieth-century Cnossus; and at the end of those seven years our Cnossus fell.

I was there when France fell; and I have written this book to mourn her.

But I have not forgotten about the grace of God.

"Almighty and everlasting God, in whose hands is all power and the right of all sovereignty, look to the help of the Christian people; that the heathen who trust in their own fierceness, may be crushed by the power of Thy right hand."

THE END

Index